J. Mackenzie

Retail Security and Shrinkage Protection

Retail Security and Shrinkage Protection

Philip P. Purpura, C.P.P.

Butterworth–Heinemann
Boston London Oxford Singapore Sydney Toronto Wellington

Copyright © 1993 by Butterworth–Heinemann, a division of Reed Publishing (USA) Inc.
All rights reserved.

Portions of Chapters 2, 4, and 10 have been adapted from the following documents
with permission from Butterworth–Heinemann.
   Purpura, Philip. *Modern Security & Loss Prevention Management.* Boston: Butterworth–Heinemann,
   1989.
   Purpura, Philip. *Security & Loss Prevention: An Introduction.* Boston: Butterworth–Heinemann, 1991.

No part of this publication may be reproduced, stored in a retrieval system, or transmitted, in
any form or by any means, electronic, mechanical, photocopying, recording, or otherwise,
without the prior written permission of the publisher.

 Recognizing the importance of preserving what has been written, it is the policy of Butterworth–
Heinemann to have the books it publishes printed on acid-free paper, and we exert our best
efforts to that end.

Library of Congress Cataloging-in-Publication Data

Purpura, Philip P.,
    Retail security and shrinkage protection / by Philip P. Purpura.
        p.   cm.
    Includes bibliographical references and index.
    ISBN 0-7506-9274-X (alk. paper) :
    1. Retail trade—Security measures.   I. Title.
HF5429.27.P87   1993
658.4'73—dc20   92-38544
                                                                             CIP

British Library Cataloguing-in-Publication Data

A catalogue record for this book is available from the British Library.

Butterworth–Heinemann
80 Montvale Avenue
Stoneham, MA 02180

10 9 8 7 6 5 4 3 2

Printed in the United States of America

Contents

Preface ix

Acknowledgments xii

I INTRODUCTION

1 Retailing and Security 3
The Evolution of Retailing 3
Crime Follows the Growth of Retailing 4
Retailing Today 7
Security and Loss Prevention 8
Notes 8

2 Planning for Retail Security 9
Retail Objectives and Problems 9
Security Planning 11
Guidelines for Planning 16
Questions during Planning 17
Planning from a Systems Perspective 18
Risk Analysis 20
Return on Investment (ROI) 21
Standards 23
Research 24
Audits 27
Marketing 27
Case Problems 29
Notes 30

3 Legal Aspects of Retail Security 31

Local and State Laws 31
Federal Laws 32
Civil and Criminal Liabilities 33
A Charge of Negligent Security 41
Preparing for a Lawsuit 43
Case Problems 48
Answers to You Be the Judge 49
Notes 49

II PROBLEMS AND COUNTERMEASURES

4 Job Applicant Screening and Employee Training 53

Human Resources in Retailing 53
Human Resources Problems in Retailing 53
Legislation and Court Decisions 54
Job Applicant Screening 57
Training 74
Case Problems 77
Notes 78

5 Protection at the Point-of-Sale 79

Management Information Systems 79
Cash Registers 79
The Point-of-Sale as a Vulnerable Location 82
Preventing Losses at the Point-of-Sale 84
Bad Checks 86
Credit Card Fraud 92
Counterfeiting 96
Refund Fraud 98
Additional POS Vulnerabilities 99
Case Problems 100
Answers to You Be the Judge 101
Notes 102

6 Internal Losses and Countermeasures 103

Shrinkage 103
The Problem of Employee Theft in Retailing 109
Employee Theft Countermeasures 117
Case Problems 127
Notes 130

7 Shoplifting and Countermeasures 132

Losses from Shoplifting 132
Characteristics of Shoplifters 133
What Can Be Done to Reduce Shoplifting? 138
Research on the Shoplifting Problem 140
Protection against Shoplifting 143
Case Problems 160
Notes 161

8 Investigation of Internal Losses and Shoplifting 162

Investigative Skills 164
Investigation of Suspected Internal Losses 170
Investigation of Suspected Shoplifting 183
Case Problems 198
Answers to You Be the Judge 199
Notes 199

9 Store Design and Physical Security 201

Store Location and Design 201
Physical Security 209
Physical Security Methods 212
Case Problems 237
Notes 237

10 Burglary and Robbery Countermeasures 240

Burglary 240
Robbery 253
Community Crime Prevention Programs 268
Case Problems 270
Notes 271

11 Risk Management 273

What Is Risk Management?   273
Risk Management Strategies   273
Job Duties of Risk Managers   274
The Insurance Industry   276
Insurance for Retailers   277
Loss Prevention   289
Investigate Insurers   290
Annual Review of Insurance Coverage   290
Safety   291
Occupational Safety and Health Administration (OSHA)   291
Fire Protection   302
Disasters   303
Comprehensive Risk Management   307
Case Problems   307
Notes   307

12 Special Topics 309

Shopping Malls   309
Gangs   314
Substance Abuse: A Drug-free Workplace   317
Technology and the Future   325
Case Problem   327
Notes   330

Appendix A   Retail Security Surveys   331

Appendix B   The Americans With Disabilities Act   342

Index   354

Preface

This book focuses on security and shrinkage protection for retail businesses. The subject matter is written for students, security practitioners, and retailers. An emphasis is placed on vulnerabilities, losses, and practical retail security countermeasures.

The job of protecting retail businesses is complex. Retail security programs with yesterday's ideas will not survive because management is requiring security practitioners to do more with less and show a return on the investment in security. Protection executives must convincingly prove a return on investment to survive budget cuts. Reduced losses and shrinkage mean continued employment. Ernst & Young's *Survey of Retail Loss Prevention Trends*, the thirteenth annual survey released in January 1992, makes the following statements in reference to retailers setting specific shrinkage goals:

> And if they failed to meet these goals? Most companies investigated the cause of the shrinkage and/or implemented additional controls. But a very large group—some 43 percent—replaced personnel at a store that has not attained the desired shrink percentage.
>
> Most of the executives believe dismissing people is a regrettable but acceptable practice and an encouraging trend. . . . But, unpleasant as this practice is, these executives applaud it as yet another demonstration of management's commitment to loss prevention.

In the retail security field, practitioners lose their jobs when protection programs do not meet management expectations, when shrinkage is too high, when not enough shoplifters or thieving employees are apprehended, or when lawsuits result from the inappropriate actions of security personnel. What makes matters worse is that certain aspects of retailing run counter to providing security, such as poor screening of job applicants and hiring of many part-time and temporary employees. Also, modern merchandising techniques are designed to facilitate the customer's accessibility to merchandise. Retailers want customers to walk freely through their stores, notice merchandise, pick it up, and then purchase it. Unfortunately, these techniques also trigger shoplifting. What are security practitioners to do? First, an understanding of retailing, its problems, and the needs of the particular retailer are vitally important. Second, despite the difficulties of the profession, the practitioner must look at problems in retailing and security as challenges that have solutions. This entails devising creative strategies that complement the goals and merchandising techniques of the retailer. This mind-set is important to succeeding as a retail security professional. This book offers answers to protection problems and provides an opportunity to think critically about and analyze contemporary retail security practices. This critical thinking is a major key to produce the best possible security program that prevents losses and preserves profits.

Chapter 1 of this book begins with a brief history of retailing and how it became a magnet for crime. Chapter 2 discusses planning and tools used to critically analyze contemporary security methods, while providing methods for producing a quality security program that is both cost-effective and shows a return on investment. Chapter 3 describes legal aspects that serve as a foundation for security programs. Chapters 4 through 12 emphasize specific vulnerabilities and countermeasures for protecting retail businesses. These topics include job applicant screening and employee training, protection at the point of sale, internal losses, shoplifting, investigations, store design and physical security, burglary and robbery, risk management, and special topics.

Several features are included in this book to assist both the reader and the educator:

Basic concepts are explained before moving on to complex topics.

Drawings and photographs are included to illustrate many security methods.

Boxed items introduce supplemental information and practical applications.

"You Be the Judge" cases, which pertain to retail security legal issues, are contained in certain chapters. Readers are asked to formulate a verdict and are then directed to the end of the chapter for the court's ruling. Also, cases from legal periodicals are boxed in some chapters.

Case problems at the end of most chapters provide a means for readers to apply chapter information and acquire problem-solving skills.

The final chapter ends with an "in basket" exercise to test the reader's knowledge and skill in dealing with the demands of retail security management. This exercise can be used by a retail business as a part of the applicant-screening process for a security position.

Appendix A contains portions of retail security surveys from the accounting firm of Ernst & Young and *Security* magazine. Appendix B contains information from the Americans with Disabilities Act of 1990.

Best wishes for a challenging and rewarding career in retail security.

Acknowledgments

Many people played a crucial role in helping me prepare this book. In previous years, retailers and retail security people gave me the opportunity to work in a variety of retail positions in and around New York City, and I thank them for the experience they afforded me. My right hand in writing is my wife Amyie. Her editorial and typing assistance were especially helpful in completing this book. I am thankful for the assistance of Ms. Laurel DeWolf, Assistant Editor at Butterworth–Heinemann, who did a superb job in coordinating this project to its completion. I would also like to thank the many people in and outside of the security field who sent me information, research results, photographs, and drawings to enhance this book. For more than ten years, Mr. Alex Vaughn, Editor of *Security Management Bulletin* (Bureau of Business Practice), has provided me with "You Be the Judge" cases and case citations that have added variety to the books I have written. I am thankful for the assistance of this creative editor and fine fellow.

The following specialists reviewed draft material and offered invaluable advice to improve this book: Francis D'Addario and Barbara Andrews.

A special thanks goes to two businesses in the security and loss prevention field that provided permission to use their research in this book. Mr. Bill Zalud, Editor of *Security*, shared information and statistical tables from *The National Retail Security Survey* (1991). This retail security survey questioned more than 400 respondents who supplied interesting information on losses and loss prevention strategies.

A special thanks also goes to Mr. Peter Gilmartin and Ms. Stephanie Shern from Ernst & Young (a professional services firm that serves the retail industry). This business (in conjunction with the International Mass Retail Association) is noted for its annual survey of retail loss prevention trends. One hundred fifty-five respondents participated in the 1990 survey, which also produced insights into losses and loss prevention strategies.

Results from both research projects are stated throughout this book and presented in Appendix A.

Part I

Introduction

1

Retailing and Security

The Evolution of Retailing

Retailing has a long history; it has existed in some form in every civilization. From the market square in ancient times, to the shops of England in the 1500s, to the millions of retail establishments in the United States today, the evolution of retailing has reflected the evolution of society in a given location.

In North America during colonial times, trading posts served as the first retail stores. Currency was not used to make purchases, so settlers and Indians bartered farm products and furs for whiskey, gunpowder, and goods from Europe. Peddlers were also growing in number during these early times, although peddling has its roots in earlier civilizations. Peddlers sold pots, pans, and other household goods as they traveled by wagon from one settlement to another. Today's concept of door-to-door sales evolved from the peddlers. As settlements grew into towns, a third retailing institution emerged to serve a growing population. During the mid-eighteenth century, the general store began to meet the increasing consumer needs of colonists. These stores stocked several lines of goods, such as groceries, household items, clothes, medicine, tools, farm equipment, and animal feed. In a departure from the barter system, cash became the dominant method of payment. At the same time, the general store instituted a service to customers that is an essential part of business today—credit. Farmers were granted credit during the year until harvest time. Customer loyalty was the result.

During the nineteenth century, westward expansion, railroads, and increased manufacturing resulted in the single-line retail store that specialized in one type of merchandise. The general store could not accommodate the increasing numbers and types of manufactured goods.

The late 1800s was a period when mail-order catalog retailing gained momentum. Richard W. Sears and Aaron Montgomery Ward (whose names are familiar even today) were pioneers of this industry.

With the mail system established, Aaron Montgomery Ward rented a small shipping room in Chicago and put out a one-page price list—the first mail-order catalogue—in August 1872. Early price lists offered bustles, wool socks, and even a backgammon set for $1.00. A lady's ring was available for $3.00 and a 'gent's cassimere coat' was $3.50.[1]

During the latter part of the nineteenth century, the chain organization developed and was the first venture into large-scale retailing in the United States. A chain organization was originally defined as two or more retail stores that were similar in nature and had a common ownership. The current definition, as used by the U.S. Bureau of the Census, defines a chain as having 11 or more retail stores. Department stores also appeared during this time. The concept of department stores essentially involves uniting many, limited-line operations under one roof, under common ownership. The luxury of one-stop shopping was now available to the department store customer.

The rigors of the Great Depression played a major role in producing a new retailing institution known as the supermarket. Prices at the supermarket were lower than those at neighborhood grocery stores, because of factors such as self-service, poor illumination, and sparse furnishings. Consumers had their pick of goods from open cartons displayed on the floor. By World War II, discount houses appeared. The merchandise sold in these establishments was low priced. These retailers had low overhead and offered radios, TVs, and other appliances in an attempt to undersell department stores. As more and more city residents moved to the suburbs during the 1950s and 1960s, planned shopping centers increased in number.

Two modern types of stores are the superstore and the hypermarket. The former contains a large supermarket and pharmacy, and also stocks a variety of household items. The hypermarket is much larger than the superstore and houses a large discount store, a supermarket, and a drugstore under a single roof. Furniture, large household appliances, and automotive repair services are also offered at hypermarkets.

Today, there are many types and classifications of retail stores, including franchises, independent retailers, chain organizations, warehouse outlets, boutiques, mail-order companies, restaurants, convenience stores, and so forth. Whenever a void is found where consumer needs are not being met, a new type of retail concept is sure to evolve.

Crime Follows the Growth of Retailing

As retailing expanded through the centuries, the industry became a magnet for crime. Shoplifting, internal theft, robbery, and burglary were as much a part of retailing in earlier years as today.

One of the earliest known accounts of shoplifting, written in 1597 in England, describes 'The Discovery of the Lifting Law,' and the 'lift,' or shoplifter. Even then, there were diverse kinds of lifts; the common and rascal sort of lift, having a fine and nimble agility of the hand, and the gentleman lifts. In describing a professional troupe, consisting of a "clout" and two "covers," only the language, but not the techniques of operation, differentiates this from a modern description.[2]

During the 1500s, England was engaged in world trade and commercial activity was expanding. Because England had a huge wool industry, more and more farms were being used to graze sheep. Consequently, a great number of poor farmers and their families migrated to the cities to seek work. This led to serious urban problems, such as crime. The merchants of England were very much dissatisfied with the protection afforded to them by the government. There was no organized police force as we know it today. Instead, a compulsory watch service existed and citizens were required to serve or pay someone to take their place. Disgusted with the protection they received, merchants began to hire private police to guard their businesses, investigate crimes, and recover property stolen from them. This movement developed into the Merchant Police of England.

As the industrial revolution gained momentum during the 1700s in England, many strategies were attempted to deal with the growing crime problem. In 1748, Henry Fielding, a magistrate, conceived the idea of preventing crime by police action. A foot patrol and a horse patrol were organized for London. The Bow Street Runners, the first detective unit, were carefully selected police who moved quickly to a crime scene to begin an immediate investigation. Despite these efforts, crime continued to rise. Vigilante groups were organized to protect life and property, and to apprehend criminals. Rewards were also offered. Citizens used wolf traps to protect their property and more and more citizens carried firearms. Punishments became increasingly severe—160 crimes were punishable by death. Stealing a loaf of bread was a hanging offense. Severe penalties did not curb crime as lawmakers expected. As pickpockets were hung, others were picking pockets among the crowd watching the executions.

The Lives of Remarkable Criminals, published in the 1920s in England, describes the desperation of shopkeepers:

> In the summer of the year 1726, shoplifters became so common and so detrimental to the shopkeepers, that they made application to the Government for assistance in apprehending the offenders; and in order thereto, offered a reward and a pardon for any who would discover their associates in such practice.[3]

During 1829, a revolution in policing occurred in England when Sir Robert Peel persuaded Parliament that a professional police department was needed.

The public also had to be convinced. This was done by reforming the criminal law and reducing the number of offenses requiring a death penalty. Respect for the police and the laws they enforced grew. The Metropolitan Police Act produced quality policing and contributed to social order.

Formal policing began in London on September 29, 1829, when 1,000 men in six divisions began to patrol the city. Their headquarters was located at a residence used by the kings of Scotland—Scotland Yard. Peel's reform was to later serve as a model for policing in the United States.

During the 1800s, cities in the United States experienced similar types of urban problems as those experienced in England. Expanding cities provided many opportunities for criminals to steal goods and money—businesses were conveniently concentrated downtown and along major thoroughfares, credit for individual shoppers did not exist in cities, and people carried cash. Businesspeople had only rudimentary methods available to protect their valuables. It was common practice for business owners to carelessly display their merchandise and leave money laying about in their offices. Security was minimal. Because of these factors, criminals encountered many tempting targets. Hardware and clothing stores were especially popular among criminals. Those shops that displayed merchandise on the sidewalk made theft easier for the passing shoplifter.

A book entitled *Our Rival the Rascal*, written by Superintendent Benjamin Eldridge and Chief Inspector William Watts of the Boston Police, describes shoplifting during the late 1800s:

> There are doubtless thousands of dabblers in shop-lifting in our country as in the countries of the old world—boys who slyly pocket an apple or a handful of candy or even a knife or a necktie when the shop-keeper's head is turned—and girls who pick up a handkerchief or a bottle of cheap perfumery from the heaps on a counter. The little pilferers would commonly shrink from any considerable theft and, probably, most of them learn to be more honest as they grow older. But these first slips on the crust of crime are demoralizing and dangerous and most of our veteran thieves can trace their downfall from such a start.[4]

Before the Civil War, plate glass became a popular method of displaying merchandise, especially among jewelers. The "smash and grab" was born, as criminals used a rock to break a window and steal the merchandise.

Thieves had a good market for their stolen goods, since unscrupulous businesspeople bought these items and were unconcerned about true ownership. Furthermore, law enforcement against the fence was in its infancy.

Another problem that plagued businesses during this era was that safecrackers displayed a technical superiority over safe manufacturers until the end of the nineteenth century. There was a lack of good burglar-resistant safes. When safe manufacturers switched from iron to steel during the 1860s, burglars began using diamond bits to crack the safes. Manufacturers then resorted to constructing their safes of multiple layers of iron, steel, stone, and wire mesh to create a time delay and discourage burglars.

As more marketing innovations appeared in the retail industry during the early twentieth century, more shoplifting opportunities attracted offenders. For example, during the Great Depression supermarkets were characterized by self-service and poor illumination. Because customers could easily handle goods without the close supervision of a salesperson, shoplifting became more tempting. These supermarket retailers had yet to realize the benefits of good lighting in increasing sales and curbing crime. One source states that the increase in the number of shoplifting arrests between 1911–1920 was probably due, in part, to the formation of enlarged protection departments at stores because of increased shoplifting. In the late 1940s, a drug chain in the East had a $1,400,000 inventory loss in six months. Management used the polygraph test on the chain's 1,400 employees and found that 75 percent of them had been stealing merchandise and cash.[5]

Retailing Today

Retail businesses exist to make a profit. Total U.S. sales for the 1.9 million retail businesses now exceed $1 trillion annually and more than 17 million people are employed in this industry.[6]

It is the job of the security practitioner to concentrate on designing protection to mesh with the retailer's plans. A few basic terms and definitions are presented here to describe the business of retailing and what it is working to accomplish.

Retailing consists of business activities involved in selling products and services to consumers. Retailers' success largely depends on the degree to which they implement the retailing concept. The retailing concept requires management to determine the needs and wants of its target markets and to direct the firm toward satisfying those needs and wants more effectively than the competition. A retail strategy statement identifies the target market toward which retailers will direct their efforts, the nature of the merchandise and services retailers will offer, and how retailers will outdo their competitors. The retail strategy is developed by management through a retail mix that satisfies the target market better than the competition. A retail mix is the combination of factors that satisfies customer needs and influences purchasing. An example of a retail mix includes types of merchandise and services offered, pricing, advertising, type of assistance to customers by salespeople, store design and display of merchandise, and convenience of the store location. Some of these elements directly affect security efforts. Customer self-service, store design, and the way in which merchandise is displayed can attract shoplifters, and the crime rate of the store location will influence losses. (These topics are covered in subsequent chapters.)

Security and Loss Prevention

Security is narrowly defined as traditional methods (security officers, fences, alarms) used to increase the likelihood of a crime-controlled, tranquil, and noninterrupted environment for an individual or organization in pursuit of objectives. *Loss prevention* is broadly defined as any method (e.g., security officers, safety, auditing, insurance) used by an individual or organization to increase the likelihood of preventing and controlling loss (e.g., people, money, productivity, materials) resulting from a host of adverse occurrences (e.g., crime, fire, accident, error, poor supervision or management, bad investment).

Although the primary focus of this book is on security and shrinkage protection, several topics in this text pertain to the broader concept of loss prevention, including risk management, safety, and fire protection.

Retailers are subject to a host of adverse incidents. Crimes, fires, and accidents are major causes of losses. However, many more perils can befall a retail business, such as natural disasters (e.g., earthquake, flood), pollution, strike, equipment or system failure, error, and waste. Retailers incur billions of dollars in losses each year due to internal theft and shoplifting. It is the job of the retail security and loss prevention practitioner to plan, implement, and monitor the best possible program to minimize losses and protect profits.

Notes

1. William H. Bolen, *Contemporary Retailing*, 3rd ed. (Englewood Cliffs, NJ: Prentice-Hall, 1991), 6.
2. Loren E. Edwards, *Shoplifting and Shrinkage Protection for Stores* (Springfield, IL: Charles C. Thomas Publishers, 1958), 4.
3. Ibid., 5.
4. Ibid., 11.
5. Ibid., 14 and 61.
6. Irving Burstiner, *Basic Retailing*, 2nd ed. (Homewood, IL: Irwin Pub., 1991), 37.

2

Planning for Retail Security

It is the job of the security manager to select cost-effective strategies to prevent and minimize losses. Rather than implementing security strategies that fail to do the job, the security manager should carefully research and plan as an essential foundation for retail protection. This chapter provides practical tools for improving decision making.

For the security practitioner, the following three factors influence management support and funding, while enhancing an effective retail security program:

1. an understanding of the objectives and problems inherent in modern retailing
2. quality security planning
3. marketing the security program and its strategies

Retail Objectives and Problems

The prime objective of retailing is to make a profit. This can be accomplished by employing a multitude of unique business strategies that differ from other retailers. A novel marketing idea can propel a retail company to huge profits. As stated in the previous chapter, management determines the needs and wants of its target market, and directs the firm toward satisfying those needs and wants more effectively than the competition.

The retail industry is filled with numerous, complex problems that result from factors in the retail environment. These factors include the ups and downs of the economy, technological innovations, changing demographics, legal regulations of the industry, and several other additional problems that are of particular concern to retail security practitioners.

Many part-time and temporary employees work in the retail industry, especially during busy holiday seasons. These employees are often young and inexperienced. The screening of these applicants prior to hiring them is typically inadequate and, once hired, the training provided is usually poor. The result is that the retailer is likely to suffer from employee errors, customer dissatisfaction, and internal theft. Turnover compounds these problems.

A universal security strategy to combat this situation is thorough screening of job applicants to prevent those individuals who have an inclination to create losses from entering the workplace. Poor screening and training practices make the job of protection much more difficult for security personnel.

Modern merchandising is another area in which the practices of the retailer can run counter to what security is trying to accomplish. Most retailers want customers to walk freely about their store, touch merchandise, and then buy it. However, the more the retailer pushes merchandise on customers through a variety of techniques, and the more the customer becomes attracted to the merchandise, the greater the likelihood of triggering a theft.

Store site selection is another security concern. Management may anticipate a profit by opening a store in a certain neighborhood without considering the safety of employees and the potential for various crimes.

Store design also affects security. Multiple access points, large plate glass windows, and the arrangement and height of fixtures affect theft prevention.

Funding is an additional problem faced by the security practitioner. Because businesses exist to make a profit, security expenditures may be perceived as a drain on profits. Management may offer limited support for security, but expect first-class protection. Store managers are typically preoccupied with daily sales volumes and deal with the fear of being forced to close because of poor sales. Consequently, security may be considered a low priority.

Security specialists are often subject to the backlash of high shrinkage (e.g., merchandise losses from theft, damage, and paperwork errors). (This topic is discussed in Chapter 6.) If shrinkage does not go down, the security manager's job may be in jeopardy. Unfortunately, security managers cannot fix loss problems by simply devising new policies and procedures for store employees. Salespeople, for example, have more on their minds than security and loss prevention. Apathy toward security is common in many retail stores.

Another problem confronted by security personnel is the possibility of a lawsuit as a result of action taken to protect the retailer. In some instances, the consequences are serious and expensive.

With security weaknesses inherent in the retail industry, what is a security specialist to do? With limited funds and support, how can retail stores be protected? Despite the difficulties of this vocation, security specialists must look at these problems as challenges that have solutions. This entails creative solutions so that security strategies mesh with the objectives of the retailer. This must be the mind-set of the security practitioner or else he/she will not succeed. The purpose of this book is to offer some answers and solutions.

Security Planning

Planning is a management function that results in a design used to achieve objectives. Planning anticipates and prepares for change. In the security and loss prevention field, planning is essential. When a critical incident occurs, panic may result. However, if the security executive is prepared with carefully conceived plans, a critical event is less likely to be shocking and severe losses can possibly be prevented. Those who say, "We'll cross that bridge when we get to it," are inviting disaster. Their heads will roll if they are not prepared for worst-case scenarios.

The reality of retail security makes planning difficult. Those working in retail security may not know how to plan effectively and, with limited personnel and funds, there is very little time for planning when one is putting out one fire after another.

Planning requires good record keeping to pinpoint trends and make informed decisions. It necessitates meeting with others to develop both ideas and strategies for action. Planning should cover not only the problems of internal theft and shoplifting, but also fire protection and safety.

All security executives should devote time to planning. It ensures success and job security. When a security plan is prepared, it should contain objectives, the names of personnel involved, job duties, policies and procedures, a training program, equipment and systems, support resources, a budget, and evaluation methods.

Turning the Tide at Eckerd Drug

Early in 1990, veteran loss prevention director Lew Shealy took over as VP, Loss Prevention, at Eckerd Drug, a $3.5 billion chain based in Largo, Florida. At the time, the chain lacked a formal program for preventing loss, and its shrinkage percentage was "moving in the wrong direction," says Shealy. Now, after setting up a formalized loss prevention organization, training staff, building awareness, and instituting procedures to monitor shrinkage, Shealy says, "the tide is going out."

The tide is what? "That phrase is part of our awareness program," says Shealy. "You always need goals and objectives in a loss prevention program, because goals and objectives generate effort. So last year we set our first goal—to stop our shrinkage from growing—and we used the slogan, "Stop the tide from coming in." Eckerd stemmed the tide in January of 1991, and now, Shealy is happy to report, shrink is coming down.

Shealy spent most of his long career in the department store field, and found drug stores to be quite different. For one thing, the Eckerd chain is on the cost method of accounting, which makes it more difficult to pinpoint shrinkage, according to Shealy.

Also, the drug chain was not as systems oriented as most department stores. There was only a limited point-of-sale system, and, as a result, very little back-office support to produce exception reports that identify employee dishonesty.

Beyond that, the company was not oriented toward preventing loss. "The program, what there was of it, was geared toward apprehension," says Shealy. "There was no awareness, no effort to prevent loss."

Organizing for prevention Shealy's challenge, then, was to set up an organization dedicated to preventing loss, and this required a commitment from senior management. Shealy started with a "bottom-line" appeal: "The best way to increase gross margin today is to reduce shrink," he says. "You can't raise prices these days."

The argument is compelling when you consider the numbers. With a $3.5 billion company, a shrinkage reduction of just one-tenth of one percent is equivalent to $3.5 million.

Once he had the attention of senior management, the next step was to establish a loss prevention organization with a reporting structure that led to the highest levels of Eckerd Drug. He started by forming a corporate shrinkage committee. Chaired by Shealy, it includes the company's CEO, president, and CFO—"all the top management," says Shealy.

Next he set up a semi-autonomous regional organization, with each of the company's eight regions forming a loss prevention committee headed by a loss prevention manager. Each committee would be ultimately responsible for its own programs, but these programs would be periodically reviewed and modified by the corporate committee.

Stressing goals and objectives In helping to design their programs, Shealy stressed goals and objectives and a heightened awareness of shrink. One of the cornerstones of the awareness program is a poster board, which has been installed in all 1,700 Eckerd Drug stores. The boards carry shrink awareness messages, track the store's known losses, and hold a supply of "Shrinkage Busting Suggestion Forms." These forms give associates a chance to participate in the effort to reduce shrink, and if an idea is implemented, the company pays the associate $25. From March 1, when the program was started, to September 30, more than 1,200 associates have sent in forms, and $9,000 has been paid out.

An emphasis on auditing Even more important than awareness, says Shealy, is the importance of auditing for compliance. "Probably the best weapon we have in loss prevention is the audit," he says. "As a result, 50 percent of our loss prevention time is spent on auditing."

This year alone, Eckerd performed 5,000 audits for loss prevention, an average of 2.7 audits per store. It is an additional burden, admits Shealy, but it forces all the stores to comply with procedures and standards, and that is a key to effective loss prevention.

Civil restitution pays dividends In his "new life" with Eckerd Drug, Shealy has also become very enamored of civil restitution. "If I was going back into a department store environment today," he says, "I would go in this direction."

Why? Because it generates revenue. Last year the company recovered over $700,000 through civil recovery, and this year expects to recover $1 million. Also, civil restitution is a practical alternative to prosecution, Shealy believes.

Eckerd takes civil action against about 95 percent of the customers it apprehends. When a manager apprehends someone, he or she gives the shoplifter a civil demand letter requesting $200. To make restitution "user-friendly," Eckerd accepts payment by credit card.

Shealy admits, however, that the professional shoplifter is the biggest enemy in a drug store. In one recently concluded case, professionals were stealing $3,000 per week worth of cosmetics and other items and selling the goods to flea markets.

With these people at least partially in mind, Eckerd is investing in a wireless closed-circuit television system, which will allow security people to monitor a store from off-premises, and an enormous new alarm system. The system, now being installed by ADT, will be the largest proprietary central alarm system in the U.S., and will save the company an estimated $500,000 per year.

Technology, though, is only a tool in the war on theft. To turn the tide on shrinkage, says Shealy, you need a commitment from your people—from senior management down, and your people have to be better business managers.

Reprinted with permission from Ernst & Young. *Source:* The Ernst & Young/IMRA Survey of Retail Loss Prevention Trends (January 1992).

At Kay-Bee Toys, Loss Prevention Only Seems Like Fun and Games

Picture this: thousands of kids a day are streaming through your stores, hungrily eyeing the latest heavily promoted toy or video game cartridge. Manning the aisles and providing your primary line of defense against theft and point-of-sale mismanagement are a limited number of sales associates. A scenario for high shrinkage? Absolutely, unless you manage it aggressively, as Kay-Bee Toy Stores does.

A division of Melville Corp., Kay-Bee Toys is a $1 billion chain of 1,263 toy stores located primarily in shopping malls. According to Dan Burns, the company's loss prevention director, the concerns in toy retailing are similar to those in the specialty apparel segment—both carry trendy product lines and draw young customers who have a tendency to shoplift.

"Toys is a fashion industry," he says. "Products like Nintendo and Cabbage Patch Dolls are heavily promoted through television, and retailers have to time the hot streaks properly. That means we have to carry large quantities and lots of SKUs, which increases our exposure to theft."

Compounding the challenge, he says, is Kay-Bee's mall locations. Youngsters like to roam in malls, making the situation "tougher to control," he says—especially when the mall stores are staffed primarily by sales people aged 17–22.

Shrinkage not a top priority in the '80s Remarkably, says Burns, Kay-Bee did not fully recognize its vulnerability to shrinkage until recently. In the 1980s, when business was brisk and margins were high, the dollars lost to shrinkage went largely unnoticed. Of course, if there was a major problem at a particular location, they addressed it. But management also had the luxury of taking markups to compensate for significant losses.

The nineties obviously presents a new reality. There is considerable pressure on margins, and shrinkage is impacting the bottom line, even at growing, profitable companies like Kay-Bee. For Burns, who joined the company in late 1990, this has meant attacking shrink aggressively. But it has also meant changing a company culture that has not fully appreciated the shrinkage problem before.

Change starts from the top Working with senior management, Burns began instituting these cultural changes in January, 1991. His first step was to scale down and redefine the role of loss prevention in the field. The new structure consists of 10 regional loss prevention managers, each responsible for approximately 110 stores.

These loss prevention managers were "empowered" to take complete responsibility for loss prevention in their regions and work closely with the regional sales managers in all aspects of the business. Education, training and prevention now play a larger role than investigation and detection.

T.O.Y.S. awareness Burns' next major initiative was to heighten awareness throughout the organization, and particularly at the sales associate level. "Our associates are our first line of defense," says Burns. "It's critical that we get and hold their attention."

Because most of Kay-Bee's associates are between the ages of 17 and 22, and because there was little awareness training before he arrived, the program includes some very fundamental things. Associates are told to make eye contact with customers, for example. They're also trained to be friendly and ask questions like, "Can I help you?"

These kinds of fundamentals are also communicated on stock-room bulletin boards. Every week, the board carries a new loss prevention message such as, "Never leave back doors unattended."

Beyond the basics, Burns has fashioned a creative awareness program known as TOYS, which stands for Take On Your Shrinkage. Associates wear TOYS buttons, which serve as constant reminders, and every month the loss prevention department holds an awareness activity aimed at the 17–22 year olds.

Back in October, Burns held a "lottery-type" event. All 17,000 Kay-Bee associates were sent a lottery-style ticket that quizzed them on basic loss prevention issues, and also gave them an opportunity to win a "grand" prize. By scratching off one of the four numbers on the ticket, an associate had a chance to win a canvas bag. (There were 300 winners.)

The company also runs loss prevention articles in its internal newsletters, and it sends out attention-grabbing messages in its payroll stuffers. Often these messages are in the form of cartoons. One recent example: Two "bandit-like" characters are talking. One says to the other, "I really like these steal one, get one free sales."

Limited use of technology Loss prevention technologies are used sparingly at Kay-Bee. According to Burns, the technological focus is on the POS. Specifically, they are now utilizing it more fully to produce exception reports and beyond that, to generate a kind of loss prevention "profile" at the store level.

The company does not use EAS, though it will be testing it in 1992. In high-shrink locations, it does use some of the traditional loss prevention devices, like mirrors. But as Burns says, Kay-Bee's primary "device" is its people.

Are they effective? Yes, says Burns. Kay-Bee's shrinkage has historically been in line with the industry standard for hardliners, somewhere between 2.00 and 2.50 percent of sales.

"Shrink can be controlled," says Burns. "You need a commitment from management, a strong organization with careful monitoring and reporting, and most of all, awareness. Fortunately, we have that commitment."

Reprinted with permission from Ernst & Young. *Source:* The Ernst & Young/IMRA Survey of Retail Loss Prevention Trends (January 1992).

Guidelines for Planning

The following list provides some basic guidelines for developing a mind-set for planning.

- A security plan must reflect the needs of the business and management's viewpoints. Both viewpoints may differ, which presents a challenge for security. For instance, a security manager may argue for more resources directed at internal theft, while management may view shoplifting as a greater threat. Record keeping and research can be used to justify expenditures.
- Although retail store design and merchandising techniques aim to generate profits, they may also expose a retailer to crime. Security managers must accept these vulnerabilities and work with the retailer to provide store protection.
- Planning is an ongoing process. Since the world is changing so quickly, retailers must respond rapidly to survive and security must keep pace with the industry. A broad view of the world, in terms of economic, social, and political factors is important for security managers.
- One of the most underused avenues of effective security planning is an interdisciplinary approach. Several fields of study hold answers to security and loss prevention problems, such as risk management and marketing. Security professionals should read and study issues outside of the security field to prevent "tunnel vision" and to foster a broader perspective of problems and solutions.
- A security manager should never remain confined in an office to design "miracle security plans." Those who are served by security (e.g., employees, customers) should be solicited for ideas to improve protection. When expensive capital investments are planned for security, a buying team can be established. This is

especially important because of rapid technological changes and the need for integration of old and new security systems. Members of the security, risk management, finance, and management information systems (MIS) departments can be part of a buying team for large corporate purchases.

Plans must be clearly stated in financial terms for management.

When security plans are presented to management for approval, ensure that there is sound justification.

Questions during Planning

As plans for protection unfold, each strategy should be screened through the following series of questions:

- Is the proposed strategy for protection really needed? Has a risk analysis been conducted? Is there a realization that security is as good as the time it takes to get through it?
- What type of security is being planned? Is it hardware, software, personnel, policies and procedures, or a combination thereof?
- What level of security is required for the retailer? Minimum, medium, or maximum? Retail stores are not prisons and increased security must be subtle and not hinder business operations or customer shopping. (One department store, for example, located near a drug-infested neighborhood, had 35 security personnel working on Saturdays, plus extensive closed-circuit television (CCTV). The security force blended into the activities of the store without being obvious.)
- What will the security strategy cost? Is it cost-effective? What is the timetable for a return on investment?
- What research has been conducted on the strategy? Any published research? What are other similar companies doing?
- Does the strategy conform to business and management objectives and needs?
- Does the strategy interfere with business operations or alienate customers?
- Will the strategy have a negative impact on employee morale?
- What are employee views on the security strategy? (For example, management can set policies and procedures, but employees must have the time to do the job.)
- Have external factors been checked for input? This includes insurance carriers, local public safety agencies, laws, and local codes.
- How will the strategy be evaluated?

Another means of planning is to use risk management techniques. These techniques are covered in Chapter 11.

Planning from a Systems Perspective

The planning process can be assisted through a systems perspective that involves inputs, processes, output, and feedback (Figure 2-1).

The input for planning can become quite extensive. Most of the topics in the input column in Figure 2-1 are discussed in this book. The more informed the security executive is with these topics, the better the chance that quality decisions will be made. Security executives must become a conduit of information for planning.

In his book *Loss Prevention through Crime Analysis*, Francis J. D'Addario emphasizes that it is of paramount importance to find out where losses are occurring so that resources can be directed at the problem. He states that analysis drives the successful prevention effort and he holds the following viewpoints:

> Crime analysis features the collection of diverse pieces of crime data: the who, what, when, where, and how. These data are then catalogued and examined for common denominators, patterns, and trends.
>
> Crime analysis enhances policy decisions, the allocation of resources, selection of hardware, and training. The methodology can be expanded to track all casualty losses including worker's compensation, public liability, and property losses.
>
> For chain stores, repeat offenders are tracked on maps that illustrate the locations of similar crimes. Embezzlers are tracked through audit trails. Serial offenders are charged with multiple counts resulting in longer incarceration. Crime analysis ensures objectivity and improves return on investment.
>
> The method of operation (MO) used by offenders is at the foundation of crime analysis. And because offenders are creatures of habit, their anonymity to avoid capture is destroyed by collecting information on their MO (e.g., type of business victimized, time, point of entry, weapon, type of property taken, and description and behavior of offender).[1]

In his crime analysis work with various fast-food restaurant chains, Francis J. D'Addario carefully studied robbery methods and then designed policy countermeasures for each type of robber. For example, the customer robber accounted for 19 percent of all robberies in one chain. This robber usually arrived 15 minutes before closing, ordered an expensive item (because the money would be taken back), sat in a key location for observing many areas

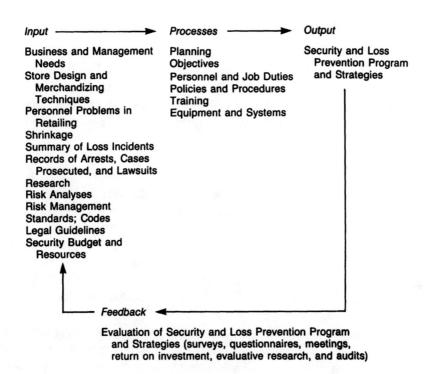

Figure 2-1 Planning from a Systems Perspective

of the store, and preferred for personnel to ignore him to reduce the chances of subsequent identification. After the MO of these customer robbers was isolated (based on robbery incident reports), training helped employees to decide whether to call police for a preventive patrol or suspicious person report. In one chain, the robbery rate was reduced by 23 percent by policy and procedure alone. The point here is that careful crime reporting and analysis can lead to successful strategies for security and loss prevention.

Also, D'Addario found that a significant percentage of crimes was misreported by retail workers (e.g., burglaries and larcenies were reported as robberies). Training and reviewing of reports by supervisors reduced this problem.

Another important revelation of crime analysis is the significant portion of crimes from within:

> In the service industry, at least one-third of the robberies are internally related, involving either current or former employees and their associates. Similarly, 90% of nonforcible entry commercial burglaries and 95% of the larcenies feature internal connections.[2]

Risk Analysis

Risk analysis is a tool for planning security; it provides input to improve planning. Three steps are involved in a risk analysis—survey the premises requiring protection, identify vulnerabilities, and determine probability, frequency, and cost. A good risk analysis can estimate the expected annual loss from specific threats. However, the methods of risk analyses vary.

Survey

The survey should be designed for the specific business that requires protection. A retail store would require a different list of survey questions than a manufacturing plant. The survey for a retail store should be broad-based and include any areas that could cause losses. Crime, fire, and accident are main concerns, but many more topics can be included in a comprehensive survey, such as job applicant screening, training, point-of-sale (POS) practices, inventory procedures, shrinkage, buying practices, vendor controls, merchandise controls, price changes, and accounting and computer controls.

The survey can emphasize the three major strategies of loss prevention: people, policies and procedures, and hardware. Targets of protection, such as employees, customers in the parking lot, merchandise, money, and equipment and systems, can also be included in the survey to study how each is being protected.

Vulnerabilities

A survey will often expose weaknesses in protection. Modifications may be made to existing methods and new methods of protection can be introduced. For example, loopholes in a customer refund system necessitate tighter accountability. Undercharged fire extinguishers require more frequent inspection and charging. A large increase in robberies should be countered by policies and procedures, training, and physical security.

Probability, Frequency, and Cost

When determining the probability, frequency, and cost of potential loss incidents, the answers are not easy to pinpoint. Sources of assistance include the security practitioner's experience, records or past incidents, industry reports, trade publications, research, communications with fellow practitioners, and special computer programs.

Security managers typically maintain records of loss incidents. These records can provide many answers. However, careful analysis of these records is required, because incorrect conclusions can result. For example, if a retail store records 100 shoplifting apprehensions for a year, this does not mean that only 100 shoplifters stole from the store. How many people stole during the year and what are the total losses? What percentage of store losses and shrinkage are attributed to shoplifting in comparison to employee theft? It is the combination of multiple sources of information that provides the best estimate of probability, frequency, and cost.

When the costs of loss incidents are calculated, direct and indirect costs should be included. For example, the direct cost from a burglary would be the amount of money stolen from the safe. Indirect costs may include repair to the point of forced entry at the building and repair or replacement of the safe, as well as losses not covered by insurance. In addition, several hours of an employee's time will have to be spent with police, repair workers, the insurer, and company security personnel. Special arrangements will have to be made to accommodate cash on the premises until the safe is repaired or replaced. This may entail frequent trips to the bank or additional expenses for extra cash pickups by an armored carrier. Lost sales must be estimated while police are processing the crime scene during normal operating hours. Total costs are often underestimated after a loss incident. *It is vital that security managers communicate true costs (direct and indirect) of incidents or potential incidents so that upper management fully understands the financial impact of losses.*

Return on Investment (ROI)

More and more business executives are demanding that security and loss prevention expenditures produce an ROI. For the protection manager, this means that planning and budgeting must be spelled out in financial language familiar to the business executive. A request for a CCTV system, for example, will not only require a detailed plan and budget, but also a sound justification for the purchase (based on a risk analysis) and a timetable that shows when the investment will show a return.

For those security managers who find this difficult to digest, they may be forced into demonstrating an ROI as a result of the following statement from a senior executive: "Look, we are facing tough economic times. Our last quarter was awful. The security budget will be cut significantly unless you can show us a return on investment."

One avenue for retail security management to demonstrate an ROI is by lowering shrinkage following an investment in security. If, for example, $2 can be returned to the company for every $1 invested in security, then the security investment shows a good return.

Another way in which an ROI may be demonstrated is through a summary of loss events in a company. This summary can show a decline in incidents, lower monetary losses, and an increase in recovery of assets. But this can get tricky, because investments in security can result in an increase in incidents reported. This may be due to more patrols and investigations, easier reporting methods (e.g., a toll-free number), rewards for information, and greater confidence in security. Unfortunately, as security improves and more crimes are reported, a crime wave may appear to exist. Be aware that an increase in reported incidents may reflect not so much an actual increase in crime, but a change in security.

Although an investment in security may result in an initial upswing in reported crimes, the level of reporting will likely stabilize as employee-offenders leave the company, security obstacles become too formidable for offenders, and job applicants with criminal motives look elsewhere for an easier target.

Retail security managers should carefully study incidents over several years and consider how security practices affect reporting of crimes and money returned to the company. The money and assets recovered, including court-ordered restitution, should be credited to those incidents that result in such a return. Also, the uncovering and firing of dishonest employees may result in a store showing improved profits. If sales increase after such an incident by, say $20,000, security should take the credit and include these figures when demonstrating an ROI.

Loss avoidance is another factor to consider when determining ROI. Estimates can be prepared of the potential losses and costs if certain security strategies are not implemented. This projection entails a risk analysis and should include direct and indirect costs based on potential losses.

The following list provides additional ideas for generating an ROI in security.

- Purchase a system that saves on personnel costs and/or serves multiple purposes—for example, a CCTV system that is capable of watching several access points and a production line.
- Demonstrate to senior management that security is contributing to profitability. For instance, undercover investigators not only perform security functions, they also work as clerks, truck drivers, and so forth. Furthermore, nonsecurity information can also be collected by the investigator, such as production problems and unsafe conditions. Several jobs are being done for the price of one.
- Work to reduce insurance premiums through security and loss prevention (S&LP) methods.
- Estimate direct and indirect losses from crimes, fires, and accidents if S&LP did not exist to curb these losses.

- Hire a bad check specialist or debt collector who recovers several times his or her salary or contract the problem to a service at a predetermined rate of return.
- Study the net result of public prosecution of employee-offenders versus private justice.
- Study the feasibility of having those subjected to security and investigative efforts pay for these costs after overwhelming evidence has been collected. This has been done in the United States and overseas.
- Perform security services (patrol, investigation) for other companies during slow seasons.
- Train other firms' security personnel for profit.
- For large companies with expensive in-house protection programs, consider establishing a subsidiary to supply security services. Savings are netted through adjustments in benefits and salaries. In-house security personnel do take a loss, but the alternative may be to let them all go, to be replaced by a contract force.
- Use an in-house central station alarm-monitoring facility to include outside accounts for a profit. Carefully consider liability. Or form a consortium among several businesses to share the central station investment. Or purchase a central station and sell it to a contractor, who agrees to lease it back and then sell it back after a set time. Proper legal, accounting, tax, and risk management input are worthwhile.
- Expand security's role to include accident management: prevention of injuries and protection against claims. Require that security patrols check for unsafe conditions. Coordinate workers' compensation claims through security to utilize investigative skills and, possibly, covert surveillance for malingering.
- Senior management must be made aware of savings generated through S&LP. One reported unsafe condition can avoid an expensive accident. One uncovered case of workers' compensation fraud can pay an investigator's salary for a year.
- Consider combining the security, safety, and fire protection departments into a loss prevention department. Through a close, coordinated effort, ROI may be easier to accomplish for these functions.
- For each ROI idea, applicable state and federal laws should be checked. Potential liabilities must be considered and risk management techniques applied.[3]

Standards

Security standards provide input for planning security. Standards promote uniformity of protection among businesses in the same industry and ensure that a specific level of protection is maintained for people and assets.

Banks are protected in this way through the Bank Protection Act, airports through the Federal Aviation Administration, and defense industries through the Department of Defense. Retailers, on the other hand, and restaurants, hotels, office buildings, and manufacturing plants do not have universally accepted standards of security and loss prevention. One reason for this is that there are so many diverse types of businesses.

The court system has essentially led the way in producing guidelines for adequate security through lawsuits over inadequate security. Consider the following scenario. A retail customer approaches his automobile in a parking lot. He is assaulted and later sues the retailer for not providing enough security. When the plaintiff's attorney shows the court that there is substantial security at area retail businesses and poor security at the crime scene, the jury is likely to rule in favor of the plaintiff and support a hefty award. Consequently, retailers should study security at nearby businesses and plan for similar protection.

Municipal codes may require certain security and safety features for businesses. For example, in certain locales businesses are required to provide dead bolts and convenience stores require two clerks to be on duty during the night shift. These municipal security codes are in addition to the typical building, fire, and safety codes found in most locales.

Many retail chains have their own security standards and the specialists to plan, implement, and inspect for protection. Policies and procedures for safety and security, and specifications for physical security, are applied to all stores in the chain.

The National Fire Protection Association (NFPA) has produced standards for fire protection equipment and construction that are adopted by governments and private industry. The Occupational Safety and Health Administration (OSHA) promotes workplace safety through the enforcement of standards.

Standards have existed for many years in the security alarm industry. Underwriters Laboratory (UL), an independent testing organization, has worked with insurance companies to establish a rating system for alarm products and installations.

Research

Feedback is vitally important to establishing an effective protection program. It helps to focus resources where problems and losses are evident. Feedback helps to eliminate ineffective strategies and promotes modification of other strategies.

There are certain security methods that are simply overrated. A barbed wire fence, for example, can be breached by going over, through, or under it. An alarm system signals an intrusion, but does not stop the offender. A response force must be dispatched. Essentially, security features are as good as the time it takes to bypass them.

Evaluative research ascertains the success of security strategies and helps to justify continued funding. The following basic research designs show how security strategies can be strengthened. Let us consider the pretest-posttest design and apply it to a new security training program. Employees are tested prior to the training and test scores are saved. The training is then conducted and concludes with a posttest. Pretest and posttest scores are compared. Higher scores on the posttest usually signify increased knowledge and employee behavior favorable to security. Another component of this research could be the recording of shoplifting incidents prior to the training and comparing the rates following the training. If shoplifting declines at the store following the training, then the training program may be the causative factor.

Another research design is the experimental control group. This tool is used universally in retailing, medicine, and many other fields. For retailing, two similar stores are studied. One store (the experimental group) receives a special security strategy (e.g., CCTV) and the other store (the control group) remains the same. Crime is monitored at each store prior to and following the experiment. The results are analyzed to determine whether the special security strategy introduced in the experimental store reduced losses. "Research Project Increases Crime" provides another illustration of this research tool.

Research Project Increases Crime

The Fastop convenience store chain, with 750 locations, was experiencing an upsurge in armed robberies. Although robbers averaged a take of $130, the greater threat of employee safety spurred management to seek a solution to the problem. The security department, in conjunction with a local college educator and consultant, decided to conduct a research project to find out what strategies would curb robberies. The research design was to use fifty stores as an experimental group and fifty stores as a control group. The former group was made less attractive to robbers by three inexpensive strategies:

1. clearing all windows of signs and display racks, and increasing lighting to provide a clear view into the store
2. training employees about safety precautions during a robbery
3. reducing available cash in stores and posting signs that indicate bank deposits are made frequently

After six months, the experimental group was compared to the control group. The experimental group showed a 40 percent decline in robberies and a 60 percent decline in money robbed when compared to the same period a year earlier. The control group had about the same number of robberies and cash taken as before.

Frequently, research reveals unexpected results. In the foregoing project, the experimental group showed a slight increase in reported robberies of managers on their way to the bank at the end of the business day. (A few managers who "staged" and reported a robbery on their way to the bank admitted to their crime.) Another component was added to the research before it was expanded to other stores: A security bulletin was prepared and sent to all experimental group stores that contained information on security and safety. One bulletin, entitled "Increasing Your Chances of Successfully Making It to the Bank," listed tips such as making sure that enough gasoline was in the car, not carrying an obvious money bag, and not giving strangers a ride. Six months later, the expanded research project showed no increase in managers robbed on their way to the bank. The research continued and the number of robberies dropped.[4]

Caution is advised when forming conclusions following research. Variables unknown to the researcher may influence research results. Repeated research will strengthen the conclusions drawn from the original research.

The scientific method is a universally applied method of conducting research. It involves a four-step process: statement of the problem, hypothesis, testing, and conclusion. The hypotheses restates the problem and provides a solution. Testing utilizes some of the previously discussed research designs.

Scientific Method

Problem:	Employee Theft
Hypothesis:	Employee theft can be reduced through CCTV.
Testing:	Experimental Group Control Group
	Store A, CCTV Store B, no CCTV
Conclusion:	Following six months of testing, Store A showed a drop in employee theft. CCTV may be the causative factor.

Following such research, other stores can be studied. Also, additional strategies (e.g., thorough job applicant screening) can be added to stores for testing.

Audits

Following the implementation of security plans, practitioners must determine whether the plans are being followed by employees. Audits evaluate protection programs and provide feedback to security management.

Audits vary widely. They can be as simple as a security officer surveying physical security or a supervisor checking to see if employees are following policies and procedures, or as complex as an accountant studying financial records. Audits are often a delicate process that require the utmost concern for positive human relations. Employees may become defensive when subjected to an audit or inspection and any recommendations that result from an audit may be difficult to implement.

Two avenues of promoting audits involve management support and personnel evaluations. When management supports audits through directives, verbal communication, and actual execution of the audit, employees are more likely to be cooperative. Personnel evaluations in conjunction with raises also play a role in generating support for audits and cooperation with suggestions for improvement.

Marketing

Marketing consists of a set of principles for choosing target markets, measuring their needs, developing want-satisfying products and services, and delivering them at a value to the customer and a profit to the company.[5]

Marketers face challenges similar to security practitioners. For example, security managers are selling protection services and resistance must be overcome from upper-management and employees throughout an organization.

The environment in which something is marketed is constantly changing. The outside institutions and forces that affect a business are known as the macroenvironment. The macroenvironment includes demographic, technological, cultural, economic, and political factors. Security managers should be in tune to the changing macroenvironment, as this knowledge will help them market security. Demographic statistics cover changes in family structure, the educational level of the populace, aging, and other topics. If there is an increase in single women in the work environment, then maybe security can design a specific program to protect them on and off the premises. With new technology constantly entering the retail environment, security must be aware of the threats it may bring. If an increased percentage of a retailer's customers read and speak Spanish, then the retailer must make changes to facilitate communication. For instance, antishoplifting signs should be printed in

English and Spanish. Economic problems can easily result in cuts in security budgets. Political factors are varied and may involve security, such as demonstrations over not hiring enough minorities or a controversy over a certain product for sale.

Retail security managers should consider various marketing concepts and strategies to improve the effectiveness of security. Market segmentation divides a market into groups of consumers who have particular needs. When a specific market segment is chosen for a certain product or service in conjunction with a precise marketing program, this is called *target marketing*. In a retail environment, the protection market can be divided into salespeople, cashiers, management, buyers, and employees. Each segment of the market can be targeted to receive a specially tailored protection program to meet each group's needs. Salespeople can receive a special training program that emphasizes the problems and countermeasures associated with shoplifting; special training for cashiers can focus on bad checks and credit cards, counterfeit money, and quick-change artists; management can be instructed on the causes of and countermeasures for shrinkage; buyers can receive concise bulletins on travel tips to prevent victimization; and employees can be provided with self-protection guidelines for parking lots, home, and so forth. The point is, security is very often general in nature and so broad in scope that it may interest very few. The retail security manager needs to pique people's interest by using basic marketing strategies (i.e., studying the various consumers of security, segmenting the market, and then targeting the various markets with specially tailored programs). The influence of security over a target group or groups is better than no influence at all.

Marketing strategies are increasingly being applied to, not only products, but also services and ideas. Security can benefit from marketing strategies, because security is a service based on certain ideas. Public police departments employ numerous strategies to sell police services and ideas to the community. "Officer Friendly" and McGruff the crime-fighting dog are advertising campaigns to promote crime prevention. Even the color and markings on the patrol cars are all carefully designed marketing strategies.4

A retail security department can improve its image in a company by following these three steps—ascertain the present image, decide on the desirable image, and prepare a marketing plan. Two specific avenues for improving image are to establish quality hiring standards and training. However, management support and an adequate budget are vital. Unfortunately, in many organizations neither support nor funding are plentiful and the security manager must be creative. Consider the following ideas for improving image:

> Ensure that all security personnel have a good appearance. This generates respect and cooperation. First impressions are lasting and

there is only one opportunity to create a first impression. Require that all security personnel act in a courteous manner. Strive to make courtesy contagious.
Establish the credibility of the security department. This occurs when people trust security personnel and believe in their competence and judgment. Credibility is established by setting a good example and through ethical leadership.[6]
Focus on all employees as loss prevention partners, not suspects.
Participate in the orientation of all new employees and in periodic training.
Prepare internal security bulletins or write a column in a company newspaper.
Implement involvement programs to cut losses.
Participate in company recreational activities.
Become involved in community programs that promote crime prevention.

Retail Security Information Sources

The following sources can be helpful for retail security planning:

American Society for Industrial Security
1655 N. Fort Myer Dr., Suite 1200
Arlington, VA 22209
(703) 522-5800

National Retail Federation
100 West 31st St.
New York, NY 10001
(212) 244-8780

National Crime Prevention Institute
University of Louisville
Louisville, KY 40292
(502) 588-6987

Also consider these academic departments at your local college: security and loss prevention, criminal justice, business, marketing, and risk management.

Case Problems

2A. As the retail security manager for a small retail chain, you are becoming increasingly concerned about security cutbacks as described by peers working for other retail companies. The five

department stores for which you are responsible have an adequate security budget. However, your intuition tells you that your boss is going to request greater financial accountability for security expenditures (i.e., proof of a return on investment) and proof that security is effective. What do you do?
2B. As a retail security manager for a large retail store, you would like to change the image of security and generate much more support and cooperation from management and employees in general. What are your strategies?

Notes

1. Francis J. D'Addario, *Loss Prevention through Crime Analysis* (Boston: Butterworth–Heinemann, 1989), 2–5.
2. Ibid., 46.
3. Philip P. Purpura, *Modern Security & Loss Prevention Management* (Boston: Butterworth–Heinemann, 1989), pp. 57–58.
4. Ibid., 31–32.
5. Philip Kotler, *Principles of Marketing* (Englewood Cliffs, NJ: Prentice-Hall, 1980), xvii.
6. Gordon S. Smith, "Head and Shoulders above the Rest," *Security Management* (December 1991): 64.

3

Legal Aspects of Retail Security

The legal environment is one of many factors that plays a role in controlling retail businesses. (Other factors include competition, consumerism, technology, and demographics.) Laws guiding security are actually a small part of the total group of laws that impact retailing. This chapter provides an overview of laws that pertain to retailing and then focuses on legal aspects of retail security.

Local and State Laws

Local laws can be numerous and confusing among jurisdictions. A zoning law may preclude a chain restaurant from building, because the design does not blend into the local architecture. When zoning laws are not applied equally, they can become a way to bar new business. Other local laws require locales to have a business license and pay a fee. A special liquor or gasoline permit may also be required. These are sources of revenue. Approval may be necessary for placing a sign in front of a business. Local governments also exercise a degree of control over retail businesses through building and fire codes, and safety and health regulations. In reference to security, a local code may prohibit barbed wire and require dead bolts.

State governments are also involved in fire, safety, and health laws. State environmental laws and their enforcement are other issues that impact businesses. Many states have minimum markup laws that prohibit sales below cost. Licensing of professions is another area in which states are involved. Retailers are affected when they employ pharmacists, optometrists, beauticians, barbers, and others. State laws may require that a pharmacy be partly owned by a pharmacist and may bar a medical doctor from owning one. Food establishments, pet shops, and other businesses often have specific state regulations to follow. Taxes are an additional legal responsibility for the retailer. Income taxes and real estate taxes must be paid. A sales tax, collected on merchandise sold to customers, goes to the state and possibly local governments. Retailers must determine which state laws apply to their business.

Federal Laws

Numerous federal laws exist that impact retail businesses. The Sherman Antitrust Act of 1890 is an early federal statute that promotes open, unrestricted competition and endorses the free enterprise system. It was enacted to curb the monopolistic business practices (e.g., price fixing) of giant trusts in the oil and railroad industries. This law held that contracts, trusts, and conspiracies that restrained trade were illegal. This means, for example, that Sears and J.C. Penney would, in all likelihood, not be permitted to merge. A violation of this law would occur if a retail trade group agreed to charge set fees for services such as delivery or alterations.

In 1914, the Clayton Act strengthened the Sherman Antitrust Act by focusing on specific illegal practices, such as discriminating in price among buyers. In other words, the Clayton Act maintains that price differentials in the same customer group must be justified.

The Federal Trade Commission Act, passed in 1914, prohibits deception, fraud, and other unfair methods of competition in interstate commerce. This act also created the Federal Trade Commission (FTC), which is the main policing agency of the federal government as far as retailers are concerned. Today, the FTC is subject to considerable media attention when a business is charged with "cheating" the public. Over the years, the FTC has been strengthened by several laws that deal with product labeling and other consumer protection laws.

The FTC takes legal action against companies involved in deceptive advertising and it requires advertised claims to be supported by valid evidence. Sometimes, retailers are accused of bait-and-switch advertising. This occurs when a retailer promotes an item at a low price to attract shoppers, but informs customers that the item is sold out. Then the retailer attempts to sell a higher priced item. The FTC is also involved in antimonopolistic activities. For example, the FTC requires companies to inform the government of their plans to merge and to seek approval from the FTC.

In 1936, the Robinson-Patman Act was passed by Congress to assist thousands of independent retailers who were victimized by questionable buying practices of the national chains. This act was especially important for small businesses during the Great Depression. It declared that discrimination in pricing was illegal in interstate commerce when such practices reduced competition. For the first time, the buyer could be held liable for receiving a discriminatory price.

The Consumer Credit Protection Act (1969), often referred to as "Truth in Lending," requires disclosure of all credit terms to consumers. The purpose of this act is to permit consumers to shop for credit. All credit terms, including annual interest rate, size of monthly payments, and number of payments, must be disclosed in any advertisement.

Federal acts also establish regulations on how products can be labeled and sold (e.g., the Child Protection and Toy Safety Act [1969]).

The Fair Labor Standards Act (1938) has a considerable impact on retail stores. This act, referred to as the Federal Wage and Hour Law, establishes minimum wage, maximum hours, and provisions for overtime compensation. Another act involving human resources is the Civil Rights Act of 1964, which prohibits employment discrimination. This law and others, along with significant United States Supreme Court cases, are discussed in Chapter 4.

Civil and Criminal Liabilities

Retailers are subject to a host of liabilities. Large retailers are subject to shareholder lawsuits that accompany mergers and acquisitions. Directors' and officers' liability insurance is a growing market for insurers. Even small retailers face a variety of legal actions. Retailers may face the following civil or criminal liabilities:

- failure to honor employment contracts
- manipulation of financial statements
- unfair labor practices
- antitrust violations
- collusion or conspiracy to defraud
- improper expenditures
- imprudent expansion that results in a loss
- conflict of interest
- unfair or illegal marketing practices
- misleading statements and forms filed with the Securities and Exchange Commission[1]

Many more liability issues face retailers, such as product tampering. Because retail stores are open to the public, just about all products are vulnerable to tampering. Many companies have strengthened their packaging to prevent tampering. However, no package is 100 percent safe. Deaths from the consumption of cyanide-tainted aspirin and cyanide-laced soup in 1986 reminded Americans that the earlier deaths from cyanide-laced Tylenol capsules, which prompted new legislation for tamper-proof containers, had not eliminated the possibility of victimization. Cases of product tampering are extremely difficult to investigate.

Terrorism is also a serious threat to retailers. When combined with media coverage, terrorism can create very serious financial losses. In 1989, terrorists injected cyanide into fruit from Chile. All US supermarkets were forced to pull Chilean fruit from their shelves.

Retail security practitioners obviously need a good foundation in law to be successful. This knowledge improves decision making and prevents litigation. Security practitioners can easily make a mistake that results in a lawsuit. A primary way in which private security personnel are controlled in our society is through tort law, which is a private or civil wrong or injury. In other words, the fear of a lawsuit influences the behavior of security personnel and retailers in general.

In contrast, public police are controlled not so much by tort law, but by citizens' rights as stated in the United States Constitution Bill of Rights. Private security is not as heavily controlled by the Constitution as public police. However, these statements are generalizations. Today, police are being sued and private security practitioners may be restricted by the Bill of Rights. Either group (private or public) can be on the receiving end of civil and criminal action.

Civil Liabilities

Civil liabilities usually fall into two categories—breach of contract and torts. Breaches of contract involve failure to perform a duty that was agreed to earlier. Retailers and other companies depend on contracts to operate their businesses. These contracts promise to deliver goods, perform services, and pay back loans.

A tort (i.e., a civil wrong) may result in injury to a person, property, or reputation. The injured party, called a *plaintiff*, sues to recover compensation for damages caused by the *defendant* or tort-feasor (i.e., the one who commits a tort). Defendants can be a person, a corporation, an association, or other entity. Tort liability is based on two premises—a person should not intentionally injure others or their property, and all people should exercise reasonable care and caution in the conduct of their affairs. The first premise resulted in several torts called *intentional torts*. The second premise involves tort liability and is referred to as *negligence*.

Intentional Torts

Intentional torts occur when an individual acts in a way designed to bring about an intended result. Since the tort-feasor has committed a willful wrong, the court may punish the defendant by imposing punitive damages (i.e., a money award to punish) along with compensatory damages (i.e., money equal to the actual loss). The following are common intentional torts.

Assault. Assault is an intentional threat to harm, or show of force, that could cause a person to feel in danger. Usually, words alone will not create a reasonable fear of harm; a threatening gesture is required. Liability may be avoided by proving self-defense.

Battery. Battery involves intentional, unwanted touching of another person or an object associated with that person (e.g., a hat, pocketbook, cane, or necklace). An improper search by security personnel could be considered battery. In addition to striking someone, battery is extended to activities such as hitting someone with a rock, spitting on someone, and even surgery done without a person's consent. Battery may likewise extend to less serious situations that can be offensive and insulting, such as kissing or pinching a stranger in public. Employees have sued their employers for assault and battery after submitting to a polygraph test. The assault is based upon extreme apprehension prior to the test and the battery results from being physically connected to the polygraph equipment.

Infliction of emotional distress. This tort involves intentionally causing emotional or mental distress in another person. This can be done by obscene or abusive language or conduct. Search-and-seizure actions by retail security personnel after an apprehension for shoplifting have resulted in damages being awarded for emotional distress. Liability does not exist for all cases of hurt feelings, ordinary insults, or vulgar language. If the average person is inclined to believe that the behavior of a defendant was outrageous, liability commonly exists.

False imprisonment or arrest. False imprisonment or arrest is intentional and forceful confinement or restriction of the freedom of movement of another person. Detention and its unlawfulness are the necessary elements to create liability.

> False imprisonment is a wrongful detention for a private purpose, with no intention to bring the detainee before a court. False arrest is a wrongful detention by someone presumed to have the legal authority to enforce the law.[2]

Malicious prosecution. Malicious prosecution is groundless initiation of criminal proceedings against another person. The plaintiff must prove five points: (1) the criminal proceedings ended in favor of the plaintiff, (2) the defendant in the lawsuit initiated the criminal proceedings, (3) there was no probable cause, (4) the plaintiff incurred damages, and (5) the initiation of the criminal proceedings was motivated by malice. Malice is "ill will; intentionally harming someone; having no moral or legal justification for harming someone."[3]

The existence of probable cause is a primary defense to this tort. However, liability can be upheld when inaccurate information is presented and when this information is the deciding factor in the decision to prosecute.

Of particular importance to the private sector is the risk of a malicious prosecution suit being brought after criminal charges in an incident have been dropped. It is to the legal advantage of security personnel if the prosecutor drops charges because of caseload problems, rather than because of a lack of probable cause. If the outcome of the prosecution results in restitution, most courts consider it a compromise settlement, not a decision in favor of the suspect. This destroys a key element in proving malicious prosecution. Also, a finding for restitution that emanates from a court is beneficial to the private sector, since it eliminates the suspicion for bribery allegations that could arise if the company made an internal decision to offer restitution. However, if a suspect agrees to restitution and signs a release to hold a company free of any civil liability, there is no guarantee for avoiding a lawsuit. A few courts have permitted the suspect-turned-plaintiff to sue in cases when the suspect acted under duress while signing the release.

Trespass to real property. This tort involves entry of private property without permission. Real property includes land and those things attached to it (e.g., buildings, trees, minerals). Examples of trespass include using someone's land as an unauthorized shortcut or for dumping. This tort encompasses chemicals, water, or anything else that escapes from one's property to another's. Government officials, such as the police, have powers of entry in certain circumstances. Private security personnel are restricted from trespassing.

Trespass to personal property. This tort is unlawful interference with the portable property of another. In other words, when possession is taken without permission, even if the property would be returned later, this action is illegal.

Conversion. This tort involves the wrongful taking of a person's personal property and converting it to one's own use (e.g., refusing to return a borrowed piece of equipment). "Conversion may be made by mistake, but if it is done intentionally it amounts to criminal theft, which is considered under the headings of larceny, embezzlement, and robbery."[4]

Invasion of privacy. Invasion of privacy is an unjustified intrusion into another's reasonable expectation of privacy. Examples of this tort are unauthorized entry or peering into a person's home, conducting an illegal search of an employee's belongings, and wiretapping. This tort also includes the unauthorized checking of a person's professional and personal records, as might be done during background investigations. ("Privacy" legislation has attempted to ensure that personal information in data banks is protected from unauthorized access.) Polygraph tests by employers have also been held by the courts to be an invasion of privacy.

Defamation. Defamation is injury to the reputation of another by publicly making untrue statements. Libel is written defamation and slander is oral defamation. Security personnel should never make defamatory statements when confronting a wrongdoer. Even yelling "Stop, thief!" can hold one liable for defamation. Searching a suspect in a public place can also be grounds for defamation. Always try a moderate approach first with a suspected lawbreaker.

Say: "Would you please accompany us to the office to discuss this matter?" This method will place security personnel in a better position if a mistake has been made.

Negligence

In addition to intentional torts, a second major area of tort liability is negligence. Negligence is the failure to exercise a reasonable amount of care in a situation that causes harm to someone or something. Negligence is an act performed in a careless manner or an omission to act. In negligence suits there is usually a failure on the part of one person to provide due care when there is foreseeable risk of harm to others. For example, when customers of a retail store are repeatedly assaulted, but management fails to take steps aimed at protection, the store may be found negligent. In a negligence case, the plaintiff has four basic elements to prove:

1. *legal duty:* Certain standards of duty must be met to protect others against unreasonable risks. Depending on the circumstances, the standards may vary. A business owner would have a higher legal duty to a customer than to a trespasser. A customer can expect protection from known and foreseeable dangers through loss prevention strategies. A trespasser must merely be warned of known dangers (e.g., hazardous substances or high voltage).
2. *lack of due care:* A judge or jury determines whether there has been a failure to exercise due care. This is determined based on case law standards, pertinent statutes, and the "reasonable person concept." The reasonable person concept asks: What degree of diligence and care can be reasonably expected under the circumstances?
3. *actual harm:* The plaintiff must prove that actual harm was suffered. Physical injury may be obvious to the court. However, humiliation, for instance, is difficult to verify.
4. *proximate cause:* The plaintiff must prove that the negligent act was reasonably connected to the plaintiff's injury. Problems arise in applying this rule when events break the sequence between an act and the injury. Suppose that a customer in a retail store slips and breaks an ankle, and during the ambulance trip to the hospital, the customer is killed in a traffic accident. The retailer's negligence was not the proximate cause of the customer's death.

You Be the Judge 3-1

The Story: *Hey, I'm practically running on fumes,* thought Bob Hoag, peering at his gas gauge. *I'd better stop somewhere and fill up.*

Hoag was driving through unfamiliar territory, but he brightened when he saw the familiar neon logo of Colossal Oil piercing the darkness, looming above a gas station just off the approaching highway exit.

Had Hoag known what was in store, he would have kept going, empty tank or not. But he unsuspectingly drove down the exit ramp and into the Colossal station, pulling up to the full-serve pumps and shutting off his automobile's engine.

He waited nearly a minute for an attendant to come out of the building, but none did. *Huh,* he thought, *I can see that two guys are in there. Don't they know I'm here?*

Impatiently, he got out of his car and walked into the gas station's office. Immediately, he wished he hadn't. An armed robbery was in progress! The gunman stood to Hoag's right, the terrified attendant to Hoag's left. In a panic, the attendant darted *behind* Hoag, trying to shield himself. The stickup man fired a shot, hitting Hoag, then ran out the door, into the night.

Hoag survived his wound but was left with partial disabilities. He asked his lawyer about suing for his injury on the grounds that the gas station employee's action had put him in harm's way.

"Well, there's no point in suing the guy who actually owns the station and is the attendant's employer," said the attorney. "He doesn't have any money to speak of, so you wouldn't collect much even if you did win. Let's go after Colossal! Their name is on the gas station, and they're the ones with big bucks."

Hoag sued Colossal Oil. Did he collect?

Make your decision; then turn to the end of the chapter for the court's decision.

Source: "You Be the Judge," including the decisions at the end of this chapter: Reprinted with permission from *Security Management Bulletin: Protecting Property, People & Assets*, a publication of Bureau of Business Practice, Inc., 24 Rope Ferry Road, Waterford, CT, 06386.

Personnel in the security field have been held liable for negligence by failing to exercise due care in the use of firearms, force, and motor vehicles. Employers and supervisors can be subject to civil litigation resulting from procedures in selecting, training, and supervising employees.

The following four items are the major defenses to negligence torts:

1. *contributory negligence:* The defendant must show that the plaintiff failed to use reasonable care or acted negligently in a way that might have contributed to the injury (e.g., a pedestrian who is reading a newspaper while crossing a street and prior to being hit by an automobile).
2. *assumption of risk:* In this defense, the defendant must show that the plaintiff was aware of the risks involved (e.g., riding in a car with a drunk driver, being a spectator close to a race track, or skydiving).
3. *comparative negligence:* Civil courts apportion damages based on the degree of fault of each party. If the plaintiff is 25 percent negligent, only 75 percent of the damages can be recovered. The purpose is to protect plaintiffs who are slightly negligent from being hindered from recovery.
4. *strict liability without fault:* Courts may hold a party strictly liable for harm to another without fault or negligence. Such cases pertain to situations in which harm cannot be avoided even when reasonable care is taken. For example, workers' compensation laws hold employers liable without fault for employee injuries. A manufacturer may be held liable for injuries caused by a defective product even if the harmed party cannot prove how the manufacturer was careless.

Malpractice

Malpractice is professional negligence in which there is a failure to exercise the degree of care that a professional calling requires. This area of tort liability has shown a significant increase for doctors, lawyers, accountants, and other professionals. Security and loss prevention practitioners in a position of authority are likewise subject to malpractice liability.

Vicarious Liability

Usually, an employer or principal is vicariously liable (substitutively liable) to a third party for wrongful acts of an employee or agent during the ordinary course of business. This can result in both civil and criminal action. Employers may be liable even though they did not direct the act, assent to it, or even if they instructed against the act. By the same token, the employee is not relieved from liability, even though actions may have been under the command of the employer.

The foundation for vicarious liability is found in the established doctrine of *respondeat superior* ("let the master respond"). Also known as the "deep pocket" theory, the employer (or "master") is in a better position to pay damages than the employee (or servant). If the tort occurs during business hours, but it can be proved that the employee was "off on a frolic" and therefore not acting within the scope of employment, negligence would not be imputed to the employer. However, the employee would still be liable.

A security officer protecting a business is clearly within the scope of employment when an on-site arrest is made. The best way for an employer to prevent liability that results from a security officer's tortious or criminal actions is to provide quality job screening and training.

Many executives erroneously believe that they can avoid the liability that results from security's bad judgment by hiring a contract security force and including a "hold harmless" clause in the service contract. Generally, such a clause carries little weight, because so many client activities are intertwined with the contract service. For example, client company policies and procedures are commonly enforced by contract security officers. Much can be questioned about this relationship, especially since the contract service was selected by the client. What criteria were used for selection? How did the client guide training for unique needs and supervision? Did the client take any actions to cut the security budget? Furthermore, courts have viewed the security function as nondelegable. Businesses can protect themselves by carefully selecting contract security firms and thoroughly investigating their training and insurance.[5]

Strict Liability

Strict liability (or liability without fault) may be imposed on persons who are engaged in abnormally dangerous activities that result in injuries to others (e.g., dynamite blasting, oil drilling, or owning vicious animals). The reasoning behind this legal doctrine is that no adequate safety methods can be taken to eliminate risk and that one who engages in such dangerous activities should be responsible for adverse consequences. Some states have imposed strict liability on contract security companies that are permitted to operate under a "certificate of authority" issued by the state.

All of the preceding torts and theories of liability should be viewed as interacting factors of a single liability system. A typical plaintiff in a civil case will use all theories of liability that could apply to the facts of the particular case, and all potentially liable individuals will become defendants. The court will study the facts of the particular case and will decide on the validity of the theories of liability presented by the plaintiff and on which defendants are liable, if any.

Damages

Damages is the term used to describe the money awarded to parties who have suffered injury. An award for damages is received by a successful plaintiff in a civil action that is the result of a tort or breach of contract.

Depending on state law, juries are charged with determining which party is to be given favorable judgment and, if the plaintiff wins, how much is to be awarded in damages. Appeals to a higher court are permissible when an award is too low or too high. The more common types of damages are as follows:

actual or compensatory damages: a sum of money equal to the real financial loss suffered by the injured party

incidental and consequential damages: awards for losses indirectly attributable to a tort, which may include emotional distress, anxiety, and embarrassment

punitive or exemplary damages: awards in excess of actual or incidental damages as a punishment to the defendant when it has been proved that the defendant acted with malicious intent and disregarded the rights of the plaintiff.[6]

A Charge of Negligent Security

Retailers, like other entities, can be charged with negligence when there is a failure to exercise a reasonable amount of care in a situation that causes harm to another. For example, a retail department store that fails to improve protection following multiple assaults in its parking lot may become a defendant in a civil suit for negligent security. In this case, the retailer has a duty to provide protection because of reasonably foreseeable dangers to those who enter the premises. The plaintiff's attorney will attempt to prove this contention. Typical questions evolving in such a case are: How many previous assaults occurred on the premises? What security measures were in place when the plaintiff was victimized? What types of security are at similar nearby locations? Can it be shown that security was substandard and negligent in operation? The plaintiff's attorney will likely attempt to obtain the following types of information during the pretrial discovery stage, during which all parties in a civil suit are allowed to discover all relevant information to avoid protracted litigation. Such information includes the following:

- number of security officers on duty during the assault
- qualifications of the officers and methods of screening applicants
- training and supervision documentation
- policies and procedures
- physical security measures (e.g., CCTV, lighting), and operation and maintenance logs
- security surveys
- reports (internal and police reports)
- statements of witnesses
- laws regulating security in the state

- whether or not the retailer followed the laws
- the amount of management support for security

When a lawsuit occurs, it means that security will undergo careful study by the plaintiff's attorney. In essence, management either pays for adequate security early on (to prevent unfortunate incidents) or pays later (following a lawsuit).

Can a Shopping Center Be Held Liable to a Customer for a Purse Snatching and Injuries? Can a Computer Printout of Area Crimes Be Admissible to Establish Foreseeability?

Rosabel Brown and her husband completed some Christmas shopping at Valley River Shopping Center in Eugene, Oregon, and walked to their car. In the parking lot an assailant grabbed Ms. Brown's purse and knocked her to the ground. Ms. Brown, 76 years old, suffered numerous injuries and sued the shopping center owner, among others. A judgment was entered in her favor and the defendants appealed.

The Court of Appeals of Oregon held that Ms. Brown was only required to show the defendants should have reasonably anticipated that careless or criminal conduct on the part of third persons would be likely to endanger the safety of a visitor.

Ms. Brown's evidence included a police report of all criminal incidents at Valley River. The defendants argued that the police report was merely a summary report and the underlying police reports should accompany the summary report. They also argued that the report was irrelevant to the case.

The court of appeals ruled that the crime report summary was relevant and properly admitted into evidence. As to the foreseeability of the crime, the court noted that there were 268 criminal incidents in or around the Valley River Shopping Center within six months before Ms. Brown's attack. An expert witness testified that criminal activity in the area increased the risk of victimization to customers. The Valley River director of security, a former police officer, was aware of the police reports of criminal incidents. Furthermore, although extra security was hired during previous Christmas seasons, no additional security personnel were hired during the Christmas season in which Ms. Brown was attacked. Judgment was affirmed.

This case was summarized from: R. Keegan Federal, Jr., and Jennifer L. Fogleman, *Avoiding Liability in Retail Security* (Atlanta: Strafford Pub., 1986), pp. 30–32. *Case Cita-*

> tion: Rosabel Brown v. J.C. Penney Company, Inc., a foreign corporation, and May Department Stores Company, a foreign corporation dba [doing business as] Meier & Frank Company; W.H. Shields, H.A. Anderson, Joseph Fought, and Allan Penney, dba Valley River Center, and H.A. Ellsworth, No. 78–8085; CA A22384, in the Court of Appeals of Oregon, decided August 10, 1983, reconsideration denied September 16, 1983, review allowed October 25, 1983, reported at 667 P.2d. 1047; *Private Security Case Law Reporter*, Vol. V, No. 1, p. 7.

Preparing for a Lawsuit

Businesses rarely receive advance notice of an impending lawsuit. Usually, the first indication of a lawsuit results from a sheriff's deputy or process server arriving on the premises with a summons and complaint. A summons is a court order to appear in court. A complaint is a pleading of facts and claims filed in court. The list that follows provides some basic guidelines for establishing advance procedures for being successful in court.

- All employees, especially those at access points (e.g., security officers, receptionists), should be trained in how to handle summons and complaints.
- Employees should not sign anything.
- Notes should be taken. Who arrived? For what purpose? Note date and time.
- Management should be notified quickly and discreetly.
- Contact the company's liability insurance carrier immediately to find out if the insurer will defend the lawsuit. If this avenue is unproductive, contact an independent attorney.
- Ensure that all communications concerning the case are directed through a designated person. Even off-the-cuff statements can be damaging to the case. The company's attorney should handle questions.
- An investigation of the incident that gave rise to the lawsuit should be handled by the company's attorney.
- Expect your company to receive court-approved requests for information and materials. These will take the form of interrogatories (questions), requests to produce (requests for documents that are required), and requests to admit (that something did or didn't occur).[7]
- A deposition, which is a collection of oral testimony given under oath, is possible. It is part of the discovery process. Depositions allow attorneys to gauge the strength of the case. Many cases are won or lost at this stage. If your deposition conflicts with your testimony given at the trial, your credibility may be questioned.

Depositions are held by agreement between attorneys or by court-approved subpoena. The subpoena requests a person's presence and possibly certain documents.

Follow basic common-sense guidelines for depositions:

Don't rehearse "pat" answers. This may leave the impression that answers are not credible.
Never guess. Ask for questions to be clarified.
Take your time.
Tell the truth.
Don't volunteer information.
Don't exaggerate.
Don't get too friendly. Act like a computer. Watch for ulterior motives of opposing counsel.
Don't get angry.
Take a break when you need to.

You Be the Judge 3-2

The Story: While checking a suspicious noise at night on his store's loading dock, a security officer at Bargain Mart was shot and killed by unknown assailants. His family then tried to recover for negligence and wrongful death by suing several parties.

They sued Bargain Mart, of course. They also sued a security coworker who had been on duty with the officer and who, they charged, should have helped protect him. Both of these suits failed, winning nothing for the family.

The oddest action by the family was a suit against Shop-O-Rama, a store situated in the same mall, 500 yards away from Bargain Mart.

The family noted that Bargain Mart and Shop-O-Rama shared a section of the mall parking lot. They introduced testimony showing that security patrols from Shop-O-Rama sometimes crossed over into Bargain Mart's half of the lot. In fact, on a couple of occasions when Shop-O-Rama security officers chased suspects, they caught them right on Bargain Mart's sidewalk.

In addition, noted the family, the generator that powered the outdoor parking lot lights (including those nearest to Bargain Mart) was located on Shop-O-Rama's property and was serviced by Shop-O-Rama employees. Bulbs in the parking lot light stanchions (again, including those next to Bargain Mart) were regularly changed by Shop-O-Rama security officers.

The family contended that all these unofficial security incursions by Shop-O-Rama into Bargain Mart's property made Shop-O-Rama partly *responsible* for security at Bargain Mart. Shop-O-Rama had assumed a special duty for security protection of persons at Bargain Mart, the family claimed.

Did the court agree?

Make your decision; then turn to the end of the chapter for the court's decision.

Source: "You Be the Judge," including decisions at the end of this chapter: Reprinted with permission from *Security Management Bulletin: Protecting Property, People & Assets,* a publication of Bureau of Business Practice, Inc., 24 Rope Ferry Road, Waterford, CT, 06386.

Civil Rights Claim Against Department Store

A man filed a civil rights action against a department store, claiming he was beaten by three security officers. He was allegedly handcuffed, dragged to the security office, and handcuffed to a chair for nearly 1½ hours until the police were called. The man claimed that store security had a "pre-arranged association" with the Philadelphia police department and that, for this reason, the security officers' acts constituted "state action" for the purpose of a civil rights suit under federal law, which involves 42 U.S.C. Section 1983, which creates a civil cause of action, enforceable in federal courts, against any person acting under color of state authority who deprives another of any rights, privileges, or immunities secured by the Constitution or laws of the United States.

The U.S. District Court for the Eastern District of Pennsylvania dismissed the man's claims.

> A store and its employees are not state actors under Section 1983 unless: (1) they have a pre-arranged retail theft detention plan with the police; and (2) under the plan, the police will arrest anyone identified as a shoplifter by the store without independently evaluating the presence of probable cause.[8] This type of plan would give private security agents the power of the state. The existence of such a plan had not been spelled out.

This case was summarized from the *Security Law Newsletter* No. 90-123 (Crime Control Research Corporation, Washington, DC). *Case Citation:* Vassallo v. Clover,

No. 90–2875, U.S. District Court, Eastern District of Pennsylvania, July 24, 1990.

Sexual Harassment

The definition of sexual harassment has varied over time. Today, the courts' definition has made it much easier for plaintiffs to prove harassment claims, and complaints are increasing.

In the 1980s the federal courts ruled that it was not a hostile environment where a superior repeatedly propositioned an employee and allowed co-workers to slap her on the buttocks and comment that she must moan and groan during sex. The court said that this did not create sufficient "anxiety and debilitation" on the employee's part (Scott v. Sears, Roebuck & Co., 798 F.2d 210 (1986)).

In another federal case in 1986 the Sixth Circuit held that the workplace was not hostile even though posters of naked women existed and workers told the plaintiff that she needed "a good lay." The court stated that there was no proof that the harassment seriously affected her psychological well-being (Rabidue v. Osceola Refining Co., 805 F.2d 611 (1986)).

Subsequent to these cases the courts have dropped their emphasis on "debilitation" as the test of whether the environment is "hostile." *The test today is whether the workplace can be seen as abusive from the perspective of a "reasonable woman."* An example is a supervisor stating that a female employee has a "great figure" or "beautiful legs." It is possible that such statements can be offensive from the perspective of a reasonable woman. Supporting cases are Lipsett v. University of Puerto Rico, 864 F.2d 881 (1st Cir. 1988) and Andrews v. City of Philadelphia, 895 F.2d 1469 (3rd Cir. 1990).

Even a well-intentioned compliment could be cause for legal action. A "polluted environment" can also result in action: this includes posters of nude women and "dirty jokes." In Radtke v. Everett, 471 N.W. 2d 660 (1991), the Michigan court of Appeals applied the reasonable-woman test and ruled that a single caress could be sufficient to establish a hostile environment.

The Americans with Disabilities Act (ADA) of 1990

Congress determined that approximately 43 million Americans have some type of physical or mental disability. One in five people in the United States will become disabled in their lifetime. These people have been subject to discrimination when seeking employment, in the workplace, and in many areas of everyday life. The crux of the problem is that disabled people are considered less equal in our society. Consequently, public law 101-336 was enacted on July 26, 1990. This legislation is divided into five sections, called titles:

Title I—Employment
Title II—Public Services
Title III—Public Accommodations and Services Operated by Private Entities
Title IV—Telecommunications
Title V—Miscellaneous Provisions

Titles I and III have a significant impact on methods of protecting businesses. Title II and a portion of Title III involve public transportation. Title IV pertains to communications for those persons who are hearing and sight impaired. In this book, Chapter 4 discusses Title I and Chapter 9 discusses Title III. Appendix B also contains information on the ADA.

The ADA is very specific as to its intent and purpose. However, it is vague in terms of how businesses must comply with the law. Court decisions that result from lawsuits by disabled persons will define the ADA and help to determine what needs to be done to adhere to the law.

The EEOC processes complaints and files lawsuits on behalf of persons alleging discrimination under the ADA. During 1992, the EEOC anticipates 12,000-15,000 lawsuits. Millions of dollars have been allocated to the EEOC by the federal government for this litigation.

Criminal Liabilities

Whereas civil law involves disputes among persons, businesses, and government, criminal law involves crimes against society. The proof required to win a civil case is a "preponderance of evidence" (i.e., believability and greater weight of facts proved). In a criminal case, the standard is "proof beyond a reasonable doubt," which is a greater weight of evidence than that required in a civil case.

The US Congress, state legislatures, and local legislative bodies specify the actions to be defined in the criminal law. In addition, courts play a role in interpreting laws. Offenses are classified into four categories:

1. *Capital crime* is most serious and results in the death penalty for the crime of murder.
2. *Felony* is a serious crime that is punishable by a year or longer in prison for crimes such as robbery, burglary, and grand larceny.
3. *Misdemeanor* is a less serious crime that is punishable by less than a year of incarceration for crimes such as shoplifting, petty larceny, and public drunkenness.
4. *Infraction* is the least serious offense and results in a fine for a traffic violation.

When a crime occurs, a prosecutor initiates legal action to punish. A single act can be a crime and a tort when society and a victim are harmed. Society punishes the guilty party, although historically the victim has not been compensated by the offender. Today, we see the criminal court system order restitution from the offender to the victim. In addition, most states have victim compensation programs.

Usually, an employer is not vicariously liable for criminal acts of employees unless the prosecution can prove that the employer knowingly and intentionally supported the employee's criminal act. An employer can be held liable for an employee's violation of a regulatory offense.

As with individuals, corporations can be criminally liable for violations involving a wide array of state and federal laws. Violations pertain to those laws stated at the beginning of this chapter. Crimes against retailers are discussed later in this book in Chapters 6, 7, and 10.

Case Problems

3A. As an assistant director of loss prevention for a retail department store chain, you have been assigned the task of designing a litigation prevention program for the security department. This program and a manual will be used by all store security managers. What strategies would you employ to prevent litigation? What would you include in the manual?

3B. As the director of security for a retail company, you will soon make your yearly pitch for funding for the security department. During the last few years, the security budget has been lean, although no major cuts have occurred. This year, you will ask for additional funds and you will add another dimension to budget justification—the danger of a charge of negligent security.

Because you will justify your budget by strategies such as ROI, you have only a minute or two to discuss the negligent security topic. Prepare such a statement.

Answers to You Be the Judge

3–1. No. The attendant who endangered Hoag was not Colossal Oil's employee, so Colossal was not responsible for what he did. He actually worked for the gas station owner, Colossal's franchisee. Sometimes, people who are not on your payroll may appear to be your representatives. These could include contractors' employees on your property (contract security officers, for example) and employees of franchisees or other firms that you supply and that display your name. Get your attorney's help in structuring agreements with these firms so that you are not liable for what their people do. (This case has been fictionalized for dramatic effect and to protect the privacy of those involved.) *Case Citation:* Burgos-Oquendo v. Caribbean Gulf Refining Corp., 741 F. Supp. 330 (D. Puerto Rico 1990).

3–2. Not even for a moment. The family's claim that Shop-O-Rama had "unofficial protective duties" toward Bargain Mart was baseless, said the judge. The slain security officer had not been Shop-O-Rama's employee; that store had no relation to him at all, much less a duty to protect him. However, this case does raise a question to discuss with your legal counsel: *Are* there circumstances in which your security programs and personnel could incur liability for events at the company next door? Overreaching patrols? Shared services? Your awareness of crime dangers? If so, what should you do? (This case has been fictionalized for dramatic effect and to protect the privacy of those involved.) *Case Citation:* Carriere v. Sears, Roebuck and Co., 893 F.2d 98 (5th Cir. 1990).

Notes

1. J. Barry Mason et al., *Retailing*, 4th ed. (Homewood, IL: Irwin Publishing, 1991), 656–657.
2. "The Legal Basis of Liability," *Security Management* 26 (December 1982): 12.
3. Daniel Oran, *Law Dictionary* (St Paul, MN: West Publishing, 1975), 200.

4. John J. Moran, *Practical Business Law* (Englewood Cliffs, NJ: Prentice-Hall, 1985), 33.
5. Philip P. Purpura, *Modern Security & Loss Prevention Management* (Boston: Butterworth–Heinemann, 1989), pp. 290–297.
6. Ibid., pp. 296–297.
7. "Get Ready to Go to Court," *Corporate Security* (May 1990): 7.
8. James R. Miller, "The Legal Deposition," *Small Business Reports* (February 1990): 68–70.

PART
II

Problems and Countermeasures

4

Job Applicant Screening and Employee Training

Human Resources in Retailing

Human resources in retailing encompasses a number of components, with the goal of providing the people who will make the organization work effectively. Examples of these components include job analysis, job descriptions, recruiting, screening, selecting, training, compensation and benefits, performance evaluations, and labor relations. Although this chapter covers only two of these components, as protection professionals we should maintain a broad perspective by understanding that job applicant screening and employee training are only a part of human resources management. At the same time, management in general should be aware that a fair and equitable human resources program will have an impact on employee behavior and losses.

Those who manage the human resources department are confronted with an increasingly complex environment as a result of numerous issues, such as testing for illegal drug use, AIDS, labor shortages, coordination of child care, undocumented foreign workers employed in the US, and the problems associated with business mergers, acquisitions, and restructuring. Today, an emphasis is being placed on increasing productivity through improved use of people and assets. More must be done with limited resources by "working smarter."

Most security professionals know that their duties do not exist in a vacuum. The key for the protection professional is to provide expertise internally where it is needed. A human resources manager is likely to be interested in cost-effective screening of applicants and training of employees, both of which show a return on investment.

Human Resources Problems in Retailing

A clear understanding of human resources problems in the security industry is especially important, because employees are the most important asset of an organization. But at the same time, employees can be a great liability. Employers should establish methods to prevent hiring employees who are a hindrance to business goals. A poorly screened, new employee can bring grief to the workplace and to management by, for example, committing a violent act against another employee or customer. The result can be a lawsuit for retailer negligence. Liability can be costly. A fraudulent workers' compensation claim or internal theft are two other examples that can produce losses that could be overcome by effective job applicant screening.

Aside from quality screening, training is another means of preventing losses. When employees know how to do their job properly, mistakes and victimization can be reduced. For example, retail employees should accept checks from customers only after certain requirements are met by each customer (e.g., proper ID is shown). A robbery may be thwarted by a salesperson's quick action to summon police when noticing a suspicious customer. However, employees must first be trained on indicators that signal that a robbery is about to occur. Crime prevention is only a portion of the benefits of training. Accountability of merchandise markups and markdowns will impact shrinkage. Service and courtesy to customers are learned through training, and generate image and repeat business. Thus, training can improve profits.

The benefits of quality screening and training are obvious. On the other hand, the hard realities of retailing make consistent, good-quality screening and training difficult. The retailing industry is noted for hiring many part-time and temporary employees. Many of these employees are inexperienced. These problems are particularly acute during busy holiday seasons when business volume is up and crowded stores require many more salespeople. Retail employees are often paid low wages and work long hours. During holidays, the work hours increase, while in other occupations the opposite may occur. Employee dissatisfaction and high turnover also characterize retailing. In fact, research shows that young employees and employees who are dissatisfied with their job are more likely to commit internal theft. (This research is discussed in Chapter 6.) What makes matters worse is the shortage of quality, low-cost employees:

> Retailers will continue to find themselves critically short of a sufficient number of low-cost employees to work the extended hours common in retailing today. Shortages in excess of 1 million workers are predicted during the decade of the 90s. Additionally, labor costs are likely to rise as a result of the probable approval during the 90s of such programs as minimum health benefits, minimum parental and medical leaves, and higher minimum wages.[1]

Legislation and Court Decisions

Six major pieces of legislation and six Supreme Court decisions follow that apply to job applicant screening. In essence, the existing legislation and court decisions require that all screening methods must be job-related, valid, and nondiscriminatory.

Federal Legislation

Equal Pay Act of 1963. This legislation requires that men and women be paid equally if they work at the same location at similar jobs. Exceptions include a seniority or merit system and earnings through quantity or quality of production.

Civil Rights Act of 1964, Title VII. This law prohibits employment discrimination based on race, color, religion, sex, or national origin. Title VII prohibits discrimination with regard to any employment condition, including recruiting, screening, hiring, training, compensating, evaluating, promoting, disciplining, and terminating. Congress established the EEOC to enforce Title VII.

Age Discrimination in Employment Act of 1967. Age discrimination is prohibited in the workplace according to this law. In 1986, an upper age limit was eliminated. However, health factors can be considered as limiting job functioning, especially for certain occupations.

Equal Employment Opportunity Act of 1972. The purpose of this federal law (EEO) is to strengthen Title VII by providing the EEOC with additional enforcement powers to file suits and issue cease-and-desist orders. Further, the EEO expands coverage to employees of state and local governments, educational institutions, and private employers of more than 15 persons. EEO programs are implemented by employers to prevent discrimination in the workplace and to offset past employment discrimination. Affirmative action plans by employers are aimed at correcting past inequities by providing opportunities for minorities underrepresented in the workforce.

Rehabilitation Act of 1973. This act requires contractors with the federal government to take affirmative action to hire those with physical or mental handicaps.

Americans with Disabilities Act of 1990. This bill aims to eliminate discrimination against the physically and mentally handicapped. The ADA gives disabled individuals a federal right of action, rather than relying on only state and local statutes. It extends the Rehabilitation Act of 1973 to the private sector. For retailers, the ADA in Title I prohibits discrimination in employment and in Title III covers public accommodations. Requirements include job criteria based exclusively on the essential skills for the job. Employers must truly consider disabled job applicants. Reasonable accommodations must be provided (e.g., a lower counter), so the disabled applicant can do the job. This bill can result in an expanded pool of job applicants for retailers.

U.S. Supreme Court Decisions

Griggs v. Duke Power (1971). In 1968, several employees of the Duke Power Company in North Carolina were given a pencil-and-paper aptitude test for manual labor. Willie Griggs and twelve other black workers sued their employer with the charge of job discrimination under the Civil Rights Act of 1964. Their contention was that the pencil-and-paper aptitude test had little to do with their ability to perform manual labor. The Supreme Court decided that a test is inherently discriminatory if it is not job related and differentiates on the basis of race, sex, or religion. Furthermore, employers are required to prove that their screening methods are job related.

Albermarle Paper Co. v. J. Moody (1975). The Supreme Court decided that tests or other screening methods that disqualify a disproportionate number of minorities have to be validated. In other words, employers must prove that a test predicts on-the-job performance.

Washington v. Davis (1976). This case involved the Washington, DC, police department, where, between 1968 and 1971, 57 percent of blacks failed the entrance exam, compared to 13 percent of whites. The department demonstrated that the exam was related to those given during recruit training. According to the Supreme Court, the police department did not discriminate. If a test is job related, it is not necessarily illegal, even though a greater percentage of minorities do not pass it. This case departed from several others in that it supported the use of tests as a screening tool.

Bakke v. University of California (1978). Reverse discrimination was the main issue of this case. Allan Bakke, a white male, sued the Davis Medical School under the "equal protection" clause of the Fourteenth Amendment because it set aside 16 of 100 openings for minorities, who were evaluated according to different standards. The Supreme Court concluded that the racial quota system was unacceptable, because it disregarded Bakke's right to equal protection of the law, and that affirmative action programs are permissible as long as applicants are considered on an individual basis and a set number of places has not been set aside. Race can be a key factor in the selection process; however, multiple factors must be considered.

Weber v. Kaiser (1979). Reverse discrimination, again, was the issue in this case. Brian Weber sued Kaiser Aluminum under Title VII of the 1964 Civil Rights Act because he had been bypassed for a position under a company-union rule that set aside 50 percent of jobs of a certain category for blacks. The Supreme Court ruled that employers can give preference to minorities in hiring and promoting for "traditionally segregated job categories." Affirmative action programs were strengthened.

Fire Fighters Local Union 1784 v. Stotts (1984). This case showed that not all affirmative action programs are acceptable. The Supreme Court ruled that a seniority system cannot be subservient to an affirmative action program during a layoff. A last-hired, first-fired plan by the union and the City of Memphis survived.

Other legal guidelines apply to job applicant screening. The Employee Polygraph Protection Act of 1988, for example, severely restricts detection of deception devices in the workplace, except under certain conditions.

If we go beyond the legal guidelines for screening applicants, and consider federal and state legislation, and court decisions for human resources management, several volumes can be written on this topic. The Fair Labor Standards Act, first passed in 1938 and amended numerous times, addresses minimum wage (originally set at 25 cents an hour) and length of the standard work week. The act applies to employees of firms that do business in more than one state and have annual sales of at least $250,000. The act also sets minimum age requirements for all workers. The Occupational Safety and Health Act of 1970 attempts to ensure a safe and healthy workplace. The National Labor Relations Act of 1935 stipulates legal rights and obligations of unions and employers. The Federal Insurance Contribution Act of 1937 pertains to Social Security.

These laws are a sample of the legal guidelines for employers. The posters that follow (Figures 4–1 and 4–2) are required by law to be posted in the workplace and reflect federal legislation. Many states and municipalities have also enacted legislation involving the workplace, and businesses are required to keep records that can be legally scrutinized by government agencies.

Job Applicant Screening

Job applicant screening should not be taken lightly, because problems are avoided when quality hiring decisions are made. The aim of screening prospective employees is to hire the most appropriate people—those who will benefit the business while at the same time not being a liability. Every business will hire its share of employees who are thieves, substance abusers, malingerers, and so forth. Human resources personnel and security practitioners should strive to hold these sources of losses to a minimum. The following pages present several strategies for quality screening.

NOTICE TO EMPLOYEES
FEDERAL MINIMUM WAGE

$3.80 per hour
Effective April 1, 1990

$4.25 per hour
Effective April 1, 1991

Most Employees in the United States qualify for both minimum wage and overtime pay under THE FAIR LABOR STANDARDS ACT. Overtime pay may not be less than 1 1/2 times the employee's regular rate of pay for hours worked over 40 in one workweek.

Certain full-time students, student learners, apprentices, and workers with disabilities may be paid less than the minimum wage under special certificates issued by the Department of Labor.

Covered Employees
- Employees engaged in interstate commerce or in the production of goods for interstate commerce (i.e., goods that travel across state lines), regardless of the employer's annual volume of business.
- Employees who work for enterprises that have an annual gross volume of sales made or business done of over $500,000.
- Employees of hospitals, residential facilities that care for those who are physically or mentally ill or disabled, or aged, schools for children who are mentally or physically disabled or gifted, preschools, elementary and secondary schools, and institutions of higher education, regardless of the annual volume of business.
- Employees of public agencies

Child Labor
An Employee must be at least 16 years old to work in most non-farm jobs and at least 18 to work in non-farm jobs declared hazardous by the Secretary of Labor. Youths 14 and 15 years old may work outside school hours in various non-manufacturing, non-mining, non-hazardous jobs under the following conditions.
No more than — 3 hours on a school day or 18 hours in a school week.
8 hours on a non-school day or 40 hours in a non-school week.
Also work may not begin before 7 a.m. or end after 7 p.m. except from June 1 through Labor Day, when evening hours are extended to 9 p.m. Different rules apply in agricultural employment.

Training Wage
A training wage of $3.35 per hour, or 85 percent of the applicable minimum wage, which ever is greater, may be paid to most employees under 20 years of age for up to 90 days under certain conditions. Individuals may be employed at this training wage for a second 90 day period by a different employer if certain additional requirements are met. No individual may be employed at the training wage, in any number of jobs, for more than a total of 180 days. Employers may not displace regular employees in order to hire those eligible for the training wage.

Tipped Employees
A tipped employee is one who regularly receives more than $30 a month in tips. Tips received by such employees may be counted as wages up to a certain percentage of the minimum wage. The minimum cash wage that employers must pay (from their own pockets) to tipped employees is $2.09 an hour effective April 1, 1990. It will rise to $2.13 an hour effective April 1, 1991. If an employee's hourly tip earnings (averaged weekly) added to this hourly wage do not equal the minimum wage, the employer is responsible for paying the balance.

Enforcement
The Department of Labor may recover back wages either administratively or through court action, for the employees that have been underpaid in violation of the law. Violations may result in civil or criminal action.
Civil money penalties of up to $1,000 per violation may be assessed against employers who violate the child labor provision of the law or who willfully or repeatedly violate the minimum wage or overtime pay provision. This law prohibits discriminating against or discharging workers who file a complaint or participate in any proceedings under the Act.

Note:
- Certain occupations and establishments are exempt from the minimum wage and/or overtime pay provisions
- Special provisions apply to workers in Puerto Rico and American Samoa.
- Where state law requires a higher minimum wage the higher standard applies.

FOR ADDITIONAL INFORMATION CONTACT the Wage and Hour Division office nearest you — listed in your telephone directory under United States Government, Labor Department

The law requires employers to display this poster where employees can readily see it.
U.S. DEPARTMENT OF LABOR
Employment Standards Administration
Wage and Hour Division
Washington, D.C. 20210

Revised April 1990

U S DEPARTMENT OF LABOR
EMPLOYMENT STANDARDS ADMINISTRATION
Wage and Hour Division
Washington, DC 20210

NOTICE
EMPLOYEE POLYGRAPH PROTECTION ACT

The Employee Polygraph Protection Act prohibits most private employers from using lie detector tests either for pre-employment screening or during the course of employment.

PROHIBITIONS
Employers are generally prohibited from requiring or requesting any employee or job applicant to take a lie detector test, and from discharging, disciplining, or discriminating against an employee or prospective employee for refusing to take a test or for exercising other rights under the Act.

EXEMPTIONS
Federal, State and local governments are not affected by the law. Also, the law does not apply to tests given by the Federal Government to certain private individuals engaged in national security-related activities.
The Act permits polygraph (a kind of lie detector) tests to be administered in the private sector, subject to restrictions, to certain prospective employees of security service firms (armored car, alarm, and guard), and of pharmaceutical manufacturers, distributors, and dispensers.
The Act also permits polygraph testing, subject to restrictions, of certain employees of private firms who are reasonably suspected of involvement in a workplace incident (theft, embezzlement, etc.) that resulted in economic loss to the employer.

EXAMINEE RIGHTS
Where polygraph tests are permitted, they are subject to numerous strict standards concerning the conduct and length of the test. Examinees have a number of specific rights, including the right to a written notice before testing, the right to refuse or discontinue a test, and the right not to have test results disclosed to unauthorized persons.

ENFORCEMENT
The Secretary of Labor may bring court actions to restrain violations and assess civil penalties up to $10,000 against violators. Employees or job applicants may also bring their own court actions.

ADDITIONAL INFORMATION
Additional information may be obtained, and complaints of violations may be filed, at local offices of the Wage and Hour Division, which are listed in the telephone directory under U.S. Government, Department of Labor, Employment Standards Administration.

THE LAW REQUIRES EMPLOYERS TO DISPLAY THIS POSTER WHERE EMPLOYEES AND JOB APPLICANTS CAN READILY SEE IT.

*The law does not preempt any provision of any State or local law or any collective bargaining agreement which is more restrictive with respect to lie detector tests.

Job Applicant Screening 59

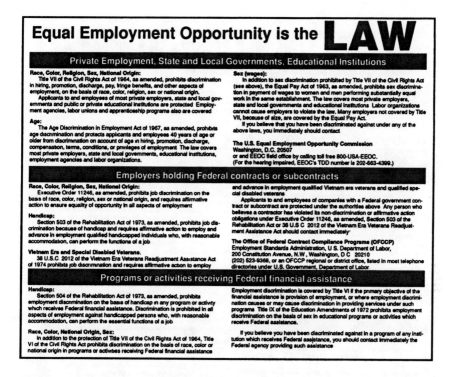

Figure 4–1 U.S. Department of Labor Poster Courtesy G. Neil Companies, Sunrise, FL.

Job Analysis

Before people can be hired, the human resources department must have a clear understanding of the job to be filled. An analysis of each job is required to provide a foundation for recruitment and training. This analysis is accomplished by observation, completion of questionnaires, and interviews. The job analysis seeks to answer the following questions:

What physical and mental tasks does the worker accomplish?
How does the person do the job? (Methods used and equipment are explored.)
Why is the job done? (This is an explanation of the purpose and responsibilities of the job.)
What qualifications are needed for this job? (A list of knowledge, skills, and personal characteristics are prepared.)[2]

Next, the job analysis provides a basis for writing a job description, which describes the content and responsibilities of the job. The job specification lists the qualifications required of a person to get the job done.

JOB SAFETY & HEALTH PROTECTION

The Occupational Safety and Health Act of 1970 provides job safety and health protection for workers by promoting safe and healthful working conditions throughout the Nation. Provisions of the Act include the following:

EMPLOYERS

All employers must furnish to employees employment and a place of employment free from recognized hazards that are causing or are likely to cause death or serious harm to employees Employers must comply with occupational safety and health standards issued under the Act

EMPLOYEES

Employees must comply with all occupational safety and health standards, rules, regulations and orders issued under the Act that apply to their own actions and conduct on the job

The Occupational Safety and Health Administration (OSHA) of the U S. Department of Labor has the primary responsibility for administering the Act OSHA issues occupational safety and health standards, and its Compliance Safety and Health Officers conduct jobsite inspections to help ensure compliance with the Act

INSPECTION

The Act requires that a representative of the employer and a representative authorized by the employees be given an opportunity to accompany the OSHA inspector for the purpose of aiding the inspection

Where there is no authorized employee representative, the OSHA Compliance Officer must consult with a reasonable number of employees concerning safety and health conditions in the workplace

COMPLAINT

Employees or their representatives have the right to file a complaint with the nearest OSHA office requesting an inspection if they believe unsafe or unhealthful conditions exist in their workplace OSHA will withhold, on request, names of employees complaining

The Act provides that employees may not be discharged or discriminated against in any way for filing safety and health complaints or for otherwise exercising their rights under the Act

Employees who believe they have been discriminated against may file a complaint with the nearest OSHA office within 30 days of the alleged discriminatory action

CITATION

If upon inspection OSHA believes an employer has violated the Act, a citation alleging such violations will be issued to the employer Each citation will specify a time period within which the alleged violation must be corrected The OSHA citation must be prominently displayed at or near the place of alleged violation for three days, or until it is corrected, whichever is later, to warn employees of dangers that may exist there

PROPOSED PENALTY

The Act provides for mandatory civil penalties against employers of up to $7,000 for each serious violation and for optional penalties of up to $7,000 for each nonserious violation Penalties of up to $7,000 per day may be proposed for failure to correct violations within the proposed time period and for each day the violation continues beyond the prescribed abatement date Also, any employer who willfully or repeatedly violates the Act may be assessed penalties of up to $70,000 for each such violation A minimum penalty of $5,000 may be imposed for each willful violation A violation of posting requirements can bring a penalty of up to $7,000

There are also provisions for criminal penalties Any willful violation resulting in the death of any employee, upon conviction, is punishable by a fine of up to $250,000 (or $500,000 if the employer is a corporation), or by imprisonment for up to six months, or both A second conviction of an employer doubles the possible term of imprisonment Falsifying records, reports, or applications is punishable by a fine of $10,000 or up to six months in jail or both

VOLUNTARY ACTIVITY

While providing penalties for violations, the Act also encourages efforts by labor and management, before an OSHA inspection, to reduce workplace hazards voluntarily and to develop and improve safety and health programs in all workplaces and industries OSHA's Voluntary Protection Programs recognize outstanding efforts of this nature

OSHA has published Safety and Health Program Management Guidelines to assist employers in establishing or perfecting programs to prevent or control employee exposure to workplace hazards There are many public and private organizations that can provide information and assistance in this effort, if requested Also, your local OSHA office can provide considerable help and advice on solving safety and health problems or can refer you to other sources for help such as training

CONSULTATION

Free assistance in identifying and correcting hazards and in improving safety and health management is available to employers, without citation or penalty, through OSHA-supported programs in each State These programs are usually administered by the State Labor or Health department or a State university

POSTING INSTRUCTIONS

Employers in States operating OSHA approved State Plans should obtain and post the State's equivalent poster

Under provisions of Title 29, Code of Federal Regulations, Part 1903 2 (a) (1) employers must post this notice (or facsimile) in a conspicuous place where notices to employees are customarily posted

More Information

Additional information and copies of the Act, specific OSHA safety and health standards, and other applicable regulations may be obtained from your employer or from the nearest OSHA Regional Office in the following locations

Atlanta, GA	(404) 347-3573	Kansas City, MO	(816) 426-5861
Boston, MA	(617) 565-7164	New York, NY	(212) 337-2378
Chicago, IL	(312) 353-2220	Philadelphia, PA	(215) 596-1201
Dallas, TX	(214) 767-4731	San Francisco, CA	(415) 744-6670
Denver, CO	(303) 844-3061	Seattle, WA	(206) 442-5930

Lynn Martin

Lynn Martin, Secretary of Labor

Washington, D C
1991 (Reprinted)
OSHA 2203

U.S. Department of Labor

Occupational Safety and Health Administration

To report suspected fire hazards, imminent danger safety and health hazards in the workplace, or other job safety and health emergencies, such as toxic waste in the workplace, call OSHA's 24-hour hotline: 1-800-321-OSHA

This information will be made available to sensory impaired individuals upon request. Voice phone (202) 523-8615; TDD message referral phone: 1-800-326-2577

Figure 4–2 OSHA Safety Poster Courtesy of G. Neil Companies, Sunrise, FL.

Several benefits emerge from these steps—job announcements are easier to write, interviewing is more productive because applicants can be asked specific questions about their skills, duties and responsibilities can be more easily explained to applicants, and relevant training can be precisely focused on the knowledge and skills required for the job.

Recruiting

Wise recruiting strategies can actually serve to screen applicants. All states have a public employment service that can assist businesses with their hiring. A public employment service can screen applicants by giving aptitude tests that signify a person's ability to learn a certain job. A private employment agency can also provide assistance, but for a fee.

If the retailer places a "Help Wanted" sign in a window, interviewing many unqualified applicants may distract the retailer from more productive duties. A newspaper advertisement can provide another source of applicants. Caution should be exercised before placing the retailer's telephone number in the ad, since numerous, unqualified applicants may call. Notices of job openings should always be carefully worded to attract qualified applicants while at the same time preventing turnover and charges of discrimination.

Selection Procedures

Not all retailers follow the same procedures for screening applicants. In fact, in the same company a sales applicant might not go through the screening that a managerial applicant would undergo. In general, procedures for screening often involve the application form, initial interview, background check, testing, and final interview. Multiple screening procedures are always suggested to improve decision making. To save money, the most expensive screening step should be the last. An application form, and the time required by the retailer to read it, costs less than paying for an applicant's physical examination.

Application Form

The application form is a very useful screening tool that is often not used to its full potential. This tool makes the task of interviewing and selection easier. Aside from the typical questions on an application form (e.g., name, address, telephone number, education, employment history), there are subtle questions answered by the applicant: Can the applicant follow directions? Print neatly? Spell and write clear sentences? Are all gaps in employment explained? Employers should be aware that the term *self-employed* is sometimes used by applicants to hide periods of incarceration or institutionalization.

Application forms and resumes often contain exaggerated or false information. When a job seeker is faced with competition, and a paycheck is at stake, the applicant may simply resort to outright lying. The Port Authority of New York and New Jersey did a study using a questionnaire to ask applicants if they had ever used certain equipment or supervised someone using this piece of equipment that really did not exist. One-third of the applicants claimed to have experience in using the equipment![3] The FBI did an extensive investigation of diploma mills and located hundreds of "graduates" of phony institutions. One hundred and seventy-one were federal and state employees.[4]

A good application form, coupled with reference checks, can verify applicant information. Some employers require an applicant to complete an application prior to the interview and mail it to the employer. Then, at a later date, while the applicant is waiting on the premises for the interview, another application is requested to be completed. Both are compared before the interview.

An application should contain sufficient space for job seekers to explain why they left their previous positions. The names of supervisors can be requested of the applicant. The application form can provide space for the job seeker to explain anything in the past that needs to be clarified.

One advantage of requiring a completed application is that if the applicant becomes an employee, a written record, signed by the employee, is preserved. Also, company policy should state that false information on an application can result in disqualification of the applicant or dismissal of the employee.

Interviews

For entry-level positions in the retail industry, a retailer may grant only one interview to save time and effort during the screening process. Another approach, especially for higher level positions, is to conduct two or possibly three interviews. The initial interview is often conducted by the personnel department and subsequent interviews are handled by the department that requires the new employee.

The completed application form can be used as an agenda for interviewing. An interviewer can check an interviewee on a number of factors: ability to communicate; education, training, and experience; opinions of past supervisors; and duties at past jobs. A two-way exchange should occur, so that the interviewee can also learn about the job and the company.

To prevent bias during the applicant selection process, antidiscrimination laws have forbidden the use of photographs and questions such as the following:

What is your age?
What is your date of birth?
What is your height and weight?

What is your religion?
What is your ethnic background?
What organizations do you belong to?
Are you married?
What is your maiden name?
Who do you reside with?
How many children do you have? Who will care for them while you work?
Do you rent or own a home?
Do you have a car?
Have you ever had your wages garnished?
Have you ever been arrested? (Questions on convictions can be asked.)
Do you have any disabilities or illnesses?

Because so many questions are prohibited, an employer may wonder what can be asked on an application or during an interview. Basic questions include name, address, telephone number, convictions, citizenship, education, experience, and references. Whatever questions are asked beyond the basics, consideration should be given to their relevance to the job. This legal requirement is known as a bona fide occupational qualification (BFOQ).

It is essential that interviewers not ask potentially discriminatory questions that could result in claims of discrimination. Rather, interviewers should rely on open-ended questions and their creative ability to explore an applicant's qualifications. Rather than asking about physical disability, ask whether the applicant can perform the job or if special accommodations are necessary. Rather than asking about family responsibilities, ask what hours the applicant can work. Can they work overtime? Rather than asking if an applicant has a car, ask how they intend to get to work?[5]

Open-ended questions are very beneficial during the interview, because lengthy responses enable the interviewer to learn more about the interviewee. Examples include, "Tell me about all your duties in all your previous retail jobs." "What would past supervisors say about your strengths and weaknesses?"

A sharp interviewer knows that much more may be communicated from the interviewee at the nonverbal level through body language and eye contact than through the spoken word. Evasiveness by the interviewee can lead to further inquiry by the interviewer. However, caution is advised against making judgments of the applicant based on nonverbal behavior.

> From a legal standpoint, employment decisions based on an interviewer's "gut reaction" to an applicant or to the applicant's non-verbal reactions would be virtually impossible to defend against a charge of discrimination.[6]

During the interview, certain factors may cause the applicant to be rejected, such as inadequate education, training, and experience; poor grooming; job hopping; and unexplained omissions in the employment record. Weeding out applicants requires tact; consideration must be given to the applicant's feelings. Critical remarks are to be avoided.

Companies may use a structured or patterned interview procedure. Specific questions are asked of all interviewees. The purpose is to make the selection process more objective.

The final part of the interview is to obtain the applicant's consent for the employer to conduct a background investigation. Retailers often do not find thorough background investigations cost-effective for sales positions. Maybe one or two references are telephoned. In any case, consent or a waiver for the employer to conduct a background investigation should contain a description of the complete preemployment screening process, a statement that the employer will conduct a background check to verify information supplied by the applicant, a clause that maintains that disqualifying factors (e.g., false information, detection of illegal substances resulting from drug tests) may bar employment, and an indication that permission is granted for the employer to discuss results with those responsible for hiring.

Background Check

The intensity of background checks will vary with the job, and the amount of time and money the retailer is willing to spend. The check may consist of one or two calls to references for a sales position, to a complete background investigation for a position that involves financial accounting. Unfortunately, job applicant screening may stop at the written application stage and never proceed to background checks and other screening tools. Background checks for part-time, temporary, and contract employees are often nonexistent. A survey reported in *Security* magazine of after-hours cleaning services revealed that more than half of the applicants who apply for such jobs have prior criminal records.[7]

Most applicants will provide references from people who look on the applicant in a favorable light. An alternative for the employer is to obtain references from references. Also, try to concentrate on previous employers who can provide information on the applicant's work habits and the ability to get along with others. When contacting references, verify the accuracy of information supplied by the applicant. Telephone calls work well, rather than using a letter, since people are reluctant to put derogatory information in writing. At the same time, there are many supervisors and managers who will not discuss past subordinates over the telephone (or by any means), because of the fear of a law suit. Another factor to consider is that positive comments may be made about an applicant by a supervisor who would like to see the individual take a job elsewhere to rid the workplace of a poor performer. In essence, the new employer will hire another employer's problem. Although background checks may be time-consuming, the growing case law on negligent hiring indicates that liability is frequently the result of an employer's failure to perform reference checks or to verify previous employment.

Public records are a good source of information on job applicants, especially for thorough investigations. Criminal records of convictions are available at most county court buildings. It is important to obtain all of the applicant's previous addresses so each county court building can be checked. Educational records are public to the extent that one may call the institution to verify attendance, years of attendance, and date of graduation. Be aware that the Family Educational Rights and Privacy Act of 1974 allows only the applicant to obtain copies of transcripts, unless a waiver has been signed. Driving records are helpful to verify name, address, date of birth, physical description, and physical limitations. Safety and substance abuse problems (e.g., excessive tickets, driving under the influence) may surface. A workers' compensation claims history will signify whether an applicant can cope with physically or mentally demanding duties. Not every state provides cooperation when these records are sought. A request in the form of a letter may be required, along with a fee. Remember that the Americans with Disabilities Act of 1990 requires job criteria based exclusively on the essential skills of the job.

If the retailer does not want to conduct background investigations by in-house staff, several firms specialize in background investigations. A large retailer may be able to negotiate low-cost background investigations with a service that can verify certain limited factors about the applicant. Private investigators can also be used; however, investigations of each applicant can easily cost hundreds of dollars.

Applicant Screening Prevents Internal Theft

With Christmas 2 months away, Peter Hodding was beginning to worry about how he could afford presents for his numerous family members. Since Peter had so many presents to buy, he decided to follow the same pattern as in the last 4 years. Every year before Christmas, he had worked in a retail store from about 6 P.M. to 10 P.M. after leaving his regular job. Each year he had worked at a different retail store and in a different type of retail department.

His plan, as usual, was to conspire with a friend to obtain merchandise at a low cost. While working in the retail store, Peter's friend would enter, select an item, and Peter would ring it up on the cash register for one-fourth of the actual price. Although Peter and his friend were able to obtain several low-cost items, this year was going to be different: both were caught by an alert store detective.

In another similar case a retail department store, during the pre-Christmas season, quickly hired numerous part-time salespeople. An experienced store detective was highly suspicious of the camera salesperson who had been working in that department during the last three Christmas seasons. When the store detective informed management about his suspicions, management appeared too concerned about other things to pay much attention to his report.

Subsequently, however, a plan was worked out whereby the suspicious store detective would enter a utility closet at 5:30 P.M. before the suspected camera salesperson began work. The store detective climbed to an upper level of the utility closet and was able to observe, with binoculars, the camera department through a removed ceiling tile. After four evenings of intense surveillance and daily pressure from management to discontinue the operation, the camera salesman rang up three dollars for a thirty-five dollar camera.

The loss prevention staff favored prosecution; however, the store management decided not to prosecute to avoid any unfavorable publicity during the holiday season when sales were extremely important. The salesperson was fired.

Stores Mutual Association

The Stores Mutual Association (SMA) is an association of retailers who share information on shoplifters and employee thieves. They operate in several metropolitan areas such as New York, Chicago, and Los Angeles. Member businesses typically provide information on convictions and confessions to an SMA. Some SMAs require members to submit copies of confessions. Each automated SMA database contains thousands of names.

SMAs vary in size of membership, costs, and rules. Businesses outside of the retailing industry may also be members. Dues range from hundreds to thousands of dollars, depending on the number of employees. A small fee of a few dollars is charged for each name search. Since only one employee thief can steal thousands of dollars, the SMA concept is cost-effective.

SMAs are restricted by the Fair Credit Reporting Act. For example, applicants must be informed if they are rejected based on information from an SMA.

Private Investigators, Databases, and Electronic Mail

In earlier years, background investigators relied on using the telephone and "leg work" to conduct investigations. Today, these methods are still employed. However, use is now being made of database services and electronic mail. A background investigation can be conducted without leaving the office by way of a personal computer and a modem connected to telephone lines to communicate with information brokers. Electronic mail (E-mail) enables a message to be sent from one computer to another. A menu displayed on the investigator's computer provides directions to an electronic request form that contains specific questions. After the E-mail is sent to an information broker, hundreds of databases are searched for applicant information. The types of information available include Social Security numbers, names, addresses, all the listed telephone numbers in the US, real property records, civil court records, a movers index derived from postal service change-of-address information, and a variety of other records. These services may have a Social Security tracking system whereby the number is entered and a person's past employers and length of employment are listed.

Professional database services employ creative methods to obtain information on people. They know that someone trying to hide from authorities is unlikely to provide the post office with a forwarding address. However, these same people may not want to miss even one issue of their favorite magazine, so a change-of-address card is completed. This is why database agencies buy magazine subscriber lists. They also purchase lists of those who enter sweepstakes.

For a retailer, such a search must be cost-effective and involve business needs. Job applicants for a key financial position may be candidates for this type of investigation. One security practitioner conducts asset searches of employees suspected of embezzlement and fraud.

Certain services do offer low-cost (under $10) reports based on Social Security numbers. Retailers should shop for the most appropriate service.

It should be pointed out that not all information brokers are alike. How accurate is the information? Is it up-to-date? Are legal guidelines for collecting information being followed?

Retailers should not overlook a simple, inexpensive source of information. The local telephone book can confirm an applicant's name, address, and telephone number.

Credit Check

A credit check may prevent embezzlement that can result from financial pressure caused by problems such as an inability to cover debts, substance abuse, or gambling. For those jobs involving access to large sums of money, a credit check can be supported as a business necessity. To avoid a challenge under privacy laws for an unwarranted intrusion into the applicant's private affairs, the employer should obtain a release and inform the applicant of the credit check. If the employer denies a job to an applicant based on a credit report, the applicant must be made aware of this decision along with the name and address of the credit reporting agency.

The use of credit checks can be challenged under Title VII (Civil Rights Act of 1964). In reference to the EEOC Guide to Pre-Employment Inquiries, rejection of applicants because of poor credit ratings has a disparate impact on minority groups and has been found unlawful by the EEOC unless supported by business necessity. Inquiries into length of residence at an address, car ownership, bankruptcy, and other aspects of financial status may violate Title VII.

Credit reports have been criticized for years because of inaccuracies that cause problems for people applying for a job, credit, housing, and insurance. At the time of this writing, Congress is considering amending and tightening the Fair Credit Reporting Act.

Testing

Several types of tests can be administered to job applicants. As with other screening methods, careful planning is a necessity, especially since all screening methods must be job-related, valid, and nondiscriminatory. The EEOC regards all screening methods as having the potential of discriminating against applicants. In some states, the word "testing" in the preemployment process is forbidden.

Because an application for employment contains information that cannot always be verified, and because the results of an interview often reflect the personal attitudes of the interviewer, many retailers are turning to various types of tests. Retailers have more on their minds than testing for honesty and substance abuse, as we will see.

Ability Test

Would you hire a secretary without testing secretarial skills, such as typing? In the retail industry, machine operation, filing, and wrapping are areas in which skills can be tested. However, there is a lack of standardization. Whatever ability or skills test is used, it should be scientifically administered and all applicants should be given the same test under the same conditions.

Aptitude Test

Does the applicant have the capacity to perform the duties of the job? In retailing, for example, aptitude tests exist for applicants for sales positions.

Intelligence Test

Certain retailers hold that each job should be filled by applicants who have an IQ in a certain range. Even those who score above the range are barred from the job because they would become bored and increase turnover.

Personality Test

This test is especially helpful when selecting applicants for supervisory and middle management positions to screen out people with emotional problems. Various traits are assessed, including sociability, self-confidence, anxiety, flexibility, and so forth. Personality tests have received considerable criticism of their validity.

Honesty Test

Because of restrictions in the use of the polygraph test, many employers have turned to honesty tests to determine the integrity of people. Millions of these tests are given each year in thousands of companies. Honesty tests are psychological tests designed to measure attitudes toward theft. A major view behind these tests and their questions is that people who tolerate stealing by others and who punish thieves lightly are more likely to steal. A test may contain less than 100 objective (multiple choice and true-false) questions. For example, one question could be the following:

As a supervisor, you catch an employee taking home five pencils. What do you do?

- A. fire the employee
- B. warn the employee
- C. ignore the behavior
- D. not sure what to do

These tests take less than an hour to complete and cost $7–$15. A computer is used to score each test.

The following guidelines will help retailers when planning and choosing an honesty test:

Thoroughly study the validity and reliability of honesty tests. Look for research by independent organizations.

Obtain a guarantee in writing from the testing firm that the test has been validated for the job for which it is to be used and it does not adversely impact any protected group.

Conform to all applicable laws. In some states, preemployment tests purporting to measure honesty are forbidden.

Require all those who take the test to sign a statement that they volunteer to be tested and that the results will be disclosed to those making hiring decisions.

Estabish a committee to select a test and to write policies and procedures. Specialists for the committee can include the human resources manager, an attorney, a college professor, and the security manager.

A survey reported in *Security* magazine revealed that two-thirds of security decision makers are ambivalent about honesty tests or say they do not detect employees most prone to dishonesty. Thirty-two percent believe these tests identify dishonest employees. Responses included, "Most people can get around these tests. . . . We've caught employees stealing from us after they pass the tests."[8]

Many companies are moving away from honesty tests because the tests only assess theft potential. Instead, greater use is being made of multipurpose tests that assess theft potential and the tendency to engage in a variety of counterproductive and productive workplace behaviors.[9]

Prior to the use of any test, careful research is vital. Tests purporting to measure intelligence, personality, and honesty can result in considerable liability for the retailer. Certain states have very strict laws on testing. A psychologist and an attorney should provide input to prevent liability.

Drug Test

Many companies use drug testing during applicant screening and randomly during employment. Employers expect workers to perform their jobs free from intoxicating substances. Furthermore, employees should not hinder productivity because of a drug problem, cause errors or accidents, or steal to support a drug habit.

There have been legal challenges to drug testing. For example, Title VII challenges may exist; the National Institute for Drug Abuse Research shows that among young adults, blacks use marijuana more frequently than whites and other minorities. Employers can avoid testing problems by adhering to strict procedures, carefully selecting a qualified laboratory, and obtaining a signed release from each person tested. Testing is easier to justify when it is designed to determine level and frequency of current drug use and may indicate an addiction to a serious and expensive substance (e.g., cocaine, heroin, barbiturates, or hallucinogens).

Employers should realize that the National Institute of Drug Abuse (NIDA) (1-800-843-4971) administers a certification program for drug testing labs. NIDA standards reinforce uniformity from lab to lab, promote strict guidelines, and greatly reduce the chances of a false positive.

Whatever drug testing program is established by an organization, the serious problem of cheating must be fully understood. If an observer is not present to carefully watch the individuals being tested, a variety of ploys may be attempted to deceive an employer. For example, people are known to secure a plastic bottle of "clean urine" under their arm and attach a tube from the bottle to their lower body, so that when their urine is requested, they use their arm to apply pressure to the bottle and somebody else's "clean" urine becomes their sample.

One survey published in *Chain Store Age Executive* showed that drug testing is finding increasing acceptance in American businesses. Fifty-five percent of 700 human resources executives test applicants and/or employees for substance abuse or are making plans to implement such programs. Only 12 percent have been challenged in court or by unions.[10] Drug testing is also discussed in the final chapter of this book.

Reliability and Validity of Tests

Employers who are planning to use tests for screening purposes should research the reliability and validity of each test, especially to ensure the test conforms to antidiscrimination laws. Reliability reveals consistent results each time the same person takes the test. Validity shows whether the test measures what it purports to measure. Many of the reliability and validity studies of honesty tests have been conducted by the major testing companies. This is a built-in bias. Two good independent sources for research on the reliability and validity of tests are the Buros Institute of Mental Measurement (University of Nebraska at Lincoln) and the American Psychological Association (Washington, DC). The Buros Institute publishes the *Mental Measurements Yearbook*, which evaluates published tests. A good library will contain a variety of publications from these organizations.

Choosing Screening Methods

The needs of the retailer and cost are two primary factors that dictate the screening methods used by retailers. Here it can be written what *should* be done; however, the reality of the retailing environment and its personnel problems leave managers with limited choices while taking chances on applicants.

Research by Hollon and Gable indicates that the interview is the dominant information source for selection purposes. Next are the application, and business and personal references. Used less frequently are the credit report, conviction check, physical examination, testing, assessment center, and handwriting analysis.[11] See Table 4–1.

How Does the Americans with Disabilities Act of 1990 Impact Applicant Screening?

Title I of this act pertains to employment. Basically, employers may not discriminate against *qualified* individuals on the basis of their disabilities. This law extends to application procedures, hiring, advancement, discharge, and terms, conditions, or privileges of employment.

Regulations state that an employer cannot ask job applicants about medical problems, medications, or their workers' compensation history. Medical examinations can be conducted after an offer of employment has been made. Employment can be conditional on whether or not the applicant passes the exam. The exam results are confidential.

The use of illegal drugs is not considered a disability. However, a person with a history of drug abuse, but who is rehabilitated, may be protected under the ADA. Tests to determine the use of illegal drugs are not considered a medical exam. The following are also not disabilities according to the ADA—kleptomania, pyromania, compulsive gambling, and homosexuality.

Legal experts in the field of personnel testing offer the following:

ADA does not restrict the timing and use of psychological tests (e.g., integrity, personality, attitude, etc.). Instead, it ensures that employers use nondiscriminatory and valid selection measures.

The ADA provisions state that medical exams may not take place at the pre-offer stage. Psychological tests are not considered medical exams, nor do they identify disabilities. They are intended to identify personality traits.

There is one testing limitation. The test may not disclose a mental or psychological disorder. Tests that are designed to disclose impairments may be used only after a conditional employment offer is made.[12]

Well-written job descriptions are a good defense against charges of discrimination. Detail is important, especially because an employer may ask applicants if they can perform the work duties as defined.

Table 4-1 Use of Pre-Employment Screening Information, National Retail Security Survey '91

	Department Store	Discount Store	Specialty Apparel	Specialty Hard Goods	Specialty Other	Home Centers	Drug Store	Grocery, Etc.	Overall Percent
Bonding	20.3%	22.2%	4.5%	17.9%	12.5%	21.0%	25.0%	11.1%	15.1%
Credit Check	43.0%	19.4%	43.9%	51.2%	37.5%	55.2%	36.1%	33.3%	41.6%
Criminal Conviction Check	53.8%	27.7%	31.8%	48.7%	41.0%	44.7%	47.2%	41.2%	43.6%
Workman Comp. Claims	10.7%	19.4%	9.0%	10.2%	12.5%	23.6%	16.6%	23.8%	14.8%
Driving History	15.3%	16.6%	15.1%	35.9%	28.5%	55.2%	36.1%	31.7%	28.1%
Honesty Test—Paper & Pencil	27.6%	50.0%	43.9%	43.5%	53.5%	42.1%	44.4%	38.1%	42.9%
Laboratory Drug Screening	15.3%	30.5%	12.1%	25.6%	25.0%	52.3%	13.8%	22.2%	23.5%
Handwriting Analysis	0.0%	0.0%	3.0%	2.5%	0.0%	0.0%	5.6%	1.5%	1.5%
Past Employment Verification	86.1%	77.7%	89.3%	87.1%	85.7%	81.5%	86.1%	76.1%	83.8%
Personal Reference Check	58.4%	52.7%	81.8%	53.8%	66.0%	71.0%	55.5%	65.6%	64.0%
Stores Mutual Service	21.5%	22.2%	19.7%	46.1%	25.0%	5.2%	16.6%	9.3%	21.0%
Multiple Interviews	43.0%	33.3%	46.9%	41.0%	50.0%	42.1%	36.1%	39.6%	41.7%
Education Verification	15.3%	19.4%	18.1%	20.5%	23.2%	13.1%	22.2%	21.8%	21.2%
Avg. Number of Screening Methods Used	4.1	4.2	4.2	4.8	4.6	5.1	4.4	4.2	

Percentages take into account the 37 stores that are classified as "other" (8.0% of total) but that are not mentioned in the table.

© 1992. *Security Magazine*. Reprinted with permission.

Training

When the topic of training enters the minds of human resources and training specialists, there is a realization that there are serious challenges faced by this fast-changing industry. In the retail environment and in retail systems, the norm is constant change, neverending competition, and the need to improve services to customers. Employees must effectively interact with new automated systems. Success in this area will affect the bottom line and shrinkage. Actually, new systems and technology require more intellectually qualified employees. Unfortunately, retailers are having to hire lesser qualified applicants than in the past, especially since the number of applicants is decreasing.

Another complication to training is changing demographics. Newer immigrants and faster population growth in certain minority groups result in cultural diversity and retailers must be sensitive to differences among employees and customers. The retailer is wise to consider all these factors in designing training programs and meeting the needs of employees, customers, and the retailer.

Plans for security training in a retail environment should consider the total training requirements of the retailer. Security training will, understandably, be in competition with other types of training, especially when training non-security employees.

When planning security training, think in terms of the interplay of training with the whole security and loss prevention program, and how its ideas and strategies are communicated. This entails a comprehensive marketing approach as discussed at the beginning of this book. Security marketing should begin when applicants make initial contact with the business, such as displaying a sign in the human resources waiting room, and making a statement on the employee application and during the interview. Messages should be positive, such as, "Loss prevention preserves jobs." Security should be marketed during orientation, training, and retraining. Other means of communicating security are through the company newspaper, a security newsletter, posters, contests, policies and procedures, and through whatever creative ideas can be developed.

Training should be a part of the socialization process in the workplace. Socialization is a learning process whereby an employee gains knowledge about the employer and how to become a productive worker. It is broader in scope than orientation and training programs, and considers, for instance, examples set by superiors. Imagine the impact on an employee who goes through an excellent training program, but is then placed with a negative supervisor who contaminates the new recruit. Sociology textbooks typically devote a whole chapter to the socialization process.

Orientation of New Employees

Orientation programs vary among retailers, but their basic objective is to introduce the new employee to the workplace. An employee handbook will provide answers to many questions. Hopefully, the security department is permitted to provide input to the handbook and to the orientation program. Some retailers give the new employee "homework" that stresses important aspects of the handbook and the job. A checklist is often used as a guide by human resources personnel to ensure that nothing is overlooked. There are many topics applicable to orientation programs, including parking and public transportation, history of the company, tour of the facility, fringe benefits, policies and procedures, security and safety, and organization. Care must be exercised so that new employees do not suffer from information overload and become overwhelmed. A good orientation program is a major building block to producing a productive, quality employee.

Benefits of Training

Several benefits result from training:

reduces error, waste, and shrinkage
improves job performance and productivity
upgrades employee skills
lowers amount of supervision required
helps to improve morale and healthy attitudes
lowers turnover
prevents litigation and strengthens a retailer's case in court
increases sales and profits

Designing Training

The designing of a properly focused and effective training program is not an easy task. The following steps should be considered:

1. Assess training needs.
2. Study the audience and their abilities, attitudes, and training needs.
3. Work with a budget or seek funding.
4. Define behavioral objectives (i.e., what the trainee is to be able to do when training is completed).
5. Prepare an outline—a step-by-step sequence for training.
6. Select the best possible instructor and training methods.
7. Implement the training program.

8. Evaluate the effectiveness of the training by sending questionnaires to the trainees and to their supervisors on the job after the training is completed.
9. Modify the training program to improve it.

The following case illustrates the importance of store policies and procedures, and an ongoing training program. Employees must be constantly reminded about loss prevention measures through training, signs, bulletins, and so forth. Companies should not hesitate to terminate employees who violate policies and procedures that result in major losses. Failure to do so may result in repeat losses.

Is Loss of $50,000 in Jewelry Just Cause for Termination?

A 13-year employee of a chain of department stores held the position of jewelry coordinator. While rearranging the jewelry displays at one store, she left two boxes containing more than $50,000 in gold chains unattended. A customer asked her several questions. When the employee returned to where she left the chains, they were gone. The employee was fired the next day.

The employee sued the store, claiming she was unfairly discharged. The court granted summary judgment to the store and the woman appealed.

A California Court of Appeal *affirmed* the summary judgment, stating that the woman was at fault for the lost jewelry. She violated company policy, which required that all merchandise, unless being shown to a customer, remain locked up at all times.

This case was summarized from the *Security Law Newsletter* No. 90-115 (Crime Control Research Corporation, Washington, DC). *Case Citation:* Moore v. May Department Stores Company, No. B 043481, California Court of Appeal, Second Appellate District, Division Two, July 31, 1990.

Training Methods

Training and its delivery must be carefully planned so as not to waste training dollars. The traditional chalk-in-hand approach has its limitations. Most peoples' minds wander during training programs. Thus, a variety of training methods should be used to hold their attention.

On-the-job training is often used in retailing, especially by small retailers who cannot afford the time to train nor to hire training specialists. Coaching is another approach whereby the new employee works with an experienced employee. These methods prove cost-effective when a retailer has a constant turnover of part-time and temporary employees.

Requiring employees to read store operational manuals and watch video tapes are other avenues for training. However, supervision and documentation of these activities is important.

One-on-one, self-paced video training programs are another approach that is gaining in popularity. Test videos are designed to ascertain whether the student understands the course content and can apply it. These programs feature scenarios that give the student a chance to choose a course of action. The consequences of wrong action are illustrated.

Large retailers have the training specialists and formal classroom facilities, including a model store with merchandise, counters, displays, and cash registers. A variety of training topics covers policies and procedures, merchandising, systems operations, sales, and customer relations.

Job rotation is another avenue for training programs. Employees are shifted to different positions within the organization. This is especially useful as part of a management development program.

Security Training

Security training begins by assessing what training is needed for retail employees in general and security personnel. Both groups should be exposed to a broad curriculum of not only security, but also safety and fire protection. All topics pertaining to losses should be discussed. Internal theft and workers' compensation fraud, for example, should be discussed openly as serious loss problems. It is the job of the security manager to design a properly focused training program that fits the needs of the retail organization and its employees.

Case Problems

4A. As a store security manager, you have been requested by the human resources manager to attend a 9:00 A.M. meeting to discuss ideas for screening part-time, temporary applicants to be hired during the holidays. The human resources manager reminds you about last season's internal theft problem. What ideas will you present at the meeting?

4B. As director of security for a chain of department stores that sells clothing, design a basic security training program for retail salespeople. Prepare a course outline with topics and indicate how many minutes will be spent discussing each topic.

Notes

1. J. Berry Mason et al., *Retailing*, 4th ed. (Homewood, IL: Irwin Publishing, 1991), 655.
2. Ibid., 273–274.
3. "Lying on Job Applications May Be Widespread," *Security* (February 1988): 13.
4. "Bogus Diplomas Present Hiring Danger," *Creative Management* (August 1987): 7.
5. Karen S. McQueen, "Are You Conducting Legal Interviews?" *Legal Management* (March/April 1990): 13–14.
6. Ira M. Shepard and Robert Duston, *Thieves At Work* (Washington, DC: Bureau of National Affairs, Inc., 1988), 60–61.
7. "Background Checks Reveal Cleaning Service Integrity," *Security* (March 1991): 10.
8. "Debate Over Honesty Testing Effectiveness Continues," *Security* (March 1991): 11.
9. John W. Jones, "Trends and Issues: Integrity Tests," *Security* (October 1991): 44.
10. "Drug Testing on the Rise," *Chain Store Age Executive* (July 1990): 21.
11. Charles J. Hollon and Myron Gable, "Information Sources in Retail Employment Decision-Making Process," *Journal of Retailing* (Fall 1979): 62.
12. "Disabilities Act Imposes Few Job Screening Restrictions," *Security* (February 1992): 51.

5

Protection at the Point-of-Sale

Management Information Systems

Management information systems (MIS) are computer-based systems designed to gather and analyze information. These systems produce computerized reports that allow retailers to find answers to their business questions almost instantly. Numerous activities can be performed with the assistance of an MIS, including performance measurement against plans, vendor analysis, and price revisions.

MISs also play a role in protecting retail stores. For example, computer-generated reports can be designed to "watch" vendors who make too many mistakes, or who may be involved in theft, fraud, or collusion with employees. Reports can include vendor name, store number, merchandise, amount received, invoice number, amount paid, and so forth. Another type of report can be used to identify truck drivers who have frequent shortages or seal discrepancies. Computer data can establish profiles of stores vulnerable to losses. Factors include local crime rates, geographic location, demographic statistics, store design, security strategies, inventory methods, and many other variables. Point-of-sale (POS) cash register systems are a component of retail MISs and provide valuable information on cashiers and sales transactions, as illustrated in the following paragraphs.

Cash Registers

Retailers have used mechanical cash registers for many years as a security device to curb employee theft. Earlier machines were actually adding machines placed on top of cash drawers. The cashier would push the appropriate buttons and crank an arm to enter information on each sale. As cash register technology evolved, a display for the price of each item was added that both the cashier and the customer could observe. Later, a record of each sales transaction was printed and the amount of change due to the customer was automatically calculated.

In the 1960s, the electronic cash register (ECR) was introduced. It uses electric light beams to enter information at a very high rate of speed. ECRs are in widespread use, especially since advances in technology have made the ECR affordable for just about all retailers. ECRs, in combination with computer systems, are increasingly being used to provide reports for management.

Computerized Point-of-Sale Cash Registers

The computerized POS cash register is the input device for many retailers. It has the ability to place sales information directly into the retailer's computer system. The information is stored in the system for retrieval when needed. Retailers can benefit from these systems in several ways. A perpetual inventory is maintained, which helps to determine shrinkage. Also, retailers can ascertain the types of merchandise that are selling most rapidly. Retailers who sell a large variety of merchandise with minimal inventory and quick turn-over find POS systems to be essential to their businesses. Automated ordering features facilitate maximum profitability. Productivity of cashiers and salespeople is also enhanced through rapid and accurate sales transactions with fewer errors. Other POS features in widespread use include price changes, third-party or in-house credit authorizations, layaways, full price look-up, and store receiving.

The speed at which POS systems operate makes them very useful. In addition to instantaneous updating of inventory, which is a primary benefit of POS systems, the speed of these systems helps to prevent losses. For example, a customer can be prevented from making several successive purchases close together and thus exceeding their credit limit. Such a scenario could easily occur under a slow record-keeping system.

Scanning and Wanding

Scanning and wanding are the primary methods of data entry at POS terminals (see Figure 5-1). The scanner is commonly used at supermarkets where bar codes are read by a fixed-slot scanner. A wand is used at general merchandise retailers to capture information. Scanning and wanding are also used in other areas of retail stores for activities such as receiving and marking. A major vulnerability of these systems is that they require human intervention to capture information. A dishonest cashier in a supermarket could pass some food items around a fixed scanner for a friend. In a clothing store, a dishonest salesperson could use a wand to capture only half the cloth-

Figure 5-1 Hand-held Laser Bar Code Scanner Courtesy of Symbol Technologies.

ing in a sales transaction. Circumvention can also occur in the receiving department of a store. Two strategies to deal with this vulnerability are CCTV surveillance and undercover investigations.

Universal Product Code

There are several merchandise marking technologies that are part of scanning and wanding systems. The standard for food and general merchandise retailing is the Universal Product Code (UPC). Consumers are increasingly seeing the telltale black and white bars on store items. The bars are codes that represent information about the manufacturer and the product (e.g., size, color, etc.). When information is captured by a scanning or wanding system, it is fed into the POS system and the price is printed on a receipt for the customer. At the same time, information, such as inventory levels, are recorded for management. These systems offer several advantages—accuracy and speed at the POS, time and labor savings, improved inventory and financial control, store-by-store feedback on customer buying patterns, and fast measurements of marketing strategies. Disadvantages include the investment required by retailers to install the systems. Also, consumer groups and unions have opposed eliminating prices on merchandise.

Protection Features

From a security and loss prevention perspective, POS systems can provide valuable information to protect retail stores. Cash register void reports, records of cashiers who repeatedly underprice, and information on bad checks and credit cards are examples of the types of reports that provide direction for security personnel to curb losses. Ratios can be programmed into systems to identify areas where losses may be occurring, such as cash-to-charge sales, refunds to sales, and meat-to-grocery sales. When a cashier is identified whose activities are outside of certain parameters, closer examination of the employee may be necessary. Data can also be maintained on employee purchases and credits, and would include the employee's name and number, dates and times of transactions, amounts, terminals, and the cashier's name and number.

Technological advances allow for the integration of CCTV cameras with the computer software that also runs the POS systems. These exception-monitoring systems enable security personnel to monitor sales transactions via CCTV systems. When an exception (e.g., refund, large sale) takes place, a CCTV camera is focused on the POS and a replication of the sales transaction is generated on the video image. The cashier, the customer, and the register tape overlay are recorded for future reference.

POS system software can also play a role in robbery protection. For example, the no-sale key that opens the cash drawer can be programmed to require a two-step procedure, such as hitting the subtotal key first. If this procedure is not followed, the POS system can send an alarm signal to a monitoring station and also activate a CCTV system.

The Point-of-Sale as a Vulnerable Location

The POS accommodates customer payment. This location is also referred to as the checkout area. Refunds and other customer services often take place at this point. Because valuables are exchanged, the POS is a very vulnerable location for retailers. Losses result from the following:

- acceptance of bad checks
- credit card fraud
- refund and exchange fraud
- acceptance of counterfeit money
- victimization by a quick-change scam
- outsider or employee stealing from the register
- failure to notice an altered price tag
- larger merchandise used to hide smaller merchandise
- cashier undercharging relatives or friends
- cashier overcharging customers for gain
- cashier failing to enter a sale in a cash register and stealing the money
- cashier discounting sales for which the customer paid full price
- pricing mistakes
- giving a customer the wrong change
- abrasive behavior by a cashier

Stealing from Cash Registers

In one case of cash register theft, a pharmacist stole thousands of dollars from his employer. When a customer paid for a prescription by check, he would ring the "no sale" button, put the check in the register, and then take out an equal amount of cash. The tape would balance at the end of the day. When confronted, the pharmacist first claimed that there were so many no sales because many customers requested change for the various machines in the store. Later, he confessed. Such a scheme can be prevented by recording all transactions in more detail (e.g., coding to identify method of payment) and reviewing register tapes as often as possible. Use the tape to review cash, checks, and credit card purchases. Don't just use the register tape to determine if the amount in the till and the amount on the tape agree.

In another case, a cashier was voiding out legitimate sales. When a customer bought something and did not wait for a receipt, the cashier would pocket the money and write "void" on the receipt with the statement "customer changed mind" or "customer did not have enough money." Two major strategies to curb these losses is to require supervisory approval of voids and to maintain records of all store voids to spot trends.[1]

Stealing from Computerized POS Registers

POS systems do offer several advantages, as discussed earlier. However, retailers must never think that employees cannot steal from a computerized POS system. Many employees brought up in the computer age are computer-literate, creative, and resourceful. Retailers should always have manual backup methods available to ensure the accuracy of computer systems. A determined thief can be challenged to outwit a computer by simple or complex means. One restaurant was victimized by a waiter who devised a simple way to go around the POS lockout feature that prevented anyone but a manager from using a void key. The waiter would spill a drink on a terminal causing it to go down. When it was down, the waiter was free to void items on manually written checks, while skimming money from customers.

In a more sophisticated case, a group of employees at a restaurant were collecting cash from customers, voiding some items on the POS system, and then pocketing the cash. Although managers were authorized to void checks, one sharp employee thief memorized the code on a manager's security key when it was in view. After obtaining a blank key from the computer company, this offender punched out all the holes with a heated paper clip and used moistened bread to fill in all but the holes corresponding to the manager's code. As the theft ring spread, just about all the manager's keys were duplicated. When management noticed excessive voids, an investigation resulted in successful prosecution.[2]

Preventing Losses at the Point-of-Sale

Training is a major strategy to prevent losses at the POS. Although training in a retail environment presents serious challenges, especially with varying degrees of turnover and numerous part-time and temporary employees, this strategy provides a foundation for reduced losses at the POS. Training should discuss the ways in which the retailer can sustain losses at the checkout and provide countermeasures. Topics should include discussions of external as well as internal offenders. Policies and procedures will provide considerable subject matter for training. An outline for training and strategies to prevent losses includes the following:

> Explain the numerous ways in which losses can occur at the POS.
> Explain techniques used to identify and prevent losses (e.g., recognizing counterfeit currency, CCTV surveillance).

Assign specific responsibilities to all employees. Have them use a specific cash register, terminal, or cash tray. If possible, require employees to log their employee number into each transaction.

Require that cash drawers be kept orderly and cash handling be done systematically to provide an improved opportunity to spot fraudulent techniques by outsiders.

Require that each transaction be done separately and the cash drawer be closed following the transaction.

Require cashiers to lock their registers when they leave.

Ensure that all customers receive a receipt. If they do not get a receipt, give them a $5 gift certificate.

Train cashiers to count change aloud to customers. Money room personnel should be required to double-check their counts, and initial and date their work. Require all deposit slips to be attached to the register tapes, initialed, and saved.

Establish policies and procedures to reduce fraudulent voids. Voids are used to eradicate and record errors by cashiers. Losses occur when a cashier voids a legitimate (no mistake) sale and pockets the cash. Assign void keys only to supervisors who must complete and sign a void form. Use the technological advantages of POS systems to make the job of controlling and recording voids easier. Use the same strategies for all "no sale" rings on registers.

Use average sale and average void reports of employees to identify potential thieves.

Many sophisticated POS terminals contain training modes that permit practice by trainees. Such practice is not included in daily sales totals. Thus, training modes must be controlled and monitored.

Use technology to investigate losses. For example, an automated price look-up system can maintain records of sales transactions that were completed for less than the proper price.

Periodically check bookkeeping and accounting records received from POS terminals or cash registers to identify irregularities.

Study records of cash overages and shortages, and look for trends. Cashiers, and their supervisors and managers, are capable of devising many ploys for illegal gain. Treat cash overages the same as shortages, because the overage may indicate an attempted theft.

Openly discuss the periodic use of an outside shopping service. Employees will not know if the customer they are servicing is really an investigator. This service tests the honesty and courtesy of cashiers, and whether they follow established procedures. One test uses a two-person team where one person pays for an item in exact change and departs, while the other person watches to see if the cashier opens the cash drawer to deposit the money.

Maintain accountability of all merchandise that is returned, due to be returned to vendor, slated for destruction, or donated to charity. These records are especially helpful for accurate inventories.

Maintain accountability of all employee purchases (e.g., type of merchandise, date, time, price, cashier, and other helpful information). Prohibit employees from completing their own sales transaction.

In training, discuss the use of overt and hidden CCTV systems that record sales transactions (including the monetary amount, date, and time) and display them on a TV monitor (see Figures 5–2 and 5–3).

Require cashiers to check with a supervisor for guidance when confronted with unusual situations.

Conduct surprise cash audits at registers and audits of money and merchandise-handling procedures. Incorporate feedback from these audits into better quality policies, procedures, and training.

Bad Checks

A bad check is not honored for payment by the bank on which it is drawn. The best way to eliminate losses from bad checks is to stop accepting checks. This is the strategy of numerous retailers. However, most retailers maintain this customer convenience, but screen the checks offered by customers.

Figure 5–2 Video Security System Courtesy of NAVCO.

Figure 5-3 Video Security System Records Theft Courtesy of NAVCO.

The problem of bad checks has persisted for many years and most retailers see it as a nuisance that is part of the business of retailing. "Check fraud" or "theft by deception" are terms that describe the act of passing a bad check. The types of bad checks include those written against insufficient funds or no accounts, forgeries, or stolen checks. Most of the time, a bad check results from honest mistakes by customers who faultered in their bookkeeping or did not accurately time their incoming funds to cover a check.

Each community has its share of offenders who habitually pass bad checks. These people are often prosecuted. However, in some communities, the limited resources of prosecutors precludes prosecution.

Bad checks also surface from professional criminals who travel around the country making a living based on fraud and deceit. These offenders may establish a new identity every few months. They may go to a cemetery, find the grave marker of a deceased person who would be their age if alive, obtain or forge a birth certificate, acquire a driver's license, and then establish a checking account and apply for credit cards. The FBI found that, in California, licenses had been issued in the names of almost 1,000 people who had been dead for years.[3] When their false identity becomes too hot, these criminals may even drop their credit cards near high schools or malls so teenagers will make the mistake of using the cards and leading police astray.

Professional check passers who travel around the country are the target of the FBI's National Fraudulent Check File. Data are maintained on their methods of operation to assist with investigation and prosecution.

Offenders usually employ several other less-sophisticated methods of passing bad checks. They often pass stolen checks obtained in a burglary, from picking someone's pocket, or from a parked automobile. This results in forgery, which is signing someone else's name to a document or changing the amount with the intent to defraud. Another ploy is to open a checking account with a small deposit and then write checks beyond the amount deposited.

Hoodwinked

The handsome, middle-aged couple strolled up to the checkout. They looked like movie stars. He wore an expensive pinstriped suit and she was adorned in gold and diamonds that highlighted her dress that cost a fortune. They selected more than $1000 worth of merchandise. The male stated he would pay cash and flashed several $100 bills. The female countered and said it was her treat. So she wrote a check and produced a driver's license. Unfortunately, the retailer was hoodwinked by an old con. The check was worthless and the driver's license a fake.

Recovery from Bad Checks

Recovery from bad checks will depend on a number of factors. Most customers often cover a bad check when notified. When this does not produce results, the best advice is to contact the local prosecutor to ascertain the procedures for recovery. For example, a retailer may send the customer a registered letter that states that payment is required within two weeks. A standard form can be used and a copy of the check and applicable law can be enclosed in the letter. If there is no response, then the retailer will sign an arrest warrant against the bad check writer. Other jurisdictions handle bad checks through the civil justice system (i.e., small claims court). The use of a collection agency is another option to recovering bad checks. Large retail chains contract collection work to specialized firms. Revco Drug Stores has done this to take the collection burden off store managers. Their collections have improved to the point that two-thirds of all dollars slated for collection are recovered. The system is centralized and each store can ascertain the status of collections. With an average of one bad check per store per day (or 1,800 bad checks per week), Revco finds this strategy cost-effective.[4]

Recovery can be a frustrating and time-consuming nuisance for the retailer. Consequently, preventive measures are especially important.

Preventive Measures

Remember that a check is nothing more than a piece of paper until the money is collected. The paper can be worthless!

Prepare clear policies and procedures for accepting checks, and include these guidelines in training. Remember that during busy shopping periods, cashiers are likely to have a limited time to screen checks and identification. Request cashier input for protection strategies.

Prohibit checks written from out of state.

Accept only checks written from the customer's checking account.

Never accept checks for amounts higher than the purchase price so the customer can receive cash.

Examine checks carefully, as shown in Figure 5–4. Make sure each check is imprinted with the customer's name and address.

Caution cashiers about offenders who try distractions or ploys during the screening of checks.

Require supervisory approval of checks written over a certain amount and when a cashier is in doubt about a check.

Consider calling the bank to find out if sufficient funds exist in the account to cover the check when checks are written for a high amount.

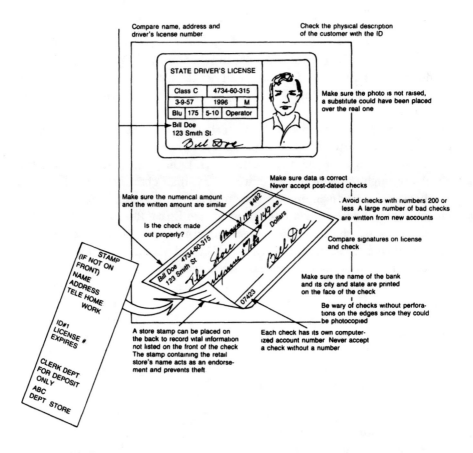

Figure 5-4 Identification and Checks

Remember that all types of checks can be forged in many different ways. Limit the types of checks accepted. A payroll check can be forged with a nonexistent company printed on it. A call to the "company" for verification may actually be to the home of a confederate. Checks certified by a bank can also be forged. Retailers should avoid accepting two-party, government, and blank checks, as well as money orders.

Traveler's checks are sold in specific denominations. The traveler signs the checks when purchased at a bank and signs them again in the presence of the person who cashes them. An offender will steal these checks and forge the second signature. Avoid accepting traveler's checks if they have been endorsed in advance. Companies issuing these checks often cover stolen ones, unless the two signatures are different.

- Request identification. This has its limitations, because a fake ID may be presented. Check the photo, date of expiration, and so forth. Does it look genuine? The key is to MATCH THE ID WITH THE CUSTOMER! Does the signature on the ID match the signature on the check? A driver's license, credit card, and employee ID are acceptable forms of identification. The cashier should record important information on the check. Unacceptable types of identification include a Social Security card, library card, or organizational membership card.
- Certain retailers copy the credit card type and number onto the face of the check. Another strategy is to record the customer's workplace information. Professional criminals may fabricate such information.
- Advertise check policies for customers.
- Keep a list of customers who have not covered their bad checks and cashiers who have accepted too many bad checks. Regular customers who write checks can be on file as a customer service to speed processing at the checkout. New customers can complete a form that includes address, telephone number, and so forth.
- Consider the cost-effectiveness of using an on-line, check-clearing service. Account numbers and customers' names are compared to data on bad checks. This service may cover a bad check if certain procedures are followed.
- Be aware that photo ID systems and requesting the customer's thumbprint on each check has had mixed results. The photo system records a picture of the check writer, the check, and the ID presented. The customer simply stands in front of a camera at the checkout, the process is completed in seconds, and the film is developed if necessary. The thumbprint takes even less time. Each method assists with prosecution. Both preventive methods are primarily deterrents that are less effective over time. In one retail store, a wall in the security office was completely covered with pictures of bad check passers. Retailers should alter their method as the deterrent value declines.
- Establish cooperative relations among retailers to prevent bad checks. A "rap sheet" on bad check writers can be shared and updated. Also, in conjunction with local police, retailers can notify each other, through an organized chain of telephone calls, that a bad check writer has been spotted.
- REMEMBER THAT MOST CUSTOMERS WHO PRESENT BAD CHECKS ARE HONEST. Cashiers should be trained to be careful with checks, but at the same time to be courteous.

> **Woman Sues Store Manager and Store for Slander following Bad Check Accusation**
>
> A woman who had been purchasing groceries at a Kroger store for a few months obtained a check-cashing card from the store. Her checks to the store were all honored. On one occasion, she purchased about $30 worth of groceries and paid with a $40 check. The check was approved by the cashier, but as she exited the store, she was stopped by an assistant manager who loudly accused her, in front of several people, of having written a bad check. He demanded that she return the groceries and the money she received as change. The assistant manager claimed that he was not aware that she had a check-cashing card. He had been informed that the woman's husband had had three checks returned; however, that was two years earlier, and the checks were forgeries following the theft of the checkbook.
>
> The woman sued the assistant manager and the store for slander. She was awarded $3,500 in compensatory damages and $7,500 in punitive damages. The assistant manager and the store appealed.
>
> The North Carolina Court of Appeals affirmed. Punitive damages are appropriate when the defendant's conduct is "malicious, wanton, or recklessly indifferent to the truth and the plaintiff's rights." The assistant manager falsely accused without making an effort to verify his information. The slander claim was proper, because of the assistant manager's loud accusations in front of others.
>
> This case was summarized from the *Security Law Newsletter* No. 90-91 (Crime Control Research Corporation, Washington, DC). Harris v. Temple, No. 8912SC649, North Carolina Court of Appeals, June 19, 1990.

Credit Card Fraud

As with checks, credit cards are a customer convenience, as large sums of cash do not have to be carried. The three major groups involved in credit card usage are credit issuers (e.g., banks, retailers), acceptors (e.g., retailers), and users. Each group is victimized by fraud, because it is easier, safer, and more profitable for criminals to steal with a credit card than with a gun. In 1988, Visa International lost $188 million and Mastercard International lost $128 million in credit card frauds.[5] Users are victimized by all sorts of scams after offenders obtain their credit card numbers. This can occur over the telephone or following the use of a credit card at a restaurant or other business.

Retailers sustain losses from various types of fraud involving credit cards. Because these cards are invalid, stolen, or subject to counterfeiting, retailers who do not follow verification procedures are likely to have difficulty recovering lost funds. An offender may simply submit to a retailer a stolen or counterfeit card in exchange for merchandise or make a purchase with a bad card at one store in a retail chain and then go to another store in the chain for a cash refund.

Credit card companies typically request that retailers confiscate and refuse sales charged to unauthorized cards. A monetary reward may be granted to a cashier who identifies and confiscates such a card. If the circumstances are not safe to keep the card, the cashier should copy the card's identifying information and the customer's name, address, and so forth. If possible, when a stolen or counterfeit card is presented, the police should be called and the suspect stalled until they arrive.

Offenders who illegally use credit cards usually forge the cardholder's signature on sales slips. They prefer to make purchases just when a store is about to close. These criminals also operate under the "floor release limit" of businesses to avoid a check on the card. This may be between $50–$100, but the level varies among types of businesses. A "zero" floor release results in a check of all cards. Professionals may have "hot card" lists obtained from dishonest retailers and they may call authorization centers to check on cards in their possession right before use. Credit card criminals prefer unsigned cards and those that are new. They may work with a mail carrier to intercept new cards. Criminals who operate interstate find illegal credit cards attractive, because of the inconvenience and expense involving witnesses and extradition. When credit card fraud is investigated, samples of handwriting are obtained from sales slips signed by the suspect and a false credit application, if available. Prosecutors must prove the elements of larceny by credit card, which include possessing a credit card obtained by theft or fraud, by which services or goods are obtained, through unauthorized signing of the cardholder's name.

Retailers are periodically found guilty of credit card fraud. Customers may be victimized when the retailer or an employee raises the amount on the charge slip or makes duplicate charge slips with the same credit card number.

Intricate Credit Card Scam

Because the going rate for hot merchandise on the street may be 10 cents to 20 cents on the dollar, criminals are devising various ways to increase their gain. One scam begins with opening a store account, usually under a false identify. A low credit limit may be requested to avoid a thorough check. Next, store merchandise is stolen, then returned to the store so the value of the items can be credited to the charge account. Gift certificates are then purchased with the fraudulent merchandise credit. An inexpensive item is then purchased with the certificate and cash is received for the difference.[6] Retailers can prevent such scams by requesting a receipt for returned merchandise and asking for two types of identification when a gift certificate is presented. In addition, any cash refunds greater than $10 could be mailed to the customer.

Preventive Measures

As with the bad check problem, policies, procedures and training are essential to preventing credit card fraud. Make sure preventive measures (such as those presented in the following list) are practical, especially when the store is busy. Follow the card issuer's procedures closely to avoid losses.

- Post procedural guidelines at cash registers.
- Examine the card. Does it look genuine? Does it look altered? The signature or the card's numbers may be changed. A razor is sometimes used to shave letters and numbers (or an iron used to flatten them) so new ones can be stamped to circumvent the verification process.
- Be aware of new technologies. Card companies are always developing new fraud prevention technologies such as holograms, ultraviolet inks, and fine-line printing. A hologram provides a three-dimensional image that is difficult to counterfeit. It can be checked by tilting the card at different angles.
- Ascertain whether the card has expired. Is it not yet valid?
- Ask the customer for a valid photo ID and record name, address, and home and workplace telephone numbers. If necessary, verify this information with the authorization center or use the local telephone book to check on the address given by the customer.
- Verify the card by checking the issuer's "hot list," telephoning the card issuer, or using an electronic authorization terminal.
- Be aware of card users. Are they trying various ploys to avoid credit card screening procedures? Are they trying to stay under the floor release limit by making small purchases?
- Make sure the card imprint is on the sales draft.
- Does the card enable an imprint on the carbon copy? Because the carbon paper has an imprint of the card number, it should be carefully destroyed or carbonless receipts should be used.

Make sure the sales draft is signed, properly dated, and complete.

Do the signatures on the card, the charge slip, and the ID match?

Require cashiers to initial each charge transaction at their register, so they can be questioned following a discrepancy.

Maintain records of credit card fraud to spot trends and to focus on problem areas.

Make sure cashiers follow procedures without being offensive. Courtesy is vital.

Remember that no preventive measure is foolproof. Cashiers only have a certain amount of time to screen the various methods of payment by customers. Preventive measures must be practical and cost-effective.

You Be the Judge 5-1

The Story: The man and woman brought several merchandise items to the department store cashier desk, and the woman proceeded to write a check in payment. When the cashier asked for identification, the woman handed over a major credit card. "If you'll wait just a moment, I'll call the card company for verification," the cashier said.

As the cashier placed the phone call, the woman shopper began fidgeting and looking edgy. "Er, I just thought of something," she told her companion. "I have to run out to the car for a minute. Be a sweetie and wait here for my packages and credit card, would you?"

"Sure, no problem," said the man agreeably as the woman nervously scurried out of sight.

His cheerful demeanor evaporated a few minutes later when a policeman suddenly loomed next to him at the cashier's desk. As he subsequently learned, the cashier's call had produced the information that his companion's card was on the card company's "stolen" list. The cashier had pressed a button that sent a code signal to Store Security, and Security had quickly called the police.

In vain, the man explained that he had just met the woman that day, was not sure where she lived or even what her name was, and certainly had not known that she was shopping with a stolen credit card. He was taken downtown and booked anyway.

The state brought him to trial for possession of a stolen credit card, but the court acquitted him, saying that the state had failed to prove him guilty.

He then sued the department store for false arrest and malicious prosecution. Did he succeed in nailing the store for damages?

Make your decision; then turn to the end of the chapter for the court's decision.

Source: "You Be the Judge," including the decision at the end of this chapter. Reprinted with permission from *Security Management Bulletin: Protecting Property, People, & Assets,* a publication of Bureau of Business Practice, Inc., 24 Rope Ferry Road, Waterford, CT, 06386.

Counterfeiting

For the retailer, counterfeiting is a multidimensional problem. It involves the unlawful duplication of something valuable. A retailer may be victimized by counterfeit clothes, jewelry, and other merchandise. Credit cards and coupons are subject to counterfeiting as well. Customers are also victimized and this impacts the retailer.

The discussion that follows focuses on counterfeit money. At the POS, counterfeit money is a periodic problem that can be prevented. The US Secret Service investigates counterfeiting cases. Unfortunately, the person who realizes that they have counterfeit money will not be reimbursed by the Secret Service. As the chain of custody is lengthened from the counterfeiter to the police, the investigation becomes more difficult.

Counterfeiting also involves what is called the currency switch. The offender modifies a $1 bill to look like a $20 bill. This is accomplished by cutting off a different corner from four $20 bills and pasting them to the four corners of a $1 bill. (Bills with three corners are still negotiable.) Careful study of the corners and knowledge of the presidential portraits on bills will expose this crime.

To prevent victimization, retailers should learn to recognize counterfeit money. This can best be done by comparing suspect money with genuine money. Figure 5–5 provides several clues for identifying a counterfeit.

Preventive Measures

Depending on the type of retail store, consider not accepting bills over a certain amount (e.g., $50 or $100).
Carefully study the currency in question without being obvious.
Once a counterfeit has been positively identified, delay the passer and contact local police.
If the passer departs, obtain a description of the person and her vehicle.
Handle the counterfeit money as little as possible.

Counterfeiting

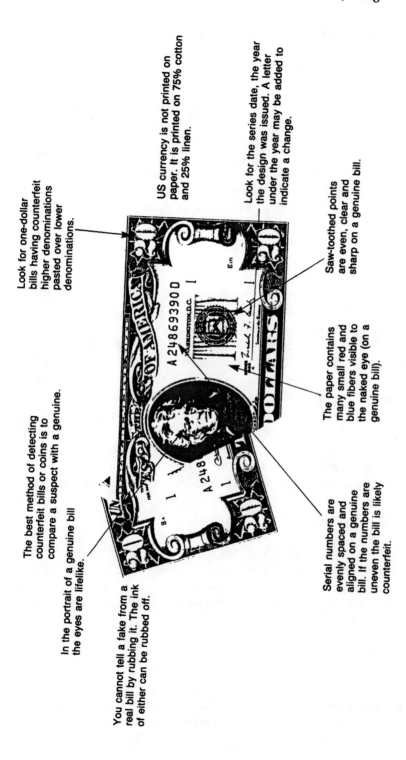

Figure 5-5 Detecting Counterfeit Currency

To deal with the problem of counterfeit money and the sophistication of color copiers that are being used more frequently, the US Treasury is gradually adding security features to currency. Protection includes a polyester strip embedded in the paper on the left side of each note between the border and the federal reserve seal. The letters "USA" and the denomination are printed on the strip. The strip can be seen, but it cannot be reproduced by a color copier. Another protection feature are the words "THE UNITED STATES OF AMERICA," micro-printed along the sides of the center portrait. Although this looks like a thin line, it can be seen more clearly with a magnifier; it does not reproduce well by using a copier.[7] At this very moment, it is likely that professional counterfeiters are devising ways in which these security features can be duplicated.

Refund Fraud

Retail employees, by themselves or in collusion with outsiders, have devised many ways to commit refund fraud. One simple method occurs when an employee keeps a customer's receipt to be used to support a fraudulent customer refund. A refund slip is completed, the receipt is attached, and the employee pockets the cash. Poor accountability of returned merchandise helps to promote such fraud. The key is for the offender to secure a receipt. A countermeasure is for the store to reward customers with $5 if they do not receive a receipt. However, offenders may search inside and outside of a store for receipts, pick up merchandise that matches the receipt, and then seek a refund for cash. Offenders are known to even walk into a store, grab merchandise, and then go directly to a refund counter to demand cash without a receipt. A bad credit card or check may be used at one store to obtain merchandise that is returned to another store for cash. Another problem for retailers is the customer who breaks or damages an item and returns it for a full refund or exchange.

Computer-literate offenders are using their home computers to duplicate sales receipts. As usual, security may stay ahead of these "third wave" criminals. Multicolor receipts for retailers are now on the market. Characters within the same line are of different colors and the retailer can change color combinations.

Preventive Measures

Offer a reward to customers who are not provided with a receipt.
Post signs that inform customers of the need for a receipt to obtain a refund. This could be a cash register receipt, credit card receipt, or cancelled check.

Study receipts for alterations.

Purchases made by check should not be refunded until after the check has cleared. Caution is also advised with credit card purchases.

Ask customers to complete a form to record name, address, telephone number, description of returned merchandise, and price. Require that both the customer and the employee sign and date the form. These forms can be numbered and can consist of multiple parts. A copy can be attached to the returned merchandise and signed by the employee who places it back on the sales floor. The form should then be sent to the cash office. Another copy should then be sent to the cash office. Another copy should be sent to the cash office by a supervisor who signs it right after the refund.

Consider mailing a check to customers for refunds over $25. This will discourage offenders who have false identities.

Management can elect to telephone those customers who received a refund greater than a certain amount to ask if the customer is satisfied. The conversation may shed light on a security weakness.

Maintain strict accountability and security of returned merchandise.

Instruct retail employees to destroy receipts found on floors and around the store.

Conduct surveillance of suspected employees if necessary.

Additional POS Vulnerabilities

When valuables are exchanged at the POS, the potential for loss exists as soon as someone devises a way to circumvent controls, if they exist. A summary of vulnerabilities and countermeasures follows.

Employees may steal from a retailer's layaway system. This is accomplished in an environment of poor accountability and inadequate supervision where, for example, employees fraudulently void layaway payments.

Following a sale, the customer pickup area is vulnerable, because employees follow a path from the stockroom to the parking lot. Constant CCTV surveillance will prevent losses.

Internal losses at a cash register may result from a cashier removing the cash register tape and inserting a new one for the last part of the business day. At closing, the old tape and corresponding money are turned in, while the newer tape and money are pocketed. The success of such a crime depends on the ingenuity of the cashier, whether the cashier can accomplish this act without being spotted, the level of supervision, and the sophistication of the cash register or POS technology. Supervisors and managers sometimes open a register for a period of time for the sole purpose of keeping the proceeds and destroying the documentation.

Depending on the type of retailer, customers may return to the POS to have their merchandise repaired. However, employees may use company time and parts to repair items for themselves or friends and even construct whole products. Close supervision of repair work orders and accountability of parts will prevent losses.

At the checkout, cashiers should always look for the container switch (i.e., merchandise that is opened and replaced with more expensive items or more items than are supposed to be enclosed). Observe merchandise that is not properly closed or sealed. Without being offensive to customers, these items should be opened for inspection.

The price switch is another problem. It is often considered as shoplifting in state statutes. Offenders simply obtain a lower price tag from an item and place it on a higher priced item before approaching the checkout. Grocery stores encounter this problem when offenders switch jar lids. Price tags that self-destruct when removed and bar codes stamped on products are two strategies to curb losses.

Quick-change artists are another thorn in the retailer's side. They go from store to store and from state to state to make their living. Their method of operation is fast talking to confuse a cashier. One common ploy is to pay for an item with a large bill and then, in the middle of the transaction, withdraw the large bill and try to pay with a smaller bill after the cashier has made change for the larger bill. The cashier should always place the money provided by the customer across the cash drawer until the transaction is complete and always complete the present transaction before moving on to another. To defend against this ploy, retain only the larger bill, provide the change for the larger bill, and close the cash drawer. Promptly report the problem to a supervisor.

Cashiers may be victimized by a team of con artists. One makes a small purchase to have the cash drawer opened for change. The other distracts the cashier with some elaborate or outrageous trickery while the first one quickly reaches into the drawer to pull out some cash. Bold offenders even pose as cashiers or salespeople to steal cash and payments from customers. "I'll be right back to bring you your change!"

Case Problems

5A. You are a security manager for a suburban shopping mall near a major city. Merchants at the mall are interested in a seminar on protection at the POS. You have only one hour for your presentation. What topics will you discuss? How will you hold their attention? Formulate an outline of specific topics.

5B. Study the identification and check (Figure 5–6) that has been presented by a customer in a retail store. List the problems associated with these items. Would you accept this check?

5C. Study the bill (Figure 5–7) that has been presented at a retail store at the POS. Would you accept it? If not, why not?

Answer to You Be the Judge

5–1. No. The store did not arrest him, the police did. The store had merely summoned police on the basis of probable cause. And not only had the store not prosecuted him maliciously, it had not prosecuted him at all. Its employees had testified in the state's prosecution of the man, but that was not the same thing as the store's pressing charges. When you have probable cause to report someone to the police, do it! Your suspicions do not have to turn out correct, they just have to be reasonable and justifiable. But be much surer of your ground before deciding to

Figure 5–6

Figure 5-7

case has been fictionalized for dramatic effect and to protect the privacy of those involved.) *Case Citation:* Nasim v. Tandy Corp., 726 F.Supp. 1021 (D.Md. 1989).

Notes

1. "Cash Registers and Sticky Fingers," *Security Management, Protecting Property, People & Assets* (April 10, 1988): 1–3.
2. Michael Sherer, "When It's Not 'On the House'," *Security Management* (March 1990): 50–57.
3. "Criminal Use of Fraudulent Driver's Licenses," *The New York Times* (April 1, 1979).
4. "Revco: Not in Collection Business Anymore," *Chain Store Age Executive* (February 1990): 104.
5. "Credit Card Business Fights Fraud," *Associated Press Release* (August 13, 1989).
6. "Credit Card Scam Prompts New Defenses," *Chain Store Age Executive* (June 1989): 70.
7. "The Feds Counter Counterfeiting," *Corporate Security* (September 1991): 4.

6

Internal Losses and Countermeasures

Shrinkage

Retail security and loss prevention practitioners are wise to maintain a broad perspective on the problem of losses. The problem goes beyond employee theft and shoplifting. Those in the protection field must think like the business people that surround them. Understanding the all-important term *shrinkage* is the first major step in this direction. Shrinkage is the amount of merchandise that disappears due to internal theft, shoplifting, damage, misweighing or mismeasuring, and paperwork errors. Also called *shrink*, the term refers to stock shortages that are determined by discrepancies between book and actual inventory values. It is expressed as a percentage of sales. A company with a sales volume of $100 million during one particular year and shrinkage of 4 percent of sales, will yield a loss of $4 million. In this case, every percentage point rise in shrinkage is equal to $1 million in losses.

Michael Levy and Barton A. Weitz, in *Retail Management*, explain shrinkage as follows:

> Shrinkage is the difference between the recorded value of inventory (at retail prices) based on merchandise bought and received and the value of the actual inventory (at retail prices) in stores and distribution centers, divided by retail sales during the period. For example, if accounting records indicate the inventory should be $1,500,000, the actual count of the inventory reveals $1,236,000, and the sales were $4,225,000, the shrinkage is 6.2% [($1,500,000–$1,236,000) ÷ $4,225,000].[1]

Another way to understand shrinkage is to realize that retailers measure their profits in mere pennies on each dollar. A net profit of 2–3 percent of sales is common for many retailers. A loss of just 1 percent of sales from theft can reduce earnings by one-third or more. Suppose a local store has annual sales of $300,000. A normal, end-of-year net profit may be in the range of $6,000–

$12,000. If shrinkage jumps to 5 percent of sales, the store is in the red; without a turnaround the business will not survive.

Retail losses can also be understood from the perspective of inventory control. A retailer can determine the value of inventory by taking a physical inventory (i.e., actually counting all of the inventory on hand). Another method is to establish a book inventory or perpetual inventory system. This avoids having to count the inventory every time a manager wants to know how much merchandise is available for sale.

If the books indicate an on-hand inventory of $100,000, but the physical inventory shows $90,000, this represents a shortage of $10,000 from shoplifting, employee theft, paperwork error, etc. If the physical count resulted in a value of $120,000, then an overage has resulted, usually from a counting error.

The result of a physical inventory will impact shrinkage and result in a shortage or an overage. Inventories must be done as accurately as possible. A security practitioner's job may depend on it.

There are several reasons that support the need for an accurate inventory. First of all, an annual inventory is required for federal income tax purposes. An inaccurate inventory will impact profit figures and taxes to be paid, and will distort the business's financial picture. Furthermore, an inaccurate inventory presents problems over multiple years—the year in which the errors occurred and the subsequent year when, and if, corrections were made following another inventory. Also, buying decisions reflect quantities in inventory. Compensation is often based on specific profit and shrinkage goals. An inaccurate inventory can cause management to panic and invest in unnecessary security services (e.g., undercover investigation) and hardware.

Can the Employees Do the Inventory Count?

At one retail lumber company, employees conducted an inventory of building products at a huge warehouse and lumber yard. Every piece of lumber was counted. The inventory showed a shortage of about $150,000. Management panicked (a common reaction following an inventory showing large losses), thinking that a serious theft problem was afoot. A security consulting firm was hastily contacted; they recommended an undercover investigation. After two months of receiving reports that contained very little substance and being billed for investigative costs of about $4,000, retail management grew impatient. Management decided to conduct another inventory and included the undercover investigator in the actual counting. To the surprise of the investigator, the management of the retail firm, and the security firm, it was discovered that some employees involved in the inventory had problems recording numbers beyond 999. These employees were unsure as to where to place commas for thousands. The second inventory was short about $60,000. A third inventory by an outside firm specializing in inventories showed a shortage of about $9,000. The total cost of trying to obtain an accurate inventory rivaled the actual shortage.

To increase the accuracy of inventories and the effectiveness of retail employees, hand–held microcomputer technology (Figures 6–1 and 6–2) is available that captures data through bar code scanning and transmits it via

Figure 6–1 Hand-held Data Collection Terminal Courtesy of Symbol Technologies.

Figure 6-2 Portable Tele-transaction Computer (PTC) Courtesy of Telxon Corp.

radio frequency data communications to management. Many helpful functions are performed by these systems including inventory taking, price changing and verifying, and product ordering. The technology can be applied as soon as merchandise arrives at the loading dock, where items are checked in and priced. Retailers have found that these systems reduce paperwork, produce a more accurate inventory, and show a return on investment.

How the shrinkage figure is compiled should be of vital concern to retail security managers. In one retail department store, security personnel (i.e., the security manager and store detectives) were replaced every year for three successive years, because management viewed the store's shrinkage as being too high. Management claimed that shrinkage was caused, for the most part, by shoplifters and since security was not making enough arrests for shoplifting, they were not doing their jobs. Employee theft and/or paperwork errors could have been the real shrinkage culprits in this store. Security practitioners should carefully study shrinkage and its causes. This brings us to the importance of understanding the many perspectives of shrinkage. Security personnel, for example, may focus on internal theft and shoplifting as the causes of shrinkage, while not paying enough attention to other important causes of shrinkage, such as paperwork errors. Other security practitioners not only study internal theft and shoplifting causes, but also stress in their work the importance of employees following store policies and procedures, especially concerning the record keeping of such activities as markdowns. Peter Berlin, in *Shrinkage Control*, states that even though errors in recording price changes (markups and markdowns) are a small percentage of reported shrinkage, the inaccurate recording of price changes is commonly considered the single largest contributor to paper shrinkage. He notes that the volume of price changes is important, because a 1 percent error rate on $5 million in markdowns will have a lot less impact on shrinkage than a 1 percent error rate on $30 million in markdowns. Retailers with markdowns of 5 percent of sales can expect less impact on shrinkage than retailers whose markdown activity is 30 percent of sales.[2]

Perceptions of shrinkage differ in retailing.

> Finance and Accounting, for example, commonly perceive high company shrinkage to be the result of the store manager's "lack of discipline in handling store paperwork." Store Operations will frequently attribute high shrinkage to inaccurate data entry and erroneous inventory adjustments in Accounting, or inaccurate store billing from the distribution center, or overall lack of support from Security. Security will commonly perceive high shrinkage to be the result of both inaccurate bookkeeping in Finance and Accounting and the lack of compliance by store managers and employees to following store policies and procedures.[3]

A persistent controversy surrounding shrinkage is the percent of shrinkage attributed to shoplifting, employee theft, and paperwork errors. For example, hourly retail employees often blame a greater portion of shrinkage on shoplifting than employee theft. Management frequently looks to employee theft as more harmful to shrinkage than shoplifting. Those employees who steal are likely to blame shoplifters, who are an elusive and convenient scapegoat. Whatever the causes of shrinkage, those in management who direct security efforts are sure to plan and prioritize security around their perceptions of the major causes of shrinkage. Table 6–1 shows perceptions of shrinkage causes as compiled by Peter Berlin.[4]

The National Retail Security Survey, a comprehensive national survey based on 456 retail respondents, found that the single largest share (38 percent) of the respondents' shrinkage was due to dishonest employees, followed by shoplifters (26.6 percent). Bookkeeping errors amounted to 22.4 percent, vendors at 4.9 percent, and the remainder (8.5 percent) was attributable to other smaller sources of loss.[5]

Table 6–1 Perceptions of Shrinkage Causes

Retail Personnel	Shoplifting	Employee Theft	Paperwork Error
Upper Management	30%	50	20
District Managers	40	30	30
Store Managers	60	20	20
Store Employees	75	10	15

Peter D. Berlin, "Different Perceptions/Different Directioins," *Shrinkage Control* (February 1990): 5.

One survey of 254 retail merchants found that these merchants have no systematic method for determining either the total amount of shrinkage or the proportion of total shrinkage derived from various sources. The researchers concluded that employers greatly underestimate the extent of employee theft.[6]

> ### Only a Very Small Portion of Shrinkage at Our Store Results from Damaged Merchandise and Employee Theft
>
> Nick Gates, a Regional Loss Prevention Manager for Mart Stores, became increasingly suspicious of Store 17, because so many employees there were blaming shrinkage on shoplifters. The store manager frequently stated, "Only a very small portion of shrinkage at our store results from damaged merchandise and employee theft." Because shrinkage had reached an unacceptable level of 5 percent, an undercover investigator was assigned to the store. Nick Gates knew the store needed to fill a vacancy in the sporting goods department. A corporate undercover investigator, who was sports minded, applied at the store, completed an application with a fictitious background, and was immediately hired because of his embellished sales experience with sporting goods. References were covered through an established system.
>
> After three weeks, the picture at Store 17 became clearer. Five employees were involved in theft, along with the store manager, as Nick suspected. There was a significant drug problem and three of the thieves were known to take orders from outsiders for 50 cents on the dollar for merchandise.

> Enforcement of policies and procedures for damaged merchandise presented another problem. When employees found discarded boxes of merchandise with all or part of the contents removed, the chain required employees to take the box and its contents to a certain storage room to be counted as damaged merchandise. However, the informal rule at the store was to throw the box away and keep the contents. Accountability for all damaged merchandise from whatever course was in disarray.
>
> The undercover investigator made some clear observations of the shoplifting problem—very few shoplifters were seen in the store, employees never confronted them, and, as Nick knew, the store had a record of zero shoplifting arrests for the past year.
>
> After confessions and signed statements were obtained, five employees and the store manager were fired. The causes of shrinkage were obviously different from what the store manager had stated earlier.

Although strategies to prevent employee theft dominate this chapter, several of these strategies are helpful for curbing paperwork errors, including quality screening of job applicants to hire competent employees and established policies and procedures. Chapter 7 focuses on shoplifting, another cause of shrinkage.

The Problem of Employee Theft in Retailing

Two words commonly associated with employee theft are *pilferage* and *embezzlement*. Pilferage refers to employees stealing in small quantities. Embezzlement involves a breach of trust whereby employees take money or property that has been entrusted to their care. Pilferage can result in greater losses than embezzlement. For example, if ten retail employees at one store each steal a small item per week, the total annual losses can exceed those accrued by multiple cases of embezzlement.

How Much Does Employee Theft Cost Retailers?

Estimates vary on the annual costs of employee theft in business. The *Hallcrest Report II* estimates that crimes against business cost $114 billion in 1990 and will cost $200 billion by the year 2000.[7] The percent of these costs attributed to employee theft in retailing is difficult to gauge. Ira M. Shepard and Robert Duston, authors of *Thieves at Work*, studied various sources on the costs of employee theft and produced the following estimates for the retail industry:

> Assuming that the shrinkage estimates of Arthur Young/NRMA [National Retail Merchants Association, now called the National Retail Federation] and others (approximately 1.8 percent of gross sales) are typical of the retail industry, then based on 1987 total retail sales of $1.51 trillion [U.S. Department of Commerce], retail shrinkage cost $27.18 billion in 1987. Applying the estimates of security and retail experts that between 40 percent and 75 percent of all shrinkage is due to theft, the annual employee theft loss in retail stores alone is between $10.87 billion and $20.36 billion.[8]

An accurate picture of employee theft in retailing must also consider indirect costs, which are easy to overlook. These include the following:

> higher consumer costs of merchandise (Estimates are 10–15 percent higher prices due to employee theft.)
> business failures
> greater demand for security
> higher insurance premiums
> difficult-to-measure problems such as low employee morale, less productivity, and damage to company image.

A precise determination of losses attributed to employee theft in retailing is difficult to obtain, because retailers use shrinkage figures to estimate employee theft and it is difficult to separate such losses from those caused by shoplifting and paperwork errors. Also, there is no centralized reporting depository (public or private) for employee theft statistics. Even if there was, companies are reluctant to report these cases because of the fear of a lawsuit and bad publicity. Many companies simply fire the thieves. Another problem is that prosecutors may refuse these cases because of limited resources. One thing is certain for retailers, employee theft is a multibillion dollar "thorn in the side" of the retail industry.

One Large Retailer's Experience

Let's take a look at some figures from a large retailer's confidential annual report on security and loss prevention. This retailer has more than 1,000 locations and annual sales of more than $1 billion. The name of the company will not be revealed; however, the following information will provide some insight into one large retailer's experience with employee theft.

The number of employees released during the year for employee theft was 620 (3 percent of the workforce of 20,666), a decrease of 20 percent from a year earlier.

Losses from employee theft amounted to $1,028,000, a decrease of 9 percent from the previous year. Shrinkage was not discussed in the report and there were no statements on the percentage of losses attributed to either shoplifting or paperwork errors.

According to the report, the probable reasons for a decrease in employee theft losses include increased awareness of loss prevention throughout the company and a significant increase in the number of security surveys by in-house security personnel. Loss prevention presentations to management increased and a toll-free number for reporting losses was established. About 950 surveys were conducted during the year, compared to 250 surveys conducted the year before.

The Security Department conducted 1,825 investigations and interviewed more than 925 individuals (mostly employees).

Total losses from all sources amounted to $2,250,000, an increase of 35 percent from the previous year due to a $220,000 theft loss at one distribution center and a $425,000 arson loss at one store. Insurance recovery is still pending.

Recoveries amounted to $1,050,000 or 47 percent, as compared to 52 percent the previous year. Insurance recovery can improve this percentage.

The number of employees prosecuted last year was 245 compared to 150 the year before, an increase of 63 percent. The company policy is to prosecute all employees caught stealing. However, many local prosecutors are reluctant to prosecute due to limited resources. A greater emphasis has been placed on cash recoveries from employees.

Salespeople account for 66 percent of all employees released for admitted theft, but they only account for 25 percent of dollar losses. Conversely, store management is involved in 28 percent of releases for admitted theft, but they account for 74 percent of all theft losses. Thus, those with the greatest accessibility to company assets have the potential to cause the greatest losses.

Employees in the 16–21 age group were involved in half of the cases of employee theft. More than 60 percent of the employees caught stealing had only been with the company for two years or less. Fifty-eight percent acted alone; 42 percent acted with another employee.

The following reasons were stated as to why employees stole from the company:

- needed money
- tempting and easy
- disliked management
- for drugs
- did not know security was that good

The control failures that allowed employees to steal included failure of management to properly approve refunds, voids, and bank deposits. This lack of proper internal controls and enforcement of procedures was constantly being written up in internal audit reports.

Recommendations in this report included the following:

Management must set a good example for subordinates to follow.

Signed preemployment statements should be requested from all prospective employees, acknowledging that they understand company policies regarding theft, the protection of company assets, and conflict of interest.

Proper screening of job applicants should include verification of all time gaps and employment references prior to employment.

Company locations not containing an alarm system should consider the protection of company assets. Systems must be approved through the Security Department.

The number of shoplifters apprehended and prosecuted during the year was 3,107. During the last three years, the number has declined. Average losses per incident vary among corporate divisions (e.g., $24 at one division versus $475 at another).

The report was critical of one corporate division of 150 locations, because only one shoplifter was caught during the last three years. Also, this same division was criticized, because its management showed a strong lack of cooperation regarding undercover operations. It was noted that these investigations were important to producing evidence, especially when documentation on losses was lacking.

The report noted that theft and other forms of counterproductive behavior should be understood as a response to the struc-

> tural and social conditions in the workplace. Theft is partly a reflection of how employees perceive management. If employees are not appreciated in the workplace, or the organization does not seem to care about theft, then there will be a higher incidence of theft.

How Do Employees Steal and What Can Be Done About It?

One of the best ways to understand and counter employee theft is to be aware of the various methods used by employees to steal from retail stores. Many employee thieves use the trash disposal system to hide stolen merchandise and believe that no one will think of looking there. Sharp security people place the trash system high on the list during inspections and investigations. Employee thieves often throw away merchandise and return to the store at night to retrieve the items. Variations of this ploy include the assistance of outsiders. Management should check trash for hidden merchandise and maintain control over who disposes of trash, where, when, and how.

Another employee theft method is to fail to ring a sale on the cash register and then pocket the money. One method to prevent this theft is to odd-price merchandise. If, for example, sales tax is 5 percent in the state, do not price items at 95 cents because the customer would not need change from the register if payment is made with a $1 bill. Stores can also offer customers $5 if the cashier does not provide a receipt. Another avenue to preventing this type of theft is to use a shopping service to detect irregularities.

Selling merchandise below the sales price or giving it away are other forms of theft. A shirt may be sold for $5 rather than $20, or two shirts may be sold for the price of one. In one case, a dishonest cashier was paying off her illegal drug bills by undercharging dealers for groceries. Items were lifted over the electronic glass scanner to avoid registering expensive products. To curb such losses, observation and surveillance should be used. CCTV systems are capable of not only displaying a video of a cashier working, but also displaying the sales price entered on the cash register.

Refund systems are often vulnerable in retail stores. Employee thieves write up a fraudulent refund and then pay themselves for items supposedly returned. Accountability is the key to prevention and investigation. Employees must complete a standard store form that requires the customer's name and address, so that a letter can be sent to them as a method of verification. It may be possible to separate the functions of writing a refund and giving the money. Two other avenues of preventing employee theft are to request supervisory approval of all refunds and to mail a check for refunded merchandise greater than a certain amount. Records should be maintained on all refunds made by all employees.

Employee thieves may arrive early for work or leave late. During these nonbusiness hours, a lax atmosphere may invite theft. Night cleanup and the restocking of shelves often occur during nonbusiness hours. If possible, these activities should take place during business hours. In one case, a cleaning crew was videotaped hiding merchandise in garbage pails and vacuum cleaners. All employees must be subject to supervision whenever they are on the premises. Supervisors also need monitoring.

As stated earlier, the National Retail Security Survey indicated that 4.9 percent of shrinkage was due to vendors. Research showed that vendor problems were most prominent in supermarkets and, to a lesser degree, in discount, home/hardware, and drug stores. However, all retailers should beware of this vulnerability. In supermarkets, for example, a vendor delivery person may deliver, stock, and display merchandise. Error and fraud may be the result.

Losses from Vendors

One convenience store chain was victimized by a bread delivery person who would take the coded tags off fresh bread and attach them to bread that was a few days old. Then he would sell the "fresh" bread to an independent grocer for a profit.

In another case, a large grocery store chain was repeatedly receiving shortages of soft drinks by a certain distributor. Several stores reported the problem to the loss prevention director. A contract investigation firm was hired and a conspiracy was uncovered among several delivery people. Management at the soft drink distributor was contacted by the loss prevention director, who possessed documented proof of the conspiracy, along with the total losses incurred by the grocery stores and the cost of the investigation. The distributor realized that continued business with the large chain was in jeopardy, so all losses, including the cost of the investigation, were reimbursed to the grocery chain. Certain delivery personnel were fired. Public police were never contacted.

Quality supervision and accountability are two primary strategies to prevent and detect vendor-related losses. Two employees should count all shipments. Employees responsible for receiving should inform the accounts payable department of discrepancies such as shortages and damaged merchandise. Accuracy is also important when merchandise is returned. Freight charges should be checked for incoming and outgoing merchandise. Good communications should take place among buyers, receiving personnel, and accounts payable bookkeepers. To strengthen controls, these job duties should be separated so each person can check on the other. Surprise checks of shipments, testing by deliberate error, and CCTV are additional strategies to curb vender-related losses.

Embezzlement is another form of employee theft. Examples include accounts payable employees who pay fictitious bills to a bogus account and then cash the checks for their own use. Other examples of embezzlement include maintaining terminated employees on the payroll and then cashing their checks for personal use. Universal accounting controls, such as clear assignment of responsibility, separation of job functions, and auditing, are effective at curbing these losses.

Research conducted by Clark and Hollinger (discussed in subsequent pages) revealed that abuse of employee discounts in retail stores was more than four times greater than theft of cash and merchandise.[9] Typically, employees will purchase items for friends and relatives who are ineligible for the discount. Also, employees sometimes defraud a retailer by purchasing items with the discount and then have a friend return it for a full-value refund. In addition to repeatedly issuing policy statements, this abuse can be curbed by detection. Employee identification numbers can be entered for all employee purchases. Periodically, a computer report can be generated that highlights those employees who have made purchases outside a "normal" range.

Many other methods of employee theft occur in the retail industry. These include padding of expense accounts for those who travel for retail companies and computer-related crimes. Theft of time is another problem. One employee may "punch out" several employees (who departed earlier) at the end of a shift. A store may have a serious problem with extended "breaks" and lunch hours.

Those striving to curb employee theft should look for indicators or signs that a theft may have occurred, such as,

- merchandise missing from boxes (In one store, a camera salesperson would steal cameras and place the empty boxes on the bottom of stacks to deceive those taking inventory.)
- employees who never seem to leave their desks or refuse to take a vacation
- complaints by customers about not having their previous payments credited to their accounts
- customers who absolutely have to be served by a particular employee
- employees who are living beyond their income levels

Who Are the Employee Thieves and How Many Are Engaged in Theft?

To assist in answering this question we will refer to the widely known University of Minnesota study, *Theft by Employees in Work Organizations*. This research was conducted by John P. Clark and Richard C. Hollinger, and was financed by the National Institute of Justice. Researchers surveyed almost 5,000 employees of 35 retail organizations, hospitals, and manufacturing companies. Most employee thieves were those who had the least to lose, such as single people in positions with little seniority or no dependents. Dissatisfied workers who were angered about insufficient raises, productivity demands, layoffs, etc., were more likely to steal. Thirty-five percent of the retail workers had been involved in at least one type of property theft. About 3 percent of dishonest retail employees steal on a daily basis, 7.6 percent steal weekly, 19.7 percent steal between four and 12 times per year, and 69.7 percent steal occasionally. About 10.6 percent of dishonest employees were responsible for 79 percent of merchandise theft.[10]

Research has shown that younger workers comprise a disproportionately higher percentage of employee thieves. One study of a large retail department store in the Midwest revealed that, although workers between 18 and 20 years old comprised 12 percent of the workforce, they accounted for 69 percent of the apprehended thieves.[11]

Another research project asked executives which employee groups are responsible for the most serious crime problems:

> ... one-third of our respondents named management or senior staff in their companies. For major fraud, managers were viewed as the primary source of the problem by 60% of our respondents. As might be expected, misconduct such as abuse of company services and petty theft are seen by two-thirds of the companies as coming from all employees or from a very broad employee group.[12]

Why Do Employees Steal?

Living in a materialistic world, and the pressures that surround us to possess and consume more and more, provide a foundation for employee theft. Retailing is in a particularly vulnerable position because this industry contains a greater share of material items desired by our consumer-oriented society. Those who work in retailing are literally right in the middle of thousands of retail items. Marketing and advertising techniques reinforce the temptation to obtain merchandise, whether through legal or illegal means.

The personal problems of employees also exert pressure that may lead to theft. Substance abuse, excessive gambling, financial problems, and domestic discord can ultimately cause losses for retailers.

Poor examples set by "pillars of society," and by managers and supervisors in the workplace, influence employee perceptions of theft. Rationalizations for theft can easily follow. "Everybody is stealing, so I should too." In retailing, with so many part-time and temporary employees earning low wages, theft can be "justified," because "they just pay us peanuts" and "the company has plenty of money; they will not miss this cash or merchandise."

Theft may be so widespread in a business that those who do not steal are considered odd. Managers sometimes believe that it is acceptable to steal and cheat customers, as long as such acts stay within "acceptable limits."

Although the focus of this book is on security, we can see that security alone can not reduce losses significantly. Management support is needed. Management should set a good example, reinforce a climate of honesty, and be as fair as possible with personnel matters.

Dr. Donald R. Cressey has studied thousands of offenders to produce an employee theft formula that contains common factors associated with these thieves and their environment:

$$\text{Motivation} + \text{Opportunity} + \text{Rationalization} = \text{Theft}^{13}$$

Motivation results from a host of sources, such as pressure in our society to obtain material possessions or drugs. The lack of security and loss prevention, and a climate of dishonesty provide the opportunity. Rationalizations are the excuses to relieve guilt (e.g., "everybody is stealing").

Employee Theft Countermeasures

Curbing employee theft is not as simple as communicating policies and procedures, and adding physical security. Employee theft is a complex problem that requires a mind-set that is broad-based when it comes to solutions. As stated in other pages of this book, the security planner must be familiar with the business of retailing and its inherent characteristics that run counter to security. These characteristics include limited access controls; merchandising techniques that not only attract buyers, but also thieves; and personnel problems such as labor shortages, low hiring standards, too many part-time and temporary employees, low wages, long hours, high turnover, and limited training.

Satisfying Employee Needs

If a retail company can respond to the basic human needs of its employees, losses are likely to be lower. When employees realize that management and supervisors care, employees are more likely to respect the company and its assets. Psychologist Abraham Maslow is famous for his hierarchy of human needs. He believes that people are always in a state of want and what they want depends on what level in the hierarchy has been satisfied (Figure 6–3). Lower needs must be satisfied before moving up the hierarchy.

Maslow's Hierarchy of Needs

Basic physiological needs. Survival needs like food, water, and the elimination of wastes can be satisfied with employer assistance. A well-run company cafeteria and clean lavatories are examples.

Safety and security needs. This need relates to order in one's life. A person needs to feel free from anxiety and fear. Adequate wages, medical insurance, and workplace safety help to satisfy these needs.

Societal needs. The need to be loved, and have friends and self-esteem can be fulfilled by supervisors. A supervisor should praise a subordinate when appropriate. Employees should receive recognition and/or awards after completing a good job. Employee socials are also helpful.

Esteem and status needs. A person needs to be competent to achieve, and to gain approval and respect.

Self-actualization needs. This need is at the top of the hierarchy of needs. It signifies that people have reached their full potential, whether as janitors, doctors, or whatever. An organization and its superiors can do a lot (e.g., training, promotion) in assisting an employee to fulfill this need.[14]

Retail organizations and stores differ on how they respond to employee needs. Many factors can distract managers and supervisors from satisfying employee needs, including limited funds, tough economic times, tight profit margins, and day-to-day operations. Furthermore, temporary employees may never get to know the efforts of management concerning employee needs. Security personnel often have a limited influence in satisfying employee needs, even though these practitioners know that such management efforts can curb losses. One retail study sheds light on these problems:

> It appears that in the high-volume stores, managers have opted for a style that emphasizes performance at the expense of employee needs. In the low-volume stores, where there is less emphasis on output, more opportunities exist for social interaction and a less hectic pace of operation. As a result, employees are more satisfied.

Figure 6-3 Maslow's Hierarchy of Needs Reprinted with permission from Butterworth-Heinemann.

Concentration on productivity and sales may well result in discontented employees and, at a point when the situation becomes irretrievable, poor performance. The problem is one of discovering the point at which both output and job satisfaction are optimized.[15]

Shepard and Duston, authors of *Thieves at Work*, add support to the preceeding viewpoints:

But human relations and security personnel largely agree that employee theft is more a symptom than a disease. While it is easier to reduce theft by increasing audits or implementing computer security systems, on a cost-effective basis it may be equally effective to use company resources to cope with the underlying cause of employee theft—morale, job security, drug abuse, and other employee relations problems.[16]

Management Support

A major strategy to reduce employee theft in the workplace is for security practitioners to generate management support for antitheft policies and procedures. Management should also set a good example.

Management support is essential to the security budget. But acquiring this support is easier said than done. We must remember that businesses exist to make a profit and this is a primary management concern. With tight profit margins in the retail industry, practitioners are being asked to do more with less resources. Consequently, security executives must show that security strategies are cost-effective and have an ROI. This is the major avenue to recruit management support. For example, by hiring an undercover investigator for a few months, management can learn about many hidden causes of losses at a retail department store. The investigator will not only report on internal theft, but also on loopholes in policies and procedures; causes of "paper shrinkage," such as unrecorded markdowns; the accuracy of an inventory; a workplace drug problem; and safety hazards.

Planning and Budgeting

Planning and budgeting must be carefully considered prior to implementing employee theft countermeasures. Earlier in this book the chapter on "Planning for Retail Security" provides essential input. The best security ideas go nowhere without careful planning and budgeting.

Human Resources Programs

If a retailer can avoid hiring dishonest individuals, or those who are incompetent, losses are averted and profits preserved. However, screening job applicants is a tricky process and most retailers do not have the time to screen adequately, especially during the holidays. Once an individual is hired, the output of the employees and their value to the organization will depend on the socialization process designed by retail management. This includes training. Employees should understand that theft reduces profits and paychecks. The National Retail Security Survey (1991) found that shrinkage levels are lower when store employees are paid more relative to the competition. When retailers pay 5 percent or less than the competition, shrinkage is 1.95 percent. Retailers who pay 15 percent or more above the competition have shrinkage of only 1.31 percent. Higher compensation can result in greater loyalty. Retailers that use salary only have 1.9 percent shrinkage, while those companies who compensate employees with salary and incentives or straight incentives have only 1.74 percent shrinkage. Profit sharing also has a positive impact on shrinkage. Research also showed retailers with low turnover have lower shrinkage.[17]

Chapter 4 discusses human resources programs that focus on screening applicants through methods such as checking references and honesty testing. It also discusses socialization, namely orientation, training, and examples set by superiors.

Policies and Procedures

Policies reflect management objectives and are used by employees as guides in their work. Procedures control the actions of employees and explain a particular way of fulfilling the requirements of a policy. For example, a policy may read that the garbage disposal system must be closely supervised. A procedure may read that trash must be taken outside by a minimum of two employees from different departments, so that each employee can witness the dumping of trash into the dumpster.

Many policies and procedures can be written to curb employee theft, such as a separate cash drawer is required for each cashier; employee coats and handbags must be kept off the sales floor; store-issued, transparent, vinyl purses are to be used; uniforms are to be worn by all employees; and uniforms can have no or very shallow pockets to reduce pocketing of merchandise.

Policies and procedures are useful to curb losses from a host of sources and are to be used when confronted with different retail situations, such as receiving bad checks and tracking fraudulent refunds, and during shoplifting arrests. It is often stated by business people that if employees could just follow policies and procedures, losses could be cut dramatically. Conversely, subordinates who are required to follow policies and procedures often complain that management frequently uncovers a problem, disseminates a policy, and expects action even though subordinates are already overburdened, do not have the personnel and resources to comply with certain policies, and have not even been queried as to alternative, "less painful" methods of solving the problem.

Management should solicit ideas from subordinates before implementing policies and procedures. Subordinates, who are "in the trenches," often have excellent ideas about solving problems and they usually follow their own ideas best. For those organizations that are overburdened with day-to-day operations and limited personnel, the only avenue is to prioritize job duties.

Policies that deal with employee theft can also involve an organizational commitment from the president on down, stating that this type of loss will not be tolerated. At the same time, top executives must set a good example. If a chief executive is known to lead a lavish life-style using corporate expense accounts, then it will be more difficult to curb employee theft.

Policies must be communicated organizationwide and enforced and applied equally. According to the Clark and Hollinger research cited earlier, those companies with strong organizational policies that address employee theft had lower rates of theft. These companies went beyond orientation programs for communicating employee theft prohibitions, and used bulletin boards and newsletters to spread the word. The research showed a fairly strong correlation between policies and theft.

Accountability, Accounting, and Auditing

Accountability defines a responsibility for and a description of something. For example, Robert Smith, a clerk on the receiving dock at ABC Department Store, is responsible for all incoming shipments. He accurately counts merchandise and maintains the proper paperwork on all merchandise arriving in the store. Expensive items are stored in a locked, caged area near the dock.

Accounting pertains to recording, sorting, summarizing, reporting, and interpreting business data. Financial statements assist management in gauging the financial health of a business. For example, profit-or-loss figures and the shrinkage level are helpful statistics used by management for business planning.

Losses are possible throughout accounting and bookkeeping operations. For example, accounts receivable must be controlled so that a clerk does not destroy bills and pocket cash. An accounts payable clerk could, in collusion with a supplier, alter invoices to embezzle money. Accounting controls are universally applied to prevent losses and include the following:

- separate duties and assign specific responsibilities, so that employees can check each others' work
- rotate employee assignments
- require employees to take vacations
- prenumber forms
- use prenumbered checks, with the company's name and address printed on them, to pay all disbursements
- require the bank to send all canceled checks to a post office box so they can be picked up and checked by an employee other than the one who writes the checks
- check all incoming merchandise against purchase orders and invoices
- test by deliberate error
- use regular and surprise audits

Auditing is a primary strategy to uncover deviations of policies and procedures, and to pinpoint losses of assets. An audit can be conducted by an external certified public accountant or by an internal accountant. For less complex audits, supervisors and security personnel can perform a variety of checks in retailing, including checking on cashiers who have excessive cash shortages or voids, checking procedures on a shipping dock, and checking physical security systems to make sure they function as intended.

Reporting and Reward Program

Reporting and reward programs work very well in many organizations. Research suggests that employee theft can be reduced through reward programs.[18] One type of program uses a toll-free number to facilitate ease of reporting loss incidents. To maintain anonymity, when callers report a loss incident, they are provided with a secret number. This number is used to pick up reward money at a bank. Written or typed letters are also part of reporting methods. One company requires employees to avoid providing any identifying information when reporting an incident. They are required to write a six-digit number two times at the end of their letters, tear off and keep one of the six-digit numbers, and mail the information to the corporate security director (see Figure 6–4). If the information proves helpful, the six-digit number will be printed in the corporate magazine to signify that a reward is waiting. The helpful employee (preferably a substitute to preserve anonymity) must bring the torn part of the letter to the corporate security director, so a comparison can be made to the letter sent earlier. A major objective of reward programs is to alert employees to the dangers of shortages and to provide a monetary incentive for giving information that results in the apprehension of offenders and/or recovery of merchandise.

Publicity is an important part of reward programs. Employees should be reminded about the program through training, bulletin boards, signs, and company publications. Publishing a six-digit number in a company magazine notifies employees that the program is active, and it acts as a deterrent.

Reward programs are used to apprehend not only dishonest employees, but shoplifters as well. One retail company's reward formula is as follows:

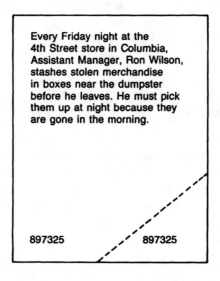

Figure 6–4 Anonymous Tip

External Theft: 10 percent of the value of the merchandise or money recovered; minimum of $25 and maximum of $2,000

Internal Theft: 100 percent of the value of the merchandise or money recovered; minimum of $100 and maximum of $2,000

During one year, this company paid $42,700 in 730 different rewards. The value of merchandise and money recovered was $127,800. This chain store provides rewards to nonemployees under certain circumstances. Executives and security personnel are exempt from rewards.

To illustrate another retailer's use of the reward strategy, Ross Stores uses points as a reward when an employee assists with an apprehension of an employee thief (or shoplifter). Points are applied to various merchandise. Employee awareness is a key objective of the program. All new Ross employees watch four 11-minute security videos. Bulletin boards are also used to increase awareness. In 1990, the program cost Ross about $30,000 and more than $100,000 worth of merchandise was recovered. Civil recovery laws provide funds for this program by allowing Ross to collect financial damages from internal thieves and shoplifters.[19]

A memorandum from one retail chain to its executives made the following observations concerning reward programs:

> ... they are nothing more than a method for buying information; there has been a marked increase in reporting and apprehensions of shoplifters and dishonest employees; stores will periodically let employees know the amount recovered and reward money paid out; publicity is important to remind employees to report losses; and the secrecy in reporting is a major deterrent to theft losses because employees do not know the informers.

Shrinkage Incentive Programs

More and more companies today are seeking to involve their employees in shrink reduction, and as they do, incentive programs are playing a larger role. The programs take many forms. Sometimes, companies set up confidential phone lines for employees to call with information about dishonesty among their fellow employees. Other times, there might be a mechanism for reporting shoplifters or suggesting ways to prevent loss. But however the system is designed, it is driven by a reward system.

In our survey, 63 percent of the participants had shrinkage reduction incentive programs in 1990. The larger the company, the more likely they were to have them. In terms of segments, 80 percent of the specialty apparel companies had incentive programs, 78 percent of the department store chains had them, and 73 percent of the mass merchant/general merchandisers used them. The least active segment in this area was supermarkets; 44 percent of these companies used incentive programs in 1990.

The most popular programs were a combination of monetary and nonmonetary recognition awards (64 percent). Thirty-two percent of the respondents used monetary awards only. Three percent used recognition awards only.

At 49 percent of the companies, all store level employees were eligible to participate. At 33 percent of the respondents, the eligible employees were all store level personnel other than security and loss personnel.

What was the basis for recognition? Seventy-five percent of the companies rewarded their employees for identifying dishonest employees, 60 percent offered incentives for reporting shoplifters, and 58 percent offered incentives for reducing shrinkage in a department or store.

The average award amount was $176. Companies with revenues below $100 million gave an average of $238. Companies with revenues of $1 billion or more gave an average of $179. In terms of segment, the specialty apparel companies gave the highest average award, $326, and drug chains had the lowest average, $57.

The average cost of these programs was $147,885. Mass merchants averaged a survey-high of $500,000, and drug chains averaged a survey-low of just $2,000.

Reprinted with permission from Ernst & Young. *Source*: The Ernst & Young/IMRA *Survey of Retail Loss Prevention Trends* (January 1992).

Signs

In Chapter 7, signs are recommended as a deterrent to shoplifting. Signs can play a similar role in reducing internal theft. A few carefully worded signs can reinforce management's concern about employee theft, and indicate the policies and procedures designed to curb it. A sign can be placed in the human resources waiting room, so job applicants can learn from the beginning that theft will not be tolerated. Signs can also be placed in high-theft locations such as shipping and receiving docks, and near garbage dumpsters. The wording of these signs should be positive (e.g., "Stop losses and ensure a steady paycheck and job security"). Managers and supervisors must set a good example and support the message in the signs; otherwise, these signs become a farce and a reminder of hypocrisy in the workplace.

Physical Security

Chapters 7 and 10 describe physical security methods that are applicable to the employee theft problem. In regard to shoplifting, one primary countermeasure is electronic article surveillance (EAS). Although this strategy is discussed in the next chapter, here we will explain how it can be used to curb employee theft. Basically, EAS "watches" stores merchandise. Items are tagged and if the tag is not deactivated after a sale, an alarm will sound when the item passes a detector at an exit. Employee theft can be countered in this way. However, because employees are more familiar with store operations, they may be able to circumvent EAS. To stay ahead of employee thieves, some stores hire a contract service to apply tags to a percentage of merchandise. Only a very few people know which items are tagged. The tags are very thin and attached to bar code labels. Only one exit should be used by employees and it should be equipped with sensors to detect the tags. Signs should be placed throughout the store that describe this security system. With these mechanisms in place, employee thieves and shoplifters are deterred.

Physical security measures to prevent burglary are also helpful in dealing with employee theft. These measures include intrusion alarms systems, strong doors and locks, safes, lighting, CCTV, and security officers.

Physical security methods against robbery also serve to curb employee theft. Examples include CCTV, lighting, and safes. Policies and procedures are another multipurpose security strategy. For instance, money-handling procedures may prevent robberies and ensure that the store's money is deposited in the bank, rather than in the pocket of a store employee.

Additional Strategies

Many other strategies are available to retailers to reduce internal losses:

- Employ an outside shopping service to test cashiers for honesty and courtesy.
- Install a "through-the-wall" security system to reduce the opportunity to hide merchandise in trash containers for later retrieval. Employees must dispose of trash through an opening in the wall that is connected to a compactor on the outside. Stolen merchandise would be destroyed. Naturally, an unlocked door nearby can render this system useless.
- Assign uniformed security officers to randomly patrol throughout the store and post them at exits during shift changes.
- Maintain access controls for employees; restrict entering and exiting to one door near a security counter (i.e., checkpoint).

Require all employee purchases to be checked and stored at the security counter until the shift ends. Prohibit employees from making their own sales transactions.

Inspect to ensure policies and procedures are being followed.

Prohibit employees from parking near shipping and receiving, and near dumpsters.

Issue company identification and require that it be worn at all times.

Periodically change locks, especially when certain employees change jobs.

Conduct random surveillance of cashiers, the cleaning crew, trash pickups, the shipping and receiving dock, and after-hours employees.

Investigate losses. Establish uniform policies on prosecution and civil recovery.

Use insurance and bonding as a last resort in a series of defenses. Fidelity bonding is basically employee honesty insurance for those who are responsible for financial matters, such as bookkeepers. To deter theft, certain companies require employees to complete bonding applications, but do not actually obtain the coverage because of the expense.

Case Problems

6A. The Supermart Distribution Center (Figure 6-5) serves a retail chain of 16 stores. A security officer is assigned to patrol the dock during the day from 8:00 A.M.–12:00 Noon and from 1:00 P.M.–5:00 P.M.—the same time other employees work. Employees, truck drivers, and visitors are permitted easy access through the facility and all its doors. Damaged merchandise is sold to employees. A janitor is responsible for trash disposal to dumpsters. An evening cleaning crew works Mondays, Wednesdays, and Fridays from 5:00 P.M.–8:00 P.M. Twice each week, on Wednesday and Friday evenings, the dumpsters are emptied by a trash collection service.

As the newly hired corporate manager of retail loss prevention, you have just completed a one-day visit to the Supermart Distribution Center. Upon returning to your office, you find a phone message from the vice president of finance. She is very concerned about the climb in shrinkage at the distribution center. She wants you to devise a countershrink plan within one week. What do you suggest?

Table 6-2 Use of Loss Prevention Programs, National Retail Security Survey '91

Source	Department Store	Discount Store	Specialty Apparel	Specialty Hard Goods	Specialty Other	Home Centers	Drug Store	Grocery, Etc.	Overall Percent
Discuss LP In New Hire Orientation	91.5%	94.5%	86.5%	89.7%	92.7%	78.9%	96.8%	83.6%	88.4%
Periodic LP Programs for Employees (LP Awareness)	88.5%	89.1%	82.0%	87.1%	90.0%	83.7%	84.38%	88.8%	87.6%
Programs Use:									
Videos	92.7%	87.8%	53.8%	68.4%	70.2%	82.3%	74.1%	81.9%	77.3%
Lectures	87.1%	85.2%	81.8%	91.8%	89.0%	80.0%	89.6%	83.6%	86.0%
Bulletin Boards/Posters	89.5%	85.7%	81.0%	75.6%	76.4%	67.6%	82.1%	75.4%	80.2%
Paycheck Stuffers	60.8%	64.4%	36.2%	36.8%	41.1%	47.2%	27.5%	32.2%	42.3%
Newsletters	71.0%	67.5%	68.2%	64.1%	53.4%	68.5%	65.6%	69.8%	66.0%
Audio Tapes/Announcements	28.9%	17.6%	9.5%	18.4%	13.7%	20.5%	13.3%	20.0%	19.5%
Hot-Line for Employee Reporting	71.4%	62.1%	59.7%	71.0%	69.0%	55.2%	71.2%	50.7%	62.7%
Incentives for Employee Reporting	72.8%	67.5%	58.2%	63.1%	61.8%	67.5%	51.6%	34.3%	59.2%
Make Apprehensions	95.8%	88.8%	89.3%	75.6%	90.7%	80.0%	82.3%	83.0%	86.1%

Percentages take into account the 37 stores that are classified as "other" (8.0% of total) but that are not mentioned in the table.

© 1992, *Security Magazine*. Reprinted with permission.

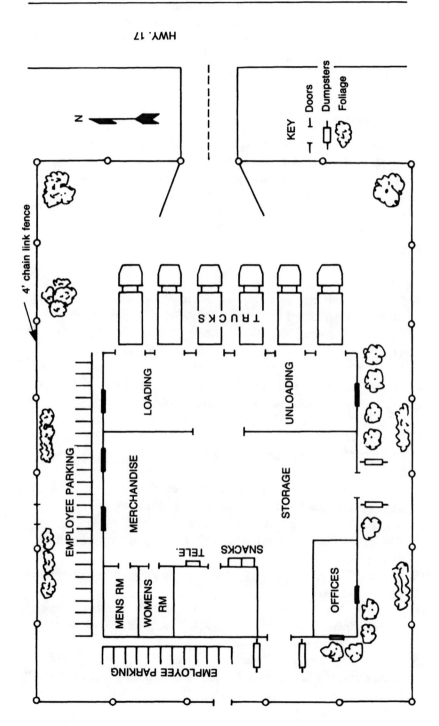

Figure 6–5 The Supermart Distribution Center

6B. Set up an internal reward program for reporting losses. The operations director wants to see your plan by the end of the week.

6C. Dan Jaffe, a reporter for *New Day News* wants to interview you regarding the speech you gave on "most employees will steal if given a chance." What do you say to support this contention?

Notes

1. Michael Levy and Barton A. Weitz, *Retail Management* (Homewood, IL: Irwin Publishing, 1992), 591.
2. Peter D. Berlin, "Markdowns: Their Impact on Shrinkage," *Shrinkage Control* (September 1990): 3.
3. Peter D. Berlin, "Different Perceptions/Different Directions," *Shrinkage Control* (February 1990): 5.
4. *Ibid.*, 5.
5. "National Retail Security Survey, 1991," (*Security* Magazine, 1992): 2.
6. Joseph F. Hair et al., "Employee Theft: Views from Two Sides," *Business Horizons* (December 1976): 25–29.
7. Hallcrest Systems, Inc., *The Hallcrest Report II—Private Security Trends: 1970 to the Year 2000* (McLean, VA: Hallcrest Systems, Inc., 1990).
8. Ira M. Shepard and Robert Duston, *Thieves at Work* (Washington, DC: Bureau of National Affairs, 1988), 19.
9. John P. Clark and Richard C. Hollinger, National Institute of Justice, *Theft by Employees in Work Organizations* (Washington, DC: US Department of Justice, 1982).
10. *Ibid.*
11. Alice P. Franklin, *Internal Theft in a Retail Organization: A Case Study* (Ann Arbor, MI: University Microfilms, 1975).
12. Michael A. Baker and Alan F. Westin, *Employer Perceptions of Workplace Crime* (Washington, DC: US Department of Justice, 1987), 10.
13. Banning K. Lary, "Thievery on the Inside," *Security Management* (May 1988): 81.
14. Philip P. Purpura, *Security & Loss Prevention*, 2nd ed. (Boston: Butterworth–Heinemann, 1991), 91–92. Reprinted with permission from Butterworth–Heinemann.
15. James H. Donnelly and Michael J. Etzel, "Retail Store Performance and Job Satisfaction," *Journal of Retailing* (Summer 1977): 28.
16. Shepard and Duston, 109.

17. National Retail Security Survey 1991 (*Security* Magazine, 1992): 8–9.
18. Hair et al., 25–29.
19. "Honesty Has Redeeming Value," *Chain Store Age Executive* (January 1991): 116–118.

7

Shoplifting and Countermeasures

Shoplifting is the theft of merchandise from retail stores by individuals posing as customers. State laws differ on how shoplifting is defined. Generally, the language of state statutes includes the following in the definition of shoplifting: taking merchandise from a retail store with intent to steal, altering any label or price, or committing an act with the intent to deprive the merchant of the full retail value of merchandise.

The basic elements to prove guilt in a shoplifting case are stated in a North Carolina case, *State v. Daye (1986)*, and they are that a person without authority willfully conceals store merchandise not purchased by that person while still on the premises. The next chapter provides in-depth coverage of investigation and prosecution of shoplifting cases.

Losses from Shoplifting

Estimates vary on the losses from shoplifting, although there is general agreement that it is a multibillion dollar problem. In the United States, the National Coalition to Prevent Shoplifting estimated annual losses at $26 billion.[1] The *Uniform Crime Report* for 1990 showed 1,271,307 reported shoplifting incidents. Losses averaged $115. Between 1986 and 1990, shoplifting was up 22% (see Figure 7–1).[2] Even though these FBI figures reveal enormous losses from shoplifting, it is important to point out that the FBI collects statistics on crimes *reported* to police departments. Retailers do not report all shoplifting incidents to the police. Shoplifters are frequently let go after signing a confession.

Security Management (Bureau of Business Practice) reports that if present trends continue, almost two million people will be charged with shoplifting each year. For every shoplifter caught, 35 get away.[3] Other estimates place detected shoplifting incidents as low as one out of 100–200.[4]

Characteristics of Shoplifters

Why Do They Shoplift?

Many theories have been advanced to explain the causes of shoplifting. The "situational approach" argues that the shoplifter has a normal personality, but steals because of environmental temptations. Another view points to shoplifting as a way in which individuals cope with anxiety and depression. The psychoanalytic perspective explains shoplifting as a result of conflicts during an individual's psychosexual development. A fourth point of view is that shoplifting is indicative of a criminal personality.[5] A universally acceptable explanation for the cause of shoplifting is difficult to construct. Although most people shoplift to "get something for nothing" or because of economic need, these two reasons do not explain all of the shoplifting incidents.

Types of Shoplifters

Shoplifters have been classified according to several categories. Two major categories are the amateur and the professional. The amateur, also known as a "snitch," represents the majority of shoplifters. These individuals often shoplift on impulse, even though they have the money to pay for stolen merchandise.

The professional or "booster" steals as a means of financial support. Orders for specific merchandise may be solicited from residents of a community and, following the theft, these items are sold at a fraction of their retail value. The going rate for hot clothing on the street is as low as 10-20 cents on the dollar.[6] Professionals employ a variety of methods to circumvent security, which will be discussed in subsequent pages. Professional shoplifters may be closely tied to a criminal culture in which they gain support for their craft, trade "war stories," and learn how to defeat security. A criminal record and associations with fences, bail bondspersons, and certain attorneys also characterize the professional shoplifter.

The kleptomaniac is an uncommon sight to retail employees. Kleptomania is characterized as a neurotic impulse to steal. These individuals may steal without regard for the value of the items or their chance of being caught. They frequently have a criminal record, although psychological therapy is likely to be more successful in dealing with the problem than prosecution.

Other categories of shoplifters include the juvenile or student, homemaker (female or male), substance abuser (the most dangerous), or retiree. Shoplifting also results from those least likely to be suspected. This category includes delivery people, assorted government inspectors, and police officers responding to a call from a retail store. Retail personnel should understand that *any-*

134 Shoplifting and Countermeasures

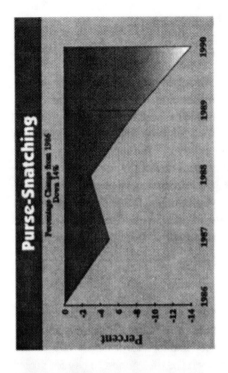

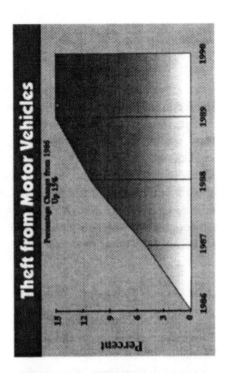

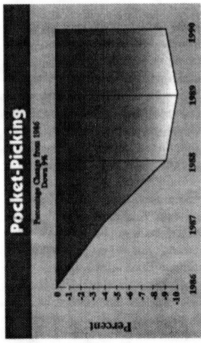

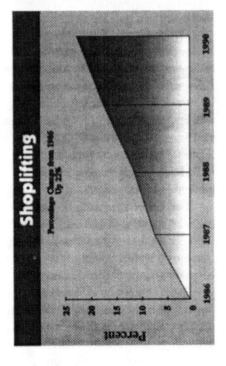

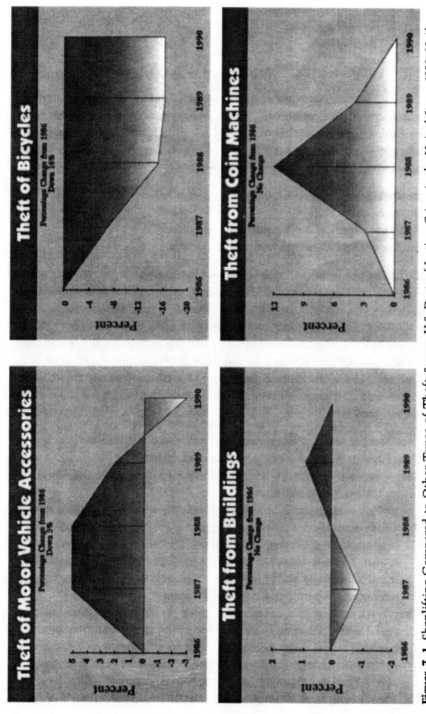

Figure 7-1 Shoplifting Compared to Other Types of Theft *Source:* U.S. Dept. of Justice, *Crime in the United States 1990, Uniform Crime Reports* (Washington, DC: U.S. Government Printing Office, 1991), 36.

one can be a shoplifter, especially since it requires no special skills and the chances for success are good.

Behavior of Shoplifters

Security personnel who deal with the shoplifting problem eventually develop a mental profile of shoplifter behavior, although not all offenders fit the profile. A profile is a list of clues that indicate a *possibility* that criminal behavior occurred, is occurring, or will occur. Suppose, as a plainclothes security officer, you notice a customer who

- constantly looks around to see who is nearby
- acts nervous
- walks past specific merchandise several times
- avoids eye contact when you browse nearby

This behavior by the suspect *may* indicate that shoplifting is about to occur. What do you do? Let us say that you make an arrest. Later, it is learned that the customer was in the store with his wife and attempted to select and purchase a gift for her without her knowledge. Always observe a suspect without taking action until you see the crime occur. In the next chapter, we learn how to produce quality shoplifting cases and prevent legal mistakes.

The behavior of shoplifters includes the techniques they use to steal. Shoplifters can be creative thieves. The following list is just a sample of the techniques they use.

They simply select a store item and put it in their pocket.

They hold or wear an item (e.g., hat) and depart.

They enter a fitting room with numerous items and conceal them under their outer clothes.

They place a price tag of a lower amount on a more expensive item.

They hide a small store item in a larger one to smuggle it past the cash register. One shoplifter bought 25 lbs. of dog food and returned to the store the next day with the empty bag. He filled it with groceries and placed it on the rack under the shopping basket and paid for the "dog food" again.

They work solo or in a coordinated group in which everyone has specific assignments. Shoplifters working in a group may pass a concealed item from one accomplice to another, which causes confusion among security personnel. If the first person is apprehended and no merchandise is recovered, litigation could result. This is why it is so important to never take your eyes off a suspect.

Adult shoplifters are known to recruit and train children to shoplift.
They use tools (e.g., scissors, stapler) and store supplies (e.g., bags, price tags) to assist in shoplifting.
They fake a handicap or a sudden illness to distract employees. They ask a salesperson to show several items beyond a number that can be controlled and switch a genuine item for a counterfeit one.
They employ devices to assist in theft, including long pockets, hooks under clothing, hollowed-out books, packages from other stores, baby carriages, wheelchairs, and so forth.
The professionals use a booster box, which appears to be a wrapped gift, but contains a hidden opening used to secrete merchandise (see Figure 7–2). This device can be designed to grab or flip an item into the box when it is placed over merchandise on a counter.
They use specially lined (e.g., foil, other metals) shopping bags to pass through electronic article surveillance systems.
Bold offenders may pick up merchandise from a rack and go right to a refund desk, without a receipt, to demand a cash refund.
They are sometimes known for their outrageous actions to avoid capture. Gypsy women, for example, may wear multiple outfits so that if they are apprehended, the ensuing confusion of several gypsy women converging on security personnel and the subsequent alteration of appearance results in difficulty in identifying the actual shoplifter. In one instance an apprehended female gypsy even exposed her breast and squeezed milk from a plastic bottle on a security officer to confuse and shock security personnel.
Women have been known to "crotchwalk." This entails standing over an item (e.g., pocketbook, small television) while wearing a dress, squatting down to pick it up with the inner thighs, standing up, and then gingerly walking out of the store.

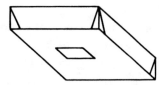 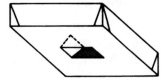

Figure 7–2 Booster Box

Crafty Shoplifters

Wednesday morning appeared to be like any other midweek morning for Phil Smith, owner and operator of Friar's Gate Jewelry Store. At about 11:00 A.M. a couple asked to see the selection of women's diamond rings. As Phil was showing the rings, he was asked by the excited female customer to let her see a necklace that she had been looking for at numerous jewelry stores. Phil turned his back to the couple momentarily to obtain the necklace of immense interest to the woman. When he faced the couple again he looked down and noticed a different ring among those on the counter. He immediately figured that the couple pulled a switch (replacing a genuine ring with a fake). Phil pointed to the ring that was new to the collection and asked the couple if they switched rings. They denied switching rings and acted insulted. Phil put the rings away, tripped the robbery alarm, and locked the front door, although he knew that if the couple was armed, he would be in trouble. He stood near where his revolver was hidden and patiently waited for the police to arrive. After a long three minutes, two officers carefully approached the front door. Phil let the officers in and explained what happened. The tray of rings was taken out and Phil identified the new ring as a fake. The officers began their questioning while several more officers and detectives arrived. The couple produced identification and a police check revealed that both had a long criminal record of shoplifting and fraud against retail stores. A search of the suspects by the police produced no diamond ring. Since the male subject had a soft drink while in the store, it was theorized that he dropped the ring in the drink and then swallowed it when he was accused. Another jeweler was brought to the store to select the fake ring from the tray. The second jeweler identified the fake immediately. Both suspects were held in detention under careful observation. Within 24 hours, a correctional officer retrieved the ring after it was eliminated by the male. Successful prosecution resulted.

What Can Be Done to Reduce Shoplifting?

Many strategies can be implemented to deal with the shoplifting problem. The degree of success varies considerably. Whatever action is taken to curb shoplifting, the following factors should be considered:

Shoplifting will continue to be a problem for retailers even though new security technology and strategies are being developed.

Although shoplifting has plagued retail businesses throughout history, this problem should be put in perspective. Many other threats face retailers and it would be foolhardy to devote disproportionate resources to counter shoplifting, while ignoring other vulnerabilities. Retailers have been guilty of exaggerating losses attributed to shoplifting. External factors are often convenient to blame for losses and shrinkage when, in fact, poor record keeping and internal theft may be more serious threats to a particular business.

Antishoplifting strategies must be cost-effective. Retail businesses exist to make a profit and not function as an arm of the justice system. Prevention is of the utmost importance. An arrest should be the last resort.

Security strategies should conform to management's philosophy and business need.

Strategies should not hinder business in any way.

Sound planning will reduce the chances of liability that may result from security efforts.

The effective use of people is a key strategy to reduce shoplifting. Security personnel and salespeople can both play a role in preventing theft.

Quality training and retraining are vital for efforts against shoplifting.

Seek cooperation from local police and prosecutors.

Evaluate antishoplifting strategies.

The Irony of Protecting Retail Stores

Retailers obviously dislike being victimized by shoplifters and suffering losses. But at the same time, retailers favor minimum access controls to facilitate customer traffic and attract customers. Increased sales are the likely result.

Compounding the difficulty of retail security are modern merchandising techniques that emphasize customer accessibility to merchandise. Retailers want customers to notice merchandise, pick it up, and then buy it. The U.S. Department of Commerce states

> Marketing techniques which make merchandise desirable to a potential buyer also make it tempting to a potential thief and offer opportunities for theft. Imaginative displays of goods, which might be overlooked, at check counters or in gondolas suggest to the customer that he needs them and can easily make his selection. Both sales and thefts increase when customers can

handle goods displayed this way because the impulsive theft is triggered by this combination of temptation and opportunity.[7]

Modern merchandising presents security problems worldwide. The debate in Germany over how to deal with the shoplifting problem included the following view.

> ... shoplifting from self-service stores is not really theft ... goods are forced on the customer. The shopowner does not resent the "taking"; in fact, he tries to seduce it. He is contributorily negligent. The wrong, moreover, is not paying, rather than taking; and not paying is more like a tort (failing to pay for something purchased on credit) than a crime.[8]

What has happened through modern merchandising is that retailers have made shoplifting easier for offenders. Also, those with an inclination toward theft are increasingly tempted, through attractive displays, to commit acts of shoplifting. Retailers find that the ROI from modern merchandising exceeds the losses from theft. Security practitioners have no choice but to employ creative solutions to the shoplifting problem, while faced with increasingly sophisticated merchandising techniques that use a variety of psychological methods to entice customers to want and need certain items.

Research on the Shoplifting Problem

A considerable amount of research has been conducted on the shoplifting problem. Three major sources of this research are in-house research conducted by security executives, research by contract firms serving the retail industry, and research conducted by college educators. All three types of research help to answer crucial questions. However, the first two sources may or may not share their information with other practitioners. College educators are eager to publish their findings.

The focus of research on the shoplifting problem is often aimed at characteristics of shoplifters. The effectiveness of security strategies is another major target for research. This is becoming increasingly important, as upper management is demanding cost-effective security with an ROI. The following is a sampling of research to illustrate the types of questions being asked about the shoplifting problem.

Arthur Young and Company, an international management consulting firm, conducts an annual survey of security and loss prevention in the retail industry for the International Mass Retail Association. Table 7–1 shows a profile of apprehended customers.

Table 7-1 Profile of Apprehended Customers[9]

	Male	Female	All
Total Apprehensions	52%	48%	—
Age			
Under 18	43	35	43
18–35	39	43	35
Over 35	18	22	22
Employment Status			
Employed	59	51	55
Unemployed	41	49	45

Modified with permission by Arthur Young & Co.

Research conducted by University of Massachusetts psychiatrist Gary Moak and his colleagues showed a countertrend in the traditional assumption that most shoplifters are young. In recent years there has been a steady increase in arrests of first offenders over age 65. Store personnel who assume that shoplifters will be among the young age ranges may need to be advised that these days it is important to keep an eye on all customers, regardless of age.[10]

JoAnn Ray of Eastern Washington University at Spokane produced research that shows that half of the shoplifters she studied were experiencing emotional stress (i.e., family separation or drug use) combined with economic problems. Added to these factors, the Illinois Retail Merchants Association reported that three-fourths of those apprehended in that state are in middle- or high-income brackets.[11]

John Carroll of MIT and Frances Weaver of Loyola University shed light on what deters shoplifters. Novice and expert shoplifters were studied. Their research showed that both types of shoplifters considered only one or two major aspects of a store before deciding to steal an item. These aspects included the level of security, store layout, the size of the item to be concealed, and the presence or absence of store employees. Alert store employees appeared to be particularly effective in deterring shoplifters. Also, only one deterrent was needed to curb shoplifting by a novice. Expert shoplifters required multiple security methods to be deterred. The implications of this study point out that if just about all of the shoplifters entering a store are novices, then multiple security measures may not be necessary to deter shoplifting.[12] Perhaps one or two well-planned and closely supervised strategies are better than several poorly conceived and implemented strategies.

A 1986 study by Murphy consisted of interviews of security personnel and shoplifters to determine the effectiveness of various prevention and detection methods including CCTV, mirrors, electronic article surveillance, and loop alarms (all discussed in subsequent pages). EAS appeared to be very effective, provided employees and the system are carefully supervised.[13]

McNees et al., in a two-part study, evaluated two strategies to prevent shoplifting. The first study evaluated the effects of antishoplifting signs that stated that shoplifting is a crime and it increases the cost of merchandise. The second study tested the effect of signs and symbols (e.g., yellow tape wrapped around the top of clothes hangers) that specifically identified merchandise frequently stolen. An inventory was conducted each day to check on missing items. The research results showed a drop in theft through the use of signs, without affecting sales. When merchandise was identified as being frequently taken, shoplifting was virtually eliminated. There was no change in the shoplifting rates for merchandise not marked with yellow tape.[14]

Evaluating Antishoplifting Strategies

The evaluation of antishoplifting strategies can expose those strategies that are not cost-effective and support the success of others. These research results will assist the planning process and budget justification. Here, we employ the scientific method discussed in Chapter 2 and apply it to the shoplifting problem.

Problem: Shoplifting
Hypothesis: Shoplifting can be reduced by training sales personnel.
Testing:
Control Group	*Experimental Group*
Store A	Store B
no change in training	short weekly training sessions for sales personnel

Conclusion: During the three months this research and training occurred, Store B significantly reduced its shoplifting problem.

This is a simplified version of how evaluative research can be conducted. Various combinations of strategies should be tested. Continued research can strengthen results. This strategy and research can be applied to other stores, following testing at one store. Local college educators, who are well versed in research methods, can be recruited to assist with research. Unsuccessful, useless security methods should be eliminated and replaced with those methods that are working to reduce shoplifting.

Protection against Shoplifting

Socialization of Employees

Retail employees are the backbone of antishoplifting programs. How employees are trained and supervised will have a significant impact on the amount of shoplifting and losses incurred.

Employers spend considerable sums of money searching for job candidates and then screening them. When a decision is made to hire an applicant, an employer should continue to invest in the hiring process and develop a productive employee who will benefit the organization. Socialization is a means of accomplishing this task. Sociologists commonly refer to this term to describe the process whereby members of a society transmit the culture of the group to new individuals. For our purposes, socialization is defined as a learning process during which employees develop an understanding of their roles and behaviors to further the goals of their employer. This process goes beyond training. Socialization in an employment environment includes an orientation program for new employees, training and retraining, and good examples set by superiors and co-workers. To reinforce appropriate behavior, a variety of strategies can be used, including good supervision, performance evaluations, praise, rewards, and recognition. Also, posters can be placed in the working environment and included in articles in a company newspaper.

Because a retailer's antishoplifting program will be a small part of the total socialization process in the workplace, security managers must understand the limited time available to impart their strategies to reduce shoplifting. Retail employees can suffer from information overload, since they are assigned specific duties, such as sales, and they often have limited interest in dealing with the shoplifting problem. In many instances, the most a security manager can expect is that when salespeople observe a shoplifting incident they contact security immediately.

If a security manager is allotted some training time, the following topics can be emphasized: economic impact of shoplifting, behavior of shoplifters, and company policies and procedures. Several other crimes (e.g., robbery and counterfeiting), in addition to shoplifting, may be important to discuss. The security manager must carefully plan the training time to cover appropriate topics and maintain the interest of the audience. To increase the retention of information and to facilitate a positive attitude toward security, consider these suggestions:

> Require participants to complete a short quiz to test their knowledge and then allow them to grade it themselves.
> Play one or two short training tapes.
> Display tools used by offenders (e.g., booster box).

Roleplay incidents.

End the training with another short quiz (i.e., posttest) that is graded by the students in the class for immediate feedback.

A key objective of these efforts is to create security-conscious employees. Awareness of loss problems and security results in greater involvement by employees and reduces losses.

Retail Management

Retail management obviously wants to reduce the shoplifting problem and associated losses. The degree to which management supports security efforts varies considerably. The primary thoughts of retail managers are daily sales figures, profits, and customer behavior. This is understandable and retail security practitioners must be perceptive to management's business concerns.

To stimulate management interest in the shoplifting problem, these strategies are recommended:

Work with management to formulate policies and procedures. Include feedback from all retail employees on the best methods to reduce shoplifting.

Provide thorough justification for budget requests for personnel and equipment.

Illustrate how security expenditures can show an ROI (e.g., through lower shrinkage).

Keep management informed on the shoplifting problem through quarterly reports that include

shoplifting statistics (e.g., losses, recovery of merchandise, apprehensions, prosecution)

short narratives of certain shoplifting incidents, including events in the store and those in the parking lot

how security personnel and salespeople cooperated

public police cooperation

training programs

crime rates of surrounding neighborhoods

comparisons to other similar stores

short comments on legal issues and cases

Salespeople

When we compare the number of security personnel with the number of salespeople in a retail store, we typically see many more salespeople than security personnel. It is the job of the security manager to recruit salespeople to enhance store protection. At a minimum, the sales force should know how to contact security. The telephone number can be placed right on the telephone or posted at convenient locations. A quick response by security is of the utmost importance. Otherwise, cooperation from the sales force can easily wane.

A primary method in which shoplifting can be prevented is through the attention given to customers by salespeople. A simple "May I help you?" can deter offenders, because they have been noticed, addressed, and eye contact has occurred. This makes most shoplifters feel uncomfortable. A few simple codes can be established and employed when salespeople and security personnel work together to thwart a shoplifter.

When salespeople are trained to play a secondary role in assisting security in apprehending shoplifters, salespeople should be taught a minimum number of vital rules, such as carefully watch a suspect, notify security, and be prepared to inform security about every detail of the incident. If possible, salespeople should also be trained in basic procedures to prevent shoplifting. This includes limiting the number of items shown to customers, keeping high-value merchandise locked up, and ensuring that price tickets are firmly affixed.

Reward Program

Because salespeople are concerned with their sales duties, they typically do not want to get involved nor do they have the time to assist security with the shoplifting problem. To increase interest, retailers have instituted reward programs in which salespeople are given cash based on a percentage of recovered merchandise following their assistance in apprehending a shoplifter. This strategy is also used to counter employee theft. Reward programs must be carefully planned and controlled. Employees need clear, simple guidelines and training to avoid liability.

Store Detectives

Store detectives are a primary strategy for detecting and apprehending shoplifters. After these practitioners have developed their skills and gained experience, many offenders are surprised when they are confronted. Experienced store detectives are usually experts on shoplifter behavior. Detectives observe the sales floor from a concealed location or use various disguises to blend into crowds of shoppers without being spotted. Because detectives act as if they are browsing through racks looking for a bargain and are, perhaps, holding some merchandise and a sales paper, offenders often dismiss a detective as just another busy shopper. Detectives must be able to

- observe without being observed
- note details for subsequent recall and report writing
- understand relevant criminal and civil laws
- apprehend a subject, possibly without assistance
- avoid physical confrontations and know self-defense techniques
- interview effectively
- follow through on a case by signing a warrant and testifying in court

Security Officers

Security officers stationed at entrances or patrolling throughout a store send a message to shoppers that the store is concerned about security. These strategies act as a deterrent to crime. One disadvantage is that shoplifters and other offenders can easily spot security officers. This knowledge helps to plan where to commit a crime in a store and how to escape.

In general, security officers should not be armed. With so many innocent bystanders in a store, the hazards and potential liability are significant.

Fitting Room Attendants

A common ploy of shoplifters is to carry several articles of clothing into a fitting room and wear these items under the outer layer of clothing. This method of theft has become so serious that retailers must take steps to prevent losses. To begin with, fitting rooms should be located in the center of a store and not near avenues of escape, such as exits or stairways. Curtains or doors in the fitting rooms should be at least 2 feet off the ground to deter theft. Some retailers lock fitting rooms and customers must ring a bell to summon an attendant to unlock the door and count the items going into the fitting room. A limit is often placed on the number of items allowed to be brought into the fitting room. More elaborate systems use color-coded cards that are given to customers by an attendant to signify the number of items going into the fitting room. Fitting room attendants may play a role in the covert surveillance of customers suspected of concealing items while in the fitting room. Those who observe must be the same sex of those being observed. Local and state laws, and relevant court decisions, should be studied prior to conducting this type of surveillance.

Physical Security

Numerous devices are on the market to assist retailers with the shoplifting problem. The planning and selection of physical security is not an easy process. Serious errors in planning and purchasing can result by omitting just one important factor, such as customer inconvenience or unexpected personnel requirements to operate and maintain physical security. Remember, even when the best possible security plans are produced, these plans are useless if the physical security devices purchased do not operate as expected.

The earlier discussion entitled "What Can Be Done to Reduce Shoplifting?" is a beginning point for planning antishoplifting strategies. When purchasing physical security, act like a wise consumer. Before vendors are contacted, it is important to properly evaluate needs. This can be accomplished through risk analysis. Purchase what is needed, not what a salesperson is trying to sell. The practitioner should read trade publications to become familiar with the latest technology and trends. All this preparation prior to a vendor visit provides a good foundation for decision making. Perhaps the best advice is to speak with a customer who has used the device or system of interest. This person will know the advantages, disadvantages, and "bugs," and will provide valuable information that may be very different than what the salesperson has to say.

Three additional factors to consider when purchasing physical security are installation, maintenance, and leasing. Ideally, the manufacturer is the best choice for installation, but subcontractors often do the job. Check to ensure compliance with manufacturer standards.

A good maintenance plan is vital, because a system is useless when it fails. Where are repair specialists based? Are parts readily available? What are the costs? These questions should be answered and provided in writing by the vendor. If the system breaks down, what in-house contingency plans are available?

Leasing is an option when a large capital outlay is not possible. In addition, the retailer can switch to newer technology when the lease expires, rather than own an outdated system. A financial specialist can offer suggestions.

Electronic Article Surveillance

During the 1960s, retail stores began tagging merchandise with magnetic strips and installing detectors at exits to deter shoplifters and recover merchandise. Known as *electronic article surveillance* (EAS) (see Figures 7–3 to 7–5), this technology has expanded tremendously in the retail industry and has many other applications. Manufacturing companies use EAS to protect finished products from employee theft, airlines curb the theft of life jackets through EAS, and prisons and hospitals use this technology to restrict the movement of people. Three technologies are used by EAS systems—microwave, magnetic, and radio frequency.

Microwave EAS systems have been used traditionally in apparel stores to protect clothing with the easy-to-recognize, large, hard tag. Once an item is

Figure 7-3 SEKURTAG Flat Pin and Dome Pin Courtesy of Security Tag Systems, Inc.

purchased by the customer, the tag must be removed with a special detacher at the POS. This technology has been criticized for slowing POS checkout procedures, damaging clothes, and embarrassing customers when a cashier forgets to remove the tag.

Magnetic EAS systems have been popular in libraries for several years to protect books. These systems emit magnetic fields to detect tags or labels that contain polarized magnetic material. The labels and tags are deactivated at the POS by making contact with a magnetic pad. This may slow activity at the checkout. Because the system contains magnetized materials, it may interfere with POS terminals, and computers and software. Also, the sensors at exits may be activated when metal objects pass. Customer embarrassment is the result if the labels or tags are not deactivated after the merchandise is sold.

Radio frequency (RF) EAS systems consist of a transmitter and receiver that, together, establish an RF field. An alarm is activated when a tag or label containing a thin, RF-printed circuit passes between the sensors. One advantage of RF EAS systems is that deactivation can occur without the cashier locating the tag or label and without the merchandise having to make contact with a dedicated device. Deactivation can be integrated into POS scanning equipment. Price scanning and deactivation of the security circuit can take place at the same time. The price tag and security circuit are combined in a single label. The cost of the paper-thin RF circuits is very low in comparison to the larger plastic tags.

Figure 7–4 Various Security Tag Systems EAS Tags Courtesy of Security Tag Systems, Inc.

Retailers choose various sized tags depending on their security strategies. Large tags of a few inches do have a deterrent value over small or hidden tags. Other retailers favor small thin tags that can be placed under price labels or bar codes. This strategy includes tagging only a certain percentage of items

Figure 7-5 Actual Single-post Installation Courtesy of Security Tag Systems, Inc.

so customers and employees do not know which items will activate an alarm. Costs range from a few pennies for one-time-use tags to $1–$2 for reusable tags.

EAS is as good as the personnel, training, and supervision supporting the system. If a salesperson does not deactivate or remove a tag, a false alarm is likely to occur and a subsequent lawsuit for false arrest may result. Personnel must respond cautiously and politely to all alarms. Quality training of the sales force and security personnel can greatly reduce errors.

Electronic Surveillance Helps Retail, Institutions Maximize Profits, Safety

Decision makers looking to protect merchandise, office supplies and people increasingly choose electronic surveillance equipment.

Versatility is electronic surveillance's charm. Hard or soft, human or inanimate, myriad objects are candidates for specialized targets and detection systems.

A Material Issue

Stores and libraries have used electronic article surveillance (EAS) for nearly 20 years. Changes in target format—perhaps more than sensors—differentiate today's systems from older systems. Lightweight targets, which serve both EAS and pricing purposes, have largely replaced cumbersome plastic tags.

Decision makers' objectives dictate the sensors or targets which best suit an application. Fluid tags or large plastic targets teamed with high-visibility sensors work most effectively if theft deterrence is top priority. Highest-scale retailers often opt for covert sensors or more aesthetically pleasing targets and sensors.

Deterring theft is half the battle when maximizing EAS potential.

"Retailers really don't want to prosecute shoplifters; these people are often the store's regular customers," says Stu Wight, sales manager, International Loss Prevention Systems, Vancouver, B.C. "Nobody wants to chase thieves down the street—you just want them to stop stealing."

And steal they do. U.S. Department of Justice statistics show that shoplifting is increasing faster than other crimes, while retail profits have taken a plunge every year since 1986.

Get to the Source

"Source tagging" is the buzzword among EAS vendors and clients.

Source tagging is the integration of EAS targets and merchandise at the manufacturing or distribution point. Targets are often placed within layers of packaging materials and deactivated at the point of sale.

In addition to saving retailers labor hours, this process expedites sales because merchandise is shipped ready to display. The drawback: Only stores which purchase the appropriate sensing gear can benefit.

"Source tagging must catch on as retail labor becomes more scarce and the minimum wage increases," says Jerry Klein, president, Checkpoint Systems, Thorofare, N.J.

The Sekurlabel from Security Tag Systems, St. Petersburg, Fla., is a deactivatible adhesive label for packaged goods. It operates on items with metallic content, such as cigarette packages. Checkpoint Systems' Impulse Program is another method for source tagging. Impulse—as well as other products conducive to source tagging applications—is non-contact deactivatable, which means that targets don't need to touch a deactivation pad.

A Matter of Taste

Vendors and users swear by their favorite detection method. Radio frequency systems most often satisfy wide-aisle and mall applications, while magnetic systems offer shorter-range coverage which is well-suited to stand alone sites. Target size affects detection range, too: Range decreases as target size decreases.

"High radio frequency systems cover wide openings, but magnetic technology's range is limited to about 40 inches," says Louis Chiera, marketing manager, Sensormatic, Deerfield Beach, Fla.

Targets or sensors can be covert, such as the Ranger DRF Overhead System from Knogo, Long Island, N.Y., that can be installed above ceilings. Knogo's Electro Thred protects audio and video products and books; it's inserted into hard cover book spines. Whispertape targets from 3M, St. Paul, Minn., also protect these high-shrink products.

Some stores and libraries choose to deactivate and reactivate magnetic targets with each transaction. Other users prefer to skip the deactivation step and instead "pass" loaned merchandise around the sensing gear.

Users deactivate targets via several methods. Detachers expedite hard tag removal. Label and soft tag users employ hand-held or counter top "pad" deactivators at the point of sale. Sensormatic's SpeedStation deactivates labels when items are placed in a merchandise bag.

Hard goods displayed in catalog warehouses and hardware stores may not require traditional EAS systems. The Squealer from Stajer Corp., Lowell, Mass., and Armed Power Strips and Boxes from Cepco, Canoga Park, Calif., alarm when these items are detached from a sensing circuit. This type of equipment also satisfies office applications where computers, typewriters and other electrical equipment need to be protected.

* * *

Stay on Target

Choices abound when it comes to EAS targets.

Generally, label-type targets protect packaged goods and hard targets protect clothing, linens and other soft goods. Many of today's targets are disposable—an attractive trait to some retailers.

Target choices include:

- Traditional hard tags. These high-visibility targets deter theft and guard soft goods. There are many varieties; some attach to merchandise straps via a lanyard.

- Fluid tags. Used alone or incorporated into EAS hard targets, fluid tags solicit rave reviews from users and industry experts. Excessive pressure causes the target's fluid vial to break and ruin the garment.

  "Ink tags are displacing EAS," says Robert DiLonardo, vice president of marketing, Security Tag Systems, St. Petersburg, Fla. "Thieves steal clothing to wear it or sell it; both purposes are defeated with these tags."
- Adhesive wires. These barely-noticeable tapes adhere to book spines, videocassettes and other hard goods.
- Pressure-sensitive labels. These fulfill both pricing and EAS tasks. They often resemble bar code labels.

Reprinted with permission from *Security* Magazine. *Source:* Brenda Moss, "Electronic Surveillance Helps Retail, Institutions Maximize Profits, Safety," *Security* (July 1991): 52–53.

Another problem stems from offenders who strive to circumvent EAS. Some shoplifters have learned how to remove EAS tags in the store. Those who work or who have worked in a retail environment are a source of information for the removal of tags. One protection strategy is to place an obvious tag and a hidden one on merchandise. If the obvious tag is removed by offenders, they will think the EAS system is defeated. This approach can be used to catch professional shoplifters and employee thieves.

To bypass EAS sensors at exits, shoplifters are using bags lined with aluminum foil or other metal. Then, in the comfort of their homes, they remove the tags. To deal with these problems, retailers are trying an idea from Sweden in combination with EAS. A tag (about 2 inches in diameter) is attached to a garment that, if removed without authorization, squirts an indelible dye and ruins the merchandise (see Figures 7–6 and 7–7). Thus, the shoplifter cannot wear the garment. Warnings are posted to notify customers of possible injury from glass, metal, plastic and ink. The dye eventually washes off one's hands, but not off the garment. When this type of tagged item is purchased at a store, the salesperson removes the tag with a special device bolted down near the cash register. As with EAS systems, offenders are striving to circumvent the dye tags. One newer system emits a beep if someone tampers with an EAS tag (see Figure 7–8). Only a retail employee can turn off the noise. EAS technology is another example that shows us that no security method is foolproof. As soon as a new strategy is implemented, offenders are eager to find a way to circumvent it. Multiple security strategies will increase protection.

Electronic Article Surveillance Systems and Fluid Tags

Company	System	RF*	(Very low frequency) EM*	M*	(High frequency) MI*	HAM*	Fluid Tags	Features, Special Applications
Checkpoint Systems	Impulse program	•						Source tagging
	QS2000	•						Disposable tags, labels (for retail)
	Alpha	•						
	Quicksilver	•						
	Signature Series	•						Wood sensors
ColorTag	ColorTag						•	
	ColorTag Mini**						•	Delicate garments
International Loss Prevention Systems	Series 4000	•						Single panel installation
Knogo	Standard SRF System	•						
	Ranger DRF Overhead	•						Covert, overhead
	Chameleon Micro-Magnetic			•				Libraries, offices
	Sentinel Micro-Magnetic	•		•				
	Silver Cloud SRF	•						
	Kno-Glo**						•	
Monarch Marking Systems	System One	•						Pricing and EAS system
	Mini-Loop System	•						
Security Tag Systems	Sekurloop	•†						Anti-kidnapping, office equipment
	Sekurpost	•†						
	Sekurlabel	•†						Packaged goods
	Inktag						•	
	Inktag II						•	
	Inktag III						•	
	Inkmate						•	Ink/EAS combination
Sensormatic	AP600/Ultra-Max					•		Industrial (AP600)
	Aisle Keeper				•			Grocery stores
	MicroMax				•			
	Standard Magnetic System			•				
	TellTag System	•						High-ticket soft goods
	Sensorink**						•	
Sentronic International	Harmless to Health System			•				Floppy disks, tools
3M	Model 2600			•				Video stores
	Model 3300			•				Pricing and EAS system

Key:
* RF = radio frequency, EM = electromagnetic, M = magnetic, MI = microwave, HAM = hybrid acoustic magneto
** = operates stand alone or interacts with sensors, † = uses very low radio frequency (frequency division technology)

Data are supplied in SECURITY Magazine's *Product, Service, Supplier's Guide* or from specification sheets. Information is as complete and correct as possible, yet non-response, market changes and other unintentional factors may affect content.

Electronic article surveillance products allow retailers to maximize profits. Those seeking a wide detection range should consider radio frequency systems. Target choice contributes to the system's visibility and affects range.

Reprinted with permission from *Security* Magazine. Source: Brenda Moss, "Electronic Surveillance Helps Retail, Institutions Maximize Profits, Safety," *Security* (July 1991): 54.

Protection against Shoplifting 155

Figure 7-6 INKTAG Two-piece Application Courtesy of Security Tag Systems, Inc.

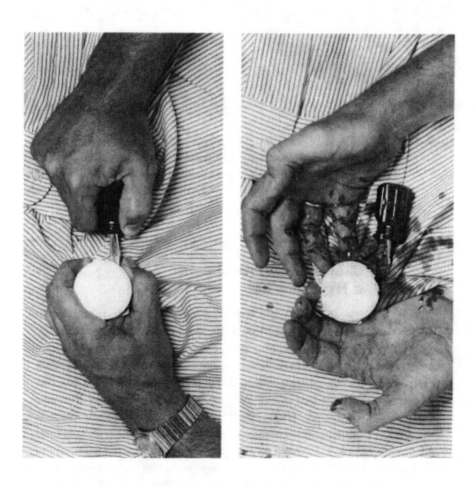

Figure 7-7 INKTAG Results Courtesy of Security Tag Systems, Inc.

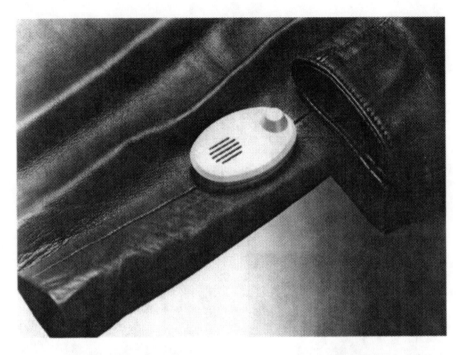

Figure 7-8 TellTag from Sensormatic Electronics Corporation Assists Sales Efforts by Permitting Open Merchandising and Increases Security While Eliminating the Need for Locked Cases, Clumsy Chains, and Wire Cables Photograph courtesy of Sensormatic Electronics Corporation.

Shoplifting Protection at a Hypermarket

The hypermarket first appeared in France in the early 1960s. It is a huge retail store that sells just about anything. The concept is appearing in the U.S. One such hypermarket in a large U.S. city has more than 300,000 square feet of space with 60 checkout lanes. EAS is used to reduce shoplifting. About 30 percent of the merchandise has tags affixed that cost less than 5 cents each. The tags are very thin and are attached to bar code labels. Deactivation occurs when the price is scanned. At the checkouts, customers pass through a scanner in case merchandise is concealed. To avoid a mistake, customers are also scanned when they enter the store, since they may have shopped earlier at the store or at another store with a similar EAS system and the tag on an item may not have been deactivated. An alarm will sound if an item has not been deactivated. To strengthen the deterrent value of EAS, signs are placed throughout the store, especially at the checkouts.

Special nonstore personnel from a contract service apply the tags to certain merchandise, so only a few individuals know which items are tagged. This reduces internal theft. Since not all items are tagged, an employee or customer does not know whether an item will set off an alarm.

What is the ROI for EAS? This hypermarket has 70 scanners in place that cost about $5,000 each, for a total of $350,000. Tags cost about $100,000 annually. Applying the tags and providing employee training for the shoplifting problem costs about $50,000. The total cost is $500,000. With sales of $300 million a year and 1 percent shrinkage (i.e., $3 million), EAS is cost-effective and shows an ROI.

Additional security at this store includes 35 surveillance cameras, 10 store detectives, 25 uniformed security officers, and a sales force of more than 700 personnel.

Closed-circuit Television

CCTV has become an effective tool to reducing shoplifting. It has a deterrent value and its surveillance capabilities enable one person to watch several locations at one time. If an offender is spotted, apprehension and prosecution are made easier through CCTV. Date and time should be displayed on all recordings to strengthen cases.

CCTV equipment consists of cameras, monitors, a recorder, a switcher to control the cameras (see Figure 7-9), and cables to connect the system. Camera features often include zoom lenses to view activities up close, remote pan to scan right or left, and tilt to scan up and down. Low-light cameras enable

Figure 7-9 Control Panel for Computerized Switching and Camera Station Control System Courtesy of Vicon Industries, Inc.

viewing when lighting conditions are poor. Overt or covert cameras are used in retail stores. Covert cameras are placed in mannequins and a variety of other locations (see Figure 7–10). The recording equipment is especially helpful for successful prosecution. CCTV is also useful for deterring other crimes and studying employee production and behavior.

For a CCTV system to be effective, the personnel who operate it must be closely supervised and their duty posts must be rotated. Unfortunately, many control rooms contain a sleeping security officer who has become fatigued from watching monitors for too long. Personnel should be switched to other posts at least every two hours.

CCD Cameras

One type of camera that is becoming increasingly popular is the charged coupled device (CCD) or "chip" camera (see Figure 7–11). A CCD is a small, photosensitive, solid-state unit designed to replace the tube in the closed-circuit camera. CCD technology has been around since the early 1950s. However, because of its complexity, it was not cost-effective to produce until the consumer market developed it through the camcorder.

There are certain advantages to the CCD camera over the tube camera. CCD cameras are more adaptable to a variety of circumstances. These color cameras are less costly and provide improved color purity. However, one point to consider is that color pictures are very dependent on lighting. Black-and-white tube or chip cameras can out-perform color cameras in most lower light situations.

Another advantage of CCD is life expectancy. Tubes last about three to five years, depending on the manufacturer and their quality. The CCD chip will average five years or longer. "Ghosting" (i.e., people in a scene appearing transparent) is less of a problem with CCD cameras, because the newer technology is less intolerant to lighting conditions. In comparison to tube cameras, CCD cameras require less power to operate, have less heat output, which necessitates less ventilation, and permit installation in a wider number of locations.[15]

Alarms

In addition to EAS, a wide assortment of alarms are capable of notifying store employees of an unauthorized movement of merchandise. Several of the alarms used to counter employee theft are also applicable to the

Figure 7-10 Camera Dome Containing CCTV Camera Courtesy of Sensormatic Electronics Corporation.

Figure 7-11 CCD Camera Courtesy of Vicon Industries, Inc.

shoplifting problem. Contact switches, as explained in Chapter 9, are often installed on display cases, drawers, storage bins, and other locations where something has to be opened to gain entry to merchandise. Loop alarms are woven through expensive appliances and clothing to complete an electrical circuit that, if interrupted, will sound an alarm. Wafer alarms are placed under items and sound an alarm when the objects are removed. Plug alarms activate an alarm when an electrical device is unplugged.

Additional Strategies

Retailers have installed other security measures to protect merchandise, such as locks, steel cables, and chains. To facilitate the detection of shoplifters, observation booths high above the sales floor enable security personnel to closely observe multiple departments. Binoculars, portable video cameras, and a good communications system will enhance security efforts. Two-way mirrors facilitate covert surveillance. Wide-angle convex mirrors permit the viewing of suspects over partitions and around corners. Dummy cameras are also used; however, unless these cameras look like the real thing, this measure is not likely to be cost-effective.

Signs that specify that "shoplifters will be prosecuted" or that "this store is protected by a security system" show varying degrees of effectiveness. Shoplifters Anonymous (headquartered in Glen Mills, Pennsylvania) reports that shoplifters are primarily concerned with whether anyone will see them steal. If they believe they cannot be seen, they assume they will succeed. Thus, signs should make shoplifters think that they will be seen. Two suggested signs are: "The last 250 people caught shoplifting in this store were all convinced that no one was watching." "This store reserves the right to use concealed electronic devices to detect shoplifters."[16]

Store layout will influence shoplifter behavior. These physical features include the arrangement of aisles, turnstiles, and corrals.

Case Problems

7A. As a security manager for a large department store in an urban area, your boss requests a report from you on the two most effective security strategies to deal with the shoplifting problem and an explanation of why both strategies would be so effective if funded.

7B. As a security specialist for a shopping mall, you have been given the task of conducting a one-hour training program on shoplifting prevention. (Apprehension and arrest will be taught by another security specialist.) List the topics you would cover, the number of minutes required to discuss each topic, and explain why you selected these topics.

Notes

1. Sue T. Reid, *Crime and Criminology*, 5th ed. (New York: Holt, Rinehart & Winston, 1988), 266.
2. U.S. Dept. of Justice, Federal Bureau of Investigation, *Crime in the United States, 1990, Uniform Crime Reports* (Washington, DC: U.S. Government Printing Office, 1991), 32–37.
3. "What Research Says about Shoplifting," *Security Management, Protecting Property, People & Assets* (January 25, 1989): 3.
4. A. James Fisher, *Security for Business and Industry* (Englewood Cliffs, NJ: Prentice-Hall, 1979), 169.
5. Esther A. Beck and Sherwood C. McIntyre, "MMPI Patterns of Shoplifters within a College Population," *Psychological Reports* 41 (1977): 1035.
6. "Credit Card Scam Prompts New Defenses," *Chain Store Age Executive* (June 1989): 70.
7. U.S. Dept. of Commerce, *Crime in Retailing* (Washington, DC: U.S. Government Printing Office, 1975), 5.
8. U.S. Dept. of Justice, *European Alternatives to Criminal Trials and Their Applicability in the United States* (Washington, DC: U.S. Government Printing Office, 1978), 33.
9. "An Ounce of Prevention," *1988–1989 Edition* (New York: Arthur Young & Co., 1990), 16.
10. "What Research Says," 3.
11. Ibid., 4.
12. F.M. Weaver and J.S. Carroll, "Crime Perceptions in a Natural Setting by Expert and Novice Shoplifters," *Social Psychology Quarterly* 48 (1985): 349–359.
13. D.J.I. Murphy, *Customers and Thieves: An Ethnography of Shoplifting* (Aldershot, England: Gower Publishers, 1986).
14. M. Patrick McNees et al., "Shoplifting Prevention: Providing Information through Signs," *Journal of Applied Behavior Analysis* 9 (Winter 1976): 399–405.
15. Charlie Pierce, "CCD Cameras Having Major Industry Impact," *Access Control* (April 1991): 1, 19.
16. *Corporate Security* (February 1986): 5.

8

Investigation of Internal Losses and Shoplifting

Before we focus on investigations of internal losses and shoplifting incidents an introduction is presented here to provide a foundation for the reader. First, it is important that we explain what an investigation is and present common factors associated with investigations.

An investigation is a search for information and facts. Typically, investigators interview victims, witnesses, suspects, and informants. Public police are more likely to collect physical evidence, such as fingerprints and shoeprints, than retail investigators.

Investigators in the private sector possess less arrest powers than public police. Private sector investigators usually have citizen's arrest powers. Simply put, from a cautious perspective, an arrest should be made only when a felony is in fact being committed and is observed by the arrestor.[1] Shoplifting, a misdemeanor, is an exception discussed later.

There are six basic questions that provide direction for all investigations. They are as follows, with questions emphasizing an employee theft incident to serve as an illustration.

1. Who? Who are the subjects involved in the theft? Who reported the theft? Any witnesses? Names, addresses, and telephone numbers should be recorded.
2. What happened? This is the chronological story of the theft incident. What happened before, during, and after the incident? What was taken?
3. Where? Where did the incident occur? Where was the merchandise prior to, during, and after the incident? Where were the participants throughout the incident?
4. When? When did the incident occur? Dates and times should be noted.
5. How? How did the theft take place? How was the subject able to circumvent security? How was the theft discovered? How can such an incident be prevented in the future?
6. Why? Why did the incident occur? Why did the participants act the way they did? The "why" question is difficult to answer;

however, the answers can point to underlying problems in the workplace, such as a climate of dishonesty, double standards, poor examples, a need for improved security, and so forth.

The "Why?" question can produce a motive and suspects can be eliminated. If a number of employees provide noteworthy information about one particular disgruntled employee, this individual should be among the suspects in a case.

During investigations, it is often difficult to answer all of these questions. Victims, witnesses, and suspects may be reluctant to speak. Investigators may have only a limited amount of time to gather information, as their caseload may be overwhelming. Also, the priority of each case will differ.

Investigations are not necessarily always targeted to crimes. In the private sector, several types of investigations are conducted. These include criminal, applicant background, accident, workers' compensation, fire, and civil investigations. Each type of investigation will differ as to how the inquiry is conducted and what laws are followed. An investigator may specialize in one or two types of investigations and become familiar with the techniques that produce results. Experience is the major factor that makes a successful investigator.

Investigators collect facts. Generally, they submit a report to their superiors and decisions are made based on the report. Action or inaction and punitive or nonpunitive results will follow. Management reviews the background of the investigator employed (e.g., security experience, former police officer or attorney), who or what will be investigated, budget restrictions, and what will be done with the facts collected.

Two major types of investigations in the private sector are proprietary and contract. A large retailer can afford proprietary (in-house) investigators, such as store detectives and corporate investigators. Retailers may also have proprietary undercover investigators and transfer them to different stores in their chain. For the small retailer who cannot afford and justify full-time investigators, an outside contract investigative firm can be hired for a fee. These firms (both one-person detective agencies and larger concerns) are regulated by government agencies (often the state police) to protect customers from felons and unethical business practices. Most of the major contract guard (security officers) companies have an investigative division. Contract undercover investigators are especially helpful to smaller retailers, because the retailer does not have to be concerned with where to place the contract agent (or operative) when the inquiry ends. This type of investigation is discussed in subsequent pages. Briefly, these investigators use a false background, apply at a company for a job, and, when hired, infiltrate employee informal groups to gather information on illegal activities. Top management of the client company is aware of the investigation. Secrecy is a top priority. Corporations are known to use a combination of proprietary and contract investigators.

Investigative Skills

The Legal System and Citizens' Rights

To be an effective investigator, certain skills are required as well as a foundation in specific subject matter. High on the list of prerequisites is a basic knowledge of the legal system and the rights of citizens. State and federal legislation, and court decisions, play a major role in providing legal guidelines for investigators. These sources inform investigators of what they can and cannot do. The Employee Polygraph Protection Act of 1988, for example, is a federal law that restricts private employers from using truth-detecting devices in the workplace except under strict guidelines as explained later.

Court cases establish standards that guide investigators. If a case is argued that deals with issues that are similar to an earlier case, the earlier case is often used as the standard (or precedent) to be followed. For instance, court cases in a particular state may contain the standard that a shoplifting conviction is more likely if retail personnel apprehended suspects right outside the store, rather than inside the store. This standard requires a stronger case to prove that the subject intended to shoplift and, at the same time, it requires a higher level of proof to protect the accused.

Knowledge of the Bill of Rights also provides guidance to investigators. These fundamental rights protect citizens. The Bill of Rights is, essentially, a list of rules that authorities must follow when dealing with citizens. The Fifth Amendment right against self-incrimination serves as an example. Private sector investigators, in addition to public police, must protect the rights of citizens. As stated in an earlier chapter, public police, who have greater arrest powers than private security, are limited in their actions by the Bill of Rights. On the other hand, private security personnel are basically controlled by the fear of a lawsuit. If a plaintiff is successful, a monetary award may be paid by the defendant (i.e., security personnel) to the plaintiff. Bear in mind that these statements are generalizations, because both public police and security personnel are subject to the twin threats of being arrested and sued following a critical incident.

Sources of Information

Skilled investigators know where and how to obtain information for their investigations.[2] They also know about the legal restrictions that exist to maintain an individual's privacy. Banks, hospitals, insurance companies, educational institutions, and credit bureaus contain information that must be safeguarded because of specific laws. Chapter 4 discusses some of these laws. Information accessible from libraries, professional and trade associations, and government agencies. Court records of convictions and law suits are also open to the public.

Investigators are known to use a variety of ploys and pretexts to obtain restricted information. Such behavior is unethical and illegal.

A growing source of information for investigators is the use of computer databases. Through the use of a personal computer, a modem, and E-mail, an investigator can send a request to a firm that searches hundreds of databases for information that pertains to addresses, telephone numbers, court records, convictions, lawsuits, real estate, and many other subjects. These databases are often used to screen job applicants, find missing people, and locate hidden assets. Caution is advised because information is not always accurate.

Networking is another avenue of information. Employees within the same industry often join similar organizations and call on each other for information and solutions to difficult problems. Retail security practitioners have shared information on known shoplifters, bad check passers, and other offenders. In addition, before purchasing a security service or system, it is always a good idea to check with a user who can explain positive and negative characteristics.

Investigators are often called to the scene of a loss, which is the starting point in an investigation. This could be the location where merchandise was taken during an employee theft or shoplifting incident. Evidence or clues can provide answers. For example, hangers or price tags may be on the floor. The price tags may provide information on the number and value of the missing merchandise. The scenes may also yield a victim or witness. Multiple loss scenes may produce a particular pattern used by the offender. This is called the *modus operandi* (MO) or method of operation. The MO of one pair of offenders was for one person to distract a cashier while the cash register drawer was open so the other person could quickly grab money from the cash drawer.

Surveillance is a popular tool of investigators for gathering information. Stationary surveillance requires patience, since the investigator stays in one spot for an extended period of time. In one case, a retail store detective watched a camera salesperson for five evenings while peering through a small hole in the door of a utility closet. Finally, the salesperson rang up an expensive camera for a fraction of the price. Moving surveillance is when a store detective carefully and unobtrusively follows a suspected shoplifter through a store.

Interviewing

There are certain guidelines for interviewing that are universally applied to all types of investigations. The guidelines listed here are appropriate for internal theft and shoplifting incidents.

First of all, interviews are conducted to learn the truth and gather facts. A confession from a suspect is often the objective of an interview. Prosecution may follow. It is important to point out that interviewing suspects is a primary information-gathering strategy of investigators, especially when confronting suspected employee thieves and shoplifters. If a suspect is unavailable, witnesses may be the only alternative for interviewing. Interviewing can also result in the elimination of suspects, the recovery of property and evidence, and corrective action.

Without a doubt, the skill of interviewing can make or break an investigator and an investigation. Knowing people, and interpreting what they are communicating both verbally and nonverbally, are essential to the successful conclusion of a case.

> Before beginning the interview, make sure you have the proper legal foundation to initiate an interview. (This is discussed in subsequent pages.)
> Identify and introduce yourself.
> Be polite and respectful.
> Maintain eye contact.
> Interview in an appropriate location, such as an office. Use an office that contains the bare essentials (e.g., desk and chairs) so the interviewee is not distracted.
> Always interview with a witness that is the same sex as the suspect.
> Plan the questioning process.
> Maintain documentation. Use standard company forms.
> Speak on a level that the interviewee can understand.
> Look for signs of nervousness and other nonverbal behavior that may indicate deception. Nonverbal behavior is often more reliable than verbal statements.
> Ask open-ended questions that require lengthy responses. For example: What are the crimes occurring at this location? What are the ways in which merchandise can be removed from the workplace? How could an employee in your type of position remove merchandise?
> Use silence and eye contact following an answer to force additional statements from the interviewee.
> Request that the interviewee repeat the story of the incident several times, so inconsistencies can be spotted. Bring the inconsistencies to the interviewee's attention.
> Test honesty by asking questions to which you know the answers.
> Do not jump to conclusions. Maintain an open mind.
> Listen closely.

Control the interview and maintain a positive attitude.

Appeal to the interviewee's conscience. Provide excuses to the suspect to be used to ease a confession: "Everyone makes mistakes." "Don't you want to get it out and feel better?"

Repeat important statements and crucial information to strengthen accuracy.

Watch out for ulterior motives of the interviewee.

Double check information when possible.

When speaking with witnesses, ask the same questions to several people to compare answers. If all witnesses state the same exact scenario of an incident, a conspiracy could be afoot. Witnesses usually have different perceptions of an incident. Record names, addresses, and telephone numbers.

Report Writing

The skill of report writing should not be taken lightly. Usually, in later years, security practitioners realize that they should have been more attentive to those earlier English and writing courses that provide a foundation for report writing. However, it is never too late to learn, especially since report writing has a definite impact on career opportunities.

Simply put, written reports reflect on the investigator. If the facts cannot be put down in a clear, concise, organized report, this will be noted by the supervisor during personnel evaluations. Many supervisors consider report writing a dominant factor when deciding on who gets promoted. This is so, because supervisors and managers use reports as guides to decision making and planning. A single, well-written report can solve a case and many of these reports can expose loss trends and show where security needs to be more sharply focused. If a case results in litigation, a quality report proves its value, since memories wane over time.

As we know, report writing begins with the six basic investigative questions. When encountering an incident, an investigator records facts in a small notebook or on a standard company form. Figure 8-1 shows a form used by a retail company for a variety of offenses.

If a narrative of the incident is to be prepared, first develop a rough outline to provide direction for writing. The outline should contain the facts of the incident in a logical order. Next, write in a narrative style (i.e., tell the story of the incident) and present the sequence of events in chronological order. For example: The subject was first spotted in the sporting goods department at 12:30 P.M. by a sales associate, Frank Wilson, from that department. Security was notified a few minutes later after Frank observed the subject conceal

Investigative Report

		Case Number
		Employee ☐ Non-Employee ☐

1. Name _____ Employment Date:
   Regular _____
   Title _____ Part-time _____
   Date Employment Terminated _____

2. Store _____ Address _____
   Telephone _____

3. Location of loss in store: _____
   _____
   _____

4. Employee Loss:
   a. Cash Theft   ☐ Date(s) _____ Time(s) _____ Value _____
   b. Merchandise   ☐ Date(s) _____ Time(s) _____ Value _____

5. Method Used to Accomplish the Loss:
   a. Cash Register   ☐   f. Transfer Voucher   ☐
   b. Credit Check   ☐   g. Work or Service Order ☐
   c. Markdowns   ☐   h. Credit Dept. Records   ☐
   d. Lay-Away Records ☐   i. Other: _____
   e. Work Order   ☐   _____

6. Non-Employee Loss: (For non-employee loss, fill in only pertinent data.)
   a. Shoplifting   ☐   c. Burglary   ☐   e. Till Tapping   ☐
   b. Charge Fraud   ☐   d. Confidence ☐   f. _____

7. Amount of Loss:*   8. a. Prosecution?   Yes/No
   a. Actual $_____   b. Conviction?   Yes/No
   b. Estimate* $_____   c. Sentence or explanation:
   c. Recovery or   _____
      Restitution $_____   _____
   d. Net Loss $_____   _____
                                  _____

9. Who discovered theft and how? _____
   _____
   _____ Date Discovered: _____

10. State method of theft. _____
    _____
    _____

11. Period of time theft went undetected. (Estimate if necessary) _____

12. Was collusion involved? Yes/No Name(s) _____

13. Recommendations for changes in procedure, internal audit, or security to prevent a recurrence: _____
    _____
    _____

_____   _____
Security Manager   Store Manager

*Report merchandise losses at retail price.

Description of Subject

Name _____ Alias _____
Address _____ Telephone _____
Place of Birth _____ Date of Birth _____
Sex _____ Hgt. _____ Wgt. _____ Hair _____ Eyes _____
Social Security Number _____
Scars/Marks or other I.D. _____
Occupation _____
Previous Convictions _____

Other Information _____

NOTE: Attach Photograph if Available.

Figure 8-1 Investigative Report

a pair of gloves. The subject was apprehended by security officer Joe Brown at 12:45 P.M.

Ensure that the report is factual. Avoid opinions. Be concise by getting to the point. Reread the rough draft to delete unnecessary words and sentences. Use a dictionary to check for spelling. Make sure the final report is neat and turned in on time.

Court Testimony

Most criminal and civil cases never make it to trial. For minor criminal (or civil) cases, a fine (or award for a civil case) may be paid by the defendant without attorneys being involved. In more serious cases, opposing attorneys typically negotiate and settle cases before reaching the trial stage. For those cases that do enter the courtroom, security personnel should be prepared to testify by reviewing reports. Witnesses and physical evidence may have to be coordinated. The services of an attorney are often helpful.

Always dress conservatively for court. The security uniform worn on the job is appropriate. Good grooming and hygiene help to make a professional appearance.

Courtroom demeanor is very important. Inappropriate behavior (e.g., getting angry) can cause the case to be lost. Remain calm by taking some deep breaths without being obvious. Carefully consider all questions before answering. If you are unsure of a question, ask for a repeat or an explanation. Never answer a question that is unclear or take a guess. If you bring notes to court, the opposing attorney can request that the notes become evidence in the case.

Be especially alert to tricks by opposing attorneys who will attempt to get you angry or confuse you in order to discredit your testimony. They may state your name incorrectly, ask rapid-fire questions, or claim that you are giving conflicting answers. State your name correctly, carefully answer questions, and speak the truth. Attorneys may act in a belligerent manner or may even be friendly. Remain calm, watch for their ulterior motives, and state the facts.

Investigation of Suspected Internal Losses

Let us first put the investigation of internal losses in perspective by making comparisons to shoplifting and burglary incidents. This will help you understand the strategies discussed in the rest of this chapter. Because employee-suspects have ties to the workplace through a paycheck, fringe benefits, and assorted personnel information, these individuals are usually easy to locate if they take flight. The situation is different when dealing with a shoplifter or a burglar. Their identities are difficult to ascertain if they flee.

A company investigator often has a time advantage when investigating employee-suspects (as opposed to shoplifters and burglars), because in the latter cases a limited amount of time may be available for interviewing. After a shoplifter or burglar is confronted and arrested, the justice system permits only a "reasonable" amount of time for interviewing prior to turning an offender over to public police. Because of an employee's ties to the workplace, interviewing and evidence gathering are likely to be more convenient for the company investigator and may continue over a longer period of time prior to confrontation and arrest. When we estimate the chances of a violent confrontation, the burglar and shoplifter are more likely to be a threat than the employee-suspect, although there are exceptions.

Guidelines

When investigating a suspected employee thief, consider these guidelines that foster caution and prevent liability:

- Be well versed on the retail company's written and unwritten policies and procedures concerning suspected employee theft incidents.
- Observe, take notes, and report to a supervisor. Let your supervisor decide the next move. The decision to approach a suspected employee-thief may be a management decision in your company.
- Remember that all executives perceive employee theft differently. Some want all thieves arrested and fired. Others want no part of the justice system, bad publicity, and loss of an experienced and trained worker. This latter group may simply want to know how much the employee is stealing, so a cost-benefit analysis can be computed.

Seek competent legal counsel for investigations. Consider potential liabilities, including violations of labor law, assault and battery, false imprisonment, defamation, and invasion of privacy.

Avoid wiretapping and electronic surveillance (bugging).

If a confrontation is the desired choice by management, be absolutely certain that company property has been stolen. A reliable eyewitness, a video recording, or paper trail are of the utmost importance. *Never* rely on hearsay.

Be prepared to prove intent—the item stolen is company property, it was concealed or removed from the premises, the suspect concealed or removed the company's property.

Make sure the suspect was positively observed concealing or stealing company property and that it was not purchased earlier. Maintain unbroken eye contact in case the property is ditched.

Consider a nonthreatening and congenial interview with the suspect and ask for an explanation of the questionable actions that were observed. The observed theft incident could really be a legitimate act. For example, a janitor is seen putting a picture frame in the trunk of his car. As it turns out, the janitor was doing a manager a favor and intended to fix the frame at home. For example, two retail employees are observed quickly loading their car with store merchandise. The store manager asked them to supply some out-of-stock items to another chain store. The proper paperwork was completed prior to the observation. In another example, a salesperson is observed concealing store supplies near a sales counter. This was done because during the busy holiday season, these supplies are difficult to obtain when the store is packed with customers.

Court Cases

In *DeAngelis v. Jamesway Department Store*,[1] a 17-year-old cashier was accused of theft by a co-worker. The jury awarded the plaintiff $10,300 in compensatory damages and $100,000 punitive damages for false imprisonment. The trial judge found evidence that the cashier was subjected to a four-hour ordeal, lectured about theft, shouted at, frightened, charged with theft, forced to sign a confession to a crime she did not commit, and told she had to stay in the room until she confessed. The appellate court affirmed, finding no privilege to conduct a custodial interrogation for a past crime and, even if a statutory shopkeeper's

> privilege applied, the defendant's conduct was unreasonable. *DeAngelis* contrasts with *Chapman v. Atlantic Zayre Inc.*,[2] where an employee reported seeing the plaintiff stealing money from a snack bar—the second report of such activity. That evening the plaintiff was interrogated and produced a $20.00 bill folded in the manner alleged. The trial court found that the co-worker's report provided the employer with probable cause to question the plaintiff that day, and therefore the qualified privilege was not abused.[3]
>
> *Case Citation 1:* 501 A.2d 561, 566 (N.J. Super. App. Div. 1985).
> *Case Citation 2:* 2 IER Cases 1255 (Ga. Super. Ct. 1987).

- For a union workplace, employees can request that a union representative be present during an interview. Compliance will avoid charges of unfair labor practices by the National Labor Relations Board (NLRB). (See *NLRB v. Weingarten Inc.* [1975] for more information.) The union employee can refuse the interview without representation and the employer may not discipline the union worker for refusing to cooperate without representation.
  For a nonunion workplace, the NLRB and courts have provided no definitive standard. The employer should exercise caution and not insist that a nonunion worker be subject to an interview without representation.
- When the suspect is confronted with solid evidence, interview in a private office, have a witness of the same sex present, and maintain documentation.
- Do not threaten, touch, search, or stop the suspect from leaving.
- If suspects will not give up company property that was *positively observed being concealed on their person*, try the following strategy. Request that the suspect come to a room that can be observed or recorded from an adjoining room. Ask the suspect to please wait in the room for a few minutes alone while management decides what to do. When suspects are alone, they may take the concealed items from their person and hide them in the room.
- If you want to search the suspect's belongings (without touching the suspect), request permission and get it in writing.
- For serious cases or difficult employee-suspects, consider calling public police. Let them conduct a search; this transfers liability.
- Never transport a prisoner to jail after an arrest has been made. Let the police perform this task to transfer liability.
- Ensure that a reliable employee, who witnessed the crime, signs the criminal complaint.

If suspects decide to confess, have them write out the confession completely and sign it (see Figure 8-2). Witnesses should also sign the confession. Do not offer suggestions on sentence structure, grammar, spelling, and so forth. Let the confession be the product of the offender. Such an approach looks good if litigation results. Also, request that the offender sign a statement that no force was applied or threats made to obtain the confession.[4]

Follow legal guidelines if the polygraph is used as a tool in the investigation. (See the boxed guidelines on subsequent pages.)

Consider the faults of private restitution. The subject may make a payment for stolen items, but then reverse the scenario and claim that the payment was a bribe. Or, the subject may make a few payments and never pay the balance of the loss. Private restitution may interfere with insurance indemnification. Consider restitution through the justice system; it may or may not be cost-effective. Also, check on civil recovery in your state.

Maintain strict confidentiality before, during, and after the investigation. Provide information only to those who have a need to know, such as the employee-suspect's supervisor, security, and human resources. This helps to prevent defamation charges.

Avoid keeping investigative reports in personnel files, because certain state and federal laws require employers to give employees access to personnel files.[5]

Investigative Tools: Pinhole Lens Cameras and Time-Lapse Recorders

Pinhole lens cameras (see Figure 8-3) permit covert surveillance of areas vulnerable to theft. The tiny lens conceals the camera to which they are attached and the lens can be placed in clocks, sprinkler heads, file cabinets, a ceiling, and just about anywhere. Because offenders can be very crafty and circumvent traditional CCTV and other investigative tools, pinhole lens cameras provide an advantage to security. One strategy is to place a pinhole lens camera in an area where an obvious CCTV camera is located. If employees disable the obvious camera, they can still be observed by the pinhole lens camera. To prevent morale problems, employees can be notified by entrance door stickers and signs that these cameras are used in the workplace. Also, monitoring personnel should be tactfully assigned, especially for locations such as fitting rooms where officers of the opposite sex are prohibited from making observations. Manufacturers offer switches with lockout features that deny unauthorized personnel access to certain cameras.

Statement

I, _____, after having been advised of my constitutional right to make no statement whatsoever and that any statement I do make may be used against me in a court of law and that I have a right to have an attorney present before making any statement, hereby make the following voluntary statement to _____, who has been identified as a Security Officer for _____, without having been threatened in any way or promised any reward for giving this statement:

On the _____ day of _____, 19____, at ____ AM or PM I stole from _____, the following described items for which I did not intend to pay:

_____

_____

_____

_____

_____

_____

_____

The total retail value of the stolen property listed above is _____.

Today's date: _____

State how you were able to steal, despite security. _____

_____

_____

WITNESS:

_____
Signature

_____   _____
Signature   Title

_____   _____
Signature   Title

Figure 8–2 Statement of Theft

Time-lapse recorders (see Figure 8-4) are enhanced video cassette recorders (VCRs) that store single frames of video at various intervals over an extended period of time. Total recording time can extend to hundreds of hours on one cassette. These recorders can switch to "real time" when an alarm condition occurs. Real time is 30 frames per second, while time lapse may record between one frame a second or one frame every eight seconds. In addition to providing surveillance of a sensitive area, time-lapse recorders are an excellent investigative tool. For example, they can indicate who exited from a certain door after an alarm and who was in a storage room during the evening when losses occurred. Features of time-lapse recorders include a quick search for alarm conditions during playback and playback according to the input of day and time.

Video alarm systems are another enhancement to CCTV and recorders. A video alarm system operates via a camera that sends a static picture to a memory evaluator. A change in the picture (e.g., someone entering a secure area) activates an alarm and a VCR.

One further note: Some states may prohibit certain forms of electronic surveillance. Connecticut, for example, prohibits electronic or video surveillance of any area designed for the health and comfort of employees, or for the safeguarding of their possessions, including restrooms, locker rooms, and lounges.[6]

Figure 8-3 Pinhole Lens Camera and Equipment Courtesy of Sperry-Vision Corp.

Figure 8-4 Time-Lapse Recorder Courtesy of VICON.

You Be the Judge 8-1

The Story: In investigating a suspected embezzlement, interrogators from the loss prevention department of Allied Services, Inc., grilled employee Jerry Boyle for two hours in a small, dusty, sparsely furnished back office. Although they established to their own satisfaction that he was guilty, they could not get him to make a formal confession. Therefore, Allied discharged Boyle but did not prosecute him.

Boyle was not so conciliatory. He took the company to court, alleging that the two-hour interrogation added up to *false imprisonment*.

To evaluate Boyle's claim, the judge asked him a series of questions:

At any time during the two hours had the interrogators told Boyle that he was not permitted to get up and leave the room? No, Boyle admitted, they had not.

Had they physically restrained Boyle in any way? His answer: no.

Had they touched him at all? No.

Had he been screamed at or yelled at in the interrogation? He had not.

Had the interrogators communicated any threat of force to Boyle, either in words, through body language, or by any other means? Again, no.

Had they given him any reason to fear for his safety? Once more, Boyle admitted that the answer was no.

Had they misrepresented themselves as police or any other type of law enforcement personnel? No, Boyle replied.

Had Boyle requested to have a lawyer sit in on the interrogation—or a union representative or any other witness or advisor? And if so, had the interrogators refused his request? No, on all counts.

The judge then had to decide whether Boyle had been falsely imprisoned.

Make your decision; then turn to the end of the chapter for the court's decision.

Source: "You Be the Judge," including the decisions at the end of this chapter: Reprinted with permission from *Security Management Bulletin Protecting Property, People & Assets*, a publication of Bureau of Business Practice, Inc., 24 Rope Ferry Road, Waterford, CT, 06386.

Undercover Investigations

Undercover investigations are effective in uncovering internal losses, especially when dealing with well-established collusion among employees and possibly outsiders. An overt investigator showing up at the workplace and interviewing employees about internal theft will likely produce less results than an undercover investigator who infiltrates employee informal groups. Note that investigations of union activities are illegal.

Undercover investigators may be proprietary or contract. Although the proprietary type are more familiar with the particular employer, placement problems can occur after an assignment, especially if a retail chain is small. Contract undercover investigators are cost-effective for short-term problems.

Security conducted a survey of businesses in general and found that 69 percent of those questioned in a national telephone survey conducted a covert investigation in their organization in the last year. Sixty-nine percent used in-house investigators, 9 percent used a contract service, and 22 percent used a combination of both.[7]

Undercover investigations cost about $500–$800 per week depending on the background of the investigator and the specializations required. A minimum of two to three months is usually needed to yield success. Questions to ask the contract firm include cost and estimated duration of the investigation, background of their investigators, training they receive, supervision, insurance, number of reports that will be generated and willingness to testify in court. The client should have an attorney, possibly a labor attorney, included in the negotiations.

The undercover investigator (UI) (with a phony background) will show up at the troubled location and apply for a job. Often, the store manager is aware of the investigation. This makes the hiring process much easier. The UI should be assigned to those areas likely to be the source of losses, such as shipping and receiving, and inventory control. Many aspects of the workplace are noted by the UI. A security and loss prevention survey should be done covertly. Where are the vulnerabilities? What is the condition of security? Are policies and procedures being followed? The UI can also participate in an inventory to find out if it is being done correctly. Employee groups are also infiltrated for information on losses. To increase the cost-effectiveness of the investigation, reports can contain factual information on a workplace problem, fire and safety hazards, production problems, waste, and so forth.

The investigator must exercise extreme caution in this vocation. A verbal slip or curious question can expose the UI. Any notes recorded in the workplace must be done quickly and in an isolated area. Daily records should be maintained. Three reports are usually prepared at home each week by the investigator and are sent to a supervisor. Reports are edited and the client may receive one report per week at the home of the executive overseeing the investigation. Unscrupulous contract firms may send frightening reports to the client and prolong the investigation. If investigators are put under too much pressure, they may withhold information for "dry weeks" and even fabricate information. Aside from these drawbacks from a few unscrupulous firms, undercover investigations are very effective in exposing offenders in the workplace.

When concluding the investigation, the client will make crucial decisions about what to do with the employees, if any, who have substantial criminal evidence against them. The prosecution decision is discussed in subsequent pages.

The Polygraph and the Psychological Stress Evaluator

In 1895, the famous Italian criminologist, Cesare Lombroso, first used an instrument to detect deception through changes in pulse and blood pressure. In 1921, Dr. John A. Larson advanced the polygraph to measure an additional factor—respiration. Then, in 1949, Leonard Keeler went one step further and designed an attachment to the polygraph to measure electrical changes on the surface of the skin, known as galvanic skin response.

Following a painless "hook up," the polygraph examiner asks questions while body changes are recorded on graph paper. The examiner can observe which questions cause considerable changes—a possible indication of deception. Interspersed between important questions are less important questions such as name and address. The purpose is to compare reactions. This acts as a "control" to gauge nervousness during important and less important questions.

The PSE is another deception detection device. The PSE was developed for the U.S. Army in 1964, but was rejected. The private sector then developed and patented a civilian version. No "hook up" is required for the PSE. It is actually a spectrum analyzer that measures frequencies of voice stress. A traveling pen moves over paper to record stress in the voice as questions are asked.

The criticisms aimed at these devices have focused on training, techniques, disputes among examiners themselves, regulation of examiners, validity, and invasion of privacy. Furthermore, the PSE can be used surreptitiously because it does not require a "hook up" to a person. The polygraph has more clout than the PSE, because it is more established, requires more intense training, and measures three bodily functions rather than one.

The culmination of much debate resulted in the Employee Polygraph Protection Act (EPPA) of 1988, which was passed by the U.S. Congress. In essence, the act prohibits most private employers from using any device that renders a diagnostic opinion regarding an individual's honesty. The Congressional Office of Technology Assessment estimated that two million polygraph exams had been conducted annually and 90 percent were conducted in the private sector. Following the act, the number dropped dramatically. Paper-and-pencil honesty tests and background investigations are examples of methods that have increased in usage.

The EPPA prohibits an employer from directly or indirectly forcing an employee to submit to such a test, or discriminating against an employee who refuses a test or who files a complaint under the EPPA to the U.S. Department of Labor. A civil penalty can be as high as $10,000. Also, individuals have the right to sue in federal and state courts.

Certain employees are exempt from the act, including those who work in national security organizations or defense industries; local, state, or federal governments; businesses involved with controlled substances; and specific security firms (e.g., armored car and alarm companies).

Proper Testing Procedures

In the course of a workplace investigation, an employer cannot suggest to employees the possible use of a polygraph instrument until satisfying these ten conditions:

1. **Economic loss or injury:** The employer must administer the test as part of an investigation of a *specific* incident involving economic loss or injury to the business, such as theft or sabotage.
2. **Access:** The employee who is to be tested must have had access to the property that is the subject of the investigation.

3. **Reasonable suspicion:** The employer must have a reasonable suspicion of the worker's involvement in the incident under investigation.

4. **Before the test:** An employer's failure to adhere to guidelines can void a test, and subject the employer to fines and liability.

    The employee who is to be tested must be notified in writing at least 48 hours, not counting weekends and holidays, prior to the test:

    - where and when the examination will take place.
    - the specific matter under investigation.
    - the basis for concluding that the employee had access to the property being investigated.
    - the reason the employer suspects the employee of involvement.
    - the employee's right to consult with legal counsel or an employee representative before each phase of the test.

    Also before the test, the employee must be provided:
    - oral and written notice explaining the nature of the polygraph, its physical operation and the test procedure.
    - copies of all questions that will be asked during the test.
    - oral and written notice, in language understood by the employee and bearing the employee's signature, advising the worker of his or her rights under the Act.

5. **Procedural requirements for polygraph examinations:**
    - The test must last at least 90 minutes unless the examinee terminates the test.
    - Either party, employer or employee, can record the test with the other's knowledge.
    - Questions cannot pertain to religious, political or racial matters; secular behavior; or beliefs, affiliations or lawful activities related to unions or labor organizations; and cannot be asked in a degrading or needlessly intrusive manner.
    - A worker can be excused from a test with a physician's written advisement that the subject suffers from a medical or psychological condition or is undergoing treatment that might cause abnormal responses during the examination.

- An employee has the right to consult with counsel before, during and after the examination, but not to have counsel present during the actual examination.
- An employee must be advised that his or her confessions may be grounds for firing or demotion, and that the employer may share admissions of criminal conduct with law enforcement officials.
- A worker can terminate or refuse to take a test and cannot be demoted or fired for doing so. But, the employer can demote or fire the worker if he or she has enough separate supporting evidence to justify taking that action.

6. **After the test:** Before an employer can take action against a worker based on the test results, the employee has a right to a written copy of the tester's opinion, copies of the questions and corresponding replies and an opportunity to discuss the results with the employer.

   An employee may be disciplined, fired, or demoted on the basis of the test results if the employer has supporting evidence, which can include the evidence gathered to support the decision to administer the test, to justify such action.

   Test results cannot be released to the public, only to: the employee or his or her designate; the employer; a court, government agency, arbitrator or mediator (by court order); or appropriate government agency if disclosure is admission of criminal conduct (without court order). The examiner may show test results, without identifying information, to other examiners in order to obtain second opinions.

7. **Qualifications of examiners:** An employer can be liable for an examiner's failure to meet requirements, which cover licensing, bonding or professional liability coverage, testing guidelines, and formation of opinions.

8. **Waiving employee rights:** A worker cannot be tested—even at his or her insistence—if the employer cannot meet procedural requirements and prove reasonable suspicion and access. Employees may not waive their rights under the Act except in connection with written settlement of a lawsuit or pending legal action.

9. **State law/collective bargaining agreements:** The Act does not preempt any state or local law or collective bargaining agreement that is more restrictive than the Act.

> 10. **Recordkeeping requirements:** Records of polygraph exams should be kept for at least three years by the employer and the examiner, who must make them available—within 72 hours upon request—to the Department of Labor.
>
> *Source:* U. S. Chamber of Commerce.

Prosecution Decision for Internal Theft Cases

The firing and prosecution of an employee-thief rids the workplace of continued losses. When caught, offenders frequently state that it was the only time they stole or it was the first time they stole. However, multiple thefts over an extended period of time can add up to huge losses. When an employee-thief is fired and prosecuted it sets an example both inside and outside of the company. Fear of the consequences if caught does play a role in reducing losses.

Civil recovery is an avenue for the employer who has been victimized by an employee-thief. Basically, money damages are sought from the offender. State civil demand statutes often refer to shoplifting incidents; however, workplace theft by employees may be part of these statutes.

There are many business executives who do not view prosecution as cost-effective. They see involvement in the criminal justice process as an inconvenience and wasteful, because their time and the time of their employees is not being expended on the business. The possibility of being sued is another concern, as is bad publicity. Firing the employee-offender appears to be the best strategy, according to this perspective. Furthermore, prosecutors may be unable to prosecute internal thieves, especially for minor crimes, because of limited resources.

There are certain regulated industries in which management is legally obligated to report theft. For example, retailers who are victimized by theft of controlled substances or firearms are required by law to report these crimes to appropriate law enforcement agencies.

Another management view is to retain the employee-offender after minor discipline has been meted out. The rationale for this approach is that the investment in an experienced and trained employee will be lost if that employee is fired.

In certain businesses, management is primarily concerned with how much is being stolen by employee thieves. Undercover investigators can estimate these figures. When employee-offenders steal more than their value to the business, then management reconsiders the decision to fire the employee. This is strictly a business decision.

According to attorneys Shepard and Duston, employee theft is a casualty loss that is deductible under the Internal Revenue Code if the loss exceeds $100 for each event and the loss is not covered by insurance or some other compensation. Such a loss has been broadly construed to include larceny, robbery, burglary, embezzlement, extortion, kidnap ransom, and blackmail. No criminal indictment and conviction is necessary to deduct the loss if the thief confesses. Legal and related expenses may also be deducted for efforts at recovering money included in taxable income. Seek the assistance of a tax specialist.[8]

Investigation of Suspected Shoplifting

Guidelines

Many of the same cautious techniques used when investigating and confronting a suspected employee-thief are applicable to shoplifting cases. The least intrusive approach is always best, because if a mistake is made by security, the problem is easier to rectify.

- When a suspected shoplifter is spotted, *never take your eyes off of the subject.* If you are observing the sales floor from, for instance, a stock room vantage point, contact a co-worker on the sales floor to maintain eye contact as you walk toward the suspect. This coordination ensures that the suspect will be observed if merchandise is concealed, ditched, or hidden.
- Prior to approaching a suspect, make sure you *see the suspect take the store merchandise off the shelf and conceal it.* This eyewitness account is good probable cause. To illustrate a mistake: John Smith, a customer, walks past the aspirin counter, which reminds him of his headache. He takes a previously purchased aspirin bottle out of this pocket, takes two aspirin, and returns the bottle to his pocket. Unfortunately, he is arrested for shoplifting based on surveillance that began while John Smith was returning the bottle to his pocket. He is found not guilty in criminal court and, following a civil suit, an out-of-court settlement is made for $25,000.
- Be prepared to prove intent (i.e., the merchandise belongs to the store, it was concealed on the person, and removed from the premises). Although certain state shoplifting statutes permit detention as soon as the suspect conceals an item, greater weight is given to the case when the suspect passes the cash register and is approached right after going out the door. Always check on the local prosecutor's requirements.

If there is uncertainty is the case or eye contact has not been maintained, never approach the suspect. Be careful of the false arrest ploy. An offender may conceal an item when a salesperson is looking, but by the time security arrives, the concealed item is back on the shelf. An arrest is made and then the subject sues for false arrest.

Never confront a suspect based on an unreliable witness, especially a customer. Depending on state statutes, only retail employees may have the legal authority to make a shoplifting arrest.

If a suspect switches a price tag, this is considered shoplifting. Check the state shoplifting statute.

If a suspect wears an item out of the store, bring it to their attention. This type of case can be difficult when trying to prove intent. A jury may favor the defendant's story.

When you approach the suspect, identify yourself and ask them to accompany you and another employee to an office to discuss a matter. Always approach with one or more employees.

Always have one employee follow behind in case the suspect attempts to ditch merchandise.

Never make an accusation, shout, state anything derogatory, or threaten the suspect. This can result in a slander suit.

Avoid touching the suspect. If the suspect flees, avoid a physical confrontation; it is not cost-effective. Obtain a good description, even if you have to go to the parking lot with a co-worker to seek vehicle information. Contact public police immediately.

Have a witness of the same sex as the suspect present at all times.

On entering the office, ask for a receipt. Also, ask for identification, which may be phony.

The major purposes in questioning a suspect are to recover all merchandise, obtain a confession, and obtain the suspect's signature on the civil release form.

Ask the suspect to hand over the concealed merchandise. Avoid a search. For difficult suspects, try the strategy stated in the employee theft section of this chapter (i.e., the suspect, left alone in an observed room, may hide the concealed merchandise). Another approach is to call the police so they can perform a search. This transfers liability. When the police arrive, the merchandise better be concealed on the suspect as observed with unbroken eye contact!

If the suspect requests to use the restroom, this could be a ploy to ditch evidence and destroy the case. A lawsuit may follow. Delay for a limited amount of time. If necessary, allow the restroom

- visit, but have at least three employees of the same sex accompany the suspect.
- Interview for a reasonable amount of time. Miranda rights are generally not required. However, in a West Virginia Supreme Court case, the court overturned a shoplifting conviction because of the increasing role in the enforcement of criminal laws by security forces. In this case, security refused the suspect access to an attorney.[9] Many private security personnel state the Miranda warnings even though the U.S. Supreme Court has not required private security practitioners to do so. Any involuntary confession will be inadmissible in court.
- Check the suspect against a list of recidivists maintained by the merchants' protection association, if a list is available.
- Document the incident completely. Use standard company forms (see Figures 8-5 to 8-7 for examples).
- During questioning, try to learn about store vulnerabilities and any "regulars" who shoplift at the store.
- Juveniles are usually handled differently than adults. Consult local authorities.
- Avoid arresting an accomplice unless there was actual participation in the shoplifting incident. Mere presence is not sufficient proof of a crime.
- Never accept money from the suspect.
- State statutes often refer to a merchant's privilege to detain shoplifters to investigate the ownership of merchandise. Detention is supported by probable cause (e.g., an eyewitness viewing of concealed merchandise). All actions by the merchant must be reasonable, and only a reasonable time span for interviewing and processing of the subject is permitted. The key distinction between detention and arrest is that in the former, the police are not called and the subject is not turned over to the police. Detention can develop into an arrest. Both require probable cause.
- If an arrest is made, the police must be called to transport the prisoner to jail. Avoid transporting the prisoner yourself because of the potential liability.
- In arrest situations, make sure the criminal complaint is signed by a reliable store employee who witnessed the shoplifting incident.
- Before the detained subject is released by the store, the security specialist should ask the subject to sign a civil release form (see Figure 8-6). These forms vary and contain some or all of the following: basic identifying information about the subject and the incident, a confession, the merchandise taken and its value, a

Shoplifting Report

Store: _____ Date: _____

Address: _____ Time statement started: _____ a.m. / p.m.

This statement is made voluntarily of my own free will; no one has threatened or in any way enticed me with any promises to make it.

_____
(Signature of Person Giving Statement)

I, _____(suspect's name)_____, do reside at _____(address)_____. While in the above-named store, on _____(date)_____, I was stopped inside/outside the store, by _____
(name of employee, owner, manager, or security officer)
_____ who did identify himself/herself first.

While in the above-named store on ____(date)____, at or about _____ a.m. / p.m., I did appropriate to my own use the item(s) listed below without first paying for, or intending to pay for, or obtaining the owner's permission:

Quantity	Item	Value

I fully understand this statement and realize that it may be used against me in a court of law.

_____
(Signature of Person Giving Statement)

Witnesses: _____   _____
                 (Signature)   (Signature)

Time Statement Finished: _____ a.m. / p.m.   Date: _____

Race	Sex	DOB	Ht.	Wt.	Build	Compl.	Hair	Eyes	Scars/Marks

Occupation _____ Employer _____ Spouse _____

Vehicle Used _____ Make _____ Model _____ Color _____ Body Style _____ License No. _____

Juvenile (Yes/No) _____ School Attends _____ Grade _____

Parents/Guardians _____ Address _____ Telephone _____

Notified by Whom _____ How Notified _____ Date, Time Notified _____

Figure 8-5 Shoplifting Report

statement that no force was applied or threats made, a statement that cooperation was voluntary, and a statement that the subject agrees not to sue. The form is often used in conjunction with a shoplifting incident form. Civil release forms actually provide

Release from Liability

I, _____, on _____ do freely and of my own volition wish to create and execute the following instrument of release.

I have been fully acquainted with the facts surrounding the detention of _____ _____ on _____ for _____ _____ at Smith Store #6. I fully understand and fully agree that the agents of Smith Store #6 who detained _____ for _____ had complete and adequate probable cause to do so and that said detention was conducted in a reasonable and professional manner and for a reasonable period of time. I am in total agreement that the entire affair has been handled reasonably and fairly and has been concluded in the best interests of all parties concerned.

In view of all of the above I, _____, do therefore, voluntarily, with no threats, pressure or coercion having been used against me, release Smith Store #6, its affiliates, agents, and employees from any and all, present and future, civil and criminal liabilities arising from the above named incident which occurred on _____ at Smith Store #6.

In affirmative acknowledgement of all the above I _____ do voluntarily affix my signature as witnessed below.

_____ date _____

Witnessed by: _____ date _____

_____ date _____

Figure 8–6 Release from Liability

limited protection against civil liability. The subject may believe he/she cannot sue. An attorney can argue that the store's forms were signed by the subject while under duress and intensive questioning. Some courts are rejecting the way in which these releases are being used. The following questions are being asked: Is an innocent person's freedom being restricted until the release is signed? Is the person being detained for an unreasonable amount of time? Is a release a contract? If so, contracts must be voluntary by all parties.[10] Aside from these drawbacks, releases are used extensively.

Notice of Prohibited Entry

To _____:

You are hereby placed on notice that you have been forbidden and prohibited from re-entering the premises of, the parking lot adjacent to, and all facilities under the control and ownership of _____, located at _____, for a period of _____, effective as of the _____ day of _____, 19_____.

If you re-enter said property during the period described, you will be *SUBJECT TO PROSECUTION* under the criminal trespass laws of _____ which provide in part:

(Insert photocopy of appropriate state code—see attached)

Served this _____ day of _____, 19_____.

_____
(Company Name)

By: _____
    Agent-Title:

Witness: _____

I, _____, hereby acknowledge receipt of this Notice of Prohibited Entry, understand its effect and meaning and knowingly and voluntarily waive all defenses to admission of this Notice of Prohibited Entry in any subsequent criminal prosecution for trespass.

This _____ day of _____, 19_____.

_____

Witnessed by:

_____

Figure 8-7 Notice of Prohibited Entry

- Always maintain a charge of shoplifting rather than larceny, because shoplifting statutes are designed to protect merchants when investigating suspected cases. Sometimes, competition among courts for fines results in charges being changed without considering legal protection for the merchant.
- It is important to point out that whatever guidelines and protection are afforded in a state shoplifting statute, the final decision on the legality and reasonableness of a merchant's actions may rest with a jury in criminal and civil court. A conviction is a good defense against a civil suit.

If a Retailer's Liability Release Was Signed by a Shoplifting Suspect under Duress, Is It Still Valid and Can the Release Be Used by the Retailer as a Defense to a Claim of False Arrest and Imprisonment?

Customer Jackie Ross was observed attempting to conceal two VCR tapes by Wal-Mart employees. Also, she was observed putting a blue shirt and a tube of lip balm in her purse. A Wal-Mart employee stopped her after she went through the checkout line and loudly accused her of attempting to steal. After Ross was taken to an upstairs office, a search of her jacket revealed the lip balm.

Ross claimed that she was threatened with arrest and forced to sign a "release." She was told that the release would simply provide for her release from the custody of the Wal-Mart representatives. Ross also claimed that her mother's request to use the telephone to call an attorney was denied and that if an attorney were called, Ross would be arrested.

The court rejected Wal-Mart's contention that Ross was barred from bringing suit because she signed the release. This was based on the evidence that she was intimidated, deprived of her own free will to make a decision, and signed the release under duress.

The court did find that Wal-Mart may have established a defense against the false imprisonment claim by showing probable cause based on the store employee who saw Ross put the lip balm in her purse.

The court dropped a slander charge and supported Wal-Mart's contention that the statements made by its employee, accusing Ross of stealing, were qualifiedly privileged. Wal-Mart argued that the statements were privileged because they were made while the employee was investigating a criminal matter. The court agreed that the accusation is privileged unless it is made with malice.

The major point of this case is that a release is to be signed without the appearance of threatening the suspect. Otherwise, the release may be invalidated.

This case was summarized from the *Private Security Case Law Reporter*, Vol. XVI, Issue 4, April 1990 (Stafford Pub., Atlanta, GA). *Case Citation:* Jackie Ross v. Wal-Mart Stores, Inc., Civ. A. No. 89–2084–0, in the U.S. District Court for the District of Kansas, decided January 17, 1990, reported at 730 F. Supp. 347.

Virginia Shoplifting Statute

§ 18.2-103. Concealing or taking possession of merchandise; altering price tags; transferring goods from one container to another; counseling, etc., another in performance of such acts.—Whoever, without authority, with the intention of converting goods or merchandise to his own or another's use without having paid the full purchase price thereof, or of defrauding the owner of the value of the goods or merchandise, (i) willfully conceals or takes possession of the goods or merchandise of any store or other mercantile establishment, or (ii) alters the price tag or other price marking on such goods or merchandise, or transfers the goods from one container to another, or (iii) counsels, assists, aids or abets another in the performance of any of the above acts, shall be deemed guilty of larceny and upon conviction thereof shall be punished as provided in § 18.2-104. The willful concealment of goods or merchandise of any store or other mercantile establishment, while still on the premises thereof, shall be prima facie evidence of an intent to convert and defraud the owner thereof out of the value of the goods or merchandise. (Code 1950, § 18.1-126; 1960, c. 358; 1970, c. 652; 1975, cc. 14,15.)

§ 18.2-104. Punishment for conviction under § 18.2-103.—(a) Any person convicted for the first time of an offense under § 18.2-103, when the value of the goods or merchandise involved in the offense is less than $200, shall be guilty of a Class 1 misdemeanor.

(b) Any person convicted of an offense under § 18.2-103, when the value of the goods or merchandise involved in the offense is less than $200, and it is alleged in the warrant or information on which he is convicted, and admitted, or found by the jury or judge before whom he is tried, that he has been before convicted in the Commonwealth of Virginia for the like offense, regardless of the value of the goods or merchandise involved in the prior conviction, or for a violation of § 18.2-95 or § 18.2-96, shall be confined in jail not less than thirty days nor more than twelve months; and for a third, or any subsequent offense, he shall be guilty of a Class 6 felony.

(c) Any person convicted of an offense under § 18.2-103, when the value of the goods or merchandise involved in the offense is $200 or more, shall be guilty of a Class 5 felony. (Code 1950, § 18.1-126.1; 1970,c. 652; 1975, cc. 14, 15; 1980, c. 174; 1987, c. 178.)

§ 18.2-104.1. Liability upon conviction under § 18.2-103.—Any person who has been convicted of violating the provisions of § 18.2-103 shall be *civilly liable* to the owner for the retail value of any goods and merchandise illegally converted and not recovered by the owner, and for all costs incurred in prosecuting such person under the provisions of 18.2-103. Such costs shall be limited to actual expenses, including the base wage of one employee acting as a witness for the Commonwealth and suit costs. Provided, however, the total amount for allowable costs granted hereunder shall not exceed $250, excluding the retail value of the goods and merchandise. (1976,c. 577.)

§ 18.2-105. Exemption from civil liability in connection with arrest or detention of suspected person.—A merchant, agent or employee of the merchant, who causes the arrest or detention of any person pursuant to the provisions of § 18.2-95 or § 18.2-96 or § 18.2-103, shall not be held civilly liable for unlawful detention, if such detention does not exceed one hour, slander, malicious prosecution, false imprisonment, false arrest, or assault and battery of the person so arrested or detained, whether such arrest or detention takes place on the premises of the merchant, or after close pursuit from such premises by such merchant, his agent or employee, provided that, in causing the arrest or detention of such person, the merchant, agent or employee of the merchant, had at the time of such arrest or detention probable cause to believe that the person had shoplifted or committed willful concealment of goods or merchandise. The activation of an electronic article surveillance device as a result of a person exiting the premises or an area within the premises of a merchant where an electronic article surveillance device is located shall constitute probable cause for the detention of such person by such merchant, his agent or employee, provided such person is detained only in a reasonable manner and only for such time as is necessary for an inquiry into the circumstances surrounding the activation of the device, and provided that clear and visible notice is posted at each exit and location within the premises where such a device is located indicating the presence of an antishoplifting or inventory control device. For purposes of this section "electronic article surveillance device" means an electronic device designed and operated for the purpose of detecting the removal from the premises, or a protected area within such premises, of specially marked or tagged merchandise. (Code 1950, § 18.1-127; 1960, c. 358; 1975, cc. 14, 15; 1976, c. 515; 1980, c. 149; 1985, c. 275.)

§ 18.2-105.1. Detention of suspected shoplifter.—A merchant, agent or employee of the merchant, who has probable cause to believe that a person has shoplifted in violation of §§ 18.2-95 or 18.2-96 or 18.2-103, on the premises of the merchant, may detain such person for a period not to exceed one hour pending arrival of a law-enforcement officer. (1976, c. 515.)

§ 18.2-105.2. Manufacture, sale, etc., of devices to shield against electronic detection of shoplifting prohibited; penalty.—It shall be unlawful to manufacture, sell, offer for sale, distribute or posses any specially coated or laminated bag or other device primarily designed and intended to shield shoplifted merchandise from detection by an anti-theft electronic alarm sensor, with the intention that the same be used to aid in the shoplifting of merchandise. A violation of this section shall be punishable as a Class 3 misdemeanor. (1984, c. 386.)

Source: State of Virginia Statutes, Office of the Attorney General.

North Dakota Retail Theft Act

51-21-02. Presumption. Any person concealing upon his person or among his belongings, or causing to be concealed upon the person or among the belongings of another, unpurchased merchandise displayed, held, offered, or stored for sale in a retail mercantile establishment and removing it to a point beyond the last station for receiving payments in the retail mercantile establishment shall be prima facie presumed to have so concealed such merchandise with the intention of permanently depriving the merchant of possession or of the full retail value of such merchandise.

51-21-03. Detention of suspect—Procedure. Any peace officer or merchant who reasonably believes that a person has committed, or is in the process of committing, theft may detain such person, on or off the premises of a retail mercantile establishment, in a reasonable manner and for a reasonable length of time for all or any of the following purposes:

1. To require the person to identify himself.
2. To verify such identification.
3. To determine whether such person has in his possession unpurchased merchandise and, if so, to recover such merchandise.
4. To inform a peace officer of the detention of the person and surrender custody of that person to a peace officer.
5. In the case of a minor, to inform a peace officer, the parents, guardian, or other private person interested in the welfare of that minor of:

51-21-04. Civil and criminal immunity for acts of detention. Any peace officer or merchant who detains any person as permitted under section 51-21-03 may not be held civilly or criminally liable for any claim for relief allegedly arising from such detention.

51-21-05. Civil remedy against adult shoplifters or the parent of a minor shoplifter. An adult who commits the offense of theft from a merchant is civilly liable to the merchant for the retail value of the merchandise, plus exemplary damages of not more than two hundred fifty dollars, costs of suit, and reasonable attorney's fees. The parent or legal guardian of an unemancipated minor who while living with the parent or legal guardian commits the offense of theft from a merchant is civilly liable to the merchant for the retail value of the merchandise, plus exemplary damages of not more than two hundred fifty dollars, costs of suit, and reasonable attorney's fees. A conviction or plea of guilty for the theft is not a prerequisite to the bringing of a suit hereunder. A parent or legal guardian of an unemancipated minor is not civilly liable under this section if it is determined by the court that one of the principal rationales for the shoplifting was a desire on the part of the minor to cause his parent or legal guardian to be liable under this section.

Source: State of North Dakota Statues, Office of the Attorney General.

Prosecution Decision for Shoplifting Cases

Many views exist on the benefits and detriments of prosecuting suspected shoplifters. The deterrent value of prosecution and its cost-effectiveness have met with considerable debate.

Retail businesses are known to maintain a strict prosecution policy at one period of time and then to relax the policy after being subjected to an expensive law suit. A soft economy and tight budgets also influence retail management's views on investments in security and prosecution. With pressure on security management to show an ROI, it may be difficult to prove the value of prosecution in financial terms. Certain retail businesses simply *claim* to have a tough prosecution policy (and communicate this to employees and customers), but in reality they do not. The purpose of this approach is to obtain as much use as possible from the psychological and deterrent value of "tough talk."

An article in *Security Management* concerning the prosecution decision, made the following observations:

The Pennsylvania Retailers Association reports that only one apprehension in ten results in arrest.

The Police Foundation (Washington, DC) found in their research that in 40 large metropolitan stores, 39 percent of all shoplifters were released without arrest.

A research study by the Police Foundation with funding from the National Institute of Justice found that for the majority of shoplifters, arrest had no deterrent effect on subsequent shoplifting offenses.

There is a need to apply arrest sanctions selectively.[11]

It is advised by one retail security specialist to prosecute only in certain situations—when the subject has no identification, resists store personnel, appears to be under the influence of drugs or alcohol, is known to have a prior criminal record, or is involved in the theft of expensive items.[12]

Another factor concerning prosecution is that the criminal justice system cannot handle all cases. Prosecutors and courts have limited resources and prioritize cases. For those cases that are prosecuted, publicizing such cases can deter others.

Prevention appears to be more cost-effective than an unwavering prosecution policy. A simple, "May I help you?" is an inexpensive beginning of a shoplifting prevention program.

Retail employees and security personnel who are eyewitnesses to shoplifting incidents provide the foundation for probable cause, which supports an arrest warrant. Their signatures on a complaint are essential for a successful case. Those working in the justice system are interested in facts. Depending on the jurisdiction, and the monetary amount of the theft, a preliminary hearing (also called a *probable cause hearing*) may be conducted to provide a judge or magistrate with an opportunity to review evidence. If the evidence is sufficient, a trial may occur. However, a trial is the exception. Most arrestees pay a fine or plea bargain (i.e., plead guilty to a lesser charge). Most court cases involving the prosecution of a shoplifter are resolved without requiring the witness—the apprehending loss prevention agent or store employee—to make an appearance in court.[13]

The security practitioner must ascertain jurisdiction requirements concerning evidence. Eyewitness testimony is crucial.

> Pictures of the shoplifter and the stolen merchandise should be taken and marked with the police case number and the police officer and the apprehending store personnel's initials.[14]

Physical evidence should be properly labeled, preserved, and stored. Photographing evidence is customary, especially if merchandise is perishable.

You Be the Judge 8–2

The Story: "Billy, you're driving Mommy crazy! If I give you some potato chips, will you please keep your hands off the shelves?" Shopper Peg Atherton took a small bag of the snacks from a display rack, opened it, and handed it to her toddler in the supermarket cart. Minutes later, when little Billy finished his greasy treat, Atherton stuffed the empty bag into the side pocket of her purse, intending to pay for it at the checkout, along with her other purchases.

The chips slipped her mind, however, and she paid for everything but them. As she approached the store exit, leading her tyke with one hand and hefting her large grocery sack with the other arm, the store security officer materialized out of nowhere and blocked her way. "If you don't mind, ma'am," he said gruffly, "I'd like to see your receipt. I don't think you paid for those potato chips that your kid ate."

Atherton realized her mistake and offered to go back and pay. The guard would have none of that. He took her to a back room and gave her a statement to sign. Cowed and confused, Atherton complied. While she signed, the security man sarcastically said, "You gonna cry? Hope not—someone swiped my tissues." In incredulity, Atherton shook her head, then led her tot from the store.

When she reached home, shaken and fighting back tears, her phone was ringing. It was the store security officer. "Hiya, Mrs. Atherton. Guess what! You left the potato chip bag here on my desk. Just wondered if you want it. Y'know—as a souvenir? Heh, heh." And he hung up.

After simmering for an hour or so in mortification, disbelief, and fury, Atherton flipped open the Yellow Pages to the "Attorneys" section. She sued the store for false imprisonment. What happened?

Make your decision; then turn to the end of the chapter for the court's decision.

Source: "You Be the Judge," including the decisions at the end of this chapter: Reprinted with permission from *Security Management Bulletin—Protecting Property, People & Assets*, a publication of Bureau of Business Practice, Inc., 24 Rope Ferry Road, Waterford, CT, 06386.

Civil Recovery

Civil recovery statutes in many states permit retailers to recover damages from shoplifters. It is much like taking (or threatening to take) someone to small claims court. These laws often extend to employee-thieves in businesses. Offenders can be held liable for attorney fees, court costs, and security expenses up to triple the damages. Basically, the losses attributed to theft are passed on to the offender.

Before seeking civil recovery, it is better to secure a guilty verdict. Civil recovery without prosecution *may* result in a lawsuit against the retailer because the case has not been proven in a court of law. Also, civil recovery may cause increased shoplifting, because the subject avoids the embarrassment of police and court system contact, plus a fine and criminal record. This civil recovery avenue results in the subject not being fingerprinted, photographed, or incarcerated.

For the retailer, civil recovery involves sending the shoplifter a demand letter (see Figure 8-8) and a copy of the state's civil recovery law. If a response is not received, a second letter is sent that informs the offender of civil court action for nonpayment. A third letter may follow. Further efforts will depend on the probability of recovery and the amount in question. Is it cost-effective to invest in additional action? Is it likely that the offender can afford to pay? How has the local court system cooperated with retailers?

A retailer can try two basic approaches to civil recovery—in-house or contract. Many retailers relinquish this administrative effort and permit an outside service firm to handle it. One firm charges 35 percent of the money collected and claims that 40–50 percent of shoplifters make some type of payment. The amount requested from a shoplifter is generally in the range of $50–$1,000, depending on state law, the value of the merchandise, the penalty, court costs, and attorney's fees.[15]

Apprehensions of Dishonest Employees and Shoplifters

The National Retail Security Survey (1991) by *Security* Magazine (which consists of more than 400 respondents) offers the following figures on methods used to apprehend dishonest employees and shoplifters.

To Apprehend Dishonest Employees

Method	Percentage
Exception Reports	35.1
Random Security Audits	20.0
Tipoff By Co-Worker	31.1
CCTV	12.8

To Apprehend Shoplifters

Method	Percentage
Floor Employees	55.0
Security Personnel	28.6
CCTV	8.7
Electronic Tags	5.1
Customers	3.6

Source: © 1992. *Security* Magazine. "National Retail Security Survey 1991," p. 10. Reprinted with permission.

Investigation of Suspected Shoplifting

Adult Demand Letter

(Store Name) _____

(Store Address) _____

_____

(Subject's Name) _____

(Subject's Address) _____

_____

Dear _____:

    This store has a report showing that on _____(date)_____, you took from us _____(list stolen items)_____ without permission, without paying for them, and to use them as your own.

    State law provides that we can demand that you pay these penalties:

for any *damages*	$_____
the *selling price* of the stolen items (even if we have recovered the items)	$_____
a *penalty* of no less than $100 and no more than $200	$_____
TOTAL AMOUNT DEMANDED	$_____

    This letter is our demand. A copy of the state law allowing this demand is attached. Please send your check or money order to _____(store name & address)_____

_____

If you do not pay by _____(date)_____, we will take this demand to civil court.

    This demand is made by this store. IMPORTANT NOTICE: The payment of any penalty demanded of you by this store does not prevent criminal prosecution under a related criminal provision and does not prevent any fines or punishment which may be handed out by the criminal courts.

    If you disagree with this demand, you may wish to contact _____(store contact)_____ _____(phone)_____. You may also wish to talk to a private attorney. If you do not pay this demand, we will file a court action. You will then have a chance to defend your position in civil court.

_____
(Signed by store owner, manager or representative)

Figure 8–8 Adult Demand Letter

Case Problems

8A. As a retail security officer, you observe a maintenance worker quickly place a typewriter in the trunk of his car and then rush back into the store. What do you do?

8B. As a store detective, you find two new radios in the garbage dumpsters behind the store. What do you do?

8C. As a store security manager, you receive an anonymous tip that the store's evening camera salesperson is selling cameras at a fraction of the sale price. What will you do? You also receive a tip that a contract security officer at the store is punching employee time cards for a fee, so that employees can leave early. What will you do?

8D. As a store detective on duty, you notice a woman shopper holding a bottle of perfume. She sprays herself and places the bottle in her pocketbook. What do you do? List your actions step by step.

8E. As a store security manager, you are informed by the store manager that he has received two complaints from angry customers who were stopped for shoplifting, then released due to lack of evidence. What will you do to stop this? To top off your day, you get another phone call—this time from the Corporate Director of Security. She's called to tell you that the company has just been slapped with another lawsuit (the fifth that year for the company and the third that year for your store) for bad shoplifting arrests. How will you clean up store security procedures?

8F. As a regional security manager, how will you respond to the following memo?

Memorandum

TO: Fred Jones, Regional Security Manager
FROM: Ralph Johnson, Corp. Director of Security
SUBJECT: Highest and Lowest Shrinkage Stores in Your Region
DATE: February 22, 1992

Please study the figures below and respond on March 10 when we meet at Store #17 at 3:00 P.M.

Store #	City	Miles from Your Home	Shrinkage (Percent)
17	Columbia	250	3.4
14	Hampton	180	2.8
12	Lake City	120	2.7

9	Florence	55	1.8
4	Chester	30	1.9
11	Newton	15	1.9

Answers to You Be the Judge

8-1. Boyle's suit failed. He had not been falsely imprisoned. In most states, false imprisonment means using force, threat of force, or misrepresentation to restrain someone's freedom of movement. Boyle was subjected to nothing of the sort. However, if you interrogate suspects in internal investigations, you definitely should consult your company lawyer about what your statutes allow. Laws differ from state to state. Missteps can make confessions inadmissible in court and, in some cases, can make a company liable. (This case has been fictionalized for dramatic effect and to protect the privacy of those involved.) *Case Citation:* Maietta v. United Parcel Service, Inc., 749 F. Supp. 1344 (D.N.J. 1990).

8-2. Atherton won her suit. The jury clobbered the supermarket chain not only for general damages but also for an even higher amount of *punitive* damages—and the inference was clear that the reason for the punitive award was the security officer's incredibly ill-considered behavior, which the plaintiff's lawyer characterized in court as "malicious and wanton." Retail security personnel who are untrained in how to treat a detained shoplifting suspect can become unexpectedly hefty items in a store's operating overhead. (This case has been fictionalized for dramatic effect and to protect the privacy of those involved.) *Case Citation:* Webster v. Dieringer's Variety, Inc., 734 P.2d 402 (Or.App. 1987).

Notes

1. For further information, see: Philip P. Purpura, *Security Handbook* (Albany, NY: Delmar Publishing, 1991), 149-154.
2. For further information, see: Wayne W. Bennett and Karen M. Hess, *Criminal Investigation*, 3rd ed. (St. Paul, MN: West Publishing, 1991), 217-253.
3. Ira M. Shepard and Robert Dustin, *Thieves at Work* (Washington, DC: The Bureau of National Affairs, 1988), 140.

4. For further information, see: Chapter 9, "Interrogations, Confessions, and Evidence Recoveries," and J. Kirk Barefoot, *Employee Theft Investigation*, 2nd ed. (Boston: Butterworth–Heinemann, 1990), 115–136.
5. Shepard and Duston, 134.
6. Ibid., 158.
7. "Covert Investigations Uncover Inside Crime," *Security* (April 1990): 67–68.
8. Shepard and Duston, 271.
9. "Do Our Store's Security Guards Have to Read Shoplifters Their Miranda Rights?" *Corporate Security* (April 1988): 5.
10. "The Trouble with Releases," *Security Management—Protecting Property, People & Assets* (October 10, 1986): 6.
11. Hubert Williams, "Stop: Should You Arrest That Person?" *Security Management* (September 1987): 52–58.
12. Thomas E. Crowley, "Attention, Shoppers: Shoplifting Program in Effect," *Security Management* (September 1988): 125.
13. For an excellent article on how to prepare for a trial, see: Roger Griffin, "Prosecuting Shoplifters," *Security Management* (March 1989): 55–60.
14. Douglas C. Espinosa, "Shoplifters: No Sale," *Security Management* (May 1989): 67–68.
15. Delany J. Stinson, "Attention, Retailers: Civil Law Provides A Tonic," *Security Management* (September 1988): 129–132.

9

Store Design and Physical Security

Store Location and Design

Store Location

Retailers are constantly searching for new locations to expand their businesses. Examples include downtown locations and enclosed malls in suburban areas. Although site selection has evolved into a science, one of the most frequent causes of failure of new retail stores is management error in locating the store. The small, independent retailer often does not subject a proposed site to scientific evaluation.[1] In fact, most independent retailers rely more on intuition than on careful study.[2]

Large retail organizations approach the location decision by employing analysts who use rating instruments and computer models that consider numerous factors such as the following:

- an area's population
- socioeconomic status of residents
- general economic conditions of the area
- buying needs of homeowners as opposed to renters
- accessibility to the site and parking availability
- nearby facilities, such as a park, stadium, office buildings, and a manufacturing plant
- available advertising media
- adequate labor force
- trends of the area

Once the area has been selected, a decision is made on the shopping district. Among the alternatives are the central business district in a city, the suburban shopping malls, or free-standing stores located on major roads. A security specialist can research several factors as input for site selection and construction:

Check area crime rates through the local police department and the *Uniform Crime Report.*

Solicit input from the local police crime prevention officer. Are there any security building codes for the jurisdiction?

What is the ratio of public police to residents in the jurisdiction? Generally, there are one or two police officers per 1,000 residents.

How often do police patrol a site?

What is the distance from police and fire agencies?

What is the condition and intensity of municipal lighting in the area?

Check the site both during the day and at night. Is it desolate at night? Are any people "hanging around" on the street? A site that is busy both day and night increases the chances that crimes will be prevented and reported.

Are other businesses in the area? What are the store hours and levels of security? Ask the retailers about the crime rate. Check with local security managers.

Use a security consultant if necessary.

Is there any potential for disaster in the area—either natural (e.g., flood) or man-made (e.g., explosion).

Store Design

Because of so much competition, retailers are increasingly concentrating on store design to generate business. Merchandise displays, fixtures, lighting, and internal traffic configuration are some of the areas considered by retailers to create innovative store personalities that differentiate their store from others. As with the decision on store location, store design involves scientific planning.

A store's exterior is advertisement that must not only attract attention, but also hold the attention of those traveling by. The exterior facade of many retail businesses aims to accomplish this objective with carefully designed signs, windows, awnings, and entrances. One strategy used at malls is called the "open front." It consists of no barrier between passing shoppers and the store, which permits very easy access. These stores are protected overnight by gates. Parking facilities are vital to a store's exterior, because an attractive store with limited parking spaces hinders sales.

Careful attention is given to the interior of modern stores. The term *atmospherics* is used to describe the conscious designing of a store to affect customers and increase sales. This is facilitated through the wise selection of specific materials and colors for walls, floors, and ceilings. Research shows that warm colors (red and particularly yellow) are good color choices for drawing customers into a store.[3]

Sound provides a store with atmosphere and gives employees and customers a psychological lift. Fast tempo music can stimulate increased customer traffic in a restaurant with limited seating capacity. Slower music is played in stores so customers stay longer and purchase more.

Lighting and its fixtures play a dominant role in highlighting the materials and colors in a store's interior, and help focus the attention of shoppers on select merchandise. Proper lighting attracts customers, holds their attention, and assists them in making decisions on merchandise (see Figures 9-1 to 9-3). Good lighting is designed to minimize glare and it reflects the true color of products on display. "Merchandise displays usually call for two to five times as much illumination as overall store lighting."[4] (Lighting also promotes safety and security, as discussed at the end of the chapter.)

Display windows also attract customers and inform them of what is in the store. Clothing stores and jewelry stores typically use displays to show shoppers the quality and prices of merchandise. Supermarkets and discount stores use large panes of glass to enclose the front of their buildings and cover the glass with large posters calling attention to sales.

Figure 9-1 Lighting Attracts Customers Courtesy of General Electric Lighting.

Figure 9-2 Lighting Helps to Hold Customer Attention Courtesy of General Electric Lighting.

Merchandise fixtures include display cases, gondolas, racks, and pegboard displays. Because these fixtures are movable, retailers can change their store design as needed. Gondolas, for example, can be easily moved. A supermarket may want to make a change by adding an array of gondolas that contain candy and cakes at the store entrance to greet customers.

Merchandise fixtures sell a store's image and its products. Fixtures send subtle messages as to whether a store is self-service or service oriented. A self-service store would permit considerable customer access to merchandise by features such as counters and racks that are accessible on all sides. Naturally, the potential for shoplifting increases. Service-oriented stores use hanging racks behind counters, and locked glass counters and cabinets that require the assistance of a salesperson.

Store layout patterns are carefully designed by retailers for maximum utilization. Two common approaches are the grid and free-form layout. The grid layout is very popular, especially with supermarkets and drugstore chains (see

Figure 9-3 Lighting Assists Customers in Making Purchase Decisions
Courtesy of General Electric Lighting.

Figure 9-4). Customers travel up one aisle and then down the next. The free-form layout (see Figure 9-5) does not encourage customers to follow a prearranged path when walking through a store. There are no rows of fixtures. Instead, irregular shapes characterize racks and counters. Customers can walk in many directions to examine merchandise. Specialty stores often use this store design. Many retailers choose a combination of designs to make their store different from others.

The Perspective of Security

The mind-set of retailers is to make a profit by using the best possible strategies when selecting a site and designing a store. Much thought goes into these plans and, typically, security is not as high a priority as the protection executive would like. In fact, site selection and store plans can run counter to security. Retail management, for example, may believe, based on

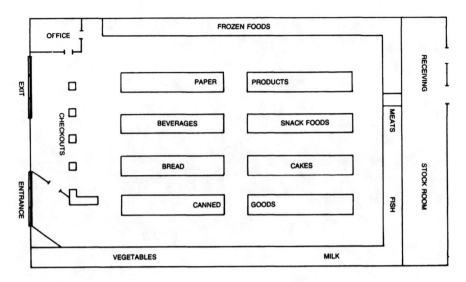

Figure 9-4 A Grid Layout

their research, that the opening of a chain store in a high-crime neighborhood will generate a profit. However, a security specialist's research may indicate that the store would be subject to numerous robberies and burglaries, necessitating extensive and expensive protection.

Consider the retail chain that plans to open new stores each with the same facade, which consist of many large windows. The strategy is to attract customers through innovative window designs that are the work of a well-known artist. One store is to be located near a sports arena, another across the street from a college campus. From a protection standpoint, many questions are raised. What are the risk management and insurance implications of the new store design? What type of glazing is to be used? What type of peril or attack can the glazing withstand?

Retail stores with large plate glass windows that are covered with posters of sale prices have one drawback in that those passing by, including police, find it difficult to observe activities (e.g., a robbery) in the store. This is also a problem when businesses are closed for the night and police patrol to check for burglars.

On the opposite side of the spectrum are those glass doors and windows that have nothing on them. They may be so clean and clear that customers walk into them and suffer serious injuries.

For department stores that have entrances on all sides, access controls are limited and anyone off the street can enter these stores. Retailers at malls who

Store Location and Design   207

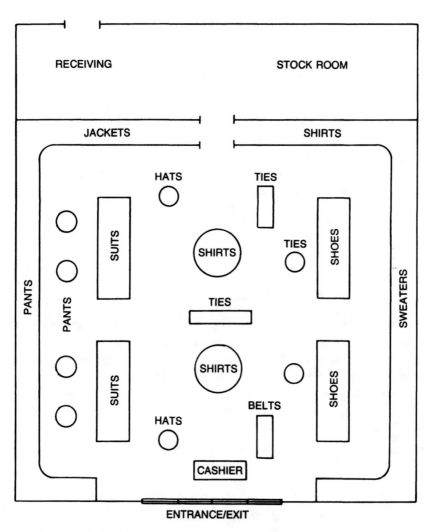

Figure 9–5 Free-form Layout

favor the "open front" concept likewise promote free access by not only shoppers, but also shoplifters and those inclined to "grab and run."

Retail merchandising is another area of store planning that can conflict with protection plans. Modern merchandising techniques emphasize customer accessibility to merchandise. Retailers want customers to walk freely through their store, notice merchandise, pick it up, and then purchase it. Marketing techniques are designed to make items desirable and to convince customers to buy. These techniques not only attract customers, but also thieves. Take, for example, a supermarket entrance that immediately meets customers with numerous gondolas that contain loose candy and nuts. Surely this sales technique will attract people who nibble without paying.

An ex-shoplifter, with 20 years of experience and an income of about $100,000 per year, made the following comments:

> When a store is built or designed, the architect or retailer never or seldom takes security into consideration. Everything is off in little rooms and boutiques. If you can't see what's going on in your store then you're gonna lose your merchandise.
>
> Merchandisers and display people know very little about security and the shoplifter. They build beautiful displays and then people steal them, plus reduce a lot of visibility.
>
> They can't leave those pillars alone! What used to be a 2-ft. square post is now an 8-ft. wall.[5]

The Role of Security

Retailers are in business to make a profit, not to cater to the perspectives of security. When we study modern merchandising, we can see that retailers have found that the investment in merchandising techniques has a return that is greater than losses from theft. With so many vulnerabilities built into retail stores, what is the role of the retail security specialist? Security's aim should be to look at the protection problems of site selection and store design as a challenge, and mesh creative security solutions into the retailer's strategies for profit. This is the role of security. Without such a mind-set, frustration and failure are likely.

Security Recommendations for Store Design

The following list emphasizes some basic protection points for store design. See the chapters on internal losses and shoplifting for additional protection strategies.

- Architects, engineers, and security practitioners should work together to design protection into retail stores prior to construction. The installation of physical security is less expensive during construction than afterward.
- Physical security should blend into store design and not be offensive or threatening.

Remember that lighting not only enhances displays and merchandise, it prevents crime.

Limit exits and install "panic" alarms on doors in case of emergency.

Plan stores for maximum visibility.

Keep stores neat and organized, so that missing merchandise is easier to spot.

Use turnstiles and barriers to ensure that customers pass through subtle checkpoints and checkouts where store employees are stationed.

Consider locating the employee lounge next to the sales floor, so employees can observe store activities while on break.

Cash registers, telephones, and other equipment should always be placed in a position so employees do not have to turn their backs to the sales floor and to customers.

Limit the height of racks, counters, and gondolas.

Use display cases with locks for high-value items. Make sure salespeople practice good security by using the lock, controlling the key, and limiting merchandise shown to customers.

Display small items near cash registers or other locations where employees are usually stationed.

Use dummy displays (e.g., empty cosmetic boxes).

Display only one of a pair.

Set up displays in a pattern, so the disturbance of the pattern can be noticed easily.

Tie merchandise to counters and racks. (Numerous devices are on the market that even contain alarms.)

Tie hangers to racks by using plastic or metal ties.

Alternate hangers to prevent the "grab and run."

Use break-away and color-coded labels to prevent ticket switching.

Control and secure store supplies (e.g., price tickets, color-coded tape, etc.).

Physical Security

How Security Defeats Itself

Physical security devices and systems such as locks and alarms are only one part of what should be an integrated approach to protection. Effective security requires planning and coordination among three major components of protection—people, policies and procedures, and physical security. There are many businesses in which the investment in security is not being realized because of poor planning and coordination among these components.

What makes matters worse is that there are many instances when a security strategy is implemented and a feeling of protection results, even though the strategy either does not live up to its expectations, is useless, or even helps offenders commit crimes. To spend money on security measures that assist criminals is unfortunate.

Let's look at the ordinary padlock used to prevent access through a gate or door. Security practitioners should test padlocks to ascertain whether they are actually providing security. Take a strong elastic band or some cord and secure it to the lock body (not the shackle) while the lock is attached to its target of protection. Jerk the elastic band or cord. Does the padlock unlock?

Are padlocks being used properly? An unlocked padlock hanging on a fence or near a door is helpful to offenders who may replace the padlock with their own, return at night for easy access, and then replace their padlock with the original.

The best door locks in the world, with the tightest key control program, are useless if an employee-thief is able to borrow a key "just for a minute" to press it into a bar of soap so a duplicate can be made.

The fallacy of the fence is important to understand. Fences, by themselves, are overrated protection. An offender can go over, under, or through a fence. The way fences are constructed can even assist intruders. Many fences have a top rail that actually provides support for someone climbing over. Without the top rail, the offender has to do a good balancing act to scale the fence. Place the rail at the bottom to hinder going under and add concrete. The strength of barbed wire arms also make an intruder's job easier. Why do these arms have to be strong enough to hold a person rather than just the barbed wire? Here, again, security assists the offender.

Don't be fooled by intrusion detectors. As the name implies, these systems detect intrusions. These systems neither protect against forced entry, delay an intruder, or block access. A false sense of security may exist in the minds of some practitioners who believe an intrusion detection system, once operational, is the solution to a protection problem. This frame of mind sets security up for failure. What is needed is an integrated approach that considers the need to delay the offender until a response force arrives. But this can be tricky. You can install a steel door with a sophisticated lock that serves no useful purpose if the offender breaks through the wall of sheetrock and wood studs. Intrusion sensors placed at a protection layer should be part of a complete delay measure (e.g., thick walls, strong door, and lock) greater than the time required for a response force to reach the scene.

Another example in which security defeats itself relates to the use of safes. These containers, if used properly, can present a formidable obstacle to offenders who also know of various methods of access without force (e.g., the owner leaves the safe combination in plain sight or hidden in an easy-to-find place, or the safe is not locked, or a "day combination" is used where the dial is set near the last number for easy access by employees).

Another set-up for failure is the use of a fire safe instead of a burglary-resistant safe to protect valuables against burglary. A fire safe has thin walls and is a burglar's delight.

CCTV systems are a costly expenditure for security departments. Without proper management and supervision of these systems this expenditure becomes wasteful. Anyone who has sat in front of TV monitors all day for several days knows that when fatigue sets in, effectiveness goes down. Sleeping, reading, and playing games are among the ways in which fatigue is handled by those monitoring the system. Job rotation every two hours is a good solution to this problem.

Another example of wasting money is to place a security officer at a shipping and receiving dock, and not ensure that a replacement is available during lunch and breaks. Security may as well put up a sign that reads: "We are not concerned about theft during the lunch hour." By establishing a security post without a relief person at the dock to cut theft, security has narrowed the time period in which thefts can occur—during lunch.

A trio of professional ex-shoplifters, when confessing their crimes, pointed out that one would distract a salesperson while the others helped themselves to merchandise. There was only one thing that ever prevented them from shoplifting and that was a knowledgable, persistent salesperson. They commented on physical security methods:

locks: Retailers commonly buy the cheapest locks to protect their most expensive merchandise.
two-way mirrors: If they went into a store and there were only two salespeople on the floor, chances are the retailer was not going to pay $6 to $8/hour to have someone stand behind the wall and peek through a mirror.
electronic article surveillance: Tag removal devices are left lying around the store.
cameras: Half of them are fake and who's watching the real ones on the monitors? It's generally the courtesy clerk who also has to answer the telephone and do paperwork.[6]

These statements were made by experienced professionals who made a career out of shoplifting. Most shoplifters are not professionals and security strategies are more effective with amateurs. A key point to remember about physical security is that it should be carefully planned and audited after implementation.

Physical Security Methods

Planning Physical Security

Before proceeding to an explanation of specific physical security methods, a list of considerations are noted here to assist with planning security.

- Mesh security with the retailer's strategies for profit.
- No security method is foolproof. Security is as good as the time it takes to defeat it.
- Security should be an integration of people, policies and procedures, and physical security.
- Avoid overemphasizing protection against any one threat (e.g., shoplifting) when other threats (e.g., employee theft) may be causing greater losses.

Another important consideration when planning physical security is the various levels of protection required at retail stores during each 24-hour period. The sales period during the day requires a free flow of customers with limited access controls. During this time, most alarms are deactivated and more doors are unlocked than at any other period. Loss prevention is a primary strategy. The second time frame, the preparation period, involves store activities in preparation for the store to open in the morning and close at the end of the day. During these times, customers are barred from the store. Perimeter doors are locked except for one door for employees. Employee and vendor theft are prime concerns at this time. The third time frame that requires intense security is during the closed period, when the store is closed for the night. All doors are locked, and all perimeter and internal intrusion alarms are activated. Burglary and hide-ins are prime concerns during this period.

Several physical security methods have been discussed already in the chapters on internal losses, shoplifting, and investigations. Here, an emphasis is placed on locks, doors and windows, alarm systems, and lighting. Figures 9–6 to 9–9 illustrate four general locations where physical security can be applied in a retail operation. These are the perimeter, entry, internal, and point. In the next chapter on robbery and burglary, physical security is also discussed. See the index as a guide.

Locks

Locks are a universally applied physical security device that have been used since ancient times. The ancient civilizations of Egypt and China designed doors with primitive keyed locks. These early locks used pegs to slide

Physical Security Methods   213

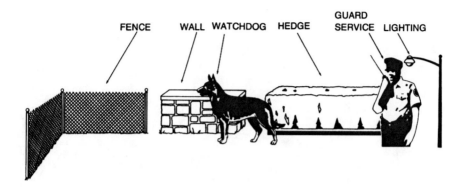

Figure 9-6 Perimeter Protection *Source:* U.S. Dept. of Justice, *Security and the Small Business Retailer* (Washington, DC: U.S. Government Printing Office, 1979), 43.

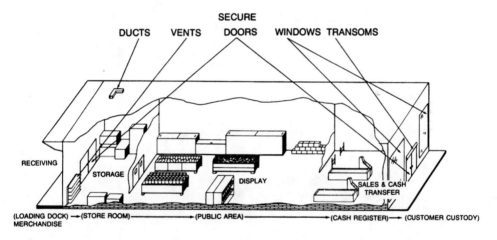

Figure 9-7 Entry Protection *Source:* U.S. Dept. of Justice, *Security and the Small Business Retailer* (Washington, DC: U.S. Government Printing Office, 1979), 52.

down into a door to secure it. A specially notched board was required to raise the pegs high enough to clear the door.

Lock selection is not an easy task. Certain retailers purchase inexpensive locks and suffer the consequences. Other retailers establish specifications for

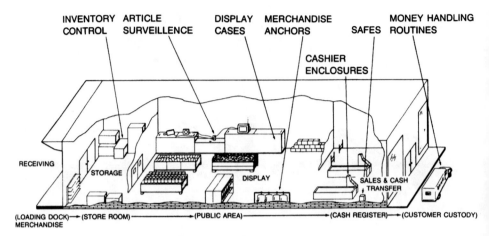

Figure 9-8 Internal (Space) Protection Emphasizes Protection of Interior Spaces or Areas *Source:* U.S. Dept. of Justice, *Security and the Small Business Retailer* (Washington, DC: U.S. Government Printing Office, 1979), 62.

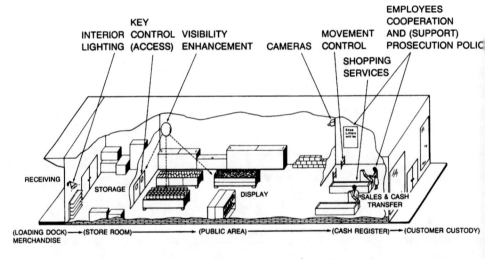

Figure 9-9 Point Protection Emphasizes Point or Object Protection *Source:* U.S. Dept. of Justice, *Security and the Small Business Retailer* (Washington, DC: U.S. Government Printing Office, 1979), 75.

locks so that all stores in their chain have good-quality locks. A locale may have a security building code that requires specific types of locks.

Retailers should use a certified locksmith to increase the competency of those who are charged with the security of people and assets. The Associated

Locksmiths of America (ALOA, 3003 Live Oak Street, Dallas, TX 75204; 214–827–1701), which has been in existence since 1956, trains and certifies locksmiths at three levels. The certified registered locksmith must pass tests that cover ten mandatory areas of expertise. The certified professional locksmith must show a knowledge of ten additional areas. The certified master locksmith, the highest ALOA rating, is qualified in at least 33 of the 35 subject areas. Locksmiths may also have to be certified by manufacturers. The ALOA has 9,000 members, but the U.S. Department of Commerce states that there are 18,000 locksmiths in this country.

Two major categories of locks are mechanical and electromechanical. The information that follows describes several locks in each category.

Mechanical Locks

Key-in-knob Lock

The key-in-knob lock (see Figure 9–10) is very common and is used widely at residences. The keyway, cylinder, and lock are in the knob. Retailers often use this type of lock on closets, fitting rooms, and other interior doors. Security is poor; there are several easy methods of defeating this lock.

Deadbolt Lock

Increased security is afforded with the deadbolt, compared to the key-in-knob lock. With the deadbolt (see Figure 9–11), a cylinder is installed in the face of the door and a key is required to move the 1-inch bolt into or out of the door frame. A thumb turn is often used on the inside where this lock is installed. To increase security further (especially if glass is located near the lock, which enables an offender to break the glass and reach the thumb turn), a double-cylinder deadbolt can be used. As opposed to the single-cylinder

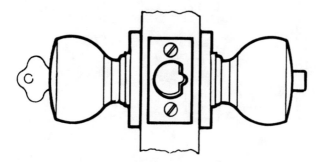

Figure 9–10 Key-in-knob Lock Reprinted with permission from Butterworth–Heinemann. *Source:* Philip P. Purpura, *Security and Loss Prevention: An Introduction,* 2nd ed. (Boston: Butterworth–Heinemann, 1991), 110.

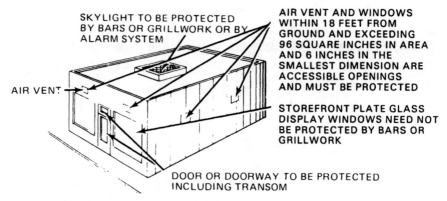

Physical Security Methods

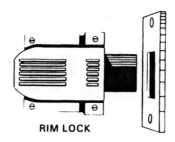

RIM LOCK

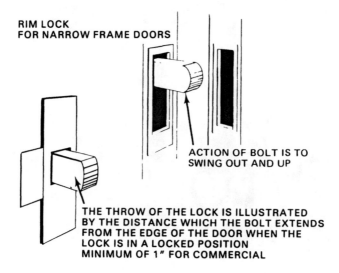

RIM LOCK
FOR NARROW FRAME DOORS

ACTION OF BOLT IS TO
SWING OUT AND UP

THE THROW OF THE LOCK IS ILLUSTRATED
BY THE DISTANCE WHICH THE BOLT EXTENDS
FROM THE EDGE OF THE DOOR WHEN THE
LOCK IS IN A LOCKED POSITION
MINIMUM OF 1" FOR COMMERCIAL

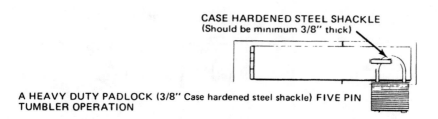

CASE HARDENED STEEL SHACKLE
(Should be minimum 3/8" thick)

A HEAVY DUTY PADLOCK (3/8" Case hardened steel shackle) FIVE PIN
TUMBLER OPERATION

THE STEEL BAR AND STAPLE OF THE HASP SHOULD BE CASE HARDENED AS IS THE PADLOCK SHACKLE RECESSED SCREWS SHOULD BE CONCEALED WHEN THE HASP IS CLOSED

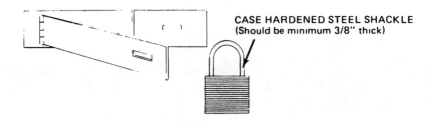

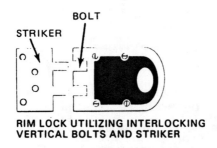

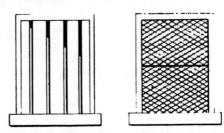

Figure 9-11 Examples of Accessible Openings and Locking Devices Referred to in the Federal Crime Insurance Program Protective Device Requirements *Source:* Federal Crime Insurance Program.

deadbolt, the double-cylinder deadbolt requires a key for both sides. A key should always be available in case of emergency. Residences and businesses often use deadbolt locks.

Mortise Lock

A mortise lock (see Figure 9-11) is rectangular in shape and is set in the outer edge of a door. This lock is noted for its spring latch, which can be locked by pressing buttons on the door edge. When the door is closed, the latch locks. A good mortise lock has both a latch and a bolt. The latch alone should never be relied on, since it can be jimmied. Use of the latch and bolt will provide good security.

Rim Lock

The rim lock (see Figure 9-11) is commonly used as a supplemental form of security to bolster protection at a door. It is installed on the inside surface of a door and a cylinder extends to the exterior of the door to permit use of a key to lock and unlock a bolt on the inside. A thumb turn or lock cylinder is employed on the inside. This is a difficult lock to defeat, especially without noise.

Padlock

The padlock, which requires a key, is often used with a hasp (see Figure 9-11) or chain to secure doors, cabinets, and other openings. Manufacturers offer a variety of padlocks with different levels of security. Low-security padlocks contain warded locks. Padlocks with higher security contain pin tumbler, disk-tumbler, or lever mechanisms. Ensure that padlocks are of hardened steel for increased security.

Combination Lock

The manipulation of a numbered dial permits access through this lock, which is often located on a safe door, vault, or high-security filing cabinet. Combination locks may have three or four dials that must be aligned for access. Although no key is required, an offender can obtain the combination through a variety of methods.

Can a Store's Failure to Reasonably Protect Customer's Goods from Burglary Be Shown by Its Failure to Use Case-hardened Locks?

James Smith, a customer, left his new motorcycle at McRary Harley-Davidson for servicing under warranty. It was stored in a shed near the main building after being serviced. Both buildings contained a burglar alarm and automatic lighting. The gate to the premises and the shed door were both padlocked.

Smith's motorcycle was stolen in a burglary. McRary admitted he discovered that the alarm was not working on the day of the burglary. Testimony by a security expert indicated that only case-hardened padlocks could resist a bolt cutter, such as the one used to gain entry to both the fence and the shed.

Smith's suit to recover the value of his stolen motorcycle was based on McRary's negligent security and Smith's reliance on the safety of the motorcycle, which created an implied contract. The trial court jury found for the shop owner and the case was dismissed, but the North Carolina Court of Appeals later ordered a new trial based on improper jury instructions.

The point to remember is that courts are allowing expert witnesses to testify as to the sufficiency of security measures and that defendants cannot absolve themselves of liability by utilizing ineffective security measures.

This case was summarized from: R. Keegan Federal, Jr., and Jennifer L. Fogleman, *Avoiding Liability in Retail Security* (Atlanta: Strafford Pub., 1986), pp. 11–12. *Case Citation:* James L. Smith v. Byrum McRary d/b/a McRary Harley-Davidson, No. 91PA82, Supreme Court of North Carolina, decided October 5, 1982, reported at 295 S.E. 2d. 444; *Private Security Case Law Reporter*, Vol. I, No. 6, p. 9.

Combination Padlock

This lock looks like a padlock except a dial is manipulated, rather than a key being inserted, to gain access. Combination padlocks are used in conjunction with a hasp or a chain.

Time-recording Lock

The advantage of the time-recording lock is that it records the time a door is opened. Businesses that use a night cleaning crew or permit employees to enter at odd hours can pinpoint when doors were opened.

Lock Mechanisms

There are four common types of lock mechanisms used in a variety of locks and padlocks. They are warded, disk or wafer tumbler, pin tumbler, and lever tumbler.

Warded

Many older buildings still have the original warded locks in doors. Warded locks are characterized by a keyway that permits observation through the door. A skeleton key is used to unlock the mechanism by making direct contact with a bolt that is forced back into the door. The warded lock affords minimum security. A piece of metal can be shaped to perform the same action as the skeleton key.

Disk or Wafer Tumbler

To unlock a door, spring-loaded, flat metal disks are aligned when the proper key is inserted in the keyway. Used for automobiles, this mechanism is also applied to file cabinets, desks, cabinets, and padlocks. More security is afforded with the disk or wafer tumbler than with the warded lock. Depending on the type of disk tumbler lock, access may be gained by using the wrong key or by forcing scissors in the keyway and turning.

Pin Tumbler

The pin tumbler lock mechanism is the most widely used. The pin tumbler operates similarly to disk tumbler mechanisms. It consists of a key, a cylinder plug, and a cylinder shell or housing (see Figure 9-12). Rather than using disks, pins form a barrier that if not aligned properly by the correct key, the cylinder will not rotate.

Lever Tumbler

The lever mechanism is different from the disk or pin tumbler in that it does not employ a rotating plug and the bolt is usually thrown directly by the key (as with the warded mechanism). Levers (which are U shaped and

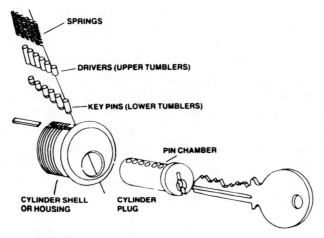

Figure 9-12 Pin Tumbler Lock Mechanism Reprinted with permission from Butterworth-Heinemann. *Source:* Philip P. Purpura, *Handbook of Loss Prevention and Crime Prevention* (Boston: Butterworth-Heinemann, 1989), pg. 229.

constructed of metal) are hinged on a post that is a fixed part of the housing. When the proper key is inserted in the keyway, the levers will be aligned to release the lock. The level of security provided by these locks depends on the number of levers. Those found in cabinets and desks usually have minimum security, while the ones in strong boxes, safe deposit boxes, and lockers provide greater security.

Electromechanical Locks

Card-operated Lock

Cards are a popular alternative to the metal key. A coded card is used to release a lock when the card is inserted into a reader or placed nearby. These locking systems can control which cards have access, based on the information programmed in the system's memory. Programming can limit access to certain days, times, inner locations, and other security requirements. A recording of all cards used will assist with investigations. The great disadvantage of this system is that a stolen card can be used to gain access if it has not been deleted from the system. Requiring a numerical code to be entered on a keypad can reduce this problem. Also, these systems enable a duress signal to be entered. Card-operated locks have been criticized over the years because of the vulnerability of "tailgating"; however, an offender can also follow an employee, who used a metal key, into a building.

Cipher Lock

The cipher lock employs a push-button panel that requires the user to press a certain combination to unlock the door. It can be used in conjunction with a variety of door operators, such as an electronic door strike.

Emergency Exit Locks

Also called panic-bar locks, these locks permit emergency exit without a key. Entrance is not permitted at these doors. Employee thieves and shoplifters are deterred by emergency exit locks, especially when an alarm is sounded if the door is opened.

There are many types of sophisticated and expensive locks and access control systems on the market. Biometric systems permit access based on fingerprints, hand geometry, retinal blood vessel patterns of the eye, and other human characteristics. Because retail businesses are generally not high-security locations, these systems are not emphasized here.

Key Control

Even though high-security locks may be installed at a certain location, this defense is useless if keys are not controlled. The foundation of key control is good accountability and record keeping of those who are assigned keys. A key should *never* be marked with identifying information that would assist an offender. Codes are more appropriate. "Do Not Duplicate" can be stamped on keys to hinder duplication. Because of employee turnover and the vulnerability of lost or stolen keys, locks should be changed at least once every six months; however, this interval is often the exception.

Interchangeable core locks can make changing locks easier for the retailer. By using a special control key, the core of the lock can be replaced by another, so a different key is required for the lock. The services of a locksmith are reduced by using interchangeable core locks.

Key control should be put in perspective, because efforts can be wasteful if a key is borrowed by an offender and is pressed into a bar of soap for subsequent duplication. This is one reason why locks should be changed periodically.

Doors and Windows

A common method used by offenders to enter a locked area is force. Although unauthorized entry can be made through a roof, air-conditioning duct, basement, and so forth, the chances are very high that forced entry will occur at a door or window. Even though a high-security lock may be installed, it is useless if forced entry takes place right through the door or window. When strong locks, doors, and windows are installed, an offender may simply break through the wall. Thus, security should be comprehensive and weak points should be eliminated. This is often called *target hardening* and it includes the gamut of physical security.

Steel doors with an optical viewer are a good form of protection for retailers. They are used at back entrances. At the front of stores, aluminum and glass are typically used. To increase security at the front of the store, metal gates are helpful in protecting the whole store front. Although an alarm system is useful to notify authorities of a break-in, the system will not stop determined intruders who may "grab and run" before security and police arrive.

On exterior doors, the hinges should be on the inside of the door to prevent the hinges from being removed. Hinges can also be welded or a pin can be placed in each hinge (see Figure 9–13).

Solid wood or steel doors can be reinforced by placing a steel bar on the inside when the store is closing for the night. A lock can be attached to the bar to prevent an offender from using the doorway to haul merchandise out if, for instance, entry was made from a window. Consider fire codes before applying this security.

Exit doors can be fitted with hardware that balances life safety and security. Fire door gear consists of panic bars or paddles tied to mechanical, electromagnetic, or electric locks. People must be afforded the opportunity to exit quickly in an emergency and security would like to be notified when an unau-

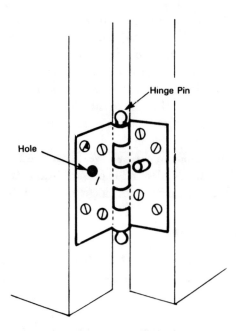

Figure 9-13 Pin to Prevent Removal of Door Reprinted with permission from Butterworth-Heinemann. *Source:* Philip P. Purpura, *Security and Loss Prevention: An Introduction,* 2nd ed. (Boston, MA: Butterworth-Heinemann, 1991), 142.

thorized door is opened. A variety of devices can be connected to these doors, such as CCTVs, VCRs, alarms, and delayed egress. The delayed egress system sets off an alarm and after 15-30 seconds, the door opens. This system is subject to criticism from life safety proponents; however, a fire or smoke alarm signal can be designed to open doors immediately.[7]

How Does the ADA Impact Physical Security at Retail Stores?

The Americans with Disabilities Act of 1990 and the U.S. Department of Justice's regulations became effective on January 26, 1992. The law and regulations apply to businesses and other organizations that operate places of public accommodation, such as retail stores, restaurants, hotels, theaters, libraries, and hospitals. The aim of the ADA is to remove barriers in existing facilities and to design new facilities to be totally accessible to the handicapped. The most critical impact on security is building access, door hardware, fire egress, and system controls. Door handles, pulls, locks, and other devices must be shaped so they are easy to grasp with one hand. Knobs are not acceptable. Push, lever, and U-shaped mechanisms are appropriate. Door closers are required to take at least three seconds to move a door to a point 3 inches from the latch. Automatic door closers must not open back-to-back faster than three seconds or require more than 15 lbs. of force to open. Revolving doors must be wide enough to allow a wheelchair to pass and provide three seconds before turning to permit passage. An accessible gate or door shall be provided adjacent to a revolving door or turnstile. Interior hinged doors must be opened with 5 lbs. of pressure or less. For elevators, buttons and controls must be 42–48 inches above the floor and the doors must remain open for three seconds. Barriers to prevent the removal of shopping carts from retail stores must not restrict the movement of those in wheelchairs. Counter tops are to be 28–34 inches off the floor. Alarm systems for emergency egress must be designed to accommodate the blind, deaf, and the nonambulatory. Public address systems and visual alarms are mandatory.[8]

Window protection should be comprehensive and include quality window frames, hardware, and glazing materials. It would be foolish to install a good window lock and strong glazing on a weak frame. Offenders have been known to pull a window right out after prying the edges.

A window lock that requires a key will provide some protection. The key should never be left in the lock, because an offender may break the window and reach in to release the lock. (The same can be said about doors with glass.) For emergency purposes, the key must be kept near the window to facilitate escape.

Windows can be protected with metal bars, metal mesh, or a sliding metal gate. Whatever physical security is used, planning must consider avenues for emergency escape.

Glazing can improve security at windows. First, the retailer must decide on the vulnerabilities of the location. Laminated glass may be chosen. This crime-resistant glass is characterized by a tough, plastic, inner layer that is pressed between two sheets of glass. Bullet-resistant and burglar-resistant glazing are other choices. The former is capable of resisting various bullet calibers. Burglar-resistant glass resists hammers, rocks, and fire, and it cannot shatter and cut people. A combination of bullet- and burglar-resistant glass is available. Polycarbonate and acrylic materials are among the materials used for this glazing. Underwriters Laboratory lists glazing according to its strength.

In addition to doors and windows, many other openings exist in buildings. Examples of other openings that require protection are skylights, roof hatchways, garage doors, and delivery chutes. Locks, metal bars, and alarms are installed for protection. If the building or store being secured joins another building or store, the security specialist should search for vulnerabilities such as shared openings, or ceilings or basements that permit entry among stores.

Alarm Systems

Any plans to install an alarm system as a form of protection should consider the fact that it will only detect and report an unauthorized intrusion to a designated party. A human response should follow. An alarm system will not physically stop an intruder. Used in conjunction with other defenses (e.g., fences, locks, etc.), an alarm system can deter criminals.

The three major components of an intrusion alarm system are sensor, control unit, and annunciator (see Figure 9–14). Sensors detect an intruder by various methods. The control unit turns the system on and off, receives information from the sensor, and then activates an annunciator (e.g., a bell or siren).

Numerous sensors are on the market for internal and perimeter security.[9] Rather than discuss sensors that apply to high-security locations such as nuclear plants and prisons, we discuss sensors commonly used by retail businesses.

Sensors

Magnetic contact switches are composed of a magnet installed on a door and a magnetically operated switch that is attached to the door frame. A magnetic field is generated when the door is closed, but when the door is opened, the interruption of the magnetic field activates an alarm. These switches are widely used on doors, windows, cabinets and many other openings (see Figures 9–15 and 9–16).

Electrical switches are similar to magnetic contact switches. However, a closed opening completes an electrical circuit that, if interrupted, triggers an alarm.

Metallic foil is glued to glass and carries an electric current that, when broken, results in an alarm. It is applied to windows (and glass on doors) in many businesses. Once installed, simple maintenance of the foil, or replacement, is an easy task.

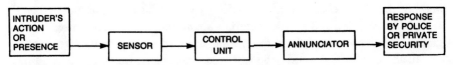

Figure 9–14 Three Components of an Alarm System *Source:* U.S. Dept. of Commerce, *Commercial Intrusion Alarm Systems* (Washington, DC: U.S. Government Printing Office, 1979), 8.

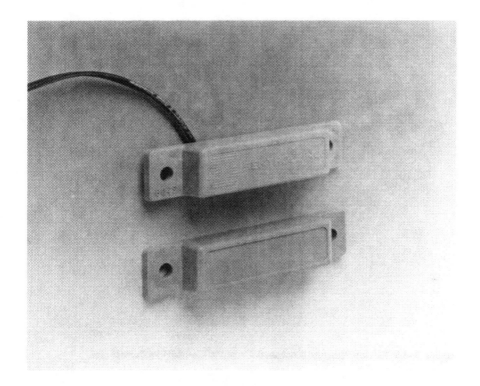

Figure 9-15 Surface-mounted Magnetic Contact with Wire Leads Courtesy of Sentrol, Inc.

Glass breakage detectors are sensitive to the sound of breaking glass. A sensor the size of a large coin is glued to the glass. One type contains a tuning fork that is tuned to the frequency produced by glass breaking. Another type employs a microphone and amplifier (see Figures 9-17 and 9-18).

Pressure mats are weight-sensitive switches that, when walked on, will close an electric contact, complete a circuit, and trigger an alarm (Figure 9-19). Commonly placed under carpeting, pressure mats are often located below doors and windows, and in halls and on stairs. (Retail stores use pressure mats to automatically open doors.) Pressure removed can also activate a variation of this sensor when an offender lifts an object (e.g., computer) that was exerting pressure on a mat.

Passive infrared (PIR) motion detectors sense infrared radiation such as heat from a body (see Figures 9-20 and 9-21). These sensors are passive,

Figure 9-16 Roller/Plunger Recessed Contact Courtesy of Sentrol, Inc.

meaning that they do not transmit a constant signal subject to interruption by an intruder. Instead, they detect a source of moving infrared radiation (the intruder) against the normal radiation environment of the room. Sources of heat from sunlight, heaters, and so forth should be avoided when this type of detector is positioned. One of the weaknesses of PIR is that it can be blinded if the lens is obscured, sprayed, or taped. However, an antimasking feature can measure the infrared reflectivity of the lense and the area in front of it, and if it increases, a trouble signal is sent. The PIR motion detector is in widespread use inside buildings.

Infrared photoelectric sensors set off an alarm when an invisible infrared beam of light is interrupted (see Figure 9-19). An offender can pass over or under the beam without detection.

Ultrasonic motion detectors transmit high-frequency, inaudible sound waves to a receiver (see Figure 9-19). When an intruder enters the area, the sound wave pattern is interrupted and an alarm is signaled. Because these sensors are highly sensitive to the environment, they are used mainly indoors. Careful installation and placement will reduce false alarms.

Physical Security Methods   229

Figure 9-17 A Glass Trap Shock Sensor Detects Intrusions by Responding to Shock Waves from Forced Entry through a Window Courtesy of Sentrol, Inc.

Microwave motion detectors trigger an alarm when an intruder interrupts a microwave or electromagnetic field. Also called radar detectors, these sensors use radio waves that have a frequency that is higher than sound waves. An alarm can be triggered if waves travel beyond the secured area and detect outside activity. Also, fluorescent lighting is a problem for

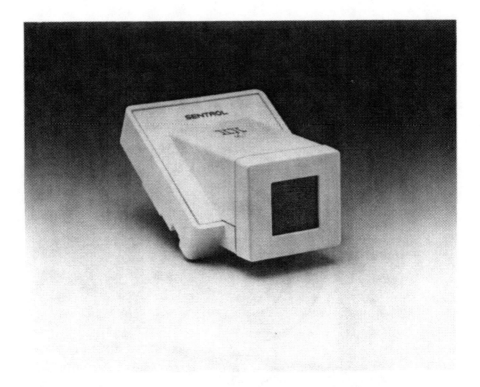

Figure 9-18 Dual Technology Acoustic/Vibration Glass Break Sensor Courtesy of Sentrol, Inc.

microwave detectors. These sensors are used inside and for high-security locations along a perimeter. For external use, there is the potential for false alarms from adverse weather and other disturbances.

Dual technology devices combine two detection technologies into a single housing. PIR and microwave serve as a popular example. Both technologies must perceive a disturbance at about the same time for an alarm to be signaled. This helps to reduce false alarms.

These sensors are the most popular for protecting retailers against intruders. Many other sensors exist and their application depends on the unique needs of the store. *Vibration sensors* detect vibrations on the surface. They are connected to doors, walls, and safes. *Capacitance sensors* protect safes and valuable objects by establishing an electrostatic field that, when interrupted, triggers an alarm. *Screen sensors* have thin wires that are electrically charged. These wires are used in a variety of defenses (e.g., doors, windows, screens).

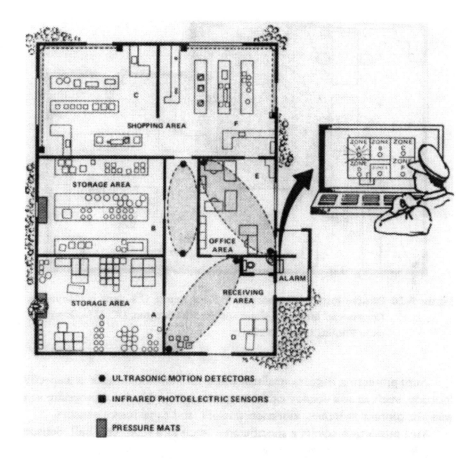

Figure 9-19 Floor Plan with Sensors and Alarms Reprinted with permission from Butterworth–Heinemann. *Source:* Philip P. Purpura, *Security and Loss Prevention: An Introduction*, 2nd ed. (Boston: Butterworth–Heinemann, 1991), 121.

When a break occurs, an alarm is sounded. *Fiber optics* is growing in popularity for intrusion detection and transmission of alarm signals. It involves the transportation of information via guided light waves in an optical fiber. This sensor can be attached to or inserted in many things requiring protection (e.g., fences, doors, windows, and cabinets). When stress is applied to the fiber optic cable, an infrared light pulsing through the cable reacts to the stress and signals an alarm.

Application of Alarm Systems

The three basic kinds of protection to consider when planning the application of alarm systems are point, area, and perimeter. Note that one type of sensor can be applied to more than one kind of protection.

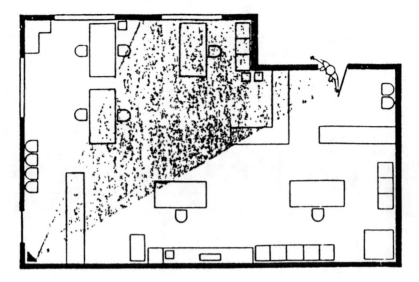

Figure 9-20 Passive Infrared Sensor (Floor Plan) *Source:* U.S. Dept. of Commerce, *Commercial Intrusion Alarm Systems* (Washington, DC: U.S. Government Printing Office, 1979).

Point protection triggers an alarm when an intrusion is made at a specific location, such as at a display cabinet or a safe. Examples of appropriate sensors are contact switches, vibration sensors, and capacitance sensors.

Area protection covers a specific area, such as a room or a hall. Sensors suitable for area protection include infrared, ultrasonic, microwave, and photoelectric beams.

Perimeter protection aims to protect the outer boundary of the building and grounds. If doors and windows make up the perimeter, which is typical for retailers, then contact switches, foil, glass breakage, and pressure mats can be applied. Many other perimeter sensors and alarm systems are on the market for a variety of applications that require increased levels of security beyond the requirements of the typical retail store.

Alarm Signaling Systems

After a sensor detects an intruder, an alarm signal must be transmitted so that a human response results. Several systems exist to accomplish this task.

Central stations are in widespread use and operate when a signal (e.g., intrusion or fire) is received at a panel located and monitored away from the protected location. Central stations are actually businesses that supply monitoring

Figure 9-21 Passive Infrared Sensor Courtesy of Sentrol, Inc.

services to the community for a fee. Radio transmissions, leased wires, telephone lines, and other methods soon to be discussed provide the connection from the protected premises to the central station.

Monitoring companies offer clients opening and closing services. This means that the central station maintains data on the client's opening and closing times.

The more professional and responsible services typically have UL- or Factory Mutual- (FM) certified monitoring equipment. Certification means that the service has more employees on duty and a higher degree of computerization. Insurers are likely to grant premium discounts for users of certified services.

Proprietary alarm systems are similar to central stations, except that the protected premises maintain the monitoring station right on the premises. This system may be cost-effective for large facilities.

Local alarms activate an annunciator on the premises and have the disadvantage of being heard only locally. These systems *may* frighten away an offender and *may* alert someone nearby to call the police. Many businesses have a silent alarm sent to a central station. The advantage is that the offender may be caught in the act.

Direct connect systems are connected by wire to a police station or some other location. A business may establish a "buddy" system with another business, whereby each acts as a receiver of an alarm and contacts police.

Automatic telephone dialers are a method of transmitting emergency messages. Basically, these systems silently dial and transmit preprogrammed messages to police and fire departments, and business owners.

New signaling technology is constantly being developed to supply the demand. This includes radio frequency, microwave, fiber optics, and cable. Advances also include remote programming that enables a central station to arm and disarm, unlock access points, and perform diagnostics and corrections.

When a retailer shops for an alarm system, it is important to consider that the lowest price is not necessarily the best choice. Reliability and maintenance are important factors. An excellent source of information, rather than a salesperson, is a user of the system being considered.

Other points to study when planning an alarm system are system growth, future integration, and hardware and software compatibility. Because retail security budgets often vary from year to year, security systems can be designed modularly and additions can be made as the budget allows.

False Alarms

More than 95 percent of alarm transmissions are false. Three primary causes are users, improper installation, and defective systems. A retailer should ensure that employees receive clear instructions on how to operate the system. False alarms are a serious problem that cause friction between the police and the business community. Many locales have enacted ordinances whereby excessive false alarms result in a fine.

Lighting

From a security viewpoint, lighting is a psychological deterrent to intrusion and it enables detection. There are many benefits of good lighting that go beyond satisfying the security and safety needs of businesses. Retail security practitioners should study the multiple benefits of lighting to provide a solid foundation when requesting budget allocations for improved lighting.

The list below contains bottom-line benefits of lighting from the National Lighting Bureau.

- Lighting is among the least costly of all security measures and is also the most effective. A business can gain a reputation for being safe and secure for shopping.
- Buildings that are well-illuminated look good. Lighting can be integrated with the building and grounds to enhance window displays and trees and shrubs. Lighting increases curbside appeal and thus more shopping by customers.
- Security lighting can prevent litigation from those who claim the business owner was negligent for failure to provide adequate lighting.
- Lighting reduces risks associated with accidents and crimes. Risk management and insurance costs can be lowered.
- The most expensive security cost is personnel. Greater reliance on lighting can reduce other more expensive security expenditures and enhance those security methods that are in place. Lighting can attract more people to illuminated areas, thus enhancing security and safety.
- Because more people work during the day, more shopping occurs at night. People look for safe locations to shop and lighting can attract customers and increase sales.
- Employee morale can improve through good lighting. Since employees feel safer, management is perceived as caring about employee safety. Also, better visibility enables people to more accurately describe offenders, criminal activity, and vehicles.[10]

New Lighting Revives Shopping Mall

Camillus, NY—Inadequate lighting in the parking lot was creating a serious problem for the owners of Fairmount Fair Mall, a major retail facility located in a suburb of Syracuse. Shoppers were concerned about their cars being broken into. Both pedestrians and drivers said they were being made uncomfortable by glare. Neighboring land owners were complaining about "light trespass." Convinced that improvements were needed, the mall's manager conducted a survey among shoppers to determine what they liked and disliked about the lighting at Fairmount and other centers they patronized. After analyzing survey responses, management decided to install a new outdoor lighting system that relied on metal halide lamps, combining good color-rendering properties with high efficiency and relatively long life. Energy was not a major issue. In fact, based on the value of energy savings alone, the new system would have to have operated more than 100 years in order to pay for itself. Payback was achieved in months, however, because of the other benefits derived.

A principal concern was reducing vandalism, especially during the Christmas season when the parking lot was filled with cars. During the first Christmas under the new lighting, vandalism was almost eliminated. And because the lighting provided such effective security, it was possible to reduce the extent of security patrols, saving $5,000 per year. The new lighting also permitted faster snow removal in the parking lot, saving another $7,500 annually. Because the lighting also called shoppers' and prospective shoppers' attention to the new parking area safety and security, traffic and sales increased, generating $90,000 annually in additional rent for the mall's owners and about $2.5 million in increased sales for retailers.

Source: National Lighting Bureau, "Lighting for Safety and Security" (Washington, DC: National Lighting Bureau, Pub.), p. 7.

Types of Lighting

Incandescent lamps are the common light bulbs that are in widespread use. They give off natural light color; however, these lamps consume the most electricity and have the shortest life (750–3,500 hours). Incandescent lamps convert electricity to light by heating a tungsten filament.

Fluorescent lamps provide high efficiency and long lamp life (ten times longer than incandescent lamps at a fraction of the power). Two drawbacks are their short range of coverage and performance problems when temperatures go below 30° F. Fluorescent and sodium lamps (described next) all use a gas discharge principle that produces light when an electric current passes through a vapor or gas.

High- and low-pressure sodium lamps produce a golden-yellow light. These lamps have a long life (7,500–24,000 hours) and are cost-effective. There are disadvantages to these lamps. The low-pressure sodium lamps especially cause color distortion, which makes it difficult for people to provide accurate descriptions of incidents at night. Also, people walking out of buildings, such as a retail store, are sometimes unable to find their vehicles at night because of the color distortion. CCTV efficiency is hindered for the same reason. Local residents living near sodium lighting have complained about effects on their sleeping.

Mercury vapor lamps are known for their pale, blue-green tint. These lamps have been criticized because of poor efficiency and color rendering. Their lamp life is between 12,000–24,000 hours.

Metal halide lamps are characterized by a bright, white light and are popular indoors where color rendition is important. Retailers use these lamps for a variety of purposes, such as for track lighting and for external illumination. Their life is between 5,000–20,000 hours.

When lighting is installed, ensure that it does not shine into the eyes of patrolling police or security. Equip each light with a sensor to set off an alarm if tampering occurs.

The selection of lighting and lighting fixtures for retailers can be complicated. Many stores employ an expert to assist with decisions, because lighting, if used intelligently, can assist in attracting customers, show the retailer's merchandise to the best advantage, and, as we know, enhance security.

Case Problems

9A. As a security specialist for a large retailer, you have been assigned to a committee responsible for making changes at Woody's Lumber Company to increase sales and profits. List and explain at least ten recommendations that you would make to improve store design and physical security (see Figure 9–22). Prioritize the list and explain why you selected the first three items as top priorities.

9B. In reference to Woody's Lumber Company (Figure 9–22), what recommendations would you make for the following vulnerabilities: internal theft, shoplifting, burglary and robbery? Establish a prioritized list of ten recommendations for each and explain why you selected the first three as top priorities in each list. This assignment can be completed in conjunction with the chapters on these vulnerabilities.

Notes

1. Gerald Pintel and Jay Diamond, *Retailing*, 5th ed. (Englewood Cliffs, NJ: Prentice-Hall, 1991), 220.
2. Irving Burstiner, *Basic Retailing*, 2nd ed. (Homewood, IL: Irwin Publishing, 1991), 260.
3. J. Barry Mason et al., *Retailing*, 4th ed. (Homewood, IL: Irwin Publishing, 1991), 458.
4. Ibid., 298.

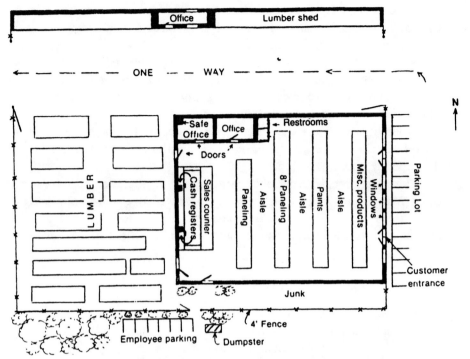

Figure 9-22 Woody's Lumber Company. Woody's lumber company has suffered declining profits in recent years. A new manager was recently hired who quickly hired six people to replace the previous crew, which was fired for internal theft. Four additional people were quickly hired for part-time work. The process for conducting business is to have customers park their cars in the front of the store, walk to the sales counter to pay for the desired lumber, receive a pink receipt, drive to the rear of the store, pick up the lumber with the assistance of the yard crew, and then depart through the rear auto exit. At the lumber company, loss prevention is of minimal concern. An inoperable burglar alarm and two fire extinguishers are on the premises. Reprinted with permission from Butterworth-Heinemann. *Source:* Philip P. Purpura, *Security and Loss Prevention: An Introduction*, 2nd ed. (Boston: Butterworth-Heinemann, 1991), 94.

5. National Crime Prevention Institute, *Confessions of an Ex-shoplifter* (Louisville, KY: NCPI, 1991), 3.
6. Ibid., 2.
7. Bill Zalud, "How to Secure the Exit," *Security* (February 1991): 31.

8. Randall Atlas, "Will ADA Handicap Security?," *Security Management* (March 1992): 37–38.
9. For further information, see: Robert L. Barnard, *Intrusion Detection Systems*, 2nd ed. (Boston: Butterworth–Heinemann, 1988).
10. National Lighting Bureau, "Lighting for Safety and Security." (Washington, DC: National Lighting Bureau, Pub.), pp. 5–9.

10

Burglary and Robbery Countermeasures

Burglary

Uniform Crime Report showed 3,073,909 burglaries *reported* in the United States in 1990—two-thirds were residential and the remainder were nonresidential. (See Figure 10-1 for percentage changes in burglary.) The annual loss was estimated at $3.5 billion. Average losses for both residential and nonresidential burglaries were about $1,100. More burglaries were reported in August, the least number in February.[1]

It should be pointed out that crimes listed in *Uniform Crime Reports* are *reported* crimes. Many crimes go unreported. Numerous victimization studies show crime being three to five times higher than what is reported to the FBI.

Crime losses often do not reflect true costs. In a burglary, for example, direct losses include the valuables stolen. Indirect losses include repairs at the point of forced entry, the need for a new safe or repairs to it, an insurance premium increase, the need to replace stolen items at present day prices, downtime at the business to recover from the burglary, and psychological harm to the victim.

Uniform Crime Reports defines burglary as the unlawful entry of a structure to commit a felony or theft. The use of force to gain entry is not required. Three subclassifications of burglary are forcible entry, unlawful entry where no force is used, and attempted forcible entry.

Burglary differs from robbery in that burglars seek to remain unseen, whereas robbers confront their victims and use force or threat of force for gain. Burglary is a crime against property. Robbery is a crime against a person.

Burglars and Their Techniques

A considerable amount of research has been published on burglary. The research focuses on burglars, their characteristics, the targets of their crime, and security measures. Most burglars are young males who are unskilled. In cities, burglars are disproportionately nonwhite. The older professionals are less common and are likely to work alone. They concentrate on "big hits," such as businesses dealing with large sums of cash or jewelry. Young and female burglars often commit their crimes in a group. Most burglars ply their trade close to where they live. Victims are chosen according to the opportunities available for unauthorized access. Locations with good security are less likely to be burglarized than those that have minimal security.[2]

Burglars choose their line of work over robbery, because they know it is safer and the chances of getting caught are lower than robbery. As one burglar explained:

> You'll get away with a hundred burglaries where you'll get away with five stickups; and indeed the proportion of crimes solved is a good bit lower for burglary than for robbery ... There is more of a chance of identifying a man who sticks up the place.[3]

This view is supported by the *Uniform Crime Report* statistics that show that of the crimes reported to police in 1990, 25 percent of robberies were cleared by arrest, while the figure is 14 percent for burglaries.[4]

Subsequent pages do not discuss the social problems underlining the crime of burglary nor the psychological makeup of the burglar. An emphasis is placed on the methods used by burglars and what security strategies can be implemented by retailers so burglars will look elsewhere to commit their crimes. We have often heard the expression "think like a thief." By understanding the techniques used by burglars, retailers can plan better defenses.

Burglars often begin their attack by checking for open doors or windows. Business people, in a rush to end the work day and go home, are known to leave a store front door unlocked. This is why foot patrol officers pull on doors in a business district during evening shifts. Offenders perform the same exact activity, often more thoroughly. Burglars frequently perform a security survey or "case" their target and look for access points that are out of sight and that have an unobstructed path for escape.[5] In addition to doors and windows, other access points of interest are garage doors, roofs and skylights, and air-conditioning ducts. Bushes, trees, and trash provide cover for the five or ten minutes, maximum, required for the break-in. If noise is not a concern, although it usually is, a burglar may do a "kick-in." A kick-in is a sharp kick at the location on the door next to the lock. A night of rain and thunder can obscure the noise. Burglars assert that most doors of houses and businesses are so poorly constructed that a kick-in will usually spring the door open.[6]

A common method to gain entry is to use a strong screwdriver or crowbar to spread or pry the door away from the door jamb where the bolt is located. The same technique can be applied to a window. Since a bolt extends about

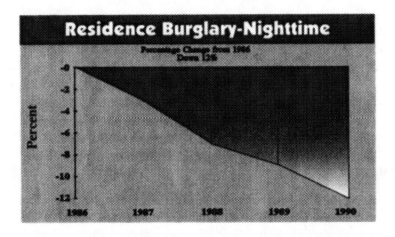

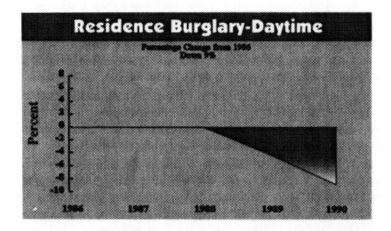

1 inch from the door lock into the door frame, by spreading or prying the frame away from the door, the door will swing open. This is called *jamb peeling*. Another technique is to use a hacksaw blade to saw the bolt.

When the door moves, the separation of contact switches, if installed, will set off an alarm. It is an axiom of professional burglars to never open doors or windows. To avoid this problem, the smart burglar will look for another, safer approach to avoid detection. For example, if foil is used on a door or window to sense intrusion, a hole can be cut through the glass at both ends of the foil so a jumper can be placed from one end to the other to enable removal of the central portion of the glass and foil while the flow of electricity con-

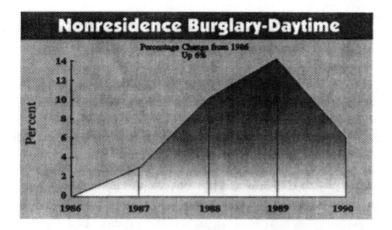

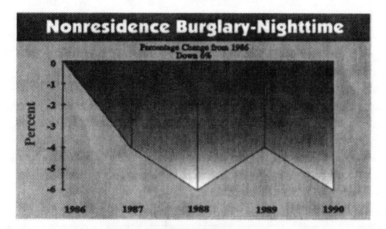

Figure 10-1 Percentage Changes in Burglary Source: U.S. Dept. of Justice, *Crime in the United States, 1990, Uniform Crime Reports* (Washington, DC: U.S. Government Printing Office, 1991), pg. 29.

tinues via the jumper wire. The same technique can be done with contact switches. Another approach is to remove a panel from a door without opening the door and setting off a contact switch or sensor. Creative burglars may even try novel approaches to avoid detection such as wearing an insulated suit to block heat emanating from the body to circumvent a passive infrared sensor.[7] Terrorists are known to own rubber suits in anticipation of scaling electrified fences.[8] Right now, there is probably a burglar who is designing a suit capable of penetrating multiple alarm systems. We can only guess as to how "stealth" technology (used in jets to avoid enemy radar) is being used by criminal minds today.

Burglars are sometimes assisted by individuals who work on the "inside." A door, window, or safe can be conveniently left unlocked; an alarm system can be turned off; or the sensitivity of a motion detector adjusted to the point where it is useless.

Alarm bells on the exterior of buildings are usually enclosed in a metal cabinet with a good-quality lock. Vents on the cabinet enable the noise to be broadcast to the surrounding area. However, if shaving cream is sprayed into the cabinet, the bell noise becomes muffled. A double box and a silent alarm to a central station are good defenses against this problem.

In reference to locks, professional burglars may pick a lock to enter a retail store. Another approach is to borrow a key, or coax an employee into borrowing a key, and press it into a bar of soap or wax so that a duplicate can be made.

Professional burglars have the skill for acquiring information about their intended target. As a retailer, exercise care when speaking with unfamiliar people, because appearances can be deceptive and anyone can purchase or prepare official-looking identification. Salespeople, maintenance workers, tourists, and so forth, whether genuine or not, may obtain answers to questions that provide just enough information for a successful burglary.

Burglars sometimes hide in restrooms or storage areas until a business is closed. Then the offender must break out after gathering the loot. Double-cylinder locks, which require a key for both sides of a door are an obstacle to the hide-in burglar.

Experienced burglars may have an accomplice outside with a walkie-talkie ready to warn of approaching police. A scanner to monitor police radio broadcasts is another tool used by burglars.

A priority for burglars is to avoid contact with anyone during the crime. Generally, the choice of burglary over robbery shows that the offender is interested in a less violent crime. However, a business person working after hours or sleeping on the premises is subject to considerable danger if a burglar gains access and a confrontation occurs. Some burglars seek to eliminate witnesses.

Police patterns may be studied by a burglar. Many know that in the early morning hours very few police are patrolling, and hiding and sleeping may be the norm for police. A diversion in the form of a fire or accident is one strategy to occupy police on the other end of town during the burglary. During the crime, the burglar may insert an obstacle in the keyway of all exterior doors, so if anyone shows up, extra time is afforded to the burglar to escape from the roof or other avenue, or to hide.

Defenses against Burglary

The previous chapter on store design and physical security provides a foundation for protection against burglary. The following pages enhance that information. In *Security and Crime Prevention*, the authors make the following comments on burglary:

> Business burglaries generally take place during nonworking hours, such as at night or on weekends. Burglaries may also occur in unattended storerooms where the offender is unlikely to meet the victim. The greatest number of burglary attempts are directed against businesses selling jewelry, men's and women's clothing, liquor, groceries, electrical and other appliances, furs, and drugs. Service stations are also frequent targets. Burglars, by the very nature of their crime, can be more selective in the goods they take and can usually take larger quantities than robbers or shoplifters.[9]

Consider a two-pronged approach to burglary protection: employee socialization (e.g., training on policies and procedures, and management setting an example through action) and physical security (see Figures 10-2 and 10-3).

Employee socialization can involve the following:

Survey possible burglar entry points.
Leave lights on (inside and outside).

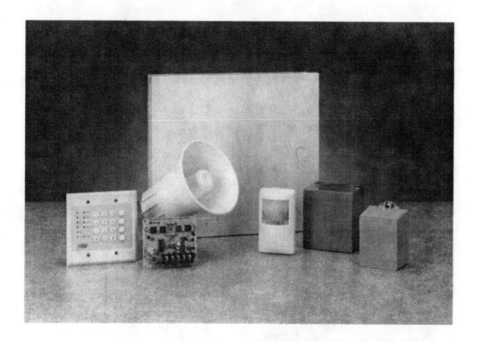

Figure 10-2 Components of a Burglar Alarm System—Keypad, Siren, Control Box, Passive Infrared Sensor, and Backup Battery Courtesy of Fire Burglary Instruments, Inc., Syosset, NY.

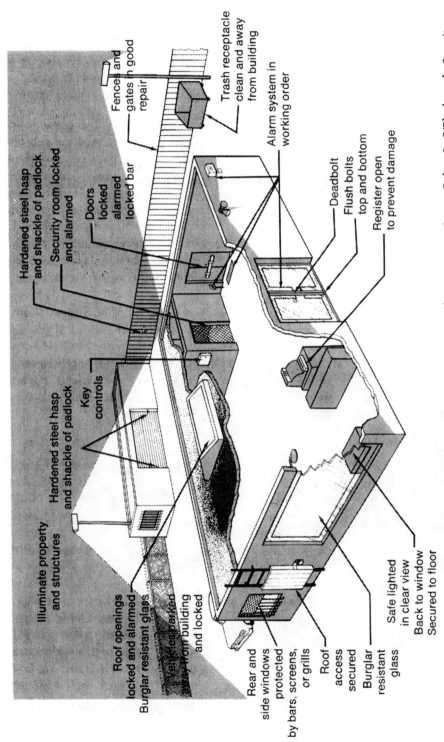

Figure 10-3 Defenses against Burglary Reprinted with permission from Butterworth–Heinemann. *Source:* Robert L. O'Block et al., *Security and Crime Prevention*, 2nd ed. (Boston: Butterworth–Heinemann, 1991), p. 309.

Overturn cash register money trays on top of opened cash register drawers at closing.

Recheck doors and windows at closing.

Recheck alarms.

Notify public and private police immediately after mistakenly activating an alarm.

Cooperate with public and private police as much as possible.

Preserve the crime scene to protect any evidence when discovering a burglary.[10]

The following list provides additional avenues for protection:

Carefully plan physical security (see Figure 10–3) and remember that its effectiveness can be measured by the time it takes to get through it.

Conduct a security survey during the day and at night. Think like a thief. Seek the services of the local police crime prevention officer.

Remove attractions when closing. Do not leave expensive merchandise in display windows.

Ensure that police and passers-by can see as much of the store as possible. Install good lighting inside, outside, and on the roof. Inside, use low counters and large, uncluttered display windows.

Place the safe and cash register up front so they can be seen easily from the outside.

Consider leaving an unleashed dog inside the store at night. Beware of potential liability if someone is hurt. Also remember that dogs can be poisoned or shot.

Keep windows and doors clean, so fingerprints of offenders can be obtained after a crime.

Do not leave vehicles, equipment, or tools in a condition that would make a burglar's job easier. Hide vehicle keys, and store equipment and tools in locked cabinets.

Use insurance as a backup if physical security defenses fail. Insurance can assist with financial recovery if losses are significant. Physical security can pay dividends by reducing insurance premiums. (See Chapter 11, "Risk Management.")

Safes

Safes (see Figure 10–4), vaults, and files can be formidable defense against burglars. However, retailers should be careful when selecting these containers since specifications and ratings vary. A common mistake is to use

Figure 10-4 Money Safe Courtesy of Diebold, Inc., Canton, OH.

a fire-resistant safe to protect against burglary. Fire-resistant safes, also called record safes, have thin steel walls that contain insulation. The insulation creates steam during a fire to cool the contents for a specified period of time (see Table 10-1). Burglary-resistant safes, also known as money safes, have thick walls and are capable of withstanding various methods of attack by burglars (see Table 10-2).

Underwriters Laboratory classifies safes after subjecting them to various tests. A 350-4 fire safe can withstand an external temperature of 2000° F for

Table 10-1 Fire Resistant Containers

Classification	Temperature	Time	Impact	Old label
UL Record Safe Classifications				
350-4	2000°F	4 hours	yes	A
350-2	1850°F	2 hours	yes	B
350-1	1700°F	1 hour	yes	C
350-1 (Insulated record container)	1700°F	1 hour	yes	A
350-1 (Insulated filing device)	1700°F	1 hour	no	D
UL Computer Media Storage Classifications				
150-4	2000°F	4 hours	yes	
150-2	1850°F	2 hours	yes	
150-1	1700°F	1 hour	yes	
UL Insulated Vault Door Classifications				
350-6	2150°F	6 hours	no	
350-4	2000°F	4 hours	no	
350-2	1850°F	2 hours	no	
350-1	1700°F	1 hour	no	

Reprinted with permission from Butterworth–Heinemann. *Source:* Gion Green, *Introduction to Security* (Boston: Butterworth–Heinemann, 1987), 173.

4 hours while the internal temperature does not exceed 350° F (the flash point of paper). The safe subject to testing is actually placed in a furnace. Another test involves the safe being dropped 30 feet into rubble to simulate the safe falling through a building (i.e., impact test) during or after a fire. Money safes are also tested by subjecting them to simulated burglary attacks as described in Table 10–2.

Burglars first attempt to enter a safe without force. This can be accomplished by simply opening the safe door that was left open or by turning the dial slowly in case the safe is set to open after passing the last number of the combination. This is often called the *day combination* and is used to facilitate quick access by employees. Sometimes, employees leave the combination in plain sight or taped under a desk drawer. A burglar may also work in collusion with an employee. Another approach is to view the safe being opened and acquire the combination via a telescope from an off-site location. A minority of burglars can open a safe through manipulation by sight, sound, and touch.

Table 10-2 UL Money Safe Classification

Classification	Description	Construction	
TL-15	Tool resistant	Weight:	At least 750 lbs. or anchored.
		Body:	At least one-inch thick steel or equal.
		Attack:	Door and front face must resist attack with common hand and electric tools for 15 minutes.
TL-30	Tool resistant	Weight:	At least 750 lbs. or anchored.
		Body:	At least one-inch thick steel or equal.
		Attack:	Door and front face must resist attack with common hand and electric tools plus abrasive cutting wheels and power saws for 30 minutes.
TRTL-30[a]	Tool and torch resistant	Weight:	At least 750 lbs.
		Attack:	Door and front face must resist attack with tools listed above, and oxy-fuel gas cutting or welding torches for 30 minutes.
TRTL-30X6	Tool and torch resistant	Weight:	At least 750 lbs.
		Attack:	Door and entire body must resist attack with tools and torches listed above, plus electric impact hammers and oxy-fuel gas cutting or welding torches for 30 minutes.
TXTL-60	Tool, torch, and explosive resistant	Weight:	At least 1000 lbs.
		Attack:	Door and entire safe body must resist attack with tools and torches listed above, plus eight ounces of nitroglycerine or its equal for 60 minutes.

[a] As of January 31, 1980, UL stopped issuing the TRTL-30 label, replacing it with the TRTL-30X6 label which requires equal protection on all six sides of the safe. Some manufacturers, however, continue to produce safes meeting TRTL-30 standards in order to supply lower-priced containers, which provide moderate protection against tool and torch attack.

Reprinted with permission from Butterworth–Heinemann. *Source:* Gion Green, *Introduction to Security* (Boston: Butterworth-Heinemann, 1987), 175.

Force is the secondary choice to enter a safe. Weak safes, such as fire-resistant safes, can be opened by ordinary tools (e.g., hammer, punch, crowbar, ax), while the stronger money safes require ordinary tools and powerful equipment (e.g., drills, torches).

Safes can be protected by ensuring that the classification is not on the outside of the safe because this informs the burglar of the types of tools required to open the safe. Capacitance and vibration sensors, and lighting, provide good protection. The safe should be placed so it can be seen from the outside and it should be bolted down to prevent burglars from stealing it. Leave as little as possible in a safe to reduce the take. This may entail frequent trips to the bank. Two important procedures to follow are to make sure the safe is locked at the end of the day and change the combination when an employee who knows it, leaves the job.

Procedures Following a Burglary

Many retailers experience the shock of being burglarized when they open their businesses in the morning. Unfortunately, the victim almost instinctively searches the whole store to survey losses and damage. This approach has several disadvantages. First, the burglar may still be in the building. Any attempt by the retailer to capture the burglar should be avoided. The burglar may be a desperate junkie and try to eliminate any witnesses. If a surprise meeting does occur, the retailer should back off and leave, or allow the burglar to escape. Obtain a good description, including unique features.

Another reason for not walking throughout the store is that valuable evidence may be destroyed, including fingerprints and shoeprints. Also, some police departments use a dog to track down burglars as long as the burglar was the last person on the premises. The retailer can destroy the burglar's scent and this investigative strategy by walking into the store. But remember, police vary in how they handle burglary calls.

When retailers realize that a burglary has occurred, they should leave the premises immediately, avoid opening for business, and contact the police by using a neighbor's telephone. Sometimes the retailer does not discover the crime until a later date. However, the police should still be called to investigate.

When police arrive, do not expect miracles or a high-quality investigation. As discussed earlier, police resources are limited and the clearance rate for property crimes is low. All police departments vary in professionalism, strategies, and skills. Do not expect a police dog to appear with police or expect fingerprints or photographs to be taken. The police will ask for basic facts and a list of missing items. This list becomes part of the public record. Insurance companies may check the list submitted to police and compare it to the list that was attached to the insurance claim. Thus, the retailer should exercise care when preparing the list. Also, the retailer is likely to need proof that the missing items actually existed.

Police Response to a Burglar Alarm

Instead of the retailer discovering a burglar in the morning, the police may receive notification that a burglary alarm has signaled an intrusion. It is a well-known fact that more than 90 percent of alarm activations are false in most communities. However, the definition of false alarm, and what causes it, are subject to considerable debate. For example, it is difficult to count those burglars who escaped from the scene upon seeing police approach in response to an alarm. These incidents are typically classified as a false alarm, when in reality the alarm system did its job.

If a community or a particular business has excessive false alarms, public police may respond in a nonchalant manner. This is dangerous for police, because this relaxed response can lead to a sudden surprise—a confrontation with a burglar.

Well-trained police approaching a potential burglary scene in response to an alarm note people and automobiles fleeing the area. The police may park a few doors away from the scene and make as little noise as possible. Their guns may be drawn. For these reasons, retailers should be very cautious and inform police if they are on the premises or en route.

If the retailer receives a call at home that their store was victimized, and police request a meeting at the store, the retailer should obtain the police officer's name and then call the police department to verify the call. Retailers have been known to respond to a bogus call and then been forced by robbers to open the business to make the crime easier for the thieves who do not have to overcome strong physical security, an alarm system, and a safe.

On the minds of police during the investigation is the possibility that the burglary was faked. If the business is faltering, the owner may see insurance fraud as a way out. Careful questioning by investigators, a thorough search for physical evidence and the point of access by the burglar, plus a check of the owner's financial status can expose fraud.

More sophisticated police departments use automated, networked databases to search for clues. These databases can include basic case information, MOs, evidence collected, and property losses. These databases can also be linked to other types of crimes. In one case, the MO of a certain burglar was to use a heavy-duty screwdriver to pry at doors to gain access. In one burglary, the tip of the screwdriver broke and remained in the door jamb. Police collected this evidence and entered the information in a database. Several months later an offender was charged with assault. A heavy-duty screwdriver was retrieved by an investigator who then searched the database. The use of a screwdriver and the collection of a screwdriver tip was spotted in the database. Burglary investigators were contacted and the screwdriver tip found earlier was matched with the screwdriver in the possession of the offender charged with the assault. After the burglar was successfully interviewed many burglaries were cleared, because the offender committed numerous burglaries using the same MO.

During their investigation, police may frequent pawnshops to search for stolen items. Informants also supply information, especially on fences and those individuals receiving stolen goods. Extremely valuable property may be entered into the FBI's National Crime Information Center, a computerized databank that contains a variety of information helpful to law enforcement authorities. The rate of recovery for stolen property varies between 25–40 percent among communities. Operation identification (discussed in subsequent pages) does assist police in returning property to the victim.

Robbery

Uniform Crime Reports showed 639,271 robberies *reported* in the United States in 1990. (See Figure 10–5 for percentage changes in robbery.) The annual loss was estimated at $501 million with an average of $783 per incident. Average dollar losses ranged from $341 for convenience store robberies to $3,244 for bank robberies. December showed the greatest number of reported robberies, while April showed the least number reported. In 1990, 42 percent of all robberies were committed with the use of strong-arm tactics, 37 percent with firearms, and 12 percent with knives or other cutting instruments. Compared to 1989, each category of weapon used increased, especially firearms at 22 percent.[11] Refer to the early discussion of burglary for comments on unreported crimes and true costs of crimes. These topics apply to robbery as well as burglary.

Uniform Crime Reports defines robbery as the taking or attempting to take anything of value from the care, custody, or control of a person or persons by force or threat of force or violence and/or by putting the victim in fear.

Robbers and Their Techniques

As with burglary, a considerable amount of research has been conducted on robbery. In one study of inmates serving time for armed robbery, it was learned that the level of criminal activity diminished with age, but as they aged, they developed an inclination toward robbery because they could do it alone and not risk being implicated by a partner. Also, robbery required fewer tools than burglary and the number of targets was endless. The researchers concluded that rehabilitative efforts had not been successful and

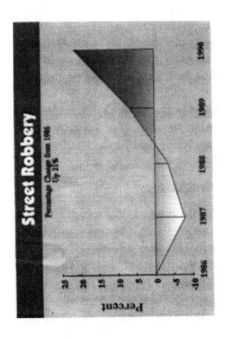
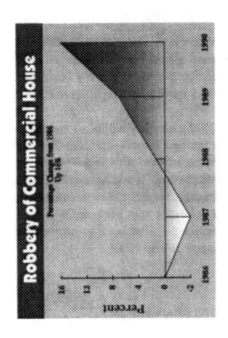
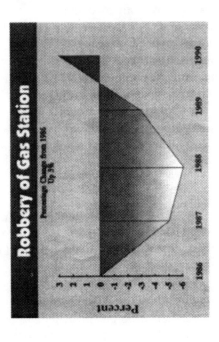
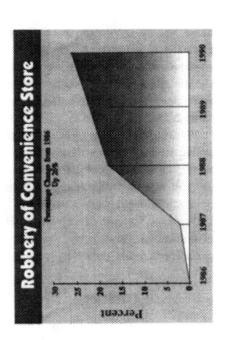

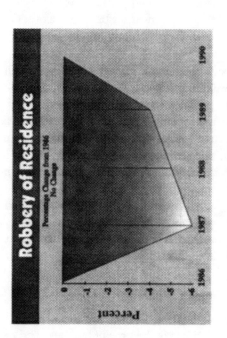
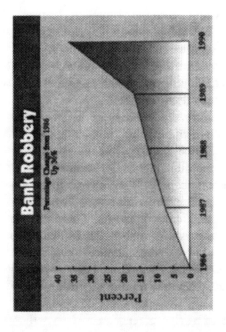

Figure 10–5 Percentage Changes in Robbery *Source:* U.S. Dept. of Justice, *Crime in the United States, 1990, Uniform Crime Reports* (Washington, DC: U.S. Government Printing Office, 1991), p. 21.

that the best approach would be to help offenders decrease their dependence on drugs and alcohol, and assist them with finding employment on their release. In another study, more than half of all robbery victims were attacked and one in 12 experienced serious injuries. Offenders displayed weapons in almost half of all robberies. Nine out of ten robbers were male and half were black or worked in groups of two or more.[12]

Only a small minority of robbers (5–10 percent) are professional criminals—those who earn their living from crime, who take pride in their expertise and in their criminal identity, and who plan their crimes with care so as to yield the largest possible income.[13] The majority of robbers (three out of four) are "opportunist robbers."[14] When these offenders see a ripe opportunity for robbery, they act. They are often young, lower class adolescents who act impulsively and do not plan their crimes. This group is more likely to rob elderly people. A third category of robbers are the semiprofessionals who do some planning and are likely to target liquor stores, convenience stores, and other small retailers. Although these three categories are general in nature, and exceptions abound, they are helpful to understand different types of robbers.

The amount of planning that precedes a robbery will vary. Professionals can take months to plan. They may make contact with an insider who can supply crucial information about cash and other valuables on hand, security systems, when valuables leave the premises, and what form of transportation is used. The professional may spend a few days involved in surveillance of the target, use a pretext (e.g., deliver a package, inspect for a gas leak, or even get a job at the location) to obtain information. On the other hand, an offender with a drug problem may walk past a convenience store once or twice before robbing it.

A portion of robbers uses some clever strategies when they rob. The "Monday robber" technique is when robbers use circumstances beyond their control to their advantage. They see a rainy Monday morning as an ideal time to rob. Employees are recovering from the weekend and coping with the "shock" of work. The rain makes wearing a long raincoat (for hiding a shotgun) and running (from the scene) appear normal. Police are less likely to get out of their patrol cars to conduct a search of an alley or other outside location in a driving rain.

The weapons employed by robbers to back up their threats are easily obtained. Guns and knives can be bought on the street or in a store, or they can be stolen during previous crimes. When these sources do not produce a weapon, a kitchen knife will do.

Planning and Research

Before implementing defenses against robbery, certain basic questions should be answered. What is the type of business and its location? Does it operate at night? Is it a high-risk business? Many more questions can be posed to focus on unique needs and produce the most cost-effective robbery defenses.

A considerable amount of research has been conducted on robberies at convenience stores and appropriate countermeasures. Research shows that when businesses keep less cash on the premises by making frequent bank deposits, the monetary incentives of robbery diminish. Also, when target hardening (i.e., physical security) is employed, it has an impact on certain forms of theft.[15] A study by the Athena Research Corporation entitled, "Robbery as Robbers See It," polled 241 robbers in prisons to find out what made targets appealing. The number one factor was the amount of money or valuables available. Close behind were ease of access and escape. Police patrols, camera systems, and alarm systems were less important. Nearly every study confirms that the amount of cash available is the major factor that attracts robbers.[16]

Security Letter noted that the security field is more an art than a science and that precious little research has been conducted on loss prevention that would meet the critical standards of the social sciences. This letter cites a 1975 study by Wayman J. Crow and James L. Bull from the Western Behavioral Science Institute in La Jolla, California. The study entitled "Robbery Deterrence: An Applied Behavioral Science Demonstration" focused on 60 experimental and 60 control "7-11" convenience stores of the Southland Corporation. It was noted that 27 percent of the 120 stores accounted for 72 percent of the robberies. Neither socioeconomic status of the store's area nor sales volume were related to robbery frequency. The researchers concluded that the attractiveness of a store to robbers can be reliably measured. Ideal considerations from the robber's viewpoint were, among other factors, availability of money, the need to terrorize the victim into giving up the money, speed in accomplishing the job, avoidance of being recognized, and a quick getaway. Countermeasures included posting signs that no more than $35 was available in the cash register and that other funds were in a locked safe not accessible to the clerk. Training for clerks emphasized greeting all customers with eye contact, maintaining vigilance, and calling police when a customer was loitering. Another strategy by these researchers was to create a "fishbowl" at the stores by clearing windows and improving lighting to put robbers "on stage" so they could be readily observed. Robberies declined by 30 percent at experimental stores. Although this research did not test a two-clerk-per-store strategy, crime prevention specialists recommend it.[17]

Research by Ronald D. Hunter of convenience store robberies demonstrated that crime prevention through environmental design works. The following variables were found to be significant in reducing robberies:

> cash registers located in the center, rather than on the side, of the store

multiple clerks
good visibility inside and from the outside
stores located next to commercial property, rather than near residential property
stores without concealed areas or escape routes (e.g., shrubbery, woods nearby)
good lighting
stores located where evening commercial activity occurred
stores with gasoline pumps[18]

A "Study of Safety and Security Requirements for 'At-Risk Businesses'" (January 1991) by the Office of the Attorney General of Florida noted that of the 322 murders on death row at the time of the study, 29 were convicted of homicides in convenience stores (that is one out of every eleven). Of the 13 convenience store murders reported for the 12-month period beginning September 1, 1989, eight victims were employees, three were customers, one was a passerby, and one was a suspect. Five police officers were killed in Florida during this same period. The Convenience Store Security Act passed by the 1990 Florida legislature has been called one of the toughest in the nation; however, it does not mandate two clerks or require bullet-resistant enclosures. A 1985 study by Dr. Richard N. Swanson for the City of Gainesville noted that the single highest predictor for selecting a robbery target was the presence of a single clerk. Other studies support this need. Although cities such as Gainesville have ordinances requiring a minimum of two clerks, heavy lobbying defeated this state legislation in Florida.[19]

A Sample of Death Row Convenience Store Cases in Florida

It was in the early afternoon hours on October 8, 1982, when shots rang out at West's Farm Market in Palmetto. When police arrived, they found the store's owner, 72-year-old Willie West, his wife, 68-year-old Martha, and an employee, Roseanna Welch, shot. The Wests died from their wounds and, although Welch had been shot five times and left for dead, she survived and was able to provide police with an account of the shooting. According to her statement, four young men had come in, ordered the three into the office before taking the $88 that was in the store's cash register. The victims, who knew the defendants, were then repeatedly shot.

On September 11, 1975, Keith Kirchaine, 16, stopped by the Zippy Mart Food Store in Hampton to visit his friend, Gene Lundgren, who was alone on duty. Authorities there discovered the body of 19-year-old Lundgren at around 10 a.m. that day but it was not until 1 p.m. that Kirchaine's body was discovered in a wooded area some four miles away from the scene. Like Lundgren, he had been shot. During Griffin's trial, it was revealed that the robbery had netted some $250 and Kirchaine had been kidnapped at gunpoint after his friend was shot and killed.

Karol Hurst, 21 and seven months pregnant at the time, was in her car at a Pantry Pride in Leesburg on February 21, 1978, when Freddie Lee Hall and Mack Ruffin decided to steal a car to use in a convenience store robbery. They chose hers. At gunpoint, they forced the young woman to drive to a heavily wooded area where she was sexually assaulted. Pleading for her life and that of her unborn child, she wrote them a $20,000 check but she was pistol whipped, robbed and then shot in the back of the head while lying face down in the dirt.

The pair then drove the stolen car to the convenience store they planned to rob. Pretending to be customers, they bought a teddy bear and two bundles of socks. A suspicious clerk had a customer call the sheriff's office and Hernando County Deputy Lonnie Coburn responded. A scuffle ensued and Deputy Coburn was shot. The deputy's body was found with the gun that killed the young mother lying next to it, along with the teddy bear and the socks.

Source: "Study of Safety and Security Requirements for 'At-Risk Businesses' " (January 1991), Office of Attorney General (FL).

A legal question that arises is whether employers in high-risk industries are responsible for the murder of their employees? One view is that they are if they fail to provide proper safety precautions. Lawsuits and regulatory law will generate attention to the need for safety and security.[20]

Defenses against Robbery

Crime prevention literature repeatedly suggests to retailers to harden the target, create a time delay, and reduce the loot. The first strategy involves physical security. An attempt to increase the time necessary to commit the crime will frustrate the offender. When less loot is on hand, losses are minimized. Table 10–3 applies these three strategies to both robbery and burglary for comparison purposes.

The following guidelines will assist retailers in planning strategies to prevent robbery.

- Of the utmost importance is quality training of employees on all aspects of robbery countermeasures, including use of equipment, and policies and procedures. Require all employees to participate in a "mock" robbery.
- Maintain good lighting both inside and outside.
- For high-risk locations consider a bullet-resistant cashier booth.
- Do not obstruct police and pedestrian observation through windows from the outside. Limit advertising posters. Make sure the checkout counter and cash register are clearly visible to observers outside.
- Lock all nonessential doors and do not unlock these doors for strangers.
- Robbers do not like to be noticed when they "case" a potential target. Thus, greet all entering customers politely and look them in the eye.
- Do not answer questions from strangers who are interested in business and security operations.
- Post emergency (e.g., police, fire) telephone numbers on all telephones.
- If a surveillance camera has been installed and a suspicious person is present, activate the camera for a few frames for possible evidence at a later time.
- Practice and advertise a cash control policy. In high-crime areas, let everyone know that the store cannot accept a $20 bill or higher. However, by posting a sign that no more than $50 is in the register, this may attract an addict robber who needs just that amount! By posting "we appreciate exact change" it is possible that employee theft may increase, since the register does not have to be opened for change!
- If possible, encourage clerks to stay away from the cash register. They can stock shelves, sweep, etc. Valuable time is expended if a robber has to coax a clerk to the register from the other side of a store.
- A pickup of excess amounts of cash should be arranged periodically. In large stores, a supervisor may walk to each register for collection while performing related paperwork. (Employees must be

Table 10-3 Robbery/Burglary Matrix

	Robbery	Burglary
Harden the target	Yes*	Yes
Create time delay	No**	Yes
Reduce loot	Yes	Yes

*For instance, a retail business hardened for robbery may include an alarm and hidden cameras. However, if the robber becomes trapped due to a metal gate that has blocked the only exit, then violence and a hostage situation may develop.

**When a robbery is in progress, a time delay can be dangerous. The exception would be if there were no threatening situation (unlikely in a robbery). Then, a time delay might aid in immediate apprehension. Time-delay safes can create a problem; warning signs are vital to deter robbers. Police agencies favor robber–police confrontations outside of the crime scene, away from innocent bystanders.

Reprinted with permission from Butterworth-Heinemann.

trained to give the money *only* to a designated supervisor.) The money is then taken to a money room for counting and preparation for transportation to a bank by retail employees or an armored car service.

- Use a safe that requires a secondary key not in the possession of the on-duty employee. Post this security precaution.
- Use a drop safe or a locked money chest that a clerk cannot open alone or that requires two keys. A time-delay safe is an alternative; it contains an inner compartment that operates on, say, a 15-minute time delay (too long for a robber to wait). Managers are often required to place the majority of funds in the time-delay section and open it only after the store has closed to count the deposit. Post information about the use of these safes on the premises for customers and robbers.

EGA Security Bulletin #17
To All Stores
"DON'T BE FOOLED BY THESE CONS"

In the last bulletin we covered "DO'S AND DON'T'S FOR ROBBERY." Here we go one step further by discussing ploys that robbers use to make their job easier by manipulating you and your job duties.

Was That a Police Officer Who Called?

Harry McCall was walking to his apartment one evening when a man pulled a gun and quickly relieved him of his wallet and keys. The next day, Sunday, Harry was surprised by a telephone call from a Sgt. Wilson who stated that police had found his wallet and keys. When Harry arrived at the downtown police headquarters, nobody had even heard of a Sgt. Wilson. While Harry was on the "wild goose chase," two groups of criminals stole from his business and apartment.

The moral: Always verify a call by telephoning authorities. Be suspicious of a telephone number supplied by the caller.

Can Time Lock Safes Really Help Robbers?

Neil Broach, a store manager, was always devising shortcuts to get the job done quicker. However, some of his methods would inevitably lead to trouble, such as the one described here. To comply with corporate security procedures, Neil used the on-site time lock safe, but his method of operation proved faulty. He would open the safe's outer door and reach inside to dial the combination of the inner door that contained a delay timer set for 15 minutes. Next, Neil would lock the outer door and then set a timer for 14 minutes. When the buzzer on the timer went off, Neil would be there to open the outer door and then turn the inner dial a few degrees to open the inner door. Ten minutes later, the scheduled armored car pickup would arrive. The guard would receive a bag of money, sign the log, and depart. Unfortunately, this routine was being watched by a customer-thief who, with an accomplice, distracted the manager the next day by becoming an irate customer and did not give the manager a chance to return to the safe after the timer rang. Thus, the armored car could not wait and left without making a pickup. Two days worth of cash would be on hand the next day, plus two robbers who showed up in a disguise. They watched Neil set the timer and closed in on him when the buzzer went off. In one minute, the robbers had hopped into a car waiting outside and departed before the armored car arrived.

The moral: Do not use a time lock safe and a timer in a location where you can be observed. Be discreet.

What Do Fishermen and Criminals Have in Common?

Some criminals plant fish nets in bank depositories. The net is arranged in the depository to prevent the money from being completely deposited so the offender can literally pull out the money. This technique works especially well at faulty depositories.

The moral: If you see such a net, or anyone near the depository, do not make a deposit. Leave quickly and call the police.

- Use a silent signal lock that triggers an alarm when a certain combination is used to open a safe during a robbery.
- Always count cash away from the public.
- When traveling to a bank to make a deposit, never use a money bag. Use a paper bag or something else that does not signal to the public that you are carrying money.
- Use irregular routes and times when banking.
- Watch for suspicious people before and after leaving. If necessary, call police and request a preventive patrol.
- Watch for suspicious people in or near the bank (e.g., someone looking over your shoulder or standing near a night depository).
- Keep some marked and recorded currency (i.e., bait money) available so it can be provided to a robber. Banks successfully use tear gas/dye packs to thwart robbers. These devices appear as a stack of currency, but emit tear gas and red smoke (that stains clothes) when taken off the premises. These packs are activated by radio transmission. The chances of recovering the money and apprehending the robber are improved with these devices.
- Place height markers at exits to assist with descriptions of robbers. Locate them at the 5', 5'6" and 6' heights. Use a different color for the 5'6" marker to prevent confusion.
- When selecting a robbery alarm system, consider the safety with which it can be activated. If a button is required to be pushed by hand, the robber may notice this action. A safer approach is a foot switch, as seen in Figure 10–6. An even safer strategy is to install a bill trap (see Figure 10–7). It is placed in one slot of a cash drawer. The last bill in the slot serves as an insulator, but when it is removed in a robbery, the metal parts touch and an alarm is sounded.
- Silent alarms are always best so as not to upset the robber.
- Integrate a robbery alarm into a hidden surveillance camera.
- Use multiple alarm signaling systems—send one to a central station or police department and another to a retail neighbor.
- Never use a robbery alarm for less serious crimes. A police response to a robbery call is usually intense. Contact local police for procedures to follow in the event of a robbery.

Figure 10-6 Foot Switch *Source:* U.S. Dept. of Commerce, *Commercial Intrusion Alarm Systems* (Washington, DC: U.S. Government Printing Office, 1979).

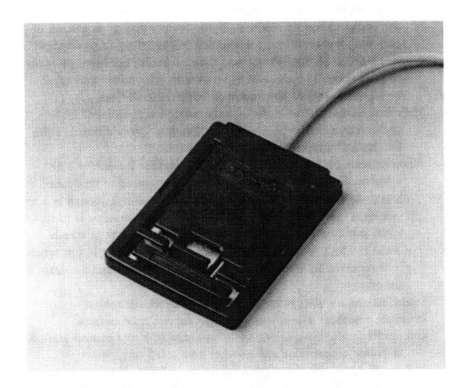

Figure 10-7 Bill Trap Courtesy of Sentrol, Portland, OR.

- Post the security methods used on the premises (e.g., CCTV, alarms, and two-key money safes that require two employees for access).
- Consider hiring security officers, but make sure they are screened, trained, armed, and alert. Seek legal advice for adequate insurance coverage and for the decision to arm officers.
- Hide keys, tools, and communications equipment in storage rooms and freezers in case a robber locks employees in these locations. Also, consider installing an alarm button.
- Most authorities do not recommend keeping a weapon on the premises for defense. The chances for serious injury or death are too great. However, because of limited police protection in certain areas and the media attention given to the crime problem, many retailers opt for being armed. Check the laws in your area concerning weapons.
- Try not to work alone. If so, give customers the impression that someone is in a back room. Play a radio in a back office, for example.
- Establish cautious opening and closing procedures. One strategy is for an employee to go inside while another waits outside for a "clear" signal. At closing, an employee can wait outside in an automobile with the engine running, doors locked, and lights directed at the exit. The availability of cellular telephones in automobiles makes an emergency call for assistance that much easier and the automobile horn can serve as a local alarm. Employees should be well versed on distress signals.
- A surprising number of armed robbers are former employees. Screen job applicants thoroughly. Take a snapshot of all new employees and keep the photos separate from personnel files (to avoid EEO problems). Use a second photo to post on a bulletin board with other employee photos.
- Consider offering free coffee to public police or employees of outside companies who use company vehicles with radios. Offer the free coffee during vulnerable hours. Allow police to write reports on the premises or come in out of the cold for a few minutes. Set up a taxi stand in front of stores prone to robbery.

Procedures during a Robbery

- When a robbery occurs, all the planning and training invested in earlier becomes extremely valuable.
- Try to remain calm. Take some deep breaths without being obvious. Robberies usually last for only a few minutes.

Think safety.

Do not resist unless your life is in imminent danger. Obey the robber's reasonable demands.

Give the robbers the valuables and do what is necessary to cause them to depart as quickly as possible.

Comply with the robber's instructions. If tens and twenties are asked for, provide just those bills.

If you have to reach under a counter to obtain a bag for the money, ask permission first.

Robbers are often substance abusers and likely to be very nervous. Never speak or act in a threatening manner, because a robber's reaction may be very aggressive. A robbery is no time for impulsive heroic action. The chances are in favor of the robber and the retailer may be injured or killed. Money and merchandise can be replaced, a life cannot!

Use your senses to your advantage. Note the unique characteristics of the robber (e.g., scars, tattoos, broken teeth). Memorize physical features and weapons used (see Figures 10–8 and 10–9 and use Figure 10–8 to write down a description after the robber departs). Did you notice any unusual odor from the robber? Examples include alcohol or a substance from a job the robber holds. Remember the things the robber touches. Fingerprints may be lifted by investigators later.

If the robber provides a demand note it could contain a valuable fingerprint and handwriting evidence. Handle it as little as possible.

Try to remember the robbers' exact words.

Do not follow robbers while they are leaving.

Be a living victim.

Note any vehicle, its unique features, model, color, and license number. This may be accomplished through the window.

Procedures after a Robbery

Notify police as soon as possible after a robbery, even if you activated a robbery alarm. Stay on the line until you provide your name, address, telephone number, and other information. Indicate whether emergency medical assistance is needed.

Follow company policies and procedures.

Request that customers wait for police to assist with the investigation. Try to obtain their names and addresses.

If you know the robber touched something, protect it so it can be dusted for fingerprints.

Write down as much as you can remember about the robber and the robbery.

SUSPECT ID CHART

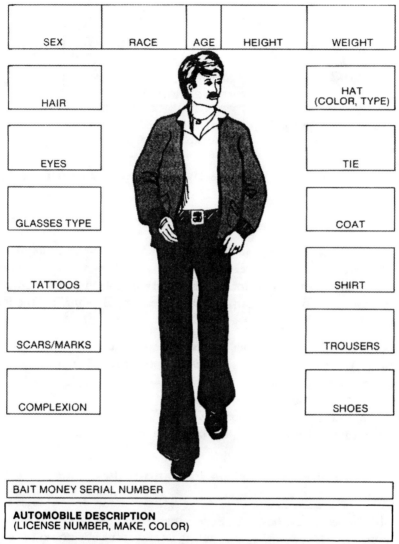

STAY ON THE PHONE!

Figure 10–8 Suspect ID Chart *Source:* Washington, D.C.: U.S. Government Printing Office.

Do not discuss the robbery with the media.
Ask police to keep the amount stolen confidential.
Prepare to assist with the prosecution of the case if the robber is caught.
Be thankful you survived.

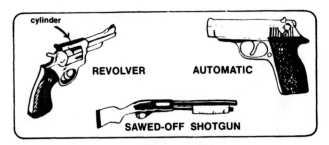

Automatic: These are flat-sided—no cylinder. The bullet clip is in the grip, where you can't see it.

Figure 10-9 Weapons *Source:* Washington, D.C.: U.S. Government Printing Office.

Police Response to a Robbery Alarm

Robbery is a violent crime and when police are en route to the scene, they are preparing themselves for a very dangerous call. Most police departments have policies and procedures to deal with robbery calls to ensure a high degree of safety for all parties. Guidelines for police include the following:

Proceed as rapidly as possible, but use extreme caution.
Assume the robber is at the scene unless otherwise advised.
Be prepared for gunfire.
Look for and immobilize any getaway vehicles.
Avoid a hostage situation if possible.
Make an immediate arrest if the suspect is at the scene.[21]

Community Crime Prevention Programs

There are thousands of police agencies in the United States and the quality varies. Many have excellent crime prevention programs and are doing a superior job in assisting community residents and businesses in combating crime.

Three primary community crime prevention programs reinforced by public police are target hardening, operation identification, and neighborhood watch. All three programs can serve residential and business locations. Target hardening is, essentially, physical security methods. Operation identification involves keeping an up-to-date inventory of merchandise and property, including office machinery. A copy should be placed in a safe deposit box or other secure location. When the inventory is being prepared, valuables should be marked with your driver's license and state initials by using an engraving tool. Also place "Operation ID" decals on windows and doors to warn offenders that property on the premises can be traced and that prosecution is made easier through Operation ID.

Neighborhood watch is popular in many communities. Residents or business people organize to watch each other's property. Those living and working on the same block know each other's routines and this makes it easier to recognize unusual behavior and things out of place. Surveillance by numerous people promotes security. Sometimes, adjacent businesses install two-way silent alarm systems so that they can signal each other to call authorities in the event of an emergency.

Several other community-based crime prevention programs exist. Crime Stoppers is run by an independent board of citizens, removed from the police, who authorize payments to citizens for information leading to the apprehension of offenders. Tipsters have the opportunity to remain anonymous. A "crime of the week" is selected to be transmitted to community residents via the media.

REACT International consists of business firms whose vehicles are equipped with two-radios that enable employees to communicate emergencies or suspicious activities to their dispatchers, who then contact the police. CB channel 9 is also monitored for emergency assistance.

Chain call warning systems have been established in many communities to notify business people of shoplifters, those who pass bad checks, and other offenders. The police call a specific business, which contacts two other businesses, and then the chain progresses until numerous businesses are aware of the suspects.

Community residents have organized other programs to reduce crime. In one community, improved street lighting resulted in less crime. Mobile drug education is another program.

Business Watch: Seattle, Washington, A Program for Commercial Crime Prevention.

In 1980 when Business Watch began, there were approximately 235,000 housing units and 26,000 businesses in Seattle. A resident of a housing unit had a one in twenty-five chance of being a victim of a residential burglary. A business person had a one in six chance of being a victim of a commercial burglary. National victimization data show that businesses are the victims in nearly 40% of all burglaries and UCR data show business burglary as one-third of the total.

For numerous years the Seattle police were involved in a well-organized residential Block Watch program with good success; however, more attention was needed to the business community. During 1980, Business Watch focused on commercial burglary, robbery, and theft. A reduction in robbery seemed less feasible because those perpetrators are less rational and rational strategies were expected to have less effect. The focus for robbery was to help business people protect themselves and reduce their losses.

The Business Watch approach had three objectives: (1) organize the merchants, (2) provide specific assistance, and (3) establish better relations with police. To introduce Business Watch to each district, a sponsor was selected who was prominent in the district. The media was also recruited. A meeting followed to introduce merchants to Business Watch.

Next, visits were conducted by Business Watch staff to: provide an introduction, distribute crime prevention materials, review crime problems, and develop a district directory of businesses. The police department printed the directories. It facilitated considerable communications among businesses, and patrolling police became less frustrated when trying to contact business owners. Many of the businesses requested crime prevention surveys as a result of the contact and communications.

The results: In each district organized, the number of burglaries declined. Decreases ranged from 25 to 50 percent. Since the program emphasized burglary countermeasures, robbery rates were not stated in the program report.[22]

Case Problems

10A. What community crime prevention programs exist in your locale? Contact the local police crime prevention officer for information.

10B. Contact local police to research how they respond to burglary and robbery calls in your community. Request a guest speaker.

10C. Return to the case problems in Chapter 9. Formulate countermeasures for burglary and robbery at Woody's Lumber Company.

10D. Use this chapter as a foundation to study a convenience store in your community to find out if it is a high-risk location for burglary or robbery. Request permission from the store's management to study the store. Inform local police about this project; they may assist. Compare convenience stores in your locale.

Notes

1. U.S. Dept. of Justice, *Crime in the United States, 1990, Uniform Crime Reports* (Washington, DC: U.S. Government Printing Office, 1991), 28.
2. Sue T. Reid, *Crime and Criminology*, 6th ed. (Fort Worth, TX: Holt, Rinehard & Winston , 1991), 319.
3. Charles E. Silberman, *Criminal Violence, Criminal Justice* (New York, NY: Vintage Books, 1978), 92–93.
4. *Crime in the United States, 1990, Uniform Crime Reports*, 21 and 28.
5. James E. Keogh, *The Small Business Security Handbook* (Englewood Cliffs, NJ: Prentice-Hall, 1981), 132.
6. Peter Letkemann, *Crime As Work* (Englewood Cliffs, NJ: Prentice-Hall, 1973), 52.
7. *Burglar Alarm Systems Defeat* (San Francisco, CA: Landis Publishing, 1974), 16.
8. Ibid., 10.
9. Robert L. O'Block et al., *Security and Crime Prevention*, 2nd ed. (Boston: Butterworth–Heinemann, 1991), 207.
10. Philip P. Purpura, *Security and Loss Prevention*, 2nd ed. (Boston: Butterworth–Heinemann, 1991), 304.
11. *Crime in the United States, 1990, Uniform Crime Reports*, 19 and 21.
12. Reid, 271–273
13. Silberman, 67.
14. For further information, see: John E. Conklin, *Robbery and the Criminal Justice System* (Philadelphia, PA: J. B. Lippincott, 1972), Ch. 4.
15. Thomas Gabor and Andre Normandeau, "Preventing Armed Robbery Through Opportunity Reduction: A Critical Analysis," *Journal of Security Administration*, 12(1) (1989): 4–6.
16. Ed McGunn, "Increase Robbery Resistance with Quick, Cheap Steps," *Security* (October 1990): 29.
17. *Security Letter*, Vol. XXI, No. 5 (March 1, 1991).
18. Ronald D. Hunter, "Convenience Store Robbery in Tallahassee: A Reassessment," *Journal of Security Administration* 13 (1 & 2) (1990): 8.
19. Office of the Attorney General of Florida, *Study of Safety and Security Requirements For "At-Risk Businesses"* (January, 1991).

20. For further information, see: Lawrence W. Sherman, "Businesses Need to React to On-the-Job Homicide Risks," *Security* (December 1987): 23–24.
21. Wayne W. Bennett and Karen M. Hess, *Criminal Investigation* (St. Paul, MN: West Publishers, 1991), 317.
22. "Business Watch: Seattle, Washington, A Program for Commercial Crime Prevention," Seattle Police Crime Prevention Unit, 610 Third Avenue, Seattle, Washington 98104.

11

Risk Management

What Is Risk Management?

Many types of misfortunes can befall a business, including fire, accident, flood, crime, negligence that results in injury or death, health hazards, business interruption, and death of a key executive. Any one of these exposures can force a company to close. Consequently, management has a responsibility to manage its risks as best as possible. Furthermore, this goal should be achieved in a manner consistent with human safety and welfare, environmental factors, ethics, and the law. The aim of risk management is to make the most efficient before-the-loss arrangement for an after-the-loss continuation of business.

Two types of risk are speculative and pure. Speculative risk exists when there is a possibility of gain or loss, such as when an investment is made in a business. Pure risk, however, involves only the possibility of loss. Retailers should take pure risk seriously and implement risk management strategies (or tools) to put themselves in the best possible financial situation if a disaster strikes.

Risk Management Strategies

Risk avoidance determines whether a business should avoid a certain venture because a specific risk is to too high. For example, a retail chain may decide not to open a store in a small town by a river because of frequent flooding, retail management may avoid selling a particular product because of numerous accidents and injuries reported by consumers, or plans for a downtown store may be scrapped following the security director's report on the crime rate.

Risk assumption requires the retailer to absorb possible losses by doing nothing and not obtaining insurance because the chance of loss is very low. A more responsible approach to managing risks is for the retailer to absorb losses by establishing a separate, internal fund that is established to cover losses. For example, a company that does a substantial mail-order business avoids paying insurance fees to the U.S. Postal Service on packages. If a loss occurs, reimbursement comes from the fund.

Risk assumption is also referred to as *risk retention* or *self-insurance*. This approach is becoming increasingly popular because of the rising cost of insurance. Only a well-qualified risk management specialist should be employed to consider the numerous variables for self-insurance.[1]

Risk abatement means that risks are decreased through loss prevention strategies. The risks are not eliminated, but if losses occur, the severity is less. An example of risk abatement is to include a sprinkler system in a store so it can reduce the damage from fire.

Risk spreading means that losses are reduced when a risk is spread among multiple locations. In a large retail store, cash registers can be spread throughout the store. Vital records stored at an off-site location spreads the risk in case of disaster.

Risk transfer relies on insurance to handle the risk in whole or in part. A premium is the price paid for the transfer. It is important not to use insurance as the major safeguard against losses. Use it as a backup to loss prevention measures; otherwise, premiums are sure to be high. Risk transfer can take other forms. Retailers, for instance, may require product liability coverage from their suppliers or may lease fixtures so the responsibility for safeguarding them is transferred to the lessor.

Job Duties of Risk Managers

Retail businesses typically seek the services of an outside insurance broker who acts as a go-between to secure insurance for the retailer. Large corporations can afford the services of full-time, in-house risk managers. However, smaller corporations use the services of an insurance broker or settle for an executive who "wears several hats." The human resources manager, for instance, may handle risk management duties.

The role of risk managers in business is becoming increasingly important in our complex world. As we know, there are many risks facing businesses. In addition to accidents, injuries, fires, and thefts, a business may be liable for violating employee rights or polluting the environment. Our courts are filled with civil and criminal actions against businesses. A risk manager will identify the particular risks facing the business and then manage the risks to ensure business survival. A retail department store will obviously have different risk management needs than a petrochemical plant.

The duties of risk managers vary among businesses. Generally, their functions involve the systematic and continuous identification of pure risk loss exposures, together with an evaluation of their nature, frequency, severity, and potential impact on the organization

the planning and organizing of appropriate risk control and risk financing techniques to minimize the cost of pure risk for the organization

the implementation of such techniques, both internally at the departmental and top management levels, and externally with loss control organizations, insurers, and other risk finance specialists[2]

In one company, a risk manager's duty may emphasize only insurance. In a large business, this duty may extend to loss prevention, safety, fire protection, and security. One coordinator may be responsible for each duty and all coordinators would report to the director of risk management.

Risk managers develop specifications of the insurance needs of their employer. These needs often include coverage required by law, such as workers' compensation insurance and vehicle liability insurance. Risk managers meet with insurance company representatives to communicate needs. The risk manager analyzes various policies and carefully considers coverage and price. Loss prevention strategies (e.g., sprinkler system to suppress fire, documented patrols by security officers) are studied as a way to reduce premiums. An investment in a sprinkler system, for example, can pay for itself over time due to reduced premiums. If premiums are too high, alternative strategies are studied to deal with risks. Deductibles are a popular strategy to reduce premiums. A small retailer, for example, may elect to absorb the first $1,000 of a loss in exchange for a lower premium that provides protection against large losses (less the deductible), which could result in serious financial difficulties. A large retailer may elect to absorb $10,000 to $250,000 in exchange for a favorable premium and good, large-loss coverage. Other avenues to deal with expensive premiums are the previously discussed risk management strategies.

In simple terms, insurance works this way: a group concerned about a certain risk purchases policies and pays a premium, which is put into a pool for the unfortunate few who experience a loss. If a risk manager finds that a premium is too high for a certain risk, or insurance is not available, the company itself may establish a special fund and contribute an amount each year that approximates what a premium would cost. During the early years of this self-insurance program, a loss could be devastating. However, loss prevention measures can be optimized to reduce the chances of a loss occurring. In later years, the fund can accumulate to the point where a loss will be sufficiently covered. When a self-insurance fund becomes substantial, other risks may be covered in the same way.

Because insurance is often expensive and at times not available, risk managers have become creative. A background in finance, accounting, and taxation are a must for this profession so the best possible financial decisions can be made for the business. To illustrate, a retailer should periodically reappraise assets (e.g., real estate, equipment) so adequate insurance coverage is maintained. The value of assets change over time, and depreciation, inflation, and replacement costs should be considered.[3]

Because potential loss exposures are evaluated in terms of expected frequency and severity of occurrence, a risk manager should be familiar with probability theory, statistical analyses, and a variety of loss-forecasting methodologies. At the same time, we should remember that the future is difficult to predict, even with these tools.

It is vital that the risk manager explain the risk management program to top executives in financial terms. The program must be cost-effective, show an ROI whenever possible, and provide financial protection. Also, the planning process must indicate the amount of risk assumed by the business, beyond that covered by insurance and loss prevention. A balance should be maintained between excessive protection and excessive exposure.[4]

Of particular importance for both the risk manager's job security and the survival of the business is a clear understanding of which risks are covered (or not covered) and to what extent are they covered. This is crucial because a surprise loss, with little or no coverage, can be financially and emotionally devastating. Also, a loss can affect shareholders, bondholders, creditors, customers, and so forth. To prevent this problem, a risk manager should have in writing, from the insurer, a list of what is covered and what is not. Insurance policies typically contain such information. Special policies or endorsements may be necessary to cover all risks. To prevent problems with claims, the risk manager should clearly know of the insurer's requirements for claims. Within what time period must a claim be made? To whom should the claim be reported? What type of proof of loss is required?

The Insurance Industry

In 1990, U.S. companies will spend nearly $150 billion in premiums for insurance to protect against property and liability losses. These same corporations will also spend almost $100 billion on risk-handling techniques that are alternatives to commercial insurance.[5] The cost to all U.S. employers in 1988 for health care benefits alone was estimated by the U.S. Chamber of Commerce to be more than $77 billion, which represents nearly 9 percent of all payroll expenses, with a growth rate of 19 percent over the previous year.[6] Added to these figures are unreimbursed costs and liability judgments for which businesses were not prepared.

There are more than 6,000 insurance companies in the United States. The Bureau of Labor Statistics estimated that, in 1989, there were 1,408,300 employees working directly for insurance companies. Property/casualty and life/health insurance companies have responsibility for assets that, at the end of 1989, totaled more than $1.8 trillion.[7]

Insurance for Retailers

Three major types of insurance that retailers should possess are property, liability, and workers' compensation.

Property Insurance

Unexpected perils can reduce the value of assets or destroy them. Fire insurance is a basic necessity, because fire can devastate and ruin assets that range from the inventory, to the interior decor, to the entire building. A retailer will find that broad coverage policies are worth the expense, since they cover a variety of perils beyond fire. By paying a small additional premium, a retailer can receive protection against such perils as windstorms, hail, sprinkler leakage, and vandalism.

Property insurance premiums are based on the physical condition of the premises, the type of building and neighborhood, and loss prevention measures, among other factors.

Liability Insurance

Retailers must protect their assets against the possibility of legal action based on negligence. This protection is especially important to retailers, because customers, employees, repair personnel, and so forth increase the possibility of someone being injured while in the store. Amounts awarded by juries in successful liability suits, and those cases settled out of court, have escalated to hundreds of thousands of dollars and even higher. Very few retailers can afford to pay such an amount to a plaintiff.

A comprehensive liability policy is a wise choice by a retailer. An insurer will defend a retailer, who becomes a defendant in a liability lawsuit, and will pay for medical treatment and the award due to the plaintiff.

Workers' Compensation Insurance

Employers have a responsibility to provide a safe working environment. Legislation and court decisions have supported this view over and over again. Even when an employer implements a variety of safety measures, employees can still have accidents and sue their employers. Worker's compensation insurance ensures protection and results in disability benefits and medical care being provided to an employee.

Some states do not require this form of insurance protection, especially when fewer than three or four people are employed. But the wise retailer, even if state law does not mandate this insurance, should obtain this type of coverage.

Workers' compensation costs are expected to double during the next five years, fueled in large part by rising medical costs. When officially reported, job-related injuries cost American employers in 1990 more than $60 billion in direct workers' compensation expenses. When retailers were surveyed, 97 percent said the major problem with the system is medical benefit costs and 92 percent said the widening definition of job-related injury is also a major problem.[8]

The unfortunate reality is that a portion of workers in the private and public sectors are unhappy with their jobs and hope to sustain a minor injury on the job, claim an inability to work, and obtain a check each month. Malingering has caused a great financial strain on the workers' compensation system. Employers and insurers find it difficult to distinguish between those who are really unable to work and those who are faking. The National Council on Compensation Insurance (New York City) notes that during a recession, claims tend to be of longer duration, especially where a worker may be facing a possible layoff.[9]

Private investigators of workers' compensation claims have a booming business. One exposed case of fraud can save a considerable amount of money over several months or years.

A workplace safety program can have an impact on fraudulent claims. Managers and supervisors should promote a strong safety environment by reinforcing policies and procedures, training, and documented inspections. If employees or customers claim to have slipped and injured themselves on a wet floor, documentation and a maintenance worker may show that the area was clean and inspected right before the person fell. Prompt and thorough investigations following an accident also helps to prevent fraud.

Another avenue to curb fraudulent claims is to thoroughly screen job applicants. A small percentage of people go from job to job to "squeeze" employers for benefits.

Other Types of Insurance

Business interruption insurance provides protection if a retailer has to close down following a fire or other disaster. The retailer is reimbursed for lost sales, utility bills, loan payments, and other obligations.

Boiler and machinery insurance covers losses from an explosion and fire involving the store's heating system.

Glass insurance covers breakage or damage to show windows, display cases, glass doors, mirrors, etc.

Group insurance includes health, accident, hospitalization, life insurance, and retirement income plans. Retailers vary in what they offer employees, especially since these plans are expensive and costs continue to escalate. Many retailers simply cannot afford basic health insurance for the employees. Other retailers share premium costs with employees.

Key person insurance provides protection from a sudden loss of a company vice-president, senior buyer, or other key executive that can result in a serious disruption of operations. Losses can include a drop in revenues, and the cost of finding and training a replacement.

Crime insurance covers vulnerabilities such as burglary and robbery. The Federal Crime Insurance Program (1–800–638–8780) provides affordable crime insurance to any property owner, tenant, or business owner in a qualified jurisdiction (i.e., 15 states, Puerto Rico, and the Virgin Islands). This program was established by Congress and began operation in 1971 to assist citizens who found it difficult to obtain adequate burglary and robbery insurance, especially in urban areas. Private insurers administer the coverage and the Federal Insurance Administration is the bearer of the risk. The program promotes crime prevention (i.e., physical security) with insurance as a backup. (See the Federal Commerical Crime Insurance Policy.)

Fidelity bonds provide protection against dishonest employees who have access to a retailer's money. Bookkeepers are usually bonded. More important, dishonest directors, vice presidents, and officers are covered if they divert money in kickback-related payouts to undisclosed business partners.

COMMERCIAL CRIME INSURANCE POLICY

The Federal Insurance Administrator, herein called the Insurer, agrees with the insured, named in the Application made a part hereof, in consideration of the payment of the premium and in reliance upon the statements in the Application, and subject to (1) the provisions of Title VI of Public Law 91-609 and Subchapter B, Parts 80 et seq., Chapter 1, Title 44 of the Code of Federal Regulations and (2) the limits of insurance, exclusions, conditions, deductibles, and other terms of this Policy with respect to the following criminal acts:

INSURING AGREEMENTS

OPTION 1 (Burglary only including safe burglary)

Option 1 includes insurance coverage only under the individually numbered Insuring Agreements I, II, III, and IV listed below.

I. Burglary; Robbery of a Watchman

To pay for loss by burglary or by robbery of a watchman, while the named premises are not open for business, of merchandise, furniture, fixtures, and equipment within the named premises provided that this Insuring Agreement does not extend to the loss of money or securities or to cash value in excess of $50 for any item of jewelry unless such property is forcibly extracted from a locked safe as provided under Insuring Agreement II entitled "Safe Burglary" which follows:

II. Safe Burglary

To pay for loss by safe burglary of money, securities and merchandise within the named premises while the premises are not open for business, but no payment shall be made for loss not forcibly extracted from a locked safe, nor for a loss in excess of $5,000 except with respect to loss by safe burglary of a safe rated for burglary resistance as Class E or better weighing at least seven hundred and fifty pounds or securely anchored to the floor.

III. Damage

To pay for damage to the named premises and to money, securities, merchandise, furniture, fixtures and equipment within the named premises by burglary, robbery of a watchman, safe burglary or attempt thereat provided the insured is the owner thereof or is liable for such damage.

IV. Policy Period, Territory

To pay for losses under Insuring Agreements I, II, and III only when occurring during the policy period within a state, the District of Columbia, the Commonwealth of Puerto Rico, the Virgin Islands and such other territories or possessions of the United States, including the Trust Territory of the Pacific Island, as defined in 12 U.S.C. 1749bbb-10a et seq. and set forth in 44 C.F.R. 80 et seq.

OPTION 2 (Robbery only)
Option 2 includes insurance coverage only under the individually numbered Insuring Agreements V, VI, VII, and VIII listed below.

V. *Robbery, Including Observed Theft Inside the Premises*
To pay for loss by robbery or observed theft of money, securities and merchandise, furniture, fixtures, and equipment within the named premises.

VI. *Robbery, Including Observed Theft, Outside of the Premises*
To pay for loss by robbery or observed theft of money, securities and merchandise, including the wallet or bag containing such property while such property is in conveyance by the insured or his messenger outside the named premises, but no payment shall be made for any loss in excess of $5,000 except when the insured or his messenger is accompanied by a guard armed with a firearm. The person carrying the insured property and the armed guard cannot be the same person.

VII. *Damage*
To pay for damage to the named premises and to money, securities, merchandise, furniture, fixtures and equipment within the named premises, by robbery, or attempted thereat, provided the insured is the owner thereof or is liable for such damage.

VIII. *Policy Period, Territory*
To pay for losses under Insuring Agreements V, VI and VII only when occurring during the policy period within a state, the District of Columbia, the Commonwealth of Puerto Rico, the Virgin Islands and such other territories or possessions of the United States including the Trust Territory of the Pacific Islands, as defined in 12 U.S.C. 1749bbb-10a et seq. and set forth in 44 C.F.R. 80 et seq.

OPTION 3 (Robbery and burglary in uniform and varying amounts)
Option 3 shall provide for uniform and varying limits of coverage under Option 1 and 2 but only in the same Policy. Both Options 1 and 2 must be applied for at the same time.

If one of the options has been selected, the other option may be added upon a renewal or upon an endorsement of the original Policy. A discount will be provided for Combined Coverage, Option 3.

EXCLUSIONS

This Policy does not apply:
(a) to loss due to embezzlement or to any fraudulent, dishonest or criminal act by any insured, a partner therein, or an officer, employee,

director, trustee or authorized representative thereof while working or otherwise and whether acting alone or in collusion with others; provided that this exclusion does not apply to robbery or safe burglary by other than an insured, an officer or a partner thereof;

(b) to loss due to war, whether or not declared, civil war, insurrection, rebellion, or revolution, or to any act or condition incident to any of the foregoing;

(c) to loss of manuscripts, records, or accounts;

(d) under Insuring Agreements I and II to loss occurring during a fire in the premises;

(e) to loss due to nuclear reaction, nuclear radiation, or radioactive contamination, or to any act or condition incident to any of the foregoing;

(f) to any loss if the premises are not equipped with the protective devices required as a condition of eligibility for the purchase of this policy or if the insured has failed to take reasonable action to maintain the protective devices in working order in accordance with the regulations of the Federal Insurance Administration, as published at the time of the inception of the current term of the policy in Subchapter B, Part 80 et seq., Chapter I, Title 44, Code of Federal Regulations.

(g) to loss of personal property of: (1) the insured, an officer or partner thereof, (2) a permanent member of the household of an insured, (3) an employee or an insured; provided that this exclusion does not apply thereof if such personal property is used in furtherance of the conduct of the insured's business;

(h) to loss of any vehicle having four or more wheels designed to be operated on any highway and for which a motor vehicle registration is required for such use;

(i) to loss from burglary or safe burglary at any embassy or consulate of any government other than that of the United States;

(j) to loss from burglary or safe burglary at any named premises which is vacant for a period of more than 60 days;

(k) to loss of property of a business (other than the insured's business) that jointly occupies the named premises with the insured but whose business area is not separated from the insured's business area by a physical barrier. In such an instance the insured shall not be deemed liable to any persons for the property of the other business or businesses despite the location of such property in the same premises named by insured in his or its location.

(l) to loss from a night depository.

CONDITIONS

1. *Definitions*
   (a) Money. "Money" means currency, coins, bank notes, and bullion; and travelers checks, register checks, and money orders held for sale to the public.
   (b) Securities. "Securities" means all negotiable and non-negotiable instruments or contracts representing either money or other property and includes revenue and other stamps in current use, tokens, and tickets, but does not include money.
   (c) Premises. "Premises" means the interior of that portion of any building at a location designated in the Application which is occupied by the insured as stated therein, but shall not include (1) showcases or show windows, not opening directly into the interior of the premises, or (2) public entrances, halls or stairways. As respects Insuring Agreements V and VI only, the premises shall also include the space immediately surrounding such building, provided such space is occupied by the insured in conducting his business.
   (d) Custodian. "Custodian" means the insured, a partner therein, an officer thereof, or any employee thereof who is in the regular service of and duly authorized by the insured to have the care and custody of the insured property within the premises, excluding any person while acting as a watchman, porter, or janitor.
   (e) Messenger. "Messenger" means the insured, a partner therein, an officer thereof, or any employee thereof who is in the regular service of and duly authorized by the insured to have the care and custody of the insured property outside the premises. In addition "messenger" includes a bonded professional guard and an employee of a bonded armored car service.
   (f) In Conveyance. Money, securities or merchandise is "in conveyance" while being transported by the insured or his messenger. If the transportation is interrupted for any purpose which is not incidental to or in furtherance of the transportation of the money or property to its destination, the conveyance ceases. Any merchandise offered for sale by the insured or messenger at a location other than the premises named in the policy is not in conveyance. However, the sale of an item of merchandise or the performance of a service, other than check cashing, related to the insured's business outside the premises which causes the insured or messenger to collect money from a customer is deemed incidental to and in furtherance of the transportation of money to

its destination and the money thus collected and any other money is and remains in conveyance.

Conveyance is interrupted and coverage ceases when (1) the money, securities or merchandise is delivered into and possession relinquished at any premises other than the premises named in the policy, or (2) the money is deposited in a bank, or (3) when an insured or a messenger collecting money, securities or merchandise previously accumulated for his pickup, from more than one location remains with such property in any location for any time longer than reasonably necessary for him to take custody of such property, or (4) when an insured or a messenger transporting money, securities or merchandise willfully and knowingly undertakes any activity that increases the likelihood of his being exposed to robbery or reduces his ability to carry out his responsibility for the custody of the money or property.

(g) *Robbery.* "Robbery" or "robbery, including observed theft" means the taking of insured property (1) by violence inflicted upon a messenger or a custodian; (2) by putting him in fear of violence; (3) by any other overt felonious act committed in his presence and of which he was actually cognizant, provided such other act is not committed by an officer, partner, or employee of the insured; (4) from the person or direct care and custody of a messenger or custodian who has been killed or rendered unconscious; (5) from within the premises by compelling a messenger or custodian by violence or threat of violence while outside the premises to admit a person into the premises or to furnish him with means of ingress into the premises; or (6) from a showcase or show window within the premises while regularly open for business, by a person who has broken the glass thereof from outside the premises.

(h) *Robbery of a Watchman.* "Robbery of a watchman" means the felonious taking of insured property by violence or threat of violence inflicted upon a private watchman employed exclusively by the insured and while such watchman is on duty within the premises.

(i) *Burglary.* "Burglary" or "burglary and larceny incident thereto" means the felonious abstraction of insured property from within the premises by a person making felonious entry therein by actual force and violence, evidenced by visible marks upon, or physical damage to, the exterior of the premises at the place of such entry.

(j) *Safe Burglary.* "Safe burglary" or "safe burglary and larceny incident thereto" means (1) the felonious abstraction of insured property from within a vault or safe, the door of which is equipped with a combination lock, located within the premises, by a person making felonious entry into such vault or such safe and any vault containing the safe, when all doors thereof are duly closed and locked by all combination locks thereon, provided such entry shall be made by actual force and violence, evidenced by visible marks upon the exterior of (a) all of said doors of such vault or such safe and any vault containing the safe, if entry is made through such doors, or (b) the top, bottom, or walls of such vault or such safe and any vault containing the safe through which entry is made, if not made through such doors, or (2) the felonious abstraction of such safe from within the premises.

(k) *Jewelry.* "Jewelry" means jewelry, watches, gems, precious or semi-precious stones, and articles containing one or more gems.

(l) *Loss.* "Loss" except as used in Insuring Agreements I, II, V and VI, includes damage.

(m) *Safe.* A "safe" is a non-portable money storage compartment not on wheels, which is reinforced with a minimum of ¼ inch solid steel plate throughout, with the exception of the door which must be at least one inch thick, solid steel plate and equipped with a combination lock which is an integral part of the door.

A Class E Safe means a steel safe having walls at least 1 inch thick and doors at least 1 and ½ inches thick, or a vault of steel at least ½ inch thick or of reinforced concrete or stone at least 9 inches thick or of non-reinforced concrete or stone at least 12 inches thick, with steel doors at least 1 and ½ inches thick.

(n) *Merchandise.* "Merchandise" includes customer property held for repair or other such work.

2. *Ownership of Property; Interests Covered.* The insured property may be owned by the insured or held by him in any capacity, whether or not the insured is liable for the loss thereof: *Provided,* That the insurance applies only to the interests of the insured in such property, including the insured's liability to others, and does not apply to the interest of any other person or organization in any of said property unless included in the insured's proof of loss.

3. *Joint Insured.* If more than one insured is named in the Application, the insured first named shall act for every insured for all purposes of this Policy. Knowledge possessed or discovery made by any insured shall, for all purposes, constitute knowledge possessed or discovery made by every insured.

4. *Books and Records.* The insured shall keep records of all the insured property in such manner that the Insurer can accurately determine therefrom the amount of loss, and if the insured maintains cash funds for the purpose of check cashing, a complete record of each check negotiated shall be kept by the insured showing the names of the maker, payee and drawee bank, and the date and amount of the check, and such records shall be maintained in a receptacle other than that used for money and securities.

5. *Limits of Liability; Settlement Options.* The Insurer shall not be liable on account of any loss unless the amount of such loss shall exceed the amount of the deductible described in the Application which is made a part of this Policy and the Insurer shall then be liable only for such excess over and above the deductible, subject to and within the limit of insurance covered by the Policy.

The limit of the Insurer's liability for loss shall not exceed the applicable limit of insurance stated in the Application, nor what it would cost at the time of loss to repair or replace the property with other property of like kind and quality, nor as respects securities the actual cash value thereof at the close of business on the business day next preceding the day on which the loss was discovered, nor as respects other property to the actual cash value thereof at the time of loss; *provided, however*, that the actual cash value of such other property held or originally acquired by the insured as a pledge, or as collateral for an advance or a loan, shall be deemed not to exceed the value of the property as determined and recorded by the insured when making the advance or loan, nor, in the absence of such record, the unpaid portion of the advance or loan plus accrued interest thereon at legal rates.

The applicable limit of insurance stated in the Application is the total limit of the Insurer's liability with respect to all loss of property of one or more persons or organizations arising out of any one occurrence. All loss incidental to an actual or attempted fraudulent, dishonest or criminal act or series of related acts at the premises, whether committed by one or more persons, shall be deemed to arise out of one occurrence.

The Insurer may pay for the loss in money or may repair or replace the property and may settle any claim for loss of property either with the insured or the owner thereof. Any property so paid for or replaced shall become the property of the Insurer. Any property recovered after settlement of a loss shall be applied first to the expense of the parties in making such recover, with any balance applied as if the recovery had been made prior to said settlement, and loss readjusted accordingly. The insured or the Insurer, upon recovery of any such property, shall give notice thereof as soon as practicable to the other.

6. *Insured's Duties When Loss Occurs.* Upon knowledge of loss or of an occurrence which may give rise to a claim or loss, the insured shall (a) give notice thereof as soon as practicable to law enforcement authorities and to the Insurer through its authorized agent and (b) file detailed proof of loss, duly sworn to, with the Insurer through its authorized agent within sixty (60) days after the discovery of loss unless such time is extended by the Federal Insurance Administrator in writing. The Administrator may, in his or her discretion, waive the requirement that the proof of loss be sworn to. Upon the Insurer's request, the insured and every claimant hereunder shall submit to examination by the Insurer, subscribe the same under penalty of 18 U.S.C. 1001 pertaining to fraud and false representation, and produce all pertinent records, all at such reasonable times and places as shall be designated, and shall cooperate with the Insurer in all matters pertaining to loss or claims with respect thereto. The insured shall as a condition of continued coverage take reasonable action immediately following the discovery of a loss to protect the premises from further loss.

7. *Other Insurance.* If there is any other valid and collectible insurance which would apply in the absence of this Policy, the insurance under this Policy shall apply only as excess insurance over such other insurance; *Provided,* That the insurance shall not apply (a) to property which is separately described and enumerated and specifically insured in whole or in part by any other insurance; or (b) to property otherwise insured unless such property is owned by the insured.

8. *Appraisal.* If the insured and the Insurer fail to agree as to the amount of loss, each shall, on the written demand of either, made within sixty (60) days after receipt of proof of loss by the Insurer, appoint a competent and disinterested appraiser, and the appraisal shall be made at a reasonable time and place within thirty (30) days after the two appraisers are appointed. If the appraisers fail to agree, they shall jointly select a competent and disinterested third appraiser and submit the question to him within fifteen (15) days thereafter. The first two appraisers shall state separately the actual cash value at time of loss and the amount of the loss. Subsequent agreement in writing by any two of the three appraisers within thirty (30) days after the third appraiser was selected shall be considered by the Insurer in determining the amount of the loss but shall not be considered binding upon him and shall not be admissible as such in court. The insured and the Insurer shall each pay its chosen

appraiser and shall bear equally the expenses of the third appraiser and the other expenses of appraisal. The Insurer shall not be held to have waived any of its rights by any act relating to appraisal.

9. *Action Against Insurer.* No action shall lie against the Insurer unless, as a condition precedent thereto, there shall have been full compliance with all the terms of this Policy and the applicable Regulations of the Federal Insurance Administration, nor until ninety (90) days after the required proofs of loss have been filed with the Insurer, nor at all unless commenced within two years from the date when the insured discovers the loss and within one year after the date upon which the claimant received written notice of disallowance or partial disallowance of the claim. Any such action shall be brought in a United States district court, as required by 12 U.S.C. 1749bbb-10a et seq.

10. *Subrogation.* In the event of any payment under this Policy, the Insurer shall be subrogated to all the insured's rights of recovery therefor against any person or organization and the insured shall execute and deliver instruments and papers and do whatever else is necessary to secure such rights. The insured shall do nothing after loss to prejudice such rights.

11. *Changes.* Notice to any agent or knowledge possessed by any agent or by any other person shall not effect a waiver or a change in any part of this Policy or estop the Insurer from asserting any right under the terms of this Policy; nor shall the terms of this Policy be waived or changed, except by endorsement issued to form a part of this Policy, as approved by the Federal Insurance Administrator.

12. *Cancellation.* This Policy may be canceled by the insured by surrender thereof to the Insurer or any of its authorized agents or by mailing to the Insurer written notice stating when thereafter the cancellation shall be effective. The grounds for cancellation of coverage by the Insurer shall be limited to those set forth in Subchapter B, Parts 80 et seq., Chapter I, Title 44 of the Code of Federal Regulations. Except as otherwise provided by such Regulations, notice of cancellation by the Insurer shall be mailed to the named insured at the address shown in this Policy, stating when not less than thirty (30) days thereafter such cancellation shall be effective. The mailing of notice as aforesaid shall be sufficient proof of notice. The time of the surrender or the effective date of cancellation stated in the notice shall become the end of the Policy period. Delivery of such written notice either by the named insured or by the Insurer shall be equivalent to mailing.

In the event of cancellation, earned premium shall be computed in accordance with the customary short rate table and procedure, unless otherwise specifically provided in said Regulations issued by the Insurer. Premium adjustment may be made either at the time cancellation is effected or as soon as practicable after cancellation becomes effective, but payment or tender of unearned premium is not a condition of cancellation.

13. Assignment. Assignment of interest under this Policy shall not bind the Insurer until its consent is endorsed hereon; if, however, the insured shall die, this Policy shall cover the insured's legal representative as insured; provided that notice of cancellation addressed to the insured named in the Application and mailed to the address shown in this Policy shall be sufficient notice to effect cancellation of this Policy.

14. Declarations. By signing the Application or by acceptance of this Policy the insured certifies and agrees, under penalty of Federal law dealing with fraud and false representation (18 U.S.C. 1001), that the statements in the Application are his agreements and representations, that this Policy is issued in reliance upon the truth of such representations, that he is aware of the applicability of the Regulations issued by the Insurer, and that this Policy and said Regulations embody all agreements existing between himself and the Insurer or any of its agents relating to this insurance.

IN WITNESS WHEREOF, the Federal Insurance Administrator has accepted the declarations of the insured set forth in the Application and has caused this Policy to be issued.

> Harold T. Duryee
> Federal Insurance Administrator

Source: Federal Insurance Administration, Federal Emergency Management Agency, Washington, D.C.

Loss Prevention

Whatever insurance program is established by a retailer, loss prevention is likely to be a key ingredient. Organizations such as Underwriters Laboratory, Factory Mutual, and the National Fire Protection Association have established standards in the security, safety, and fire protection areas. Moreover, insurance carriers (and municipalities) typically require certain levels of loss prevention through specifications or codes stipulated by the aforementioned organizations. Without adherence to these specifications, an insurer can refuse insurance, invalidate a claim, or reduce indemnification from a loss.

The basic purpose of loss prevention is to reduce the chances of a loss. This, in turn, reduces insurance premiums.

Investigate Insurers

Unfortunately, several insurance companies are experiencing financial troubles from poor investments in junk bonds, real estate, etc., and from mismanagement and fraud. State regulatory agencies have often failed to detect warning signs of impending failures and state insurance funds are supposed to support those insurers who become insolvent. The government has its limit in providing financial support to the private sector. During 1989, according to the National Association of Insurance Commissioners (NAIC), 23 insurers became insolvent (in contrast to 328 savings and loans), which cost state guaranty funds $775 million.[10] A retailer should check on the financial soundness of a prospective insurer. This can be accomplished by requesting a copy of the insurer's rating from A.M. Best Co. in Oldwick, New Jersey. Libraries and banks may have these reports. This firm ranks thousands of insurers on a scale from A+ to C−. These ratings measure, among other factors, competency, strength of reserves and investments, and capital relative to risks assumed.

Annual Review of Insurance Coverage

Whatever insurance is purchased by a retailer, it is important to review the coverage annually. In one case, a chain of stores decided to expand its men's wear departments into sporting goods departments. A section of each store was designed for sporting goods and a buyer was hired. After this business plan was implemented, a customer was hurt while handling some sports equipment in a store. The customer sued the chain. On checking the insurance coverage, the chain discovered that injuries from men's wear were covered, but not injuries from sporting goods. This example shows the importance of reviewing insurance as needs change and on an annual basis. Those retailers who rely on an outside broker may find that after the sale, the broker often does not update coverage and that the policy is renewed automatically each year. On an annual basis, an insurance broker should contact the retailer to find out if the business is expanding or cutting back. Does the retailer have more or less employees or inventory? Retailers should contact insurance brokers when changes in operations occur. Too little coverage can be more costly than having too much. Frequently, retailers do not have adequate coverage and are not aware of precisely how much coverage to obtain. One avenue of answering this question is to research the cost of litigation against similar retailers.

Safety

The number of accidental deaths in the workplace are declining each year in the U.S. In 1989, they dropped by 400 to 10,400. Workplace injuries also continue a downward trend to 1,700,000. At the same time, there are yearly increases in the work force. The dollar cost of work accidents in 1989 was $47.6 billion. This includes wages lost and medical expenses, plus indirect losses that result from damaged equipment and materials, time lost by workers, and administrative costs of insurance.[11]

Homicide Is the #1 Cause of On-the-job Deaths among Women

The Centers for Disease Control reported that the leading killer of American women in the workplace is homicide. Forty-two percent of the deaths of American women resulting from on-the-job injury from 1980 to 1985 were homicides. (The figure was 12 percent for men.) The Center's National Institute for Occupational Safety and Health identified 950 killings of women over the six-year period. Of this number, 389 (or 41 percent) worked in the retail field. It appears that robbers, not co-workers, are responsible for most of the killings. Sixty-four percent of the killings were shootings and 19 percent were stabbings. Improved lighting, safer cash-handling procedures, and bulletproof barricades are recommended.[12]

Occupational Safety and Health Administration (OSHA)

During the 1960s, accidents and injuries began to increase in the workplace. Congress responded by passing the William Steiger Occupational Safety and Health Act of 1970, which became effective on April 28, 1971. OSHA is a federal agency under the U.S. Department of Labor. The basic purpose of OSHA is to provide a safe working environment for employees (see Figure 11–1).

The National Institute for Occupational Safety and Health (NIOSH) assists OSHA through research, the development of standards for safety and health, training, and publications. NIOSH is under the U.S. Department of Health and Human Services.

JOB SAFETY & HEALTH PROTECTION

The Occupational Safety and Health Act of 1970 provides job safety and health protection for workers by promoting safe and healthful working conditions throughout the Nation. Provisions of the Act include the following:

EMPLOYERS

All employers must furnish to employees employment and a place of employment free from recognized hazards that are causing or are likely to cause death or serious harm to employees. Employers must comply with occupational safety and health standards issued under the Act.

EMPLOYEES

Employees must comply with all occupational safety and health standards, rules, regulations and orders issued under the Act that apply to their own actions and conduct on the job.

The Occupational Safety and Health Administration (OSHA) of the U.S. Department of Labor has the primary responsibility for administering the Act. OSHA issues occupational safety and health standards, and its Compliance Safety and Health Officers conduct jobsite inspections to help ensure compliance with the Act.

INSPECTION

The Act requires that a representative of the employer and a representative authorized by the employees be given an opportunity to accompany the OSHA inspector for the purpose of aiding the inspection.

Where there is no authorized employee representative, the OSHA Compliance Officer must consult with a reasonable number of employees concerning safety and health conditions in the workplace.

COMPLAINT

Employees or their representatives have the right to file a complaint with the nearest OSHA office requesting an inspection if they believe unsafe or unhealthful conditions exist in their workplace. OSHA will withhold, on request, names of employees complaining.

The Act provides that employees may not be discharged or discriminated against in any way for filing safety and health complaints or for otherwise exercising their rights under the Act.

Employees who believe they have been discriminated against may file a complaint with the nearest OSHA office within 30 days of the alleged discriminatory action.

CITATION

If upon inspection OSHA believes an employer has violated the Act, a citation alleging such violations will be issued to the employer. Each citation will specify a time period within which the alleged violation must be corrected. The OSHA citation must be prominently displayed at or near the place of alleged violation for three days, or until it is corrected, whichever is later, to warn employees of dangers that may exist there.

PROPOSED PENALTY

The Act provides for mandatory civil penalties against employers of up to $7,000 for each serious violation and for optional penalties of up to $7,000 for each nonserious violation. Penalties of up to $7,000 per day may be proposed for failure to correct violations within the proposed time period and for each day the violation continues beyond the prescribed abatement date. Also, any employer who willfully or repeatedly violates the Act may be assessed penalties of up to $70,000 for each such violation. A minimum penalty of $5,000 may be imposed for each willful violation. A violation of posting requirements can bring a penalty of up to $7,000.

There are also provisions for criminal penalties. Any willful violation resulting in the death of any employee, upon conviction, is punishable by a fine of up to $250,000 (or $500,000 if the employer is a corporation), or by imprisonment for up to six months, or both. A second conviction of an employer doubles the possible term of imprisonment. Falsifying records, reports, or applications is punishable by a fine of $10,000 or up to six months in jail or both.

VOLUNTARY ACTIVITY

While providing penalties for violations, the Act also encourages efforts by labor and management, before an OSHA inspection, to reduce workplace hazards voluntarily and to develop and improve safety and health programs in all workplaces and industries. OSHA's Voluntary Protection Programs recognize outstanding efforts of this nature.

OSHA has published Safety and Health Program Management Guidelines to assist employers in establishing or perfecting programs to prevent or control employee exposure to workplace hazards. There are many public and private organizations that can provide information and assistance in this effort, if requested. Also, your local OSHA office can provide considerable help and advice on solving safety and health problems or can refer you to other sources for help such as training.

CONSULTATION

Free assistance in identifying and correcting hazards and in improving safety and health management is available to employers, without citation or penalty, through OSHA-supported programs in each State. These programs are usually administered by the State Labor or Health department or a State university.

POSTING INSTRUCTIONS

Employers in States operating OSHA approved State Plans should obtain and post the State's equivalent poster.

Under provisions of Title 29, Code of Federal Regulations, Part 1903.2 (a) (1) employers must post this notice (or facsimile) in a conspicuous place where notices to employees are customarily posted.

More Information

Additional information and copies of the Act, specific OSHA safety and health standards, and other applicable regulations may be obtained from your employer or from the nearest OSHA Regional Office in the following locations:

Atlanta, GA	(404) 347-3573	Kansas City, MO	(816) 426-5861
Boston, MA	(617) 565-7164	New York, NY	(212) 337-2378
Chicago, IL	(312) 353-2220	Philadelphia, PA	(215) 596-1201
Dallas, TX	(214) 767-4731	San Francisco, CA	(415) 744-6670
Denver, CO	(303) 844-3061	Seattle, WA	(206) 442-5930

Lynn Martin

Lynn Martin, Secretary of Labor

Washington, D.C.
1991 (Reprinted)
OSHA 2203

U.S. Department of Labor
Occupational Safety and Health Administration

To report suspected fire hazards, imminent danger safety and health hazards in the workplace, or other job safety and health emergencies, such as toxic waste in the workplace, call OSHA's 24-hour hotline: 1-800-321-OSHA

This information will be made available to sensory impaired individuals upon request. Voice phone (202) 523-8615; TDD message referral phone: 1-800-326-2577

Figure 11–1 OSHA Safety Poster Courtesy of G. Neil Companies, Sunrise, FL.

OSHA has developed a four-point program to promote safety in the workplace. This program is summarized in the following paragraphs:

1. *Management Commitment and Employee Involvement.* This point emphasizes the importance of management in setting an example and promoting job safety and health in the workplace. Employees should be involved in planning and resolving related issues. Consider forming a safety committee to facilitate communications. Require inspections, training, and the investigation of accidents. Provide the time and funds to get these jobs accomplished. Each year, evaluate the whole safety program, and establish objectives.
2. *Worksite Analysis.* The purpose is to make sure management and subordinates know what is needed to maintain a safe workplace. A request can be made of your state's consultation program, which covers safety and health, to receive a survey of hazards on the premises. Begin with the OSHA office in your state. A self-inspection can be done by using a check list such as the one shown in this chapter. Items can be added and deleted depending on the retail business. Management should provide an avenue for feedback when unsafe conditions exist in the workplace. Also, past records of inspections, accidents, and so forth, should be studied for patterns and corrective action.
3. *Hazard Prevention and Control.* When hazards and potential hazards are known, preventive and control measures can be implemented. Examples of control measures include less toxic materials, safety guards, personal protective equipment, and regular maintenance. Your state's consultation program can assist. One very important measure is to establish safe work procedures that are supported by the enforcement of rules. When employees are asked to set up a disciplinary system, there will be greater cooperation in the workplace than if management fully controlled such a system. Plans and procedures are also vital for emergencies such as employee injuries, fires, and natural disasters. Contact local emergency services to ensure coordination in case of a serious accident. Post emergency telephone numbers on telephones.
4. *Training for Employees, Supervisors, and Managers.* This point ensures that employees are properly trained in their jobs and know how to perform it safely. In retailing, turnover is a chronic problem and training becomes especially important. A creative training program using multimedia strategies can produce good results.[13]

SELF-INSPECTION CHECKLISTS

These check lists are by no means all-inclusive. You should add to them or delete portions or items that do not apply to your operations. However, carefully consider each item as you come to it and then make your decision.

EMPLOYER POSTING
- ☐ Is the required OSHA workplace poster displayed in a prominent location where all employees are likely to see it?
- ☐ Are emergency telephone numbers posted where they can be readily found in case of emergency?
- ☐ Where employees may be exposed to any toxic substances or harmful physical agents, has appropriate information concerning employee access to medical and exposure records, and "Material Safety Data Sheets," etc., been posted or otherwise made readily available to affected employees?
- ☐ Are signs concerning "Exiting from buildings," room capacities, floor loading, exposures to x-ray, microwave, or other harmful radiation or substances posted where appropriate?
- ☐ Is the Summary of Occupational Illnesses and Injuries posted in the Month of February?

RECORDKEEPING
- ☐ Are all occupational injury or illnesses, except minor injuries requiring only first aid, being recorded as required on the OSHA 200 log?
- ☐ Are employee medical records and records of employee exposure to hazardous substances or harmful physical agents up-to-date?
- ☐ Have arrangements been made to maintain required records for the legal period of time for each specific type record? (Some records must be maintained for at least 40 years.)
- ☐ Are operating permits and records up-to-date for such items as elevators, air pressure tanks, liquefied petroleum gas tanks, etc.?

SAFETY AND HEALTH PROGRAM
- ☐ Do you have an active safety and health program in operation?
- ☐ Is one person clearly responsible for the overall activities of the safety and health program?
- ☐ Do you have a safety committee or group made up of management and labor representatives that meet[s] regularly and report[s] in writing on its activities?
- ☐ Do you have a working procedure for handling in-house employee complaints regarding safety and health?

☐ Are you keeping your employees advised of the successful effort and accomplishments you and/or your safety committee have made in assuring they will have a workplace that is safe and healthful?

MEDICAL SERVICES AND FIRST AID

☐ Is there a hospital, clinic, or infirmary for medical care in proximity of your workplace?
☐ If medical and first aid facilities are not in proximity of your workplace, is at least one employee on each shift currently qualified to render first aid?
☐ Are medical personnel readily available for advice and consultation on matters of employees' health?
☐ Are emergency phone numbers posted?
☐ Are first aid kits easily accessible to each work area, with necessary supplies available, periodically inspected and replenished as needed?
☐ Have first aid kit supplies been approved by a physician, indicating that they are adequate for a particular area or operation?
☐ Are means provided for quick drenching or flushing of the eyes and body in areas where corrosive liquids or materials are handled?

FIRE PROTECTION

☐ Is your local fire department well acquainted with your facilities, its location and specific hazards?
☐ If you have a fire alarm system, is it certified as required?
☐ If you have a fire alarm system, is it tested at least annually?
☐ If you have interior stand pipes and valves, are they inspected regularly?
☐ If you have outside private fire hydrants, are they flushed at least once a year and on a routine preventive maintenance schedule?
☐ Are fire doors and shutters in good operating condition?
☐ Are fire doors and shutters unobstructed and protected against obstructions, including their counterweights?
☐ Are fire door and shutter fusable links in place?
☐ Are automatic sprinkler system water control valves, air and water pressure checked weekly/periodically as required?
☐ Is the maintenance of automatic sprinkler systems assigned to responsible persons or to a sprinkler contractor?
☐ Are sprinkler heads protected by metal guards, when exposed to physical damage?
☐ Is proper clearance maintained below sprinkler heads?
☐ Are portable fire extinguishers provided in adequate number and type?
☐ Are fire extinguishers mounted in readily accessible locations?

- ☐ Are fire extinguishers recharged regularly and noted on the inspection tag?
- ☐ Are employees periodically instructed in the use of extinguishers and fire protection procedures?

GENERAL WORK ENVIRONMENT
- ☐ Are all worksites clean and orderly?
- ☐ Are work surfaces kept dry or appropriate means taken to assure the surfaces are slip-resistant?
- ☐ Are all spilled materials or liquids cleaned up immediately?
- ☐ Is combustible scrap, debris and waste stored safely and removed from the worksite promptly?
- ☐ Are accumulations of combustible dust routinely removed from elevated surfaces including the overhead structure of buildings, etc.?
- ☐ Is combustible dust cleaned up with a vacuum system to prevent the dust going into suspension?
- ☐ Is metallic or conductive dust prevented from entering or accumulating on or around electrical enclosures or equipment?
- ☐ Are covered metal waste cans used for oily and paintsoaked waste?
- ☐ Are all oil and gas fired devices equipped with flame failure controls that will prevent flow of fuel if pilots or main burners are not working?
- ☐ Are paint spray booths, dip tanks, etc., cleaned regularly?
- ☐ Are the minimum number of toilets and washing facilities provided?
- ☐ Are all toilets and washing facilities clean and sanitary?
- ☐ Are all work areas adequately illuminated?
- ☐ Are pits and floor openings covered or otherwise guarded?

WALKWAYS
- ☐ Are aisle and passageways kept clear?
- ☐ Are aisles and walkways marked as appropriate?
- ☐ Are wet surfaces covered with non-slip materials?
- ☐ Are holes in the floor, sidewalk or other walking surface repaired properly, covered or otherwise made safe?
- ☐ Is there safe clearance for walking in aisles where motorized or mechanical handling equipment is operating?
- ☐ Are materials or equipment stored in such a way that sharp projectives will not interfere with the walkway?
- ☐ Are spilled materials cleaned up immediately?
- ☐ Are changes of direction or elevations readily identifiable?
- ☐ Are aisles or walkways that pass near moving or operating machinery, welding operations or similar operations arranged so employees will not be subjected to potential hazards?

- ☐ Is adequate headroom provided for the entire length of any aisle or walkway?
- ☐ Are standard guardrails provided wherever aisle or walkway surfaces are elevated more than 30 inches above any adjacent floor or the ground?
- ☐ Are bridges provided over conveyors and similar hazards?

FLOOR AND WALL OPENINGS

- ☐ Are floor openings guarded by a cover, a guardrail, or equivalent on all sides (except at entrance to stairways or ladders)?
- ☐ Are toeboards installed around the edges of permanent floor opening (where persons may pass below the opening)?
- ☐ Are skylight screens of such construction and mounting that they will withstand a load of at least 200 pounds?
- ☐ Is the glass in the windows, doors, glass walls, etc., which are subject to human impact, of sufficient thickness and type for the condition of use?
- ☐ Are grates or similar type covers over floor openings such as floor drains, of such design that foot traffic or rolling equipment will not be affected by the grate spacing?
- ☐ Are unused portions of service pits and pits not actually in use either covered or protected by guardrails or equivalent?
- ☐ Are manhole covers, trench covers and similar covers, plus their supports designed to carry a truck rear axle load of at least 20,000 pounds when located in roadways and subject to vehicle traffic?
- ☐ Are floor or wall openings in fire resistive construction provided with doors or covers compatible with the fire rating of the structure and provided with self closing feature when appropriate?

STAIRS AND STAIRWAYS

- ☐ Are standard stair rails or handrails on all stairways having four or more risers?
- ☐ Are all stairways at least 22 inches wide?
- ☐ Do stairs have at least 6'6" overhead clearance?
- ☐ Do stairs angle no more than 50 and no less than 30 degrees?
- ☐ Are stairs of hollow-pan type treads and landings filled to noising level with solid material?
- ☐ Are step risers on stairs uniform from top to bottom, with no riser spacing greater than 7½ inches?
- ☐ Are steps on stairs and stairways designed or provided with a surface that renders them slip resistant?
- ☐ Are stairway handrails located between 30 and 34 inches above the leading edge of stair treads?

- ☐ Do stairway handrails have at least 1½ inches of clearance between the handrails and the wall or surface they are mounted on?
- ☐ Are stairway handrails capable of withstanding a load of 200 pounds, applied in any direction?
- ☐ Where stairs or stairways exit directly into any area where vehicles may be operated, are adequate barriers and warnings provided to prevent employees stepping into the path of traffic?
- ☐ Do stairway landings have a dimension measured in the direction of travel, at least equal to the width of the stairway?
- ☐ Is the vertical distance between stairway landings limited to 12 feet or less?

ELEVATED SURFACES
- ☐ Are signs posted, when appropriate, showing the elevated surface load capacity?
- ☐ Are surfaces elevated more than 30 inches above the floor or ground provided with standard guardrails?
- ☐ Are all elevated surfaces (beneath which people or machinery could be exposed to falling objects) provided with standard 4-inch toeboards?
- ☐ Is a permanent means of access and egress provided to elevated storage and work surfaces?
- ☐ Is required headroom provided where necessary?
- ☐ Is material on elevated surfaces piled, stacked or racked in a manner to prevent it from tipping, falling, collapsing, rolling or spreading?
- ☐ Are dock boards or bridge plates used when transferring materials between docks and trucks or rail cars?

EXITING OR EGRESS
- ☐ Are all exits marked with an exit sign and illuminated by a reliable light source?
- ☐ Are the directions to exits, when not immediately apparent, marked with visible signs?
- ☐ Are doors, passageways or stairways, that are neither exits nor access to exits and which could be mistaken for exits, appropriately marked "NOT AN EXIT," "TO BASEMENT," "STOREROOM," etc.?
- ☐ Are exit signs provided with the word "EXIT" in lettering at least 5 inches high and the stroke of the lettering at least ½-inch wide?
- ☐ Are exit doors side-hinged?
- ☐ Are all exits kept free of obstructions?
- ☐ Are at least two means of egress provided from elevated platforms, pits or rooms where the absence of a second exit would increase the risk of injury from hot, poisonous, corrosive, suffocating, flammable, or explosive substances?

Occupational Safety and Health Administration (OSHA)

- ☐ Are there sufficient exits to permit prompt escape in case of emergency?
- ☐ Are special precautions taken to protect employees during construction and repair operations?
- ☐ Is the number of exits from each floor of a building and the number of exits from the building itself, appropriate for the building occupancy load?
- ☐ Are exit stairways which are required to be separated from other parts of a building, enclosed by at least 2-hour fire-resistive construction in buildings more than four stories in height, and not less than 1-hour fire-resistive construction elsewhere?
- ☐ Where ramps are used as part of required exiting from a building, is the ramp slope limited to 1 ft. vertical and 12 ft. horizontal?
- ☐ Where exiting will be through frameless glass doors, glass exit doors, storm doors, etc., are the doors fully tempered and [do they] meet the safety requirements for human impact?

EXIT DOORS

- ☐ Are doors which are required to serve as exits designed and constructed so that the way of exit travel is obvious and direct?
- ☐ Are windows which could be mistaken for exit doors, made inaccessible by means of barriers or railings?
- ☐ Are exit doors openable from the direction of exit travel without the use of a key or any special knowledge or effort when the building is occupied?
- ☐ Is a revolving, sliding or overhead door prohibited from serving as a required exit door?
- ☐ Where panic hardware is installed on a required exit door, will it allow the door to open by applying a force of 15 pounds or less in the direction of the exit traffic?
- ☐ Are doors on cold storage rooms provided with an inside release mechanism which will release the latch and open the door even if it's padlocked or otherwise locked on the outside?
- ☐ Where exit doors open directly onto any street, alley or other area where vehicles may be operated, are adequate barriers and warnings provided to prevent employees from stepping into the path of traffic?
- ☐ Are doors that swing in both directions and are located between rooms where there is frequent traffic, provided with viewing panels in each door?

PORTABLE LADDERS

- ☐ Are all ladders maintained in good condition, joints between steps and side rails tight, all hardware and fittings securely attached and moveable parts operating freely without binding or undue play?

- ☐ Are non-slip safety feet provided on each ladder?
- ☐ Are non-slip safety feet provided on each metal or rung ladder?
- ☐ Are ladder rungs and steps free of grease and oil?
- ☐ Is it prohibited to place a ladder in front of doors opening toward the ladder except when the door is blocked open, locked or guarded?
- ☐ Is it prohibited to place ladders on boxes, barrels, or other unstable bases to obtain additional height?
- ☐ Are employees instructed to face the ladder when ascending or descending?
- ☐ Are employees prohibited from using ladders that are broken, missing steps, rungs, or cleats, broken side rails or other faulty equipment?
- ☐ Are employees instructed not to use the top step of ordinary stepladders as a step?
- ☐ When portable rung ladders are used to gain access to elevated platforms, roofs, etc., does the ladder always extend at least 3 feet above the elevated surface?
- ☐ Is it required that when portable rung or cleat type ladders are used, the base is so placed that slipping will not occur, or it is lashed or otherwise held in place?
- ☐ Are portable metal ladders legibly marked with signs reading "CAUTION—Do Not Use Around Electrical Equipment" or equivalent wording?
- ☐ Are employees prohibited from using ladders as guys, braces, skids, gin poles, or for other than their intended purposes?
- ☐ Are employees instructed to only adjust extension ladders while standing at a base (not while standing on the ladder or from a position above the ladder)?

HAZARDOUS SUBSTANCES COMMUNICATION

- ☐ Is there a list of hazardous substances used in your workplace?
- ☐ Is there a written hazard communication program dealing with Material Safety Data Sheets (MSDS), labeling, and employee training?
- ☐ Is each container for hazardous substance (i.e., vats, bottles, storage tanks, etc.) labeled with product identity and a hazard warning (communication of the specific health hazards and physical hazards)?
- ☐ Is there a Material Safety Data Sheet readily available for each hazardous substance used?
- ☐ Is there an employee training program for hazardous substances? Does this program include:
  - ☐ (1) An explanation of what an MSDS is and how to use and obtain one.
  - ☐ (2) MSDS contents for each hazardous substance or class of substances.

- ☐ (3) Explanation of "Right to Know."
- ☐ (4) Identification of where an employee can see the employer's written hazard communication program and where hazardous substances are present in their work areas.
- ☐ (5) The physical and health hazards of substances in the work area, and specific protective measures to be used.
- ☐ (6) Details of the hazard communication program, including how to use the labeling system and MSDS's.

MATERIAL HANDLING

- ☐ Is there safe clearance for equipment through aisles and doorways?
- ☐ Are aisleways designated, permanently marked, and kept clear to allow unhindered passage?
- ☐ Are motorized vehicles and mechanized equipment inspected daily or prior to use?
- ☐ Are vehicles shut off and brakes set prior to loading or unloading?
- ☐ Are containers of combustibles or flammables, when stacked while being moved, always separated by dunnage sufficient to provide stability?
- ☐ Are dock boards (bridge plates) used when loading or unloading operations are taking place between vehicles and docks?
- ☐ Are trucks and trailers secured from movement during loading and unloading operations?
- ☐ Are dock plates and loading ramps constructed and maintained with sufficient strength to support imposed loading?
- ☐ Are hand trucks maintained in safe operating condition?
- ☐ Are chutes equipped with sideboards of sufficient height to prevent the materials being handled from falling off?
- ☐ Are chutes and gravity roller sections firmly placed or secured to prevent displacement?
- ☐ At the delivery end of the rollers or chutes, are provisions made to brake the movement of the handled materials?
- ☐ Are pallets usually inspected before being loaded or moved?
- ☐ Are hooks with safety latches or other arrangements used when hoisting materials so that slings or load attachments won't accidentally slip off the hoist hooks?
- ☐ Are securing chains, ropes, chockers or slings adequate for the job to be performed?
- ☐ When hoisting material or equipment, are provisions made to assure no one will be passing under the suspended loads?
- ☐ Are material safety data sheets available to employees handling hazardous substances?

Source: U.S. Dept. of Labor, Occupational Safety and Health Administration, *OSHA Handbook for Small Businesses* (Washington, DC: U.S. Government Printing Office, 1990), 21–24, 32, 33, and 35.

Fire Protection

According to the National Fire Protection Association, there were 688,000 structural fires in the U.S. in 1989. Of these 34,500 were at stores and offices. Total property damage for fires in structures amounted to $7.5 billion, with an average loss per fire at $10,927.[14]

$3 Million Fine Sought by OSHA against Retailer

A major retailer was cited by OSHA for alleged fire safety violations resulting from a fire set by a security employee in May of 1991. Two other employees died in the fire. The alleged violations included locked exit doors. Store employees found six or eight doors locked when they tried to escape. OSHA proposed a fine of $49,000 for each locked door. Failure to train for emergency evacuation and failure to hold periodic fire drills were other alleged violations. Other problem areas noted by OSHA were blocked sprinkler heads due to material storage, lack of emergency illumination, and failure to maintain the fire alarm system. The company is expected to appeal the fines.[15]

Fire prevention involves efforts to avoid a fire. Examples are NO SMOKING areas and refraining from overloading electrical circuits. Fire suppression aims to extinguish a fire after it begins, using personnel and equipment. Both prevention and suppression strategies are the components of fire protection.

A retailer can take an active role in fire protection. The OSHA checklist contains fire protection and exiting suggestions. Additional suggestions are provided here.

Fire Prevention

Use fire-resistive building materials and furnishings, and fire walls and doors to prevent the spread of fire.
Follow fire codes and insurer recommendations.
Invite fire officials for inspections and recommendations.
Train employees to prevent fires.
Maintain good housekeeping.
Properly store hazardous substances.

Fire Suppression

Install smoke and fire detection devices.

Communicate policies and procedures, and conduct training exercises. Do employees know exactly what to do in case of fire?

Ensure that failsafe procedures exist for notifying the fire department immediately after a fire is discovered.

Ensure that fire exits are clearly identified and unobstructed.

Install emergency lighting and fire escapes, and make sure escape procedures are clearly understood by those on the premises.

Post signs in elevators to warn people to use the stairs during a fire.

Have plenty of multipurpose, dry chemical fire extinguishers on hand to fight several types of fires. Check fire codes. ABC extinguishers enable employees to extinguish a variety of classes of fires. Only very minor fires should be fought without calling the fire department. The classes of fire are

> Class A fires, which consist of ordinary combustible materials such as paper, wood, and cloth
>
> Class B fires, which involve flammable liquids such as gasoline and cleaning solvents
>
> Class C fires, which occur in electrical circuits or equipment such as copying machines
>
> Class D fires, which are rare and involve combustible metals such as magnesium.

Multipurpose extinguishers are the best to use, because employees do not have to be concerned about the danger of fighting a Class B or C fire with water. A grease fire fought with water can cause the grease fire to travel on the water. An electrical fire fought with water can cause electrocution.

Ensure that specific employees are assigned responsibility for fire suppression systems such as sprinkler, standpipes, and hose systems. Sprinkler systems are automatic, while standpipes and hose systems enable fire fighters to fight fires in upper levels of a building. Vertical standpipes run up the wall of a building at fire escape stairways with a hose connection on each floor. They can be recognized by a wall cabinet with a glass door and a folded hose inside.

Periodically check fire suppression equipment for readiness.

Disasters

Accidents and fires are not the only disasters that can cause losses for a retailer. A host of man-made and natural disasters can befall a business. Examples of the former are bomb threats (see Figure 11–2), explosions,

FBI BOMB DATA CENTER

PLACE THIS CARD UNDER YOUR TELEPHONE

QUESTIONS TO ASK:
1. When is bomb going to explode?
2. Where is it right now?
3. What does it look like?
4. What kind of bomb is it?
5. What will cause it to explode?
6. Did you place the bomb?
7. Why?
8. What is your address?
9. What is your name?

EXACT WORDING OF THE THREAT:

_____
_____
_____
_____
_____
_____
_____
_____

Sex of caller: _____
Race: _____
Age: _____
Length of call: _____
Number at which call is received:

Time: _____
Date: _____

REPORT CALL IMMEDIATELY TO:
_____
_____
Phone number: _____
_____
Date: _____
Name: _____
Position: _____
Phone number: _____

CALLER'S VOICE:
- ☐ Calm
- ☐ Angry
- ☐ Excited
- ☐ Slow
- ☐ Rapid
- ☐ Soft
- ☐ Loud
- ☐ Laughter
- ☐ Crying
- ☐ Normal
- ☐ Distinct
- ☐ Slurred
- ☐ Whispered
- ☐ Nasal
- ☐ Stutter
- ☐ Lisp
- ☐ Raspy
- ☐ Deep
- ☐ Ragged
- ☐ Clearing throat
- ☐ Deep breathing
- ☐ Crackling voice
- ☐ Disguised
- ☐ Accent
- ☐ Familiar

IF VOICE IS FAMILIAR, WHO DID IT SOUND LIKE?

_____
_____

BACKGROUND SOUNDS:
- ☐ Street noises
- ☐ Crockery
- ☐ Voices
- ☐ PA system
- ☐ Music
- ☐ House noises
- ☐ Motor
- ☐ Office machinery
- ☐ Factory machinery
- ☐ Animal noises
- ☐ Clear
- ☐ Static
- ☐ Local
- ☐ Long distance
- ☐ Booth
- ☐ Other

_____
_____

THREAT LANGUAGE:
- ☐ Foul
- ☐ Irrational
- ☐ Well spoken (educated)
- ☐ Incoherent
- ☐ Taped
- ☐ Message read by threat maker

REMARKS: _____
_____
_____

Figure 11-2 Bomb Threat Form *Source:* Federal Bureau of Investigation, Washington, D.C.

strikes, riots, and utility failure. Examples of the latter are floods, earthquakes, tornadoes, and hurricanes. The most important risk management strategy for disasters is planning. For example, are plans in place in case company computers and records are destroyed? Is a copy of the records maintained in a safe, off-site location? Larger retailers in particular should have plans in place to effectively deal with disasters. These plans should have three primary objectives: prevent injury and death, protect assets, and continue business as soon as possible.

Risk Management at Burger King
Loss Prevention and Control

Burger King (BK), like most other companies, has realized that the transference of risk (i.e., insurance) is not the only strategy to hold down the costs of risks. An effective loss prevention and control program is also important. BK emphasizes engineering, training, and quick and fair settlement of claims. A key factor for success is management's awareness that an effective program cannot succeed without the support and cooperation of the entire organization and must consider basic, day-to-day activities at BK.

To prepare a loss prevention and control program, problems must be clearly defined. Research questions pertain to accident type, frequency, severity, cause, location, time, and so forth. These factors have a definite impact on insurance premiums.

In a restaurant environment, the fire potential from both an employee, property, and customer standpoint are major concerns. BK installs basic fire protection equipment for cooking appliances. Portable fire extinguishers are also available. Automatic fire sprinkler systems are installed in many restaurants. Complete systems are very expensive and are usually not installed unless required by code. An emergency fire training program is available for employees via a videotape and loss control manual.

Slips and falls are BK's major area of loss for customers and employee injuries. Ninety percent of BK general liability claims relate to falls in the restaurant or parking lot. Prevention measures include mats at critical areas (e.g., entrances, self-service drink station) and slip-resistant shoes for employees. In the parking lots, prevention involves repair of cracked sidewalks, holes, missing grates, grease spots, and wet weather surfaces.

Cuts are the most frequent cause of employee injury. The Whizard Glove provides protection; however, supervisors must make sure they are used.

As we know, training is vital. Unfortunately, the average fast-food restaurant annual turnover rate of hourly employees is 300–400 percent, 75–125 percent for assistant managers, and 25–50 percent for managers. BK deals with this problem with four or five visits per year to each restaurant by a loss control manager in addition to an annual inspection by the insurer. There is frequent distribution of information to employees via training, loss control bulletins, safety brochures and posters, videos, and articles in company publications. A safety incentive program aimed at reducing accident costs was also introduced. Furthermore, a loss allocation system was established whereby restaurants are charged for every loss from a customer or employee injury. This relates to profit and loss, and offsets bonuses.

BK knows that claims management is a crucial aspect of risk management. Clear, concise reporting procedures include a simple incident form and a 24-hour hot line for guidance for BK managers. Quick reporting is essential, because without it, BK is likely to wind up in litigation that raises settlement costs by a factor of ten for relatively inexpensive customer claims.

Training on claims is essential to avoid the worst-case scenarios of an employee telling an injured party about other injuries on the premises or signing statements prepared by plaintiff attorneys in an effort to please customers. BK has prepared a training video for customer incidents. It deals with comforting a victim, calling for medical assistance, record keeping, and other procedures.

BK's headquarters handles all general and automobile liability claims, and food product liability claims. Workers' compensation claims are reported directly to insurance carriers because the law differs among states and centralization at headquarters would be difficult. Audits of claims are necessary to ensure that the insurance carriers are meeting performance standards, especially since BK has a high self-insured retention.

BK's philosophy is to verify the validity of claims and settle quickly. Litigation is avoided; however, the company strongly resists cases where it believes it has no liability. For serious cases, a team approach is used and it includes in-house, outside, and insurance carrier attorneys, and investigators and claims specialists.

Before a loss prevention and control program is implemented or changed, it is reviewed with those employees who are going to be involved in the program. When the program is ready to go, it is launched with a written commitment from the chief executive. Following implementation, audits reveal performance and help to improve the program. Claims management is also audited to ensure that losses are reported quickly and that contact is made with the claimant immediately. This is significant in lowering the costs of settling claims.[16]

Adapted from Donald Herbstman, "Controlling Losses the Burger King Way" and "Handling Claims the Burger King Way," *Risk Management*, March and April, 1990. Used with permission.

Comprehensive Risk Management

Retailers are wise to maintain a comprehensive risk management program. This approach considers all vulnerabilities that can harm business operations and profits. Crimes, fires, accidents, disasters, pollution, health hazards, and so forth, should be studied to establish the most efficient plans prior to a critical incident. Also, for example, a shoplifting prevention program should not be overemphasized in a retail store at the expense of preventing accidents and controlling workers' compensation costs. If a vulnerability is overlooked, if an important prevention measure is neglected, or if insurance needs are miscalculated, any one of these mistakes can ruin a business.

Case Problems

11A. You have been director of loss prevention for a large convenience store chain for more than eight years. The VP of risk management has resigned and you have been asked to apply for this position. All candidates are required to prepare objectives as to how they would provide a return on investment for risk management services. Prepare at least five objectives.

11B. As manager of loss prevention for a retail lumber chain, the director of risk management contacts you with the following message: "I'm concerned about two yard men injured in the last three months at Yard #14. One was hurt when a lumber pile fell on his arm and the other broke his toes when he dropped a box of nails on them." What action will you take to deal with this problem?

Notes

1. For additional information, see: Augustino Turner, "Risk Retention," *Small Business Reports* (April 1989): 83–88.

2. American Risk and Insurance Association, "Risk Management: An Essential Part of the Common Body of Knowledge for Business" (A position paper published and distributed through a grant from the Risk and Insurance Management Society, Inc., 1990), 5.
3. For additional information, see: Robert M. Bieber, "The Making of a Risk Manager—Part One," *Risk Management* (September 1987): 23–30.
4. For additional information, see: Luther T. Griffith, "10 Survival Skills for Managing Corporate Risks in the Future," *Risk Management* (January 1989): 16–20.
5. Michael Bradford, "Risk Financing Options Grow," *Business Insurance* (January 29, 1990): 3–6.
6. Jerry Geisel, "Health Benefit Tab Rises 19% to New High," *Business Insurance* (December 11, 1989): 1 and 36.
7. Insurance Information Institute, *Property/Casualty Insurance Facts, 1991* (New York: Insurance Information Institute, 1991): 5 and 13.
8. "Workers' Compensation Costs Up," *Chain Store Age Executive* (April 1991): 17.
9. "Workers' Compensation Fraud," *Corporate Security* (June 1991): 2.
10. Insurance Information Institute, 8.
11. Ibid., 87–88.
12. "Homicide Is Top Cause of Death from On-Job Injury for Women" (Associated Press Release, August 17, 1990).
13. U.S. Dept. of Labor, Occupational Safety and Health Administration, *OSHA Handbook for Small Businesses* (Washington, DC: U.S. Government Printing Office, 1990), 7–12.
14. Insurance Information Institute, 65.
15. "Retailer in Hot Water," *Chain Store Age Executive* (March 1992): 128–129.
16. This case was paraphrased from the following articles: Donald Herbstman, "Controlling Losses The Burger King Way," *Risk Management* (March 1990): 22–30 and Donald Herbstman, "Handling Claims The Burger King Way," *Risk Management* (April 1990): 89–94.

12

Special Topics

Shopping Malls

Although downtown shopping districts are of great importance to retailers, suburban shopping malls have become the best locations for expansion. The success of the suburban shopping mall has resulted from the following factors:

- Since 1945, a massive population exodus has occurred from the cities to the suburbs. Millions of upper- and middle-class families, with their disposable incomes, have left cities and caused a decline in urban per capita income. At the same time the purchasing power in the suburbs has skyrocketed. Retailers, likewise, have followed the exodus.
- The reliance on the automobile has made downtown traffic and parking extremely stressful for consumers. They favor the traveling and parking ease of the suburban malls.
- As suburbia grows, it too becomes crowded as families move further away, thus making cities less likely targets for shopping.
- The availability of space, cheaper rents, better planning, and flexible design have made suburban malls more attractive to retailers when compared to urban locations.[1]

Shopping malls offer a variety of conveniences for consumers. Numerous large and small retailers are at one location to facilitate one-stop shopping for consumers. Also, restaurants and movie theaters offer a break while shopping. Malls have the advantage of providing a controlled climate and protection against adverse weather. Where a shopping mall is booming with business, security is likely to be in place to protect people and merchandise.

The International Council of Shopping Centers (ICSC) (665 Fifth Avenue, New York, NY 10022; 212-421-8181) is a trade association of shopping center developers, retailers, and lending institutions. It was founded in 1957 and has a membership of 29,000. The ICSC helps members develop their business through education, professional certification, research, publications, and action related to legislation and regulation. According to the ICSC, during 1989, shopping centers employed 9.9 million people, produced $676 billion in retail sales, and generated $25.9 billion in state sales taxes.

Problems and Countermeasures

A shopping mall security program should be as comprehensive as possible and, if practical and with management support, advance to a loss prevention program that includes security, safety, and fire protection. However, the priorities and direction of the program must reflect merchant needs.

A mall security program is best centralized under mall management and headed by an executive. Periodic security meetings and a newsletter are useful to communicate and share ideas among merchants. Unfortunately, certain merchants may not want to take the time to attend meetings or attend special security seminars. The experienced security executive is familiar with such problems. Marketing strategies can be used by the security executive to generate interest among retailers. The executive should spend time on selling the security program and its ideas and strategies. (See Chapter 2 for marketing information.)

Parking lot problems are typical of malls. This includes the need for an orderly flow of traffic and organized parking. Common crimes include car thefts, break-ins, and vandalism. Policies and procedures should be in place to deal with these and other conditions such as dead batteries and keys locked in autos.

> The parking lot is where the shopper is the most vulnerable to crime because that is where they are most attractive to the criminal. Going into a store the shopper has money to buy items and leaving the store they have the merchandise.[2]

The parking lot should have good lighting and be subject to frequent patrols by security officers. Fencing and thick shrubbery limit access and egress, act as a deterrent, and complicate a criminal's getaway. CCTV (see Figure 12-1) is another form of protection that is widely used in parking lots. These strategies afford reasonable protection for customers, create a safe environment, and prevent crime and litigation. During holiday seasons and special sales and events, advanced planning and additional officers will increase safety and security.

Because of increasing austerity among municipal budgets, public law enforcement services have experienced slow growth. This impacts police assistance with mall crime problems. However, these problems can be solved through creative solutions. Certain malls provide office space for police, including a telephone and a room for questioning subjects. Other malls contain a

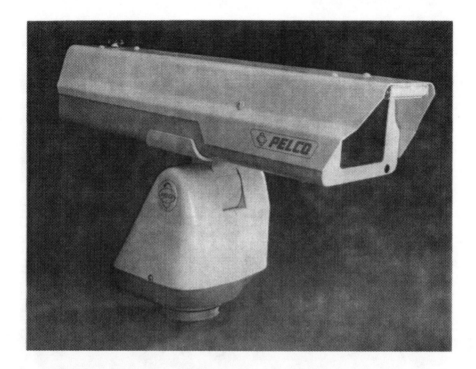

Figure 12-1 Closed-circuit Television Courtesy of PELCO.

police substation that is used for routine police work and to render assistance to retailers and customers. In locales that have considerable crime at malls, a police presence is important. "Last year 5,000 crimes were reported in Paramus' [New Jersey] shopping centers, about 75% of the total crimes committed in the town."[3]

Protection problems are varied inside malls. Figures 12-2 and 12-3 show chain closures to protect stores during off-hours.

Good communication is essential among the security force and all merchants. When shoplifters, bad check writers, and so forth, victimize a store, all appropriate parties should be properly informed and a response force dispatched to cautiously deal with the problem. If the incident is serious or if an arrest is made, public police are a necessity. Cooperative plans, and policies and procedures among individual store security departments, the mall security force, and public police will ensure a smoother response when adverse incidents occur.

It should be pointed out that the industry has no established standards for security. However, legislation is being debated in at least three states (New Jersey, Massachusetts, and Texas) that would require shopping centers of a certain size (i.e., 400,000 square feet or more) to have a security officer on duty

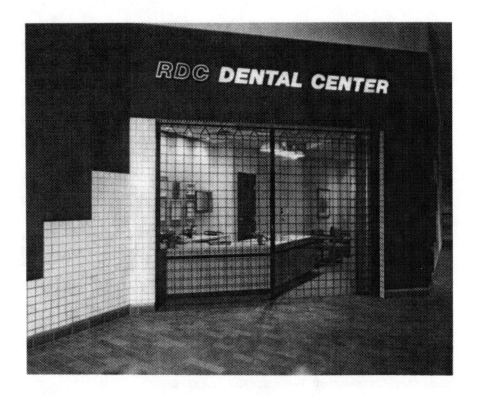

Figure 12-2 Chain Closures Courtesy of Roll-o-matic, Inc.

at all times and another officer for every additional 200,000 square feet. Also, mall owners would have to file a security plan with the local police department. The International Council of Shopping Centers opposes such legislation, because, among other reasons, the laws would not take into account the varying crime rates in different areas.[4]

> ### Security Strategies from Malls across the United States
>
> *Woodfield Shopping Center, Schaumburg, Illinois.* With the use of two rubber suction cups, the man lifts the countertop glass and steals a handful of sunglasses. Such a demonstration is part of the security awareness training for merchants. Also included in the demonstration is a shopping bag lined with aluminum foil used to try to circumvent electronic article surveillance. Security at Woodfield goes the extra mile

to not only lecture about the crime problem, but also show how offenders operate. This has a greater impact on merchants. The security team at Woodfield conducts one or two general meetings a year for the 225 tenants and also schedules programs for individual stores. Furthermore, crime prevention strategies are taught to the shopping center landscapers and the maintenance crew. Another feature of security awareness is that security officers have given out more than 5,000 awareness messages to shoppers warning them of unsafe habits such as leaving a package on a car seat or not locking a car door.[5]

Northwest Plaza, St. Ann, Missouri. The Northwest Plaza represents one-third to one-half the municipality's annual revenue. There are 160 small stores in this shopping center and none have their own security. Thus, the security officers (30 among three shifts—20 full-time and ten part-time) respond to calls for assistance. Officers are not armed and approach each incident cautiously. They wait for a moment before entering a store to ensure than an armed robbery is not in progress. When they enter, two questions are often asked: "Did someone here see the theft?" and "Will the store prosecute?" A "yes" to both questions will cause the officer to detain the suspect for police. A store may also call for a walk-through to deter juveniles or a suspicious character. Two or three patrol cars are used to patrol the parking areas where 30 million cars are parked each year. Also, an officer is posted on the roof with binoculars to watch for auto theft and other crimes. Increased security has resulted in a drop in annual auto thefts from 135 to 30–40 thefts. Mall security has an excellent relationship with the St. Ann Police Department. Police officers are hired during busy holiday seasons. Also, security officers have a second channel on their walkie-talkies so that they can contact police cars in the area.[6]

Park Fair Mall, Omaha, Nebraska, and Fort Worth Town Center Mall, Texas. Park Fair Mall restricts teenagers from access during weekday afternoons and evenings. Fort Worth Town Center Mall does not permit teenagers younger than 19 to enter the mall on Saturdays from 1:00–9:00 P.M., unless escorted by a parent. These policies resulted from situations that got out of hand. Loitering, nonshopping teens blocked entrances to stores and customers were intimidated. Park Fair Mall experienced an incident of noise and disruption that culminated in a fracas that involved more than 200 students. Security had to call in numerous police units to contain the problem. Although teen restrictions began as a risky public relations decision, after implementation people called to express their appreciation.[7]

Figure 12-3 Chain Closures Courtesy of Roll-o-matic, Inc.

The International Council of Shopping Centers hired the Gallup Organization in 1990 to conduct a survey of public perceptions of shopping centers. Respondents were asked to agree or disagree with a host of statements. The security/safety questions and responses are listed below:

"Shopping centers are a safe place for me and my children to visit."—86% AGREED

"I feel just as safe in the parking lot of a center as I do in the shopping center."—58% AGREED

"The presence of large groups of teenagers in a center bothers me."—37% AGREED

Gangs

Problems

Retailers are sometimes confronted with the age-old problem of gang activity. The following pages present some basic information about the problem, how the justice system is helping to curb illegal gang activities, and some practical, business-oriented approaches for retailers.

The definition of the term *gang* and what constitutes gang-related crime varies from jurisdiction to jurisdiction and in the literature. The U.S. Department of Justice provides the following definition:

> A gang for criminal justice purposes is a somewhat organized group of some duration, sometimes characterized by turf concerns, symbols, special dress, and colors. It has special interest in violence for status-providing purposes and is recognized as a gang both by its members and by others.[8]

Gangs are characterized by allegiance based on various social needs. They engage in acts injurious to public health and morals, and create fear and intimidation in a community. Gangs can be involved in the drug trade, extortion, armed robbery, and terrorism.

> A 1989 survey of law enforcement officials in 45 cities across the country produced the startling estimate of nearly 1,500 youth gangs nationwide, with more than 120,500 members. African American and Hispanics made up 87 percent of gang membership, far in excess of their representation in the general population.[9]

In another survey, the Los Angeles Police Department estimates about 600 gangs and 100,000 members in that city.[10] Although African Americans and Hispanics seem to dominate gang membership, other ethnic groups are involved, such as Chinese and Vietnamese. Gangs are also cross-cultural.

In 1990, gang homicides reached an all-time high of 329 in Los Angeles and 98 in Chicago. This represented 34 percent and 11 percent of total homicides in each city, respectively.[11] Gang homicides involve drive-by shootings, turf warfare, drug trafficking, and killings of informers. Research by the U.S. Department of Justice shows that adults who adopt leadership roles also engage in the greatest violence and their victims include, in addition to other gang members, innocent bystanders and professionals such as teachers and police officers.

Unfortunately, in certain communities, law-abiding citizens are prisoners in their own homes and live in fear. Drug dealing takes place openly and urban decay is evident. The social disorganization and failure of institutions such as the family and schools, and lack of employment opportunities, are causal factors influencing gang membership. Gangs fulfill socialization and survival functions for youths in poverty.

For public police, controlling the gang problem is difficult, especially since the social and political factors influencing inner city decay are beyond the control of police agencies.

Witnessing the deadly consequences of turf wars and the destruction of familial and societal structures by the combined effects of inner city violence, poverty, drug abuse and AIDS is making police officials increasingly cynical about their agency's ability to stem the tide.[12]

Although faced with difficult challenges in a difficult environment, and tight budgets, public police should do the best possible job to reduce crime. This requires research, innovation, and sensitivity to community needs.

Countermeasures

The following information highlights the strategies used by cities (percentage also noted) to counter gang activity as researched by the Office of Juvenile Justice and Delinquency Prevention, U.S. Department of Justice.

suppression: prevention, arrest, prosecution, imprisonment, supervision, and surveillance (44 percent)

social intervention: crisis intervention, treatment for youths and their families, outreach, and referral to social services (31.5 percent)

social opportunities: basic and remedial education, training, work incentives, and jobs (4.8 percent)

community mobilization: improved communication and joint policy and program development among justice, community-based and grassroots organizations (8.9 percent)

organizational development or change: special police units and youth agency crisis programs, which play a role in modifying the other four strategies (10.9 percent)[13]

During the 1950s and 1960s, the primary strategy was to reach out to youths and prevent gang involvement or intervene with social services. In the 1970s and 1980s, the police suppression approach prevailed. Unfortunately, there is no clear evidence that either approach was successful. Present day research by the U.S. Department of Justice is asking: What works and what doesn't work? Community residents and retailers are asking: What, if anything, is being done to deal with gangs? To many residents in inner city areas that are infested with gangs, the situation is almost hopeless, especially when dealing with tight municipal budgets. Community groups do what they can to bring opposing gangs together to communicate. Police use their limited resources to respond to gang incidents and contain violence. The inner city problems of poverty, crime, and gang violence dissuade retailers from continuing operations in certain neighborhoods and turn off those retailers involved in site selection. However, community mobilization was the factor that most powerfully correlated with a decline in the gang problem.[14] If community organizations, schools, churches, businesses, police, and so forth, are willing to put forth a concerted effort, gang activity can be reduced.

A retailer should consider basic risk management techniques when responding to gang activity. The risks may be too great to open a business or continue business in a gang-infested area. Considerable target hardening (i.e., physical security) is required to adequately protect a business in a high-crime area. Posting contract security officers at a retail location in a gang-infested area may actually provide another target for gangs. Public police would have to be close enough to provide fast backup. Contact the local police gang specialist to obtain suggestions for protection.

For information on gangs and countermeasures, contact the following sources:

Office of Juvenile Justice and Delinquency Prevention U.S. Department of Justice Washington, DC 20531	National Criminal Justice Reference Service U.S. Department of Justice 1-800-851-3420	The School of Social Service Administration University of Chicago 969 East 60th Street Chicago, IL 60637

Substance Abuse: A Drug-free Workplace

Strategies Recommended by the Drug Enforcement Administration

Until recently, many companies did not perceive a role for themselves in the battle against drug abuse. Indeed, they were adamant in not wishing to be viewed as surrogates of law enforcement. That view is changing, however, because drug abuse is now entrenched in mainstream America.

Money diverted from legitimate business enterprises to buy illegal drugs could be as much as $100 billion a year (2.5 percent of GNP and 8 percent of discretionary spending), while the costs to individual companies usually exceeds 2.5 percent of payroll. Having acknowledged the overwhelming financial burden levied on our economy by drug abuse, companies are now searching for ways to help eliminate this national dilemma.

Drug abuse is sustained by an economic fundamental—supply and demand. The Drug Enforcement Administration and other law enforcement authorities have worked for years to reduce supply in the hope that interrupting the flow of drugs to consumers would eliminate the problem. It is clear that those efforts alone cannot succeed if there is increasing demand.

Thus, a new strategy called "demand reduction" has been added as an essential element to address the drug abuse problem. Since the vast majority of money spent on drugs is provided by working men and women, creating a drug-free workforce will greatly enhance our economy. Significantly, if employers force a major portion of the country's drug users to abandon drug use to stay on the job, they will help strangle the drug trade by knocking out the economic underpinnings of the drug "business." A corporate response to the drug issue is essential—it is an absolute necessity in order to minimize drug-related operation costs, uphold investor or shareholder interests, protect loyal employees, provide quality products and services, and assure America's economic leadership. Indeed, America's employers may be the pivotal force in the struggle against drug abuse. This information provides guidance to assist employers in reducing the economic and social impact of drug abuse in their companies—a positive action that will simultaneously serve to extend a helping hand to employees as well as aid the country in our fight against drug abuse.

Recommendations

- Every employer should prepare a written statement, to be circulated and acknowledged by all employees, that illegal drugs will not be tolerated and that job performance deterioration resulting from abuse of drugs will result in an adverse personnel action. The statement should explain that drug use creates both economic and social consequences that are unacceptable to the company and the community.
- Employers should provide an Employee Assistance Program (EAP), to which employees may be referred to evaluate the problem and determine the appropriate course of action. The EAP should operate on a confidential basis, thereby ensuring the employees' trust and cooperation.
- Drug trafficking by employees should result in termination, even if the employee is a drug user who would otherwise be a candidate for treatment.
- A drug education program should be provided to all employees, in which they can be advised of the company policy, and the drug-related economic, health, and legal liabilities that brought about the policy.
- A drug testing program should be considered to detect non-medical drug use. If testing is adopted, it should be beyond reproach as to professionalism and confidentiality.
- Supervisory training should be offered, particularly to first-line supervisors, on the identification of work performance problems and behavior changes and the procedures for dealing with suspected drug-using and other problem employees.
- A mechanism for monitoring cost-effectiveness and success of the program should be established and routinely reviewed.

The four major elements of a workplace drug abuse program—employee assistance programs, employee education, supervisory training and identification of drug users—are essential in order to provide the most comprehensive and effective program possible.

Policy

Companies must have a clearly delineated policy on drugs in the workplace. A policy must have the support of top management, and should be developed in close consultation with all of the necessary departments, including: union, personnel, security, legal, employee assistance, occupational safety and health representatives.

In the interest of fairness and good business practice, a policy statement should be created and announced to the workforce before instituting the policy. The policy should be written, clear, acknowledged by each employee, and applied in a fair and consistent manner.

Drug policies should address issues such as:

> The company's overall position on drug use, including alcohol
> The organization's position on job performance as it relates to drug use
> The organization's position on safety of the public and co-workers as it relates to drug abuse
> Any drug deterrence technique, including urinalysis, which will be utilized
> The consequences of testing positive, including adverse personnel actions and/or mandatory treatment requirements
> The responsibility of the employee to seek treatment for addiction problems
> The assistance which will be available to employees with addiction problems
> The need for strict confidentiality for employees who are in treatment, and the procedures for dealing with the violation of confidentiality.

A drug policy will be accepted and supported by employees if it is clearly delineated and the rationale is understood.

Employee Assistance Programs

Occupational alcoholism programs came about in the 1940's and were designed to address the problem of alcohol abuse in the workplace. Today, employee assistance programs (EAPs) address a much broader range of issues, including alcohol, drug abuse, and other personal issues. The services of the employee assistance program are typically free and may also be available to family members of employees.

EAPs vary in size and structure depending on the needs of the company, the number of employees, and the range of services offered. Companies may hire their own EAP professionals or contract with outside professionals to provide services. Typically, employees are referred to an employee assistance program because of a job performance problem or because of a positive drug test result. The problem is evaluated and an appropriate course of action is determined.

EAP professionals develop a community referral network in order to provide the best possible assistance to the employees at the most reasonable cost for the employer and/or employee. Treatment costs for drug addicted employees vary according to the type of treatment necessary for the individual. Inpatient programs as well as intensive outpatient programs are typical modes of treatment.

The EAP should operate on a confidential basis, thereby ensuring the employee's trust and cooperation.

Employee Education Programs

The drug education program is crucial to the success of a company's drug policy. The company policy on drug abuse may be communicated to all employees within the context of a drug education program.

A drug education program should include:

The effects of licit and illicit drugs, including alcohol
Information about how drugs affect the health of the employee and his/her family
Information on how drugs actually affect their company's productivity
Information on how drugs affect their community and society as a whole.

Employee education may be conducted in various ways, such as: bulletin board notices, paycheck stuffers, brown-bag luncheon seminars, articles in the company's newsletters, even loaners of drug education videotapes for employees to watch with their families at home.

Supervisory Training

Supervisors play a crucial role in the implementation of a drug policy. For this reason supervisors need training on the identification of problem employees, how to confront problem or drug abusing employees, and how to refer them to employee assistance programs.

Supervisors should also be given information on the physiological and psychological aspects of addiction as well as other pertinent issues such as drug testing, drug trafficking and employee drug education.

Supervisors should not be expected to be amateur diagnosticians, but instead should concentrate on a general approach of whether chemicals may be interfering with the performance of those working for them.

Another way of spotting problem employees is based on the fact that people who abuse drugs, either at work or off the job, perform differently from those who do not. And those differences can be measured, either by observation or with the aid of an electronic data base.

A summary of drug-related performance indicators follows:

Is late for work 3 times more often.
Requests early dismissal or additional time off 2.2 times more often.
Uses 3 times more sick leave.
Is 5 times more likely to file a worker compensation claim.
Is 3.6 times as likely to have an accident at work and 9 times more likely to have a domestic or car accident away from work.
Has inconsistent work quality and lowered productivity.
Has increased mistakes, is careless, and makes judgment errors.
Shows mood swings, which seem to occur at similar times of the day.
Is overly reactive to supervisory admonishments or compliments.
Deliberately avoids co-workers and supervisors, especially supervisors who have been trained to spot abusers.
Has a deteriorating personal appearance, hygiene, or ability to get along with co-workers.
Evidence of poor morale or reduced productivity among co-workers, the result of "covering" for the abuser, or frustration at management ignorance of or inaction toward what is perceived by many workers as an obvious drug problem.
Needless risks taken to raise productivity after supervisory admonishments.
Careless handling and maintenance of machinery, equipment, or office supplies.
Disregard for co-workers' safety.
Increasing complaints about problems at home or with family and friends.
Frequent and recurring financial problems, including borrowing from co-workers or supervisors to get to paydays.

Close observation and documentation of the signs of drug abuse should only be asked of supervisors who have had training in such techniques. A clear policy statement in combination with the training of supervisors will allow for the identification, intervention and treatment of drug dependent workers in a manner consistent with the law and good personnel practices.

Drug Testing

Urinalysis to detect drug use has become a standard practice for many companies throughout America. Before a drug testing program is implemented employers must first determine who will be tested, what methods will be utilized and what the consequences will be for employees who test positive.

Employees may be tested in one or more of the following situations:

Pre-employment screening of job applicants.
As part of an annual physical.
Post-accident testing.
When referred by management for reasonable suspicion.
When employees are in safety-related and/or sensitive positions.
As a follow-up to drug treatment.
As part of a random testing program.

Normally, urine is screened for drug use with a relatively simple and inexpensive procedure. Positive screen results are then subject to a highly accurate, but markedly more expensive, confirmation procedure. No adverse personnel action should ever be taken before completing the two-step procedure.

Most employers look for a vendor to handle their drug testing requirements.

In determining how to go about drug testing and what facility to use, consider the following:

The laboratory should provide guidance in the development of procurement procedures to assure that samples are properly obtained and not falsified. The vendor should provide all materials to collect samples and specific written instructions for doing so. These may include: container, chain-of-custody and report forms, evidence tape, prepaid tamper-proof mailers, and labels. The contract price should include these items, as well as courier service. Separate financial arrangements may be needed if a urine collection vendor is required in addition to the laboratory services.
Containers should not contain preservatives that might alter the drugs or metabolites being sought.

The laboratory and its personnel must comply with state and/or applicable federal licensing and certification requirements.

There must exist a clear, up-to-date laboratory methods procedure manual.

Tests must be performed only by technicians trained and experienced in the specific drug test procedures.

The laboratory must furnish an analytical plan to assure that a positive test is followed by a confirmatory test and that no results are transmitted to the company based solely on a screening result. In other words, all positives should automatically be submitted for confirmation and quantification.

The limits for sensitivity and specificity for each test procedure should be defined. Any change from the laboratory's normal thresholds for detection should be agreed upon in writing.

The technical and administrative procedures used should differentiate legitimate therapeutic drug use from illicit drug use. In other words, a list of prescribed medication used by the donor should accompany the urine specimen.

The laboratory should be asked to identify any of the normally abused drugs or their metabolites and to offer several "panels" or combinations of tests as a cost-effective option to general testing.

Upon arrival of the specimen by approved courier, verbal report should be available within 24–48 hours and a written confirmation of the test should be available shortly thereafter. Procedures should be established to maintain confidentiality both at the laboratory and in the company, and deep freeze storage of positive samples should be offered for at least six months at no extra charge.

The National Institute on Drug Abuse has published "Mandatory Guidelines for Federal Drug Testing Programs" (*Federal Register*, Vol. 53, No. 69, April 11, 1988). All employers are urged to adhere to these guidelines in order to assure that employees and applicants are offered all possible safeguards.

Legal Issues

Ignoring the drug problem in the corporate setting can bring legal problems. Conversely, reasonable and well-intended drug prevention programs may also be challenged in arbitration or in court. However, experience reveals a relatively large legal exposure by waiting to address the issue, which is a reactive posture, versus potentially small penalties in trying to mitigate the problem of drugs in the workplace, that is taking a proactive stance. Ultimately, an employer must decide the potential legal cost from instituting a prevention program and the occasional legal challenge from an affected employee versus the much larger potential losses from not instituting a program.

Drug-related actions have thus far been concentrated in the following five areas:

Right to privacy
Freedom from unreasonable searches
Due process
Negligence (including negligent hiring, supervision, libel, and slander)
Contract law

Cases brought under the first three categories usually involve public employment, although there have been exceptions. Private companies need not be as concerned about those issues if they already exercise good personnel practices. However, the last two, negligence and contracts, clearly apply equally to all employers.

In drug testing, employers must balance:

Legal liability from lawsuits brought by:
Applicants not hired
Employees who refuse to take the test
Employees discharged or disciplined because of positive tests

versus

Legal liability from lawsuits brought by:
Business invitees
Fellow employees
Members of the general public injured or affected by a drug-using employee

Settlements in the first category are usually in the low thousands of dollars while those in the latter are often in the millions.

It is likely that in the next few years, courts are going to hold more and more companies liable for incidents caused by drug-using employees if the company has no formal drug abuse policy or guidelines. As courts have declared, there is enormous liability when a company does nothing or does the wrong thing in the face of the clear evidence of drug abuse throughout the workplaces of our country.

Internal Investigations

Internal drug investigations conducted by a company, even in the best of circumstances, can be fraught with problems. Thus it is essential that companies carefully examine the pros and cons of such an undertaking and then scrupulously correct investigative procedures if they adopt such a technique.

Reports alleging drug use or trafficking may prompt the suggestion for an inquiry. Information should be evaluated for both content and motivation. Investigations can begin with surveillance of work areas and suspected workers by assessing, approaching, and interviewing loyal and trustworthy employees, or by inserting undercover operatives into the workforce.

As in drug testing, managers should clarify at the outset what is to be achieved by an internal investigation. It must be remembered that not only should normal work rules, personnel practices, and contracts be considered, but also that laws regulating privacy, eavesdropping, and collection of evidence should be strictly complied with.

The workplace drug investigation should involve only those with a need to know, and it must be decided whether the company tasks its own security department or whether an outside private investigator is hired. In all cases, manpower, money, time, equipment, and internal political disputes will have to be weighted and estimated.

In determining whether to conduct the investigation in-house or hire an outside resource, a senior manager will have to determine his company's ability to maintain evidence, conduct surveillance or searches, handle informants, and conduct undercover operations.

The concept of internal drug investigations in the work setting is controversial at the least, and disruptive and counterproductive at worst. Done sloppily or without discipline, such an undertaking can be non-productive and damage the company image. However, odds of success increase when procedures promulgated by law enforcement authorities are followed or if cooperative inquiries are made with such officials.[15]

Technology and the Future

As technological innovations appear, virtually every aspect of retailing is affected. Those companies that do not keep pace with new technology and modern methods of retailing may find that their sales are being lost to shrewd and aggressive retailers who use new technology as a means of surpassing their competitors. As new technology is introduced to the retail environment, criminals are sure to follow, as they exploit the technology for ill-gotten gain. Consequently, security practitioners should study new technology and systems as soon as they are introduced, because it won't be long before a creative employee or outsider finds a loophole that results in losses for the retailer.

Although new technology can have drawbacks and can present security vulnerabilities for retailers, it can also prevent losses. This is illustrated by the electronic funds transfer system (EFTS) that is bringing us into a cashless/checkless society. The benefits of EFTS are that by using a terminal, a retailer can contact a bank to check on a customer's credit, process credit card sales, ensure the validity of a check written by a customer, and transfer funds from the customer's account to the retailer's account during the sale.

Because retailers experience problems approving checks and collecting on those that are bad, stores are experimenting with customer-operated terminals from which the customer obtains approval directly from the bank.

The use of the debit card is growing. This card allows funds to be shifted from the customer's account to the retailer's account during a sale.

Automatic authorization of credit and EFTS help retailers to eliminate float. *Float* is the lag time between when a customer presents a check and when the funds are deposited in the retailer's account.

The complexities of modern retailing, compounded by expanded markets and multiple locations, have forced retailers to adopt a systems approach to merchandise and information flow. The universal product code (UPC) has become a great asset in assisting with the transmission of product information. It is, essentially, the "language" for transmitting product information. The electronic data interchange (EDI) is the computer-to-computer transmission of UPC information and business documents from buyer to vendor and back again. Other important components of modern retailing are the POS systems that generate, record, and transmit sales data for management decision-making purposes. The quick response (QR) delivery systems, also known as just-in-time (JIT) systems, utilize UPC, EDI, and POS systems to enable retailers to receive merchandise quickly from vendors. QR systems also lower inventory investment and improve customer service.

QR systems require retailers and their vendors to share data through the EDI. An apparel manufacturer, for example, can fill an order quickly, because the retailer is sharing sales data with the manufacturer on an ongoing basis. The manufacturer helps the retailer manage inventory. The manufacturer shares information with the textile vendor to speed the process. Both the apparel and textile businesses can forecast how much merchandise the retailer will need. With such an interrelated system of sharing information and inventory management from the outside, retail security must look for loopholes in the system. Proprietary sales information must be protected, and the inventory system should be sound and subject to periodic audits.

Whatever technology and systems are employed by a retailer, the protection specialist should keep the crime threat in perspective. Other more serious vulnerabilities can impact a retailer and create greater losses. One source notes that the vast majority of annual losses from public and private sector information systems result from

insider acts such as human errors, accidents and omissions (50–60 percent)
dishonest employees (10 percent)
disgruntled employees (10 percent)
physical disruptions of fire (15 percent) and water (10 percent)
threats from outsiders or hackers (less than 3 percent of annual dollar losses)[16]

Another study (conducted in England) revealed that 41 percent of computer disasters resulted from software malfunctions, followed by power failure (26 percent), and fire and explosion (18 percent).[17]

Another area requiring protection is a retailer's marketing strategies, especially since marketing is a key avenue to profits in a fiercely competitive business world. Micromarketing, for example, is the targeting of specific customers and requires retailers to maintain a database of various categories of customers along with their needs and wants. A chain clothing store, for instance, can keep records of those customers who prefer a certain type of clothing and send out flyers when those items arrive for sale. From a security perspective, this proprietary information must be protected, since it equates with improvements in sales. In fact, any type of proprietary information deserves protection, especially if it provides the edge to outdo the competition.

Security practitioners must keep up with changes in the fast-paced world of retailing. As new technology, systems, and marketing strategies are introduced to surpass the competition, the primary job of security management is to protect the retailer by incorporating protection methods into business plans. Insurmountable security problems should be looked on as challenges that necessitate creative solutions.

Case Problem

12A. You are a candidate for the position of security manager for a large shopping mall near a major city. The number of candidates has been narrowed to six and the mall human resources manager has decided to use an in-basket exercise to further narrow the list of candidates. The in-basket exercise consists of a series of memoranda, telephone calls, and radio transmissions that the mall security manager would encounter in the job. Your task is to read all items, prioritize them, state what action you would take, and present the reasoning behind your actions and the priority you placed on each item. The time to complete this case is 60 minutes. First list the item number and then the priority number before responding to each item. It is possible that all candidates will be handed additional memoranda, telephone messages, or radio transmissions during the exercise. On the job, no one hands you a pile of work and leaves you to work in peace. A review panel (police captain, firefighter, college educator, and mall security officer) will evaluate each candidate's work without knowing the identity of the writer.

ITEM 1
TO: Mall Security Manager
FROM: Mall Manager
SUBJECT: Security Seminar
DATE: September 20

Several merchants would like a seminar on security before the busy holiday season. Please get back to me as soon as possible.

ITEM 2
TO: Mall Security Manager
FROM: Human Resources Manager, Bigmart Department Store
SUBJECT: Selection of Store Detective
DATE: September 24

Please walk over to review the applications for store detective. I have no idea who would be the best one.

ITEM 3
Telephone Message: September 21

Mr. John Poston, a mall customer, called again. He is still irate about the damage to his car window when Security Officer Mallory broke into the vehicle after Mr. Poston left his keys in the ignition. Mr. Poston is threatening to sue.

ITEM 4
Telephone Message: September 20

Mrs. Johnson, owner of the Befit Health Store, thinks someone is entering the store at night. She is very upset and worried, and wants you to meet her at her store.

ITEM 5
TO: Mall Security Manager
FROM: Mall Manager
SUBJECT: Application Verification

DATE: September 22

The Westwood Mall office called to verify your application for their job opening in security. Are you planning to begin another job? Please let me know immediately. Let's talk.

ITEM 6
Radio Transmission: September 24, 11:15 A.M.

"Four year old boy lost at south end of mall. We have not been able to locate for one hour."

ITEM 7
Telephone Message: September 23

Attorney for the plaintiff who was assaulted in the parking lot last month wants you to call him right away.

ITEM 8
TO: Mall Security Manager
FROM: Mall Manager
SUBJECT: Security/Safety Plan
DATE: September 16

In speaking with other mall managers at a recent seminar, they mentioned their security/safety plan. We probably need to have one too. Please respond.

ITEM 9
Radio Transmission: September 24, 11:20 A.M.

"Small fire in stock room of Smith's Department Store. We can put it out."

ITEM 10
TO: Mall Security Manager
FROM: Paula Reed, Security Officer
SUBJECT: Pay Raise
DATE: September 23

I am not pleased about my raise of only $0.15 per hour. I have been doing a good job and I really work hard when we get busy. The male security officers are making much more than my rate per hour. I believe that this difference is because I am a black woman. We have talked about this already, but you haven't done anything about it. I want something done right away or I will take legal action.

ITEM 11
Telephone Message: September 22

The manager of Hall Stuart Clothes wants to know why it took so long for security to respond to a shoplifting incident yesterday.

Notes

1. Gerald Pintel and Jay Diamond, *Retailing*, 5th ed. (Englewood Cliffs, NJ: Prentice-Hall, 1991), 223–224.
2. Geoffrey Richards, "Loss Prevention Tactics Require Planning," *Access Control* (August 1991): 22–23.
3. Heidi Gralla, "Mall Security," *Shopping Center Today* (March 1991): 8.
4. Maura K. O'Brien, "Can Owners Prevent Liability Lawsuits?" *Shopping Center Today* (March 1991): 9.
5. "Individual Attention Marks Successful Mall Security," *Security* (March 1988): 22.
6. "Mall Security—A Large Part of a Small-Town Force," *Corporate Security* (February 1990): 3–6.
7. "Malls Restrict Teen Entry; Patron Access Cited," *Security* (January 1991): 12.
8. Irving A. Spergel and Ronald L. Chance, "National Youth Gang Suppression and Intervention Program," *National Institute of Justice Reports* (June 1991): 23.
9. Jimmy Gurule, "Office of Justice Programs Initiative on Gangs," *National Institute of Justice Reports* (June 1991): 5.
10. "Crips Coming to Town?" *Security Management: Protecting Property, People & Assets* (January 25, 1991): 8.
11. Spergel and Chance, 21.
12. James Sutton, "Gangs: A Challenge to Law Enforcement," *Criminal Justice International* (July-August 1991): 1.
13. Spergel and Chance, 22.
14. Ibid., 23.
15. U.S. Department of Justice, Drug Enforcement Administration, *Drug Free Workplace* (Washington, DC: U.S. Government Printing Office), pp. 3–16.
16. Carl B. Jackson, "Making Time for DP Risk Analysis," *Security* (March 1986): 69.
17. "Computer Disaster Culprits," *Corporate Security International* (July 1987): 5.

APPENDIX
A

Retail Security Surveys

Portions of the National Retail Security Survey and the Ernst & Young's Survey are used throughout this book. The former survey questioned more than 400 respondents and asked different questions than the latter survey, which had 155 respondents. The methodology of each study differs, which makes comparisons difficult.

Ernst & Young's Survey (1990) of Retail Loss Prevention Trends

With this report, Ernst & Young has completed its thirteenth year of surveying loss prevention in the retail industry. The co-sponsor is the International Mass Retail Association, and for the second straight year the publisher is Chain Store Age Executive.

A total of 155 companies participated in this survey. There were 23 department stores, 11 drug chains, 22 general merchandise/mass merchants, 21 specialty apparel retailers, 22 specialty hardlines companies, and 19 supermarkets. In addition, there were 37 companies from "other" segments, including convenience stores and mail order companies. Fifty-three companies had annual revenues of less than $100 million, 41 had revenues of $100–$399 million, 25 had revenues of $400–$999 million, and 36 had revenues of $1 billion or more.

Loss Prevention Trends in Retail: An Executive Overview

With their eyes fixed firmly on the bottom line, retailers today are devoting a significant amount of attention to shrinkage.

Retailers have never taken loss lightly, of course. But this year's survey results, which found shrink percentages down, and comments by some of the industry's leading loss prevention executives, suggest companies are now attacking this age-old problem with as much zeal as they ever have before.

Our survey found that 1990 shrinkage at retail was down seven percent, from 2.23 percent as a percent of sales to 2.08 percent. At cost, shrink declined from 1.73 percent to 1.58 percent.

To some, this is surprising. With the economy in decline since late 1990, one might expect shrinkage to be up. But the majority of the executives we spoke with were not surprised. Companies are paying more attention to "bottomline" functional areas, they say—especially loss prevention.

Shrinkage targets To reinforce this commitment, retailers are now setting specific shrinkage goals. Some 74 percent of our participants had a shrinkage target in 1990. At retail, that target was 1.84 percent of sales; at cost it was 1.15 percent.

And if they failed to meet these goals? Most companies investigated the cause of the shrinkage and/or implemented additional controls. But a very large group—some 43 percent—replaced personnel at a store that has not attained the desired shrink percentage.

In some cases, this meant dismissing employees—an action that troubles one loss prevention executive, who feels that this kind of punitive action could actually cause more trouble than it corrects. "It sets up a situation where people might fudge paperwork to cover their tracks," he says.

Most of the executives believe dismissing people is a regrettable but acceptable practice and an encouraging trend. It should certainly be a last resort, they say, and it must be clearly justifiable. But, unpleasant as this practice is, these executives applaud it as yet another demonstration of management's commitment to loss prevention.

An emphasis on people Also good, say the loss prevention executives, is the current shift toward people as a primary weapon in the battle against shrinkage. As our survey found, retailers are spending the majority (63 percent) of their loss prevention budgets on people-related expenses. Moreover, they have identified employee awareness programs as both the most effective and most commonly used loss prevention "device."

"People, especially a retailer's own employees, are now universally considered the most important factor in loss prevention," says Ernst & Young senior adviser Burnett Donoho. "Without the involvement of your people," says the former president of Marshall Field's, "you simply cannot prevent shrink effectively."

One of the most basic manifestations of "people power" is the presence of sales associates on the selling floor. "The floor people," as one loss prevention director puts it, "are your first and probably best line of defense." Beyond this, employee awareness programs are now as fundamental to loss prevention as locks and chains were 20 years ago. "Companies are putting their faith in awareness, and they're right to do it," says Lew Shealy, VP, Loss Prevention for Eckerd Drug. "You get your best return on investment from awareness."

Focus on the point of sale In retail companies large and small, the point of sale is one of the most difficult-to-police areas—and a prime area of employee theft. For this reason, loss prevention professionals now regard POS systems as security devices, and as such, they are very popular. These systems were the second most frequently used devices, ranking just behind employee awareness programs. Many loss prevention people are now combining closed circuit television cameras with POS systems to monitor transactions and even generate exception reports.

Employee theft Today, much of the focus in loss prevention—especially when it comes to technical advances—is on employee theft. The reason is simple: dishonest employees inflict the heaviest damage in terms of dollars lost. As our survey found, employees accounted for only seven percent of the apprehensions in 1990 but 38 percent of the dollars recovered.

In recent years, some have questioned whether this kind of dramatic statistic is accurate. Perhaps, they suggest, retailers are simply doing a better job of monitoring and accounting for employee theft. But there was no doubt among the executives we spoke with that the greatest "exposure" is in the area of employee theft. "No question," says Shelley Connors, Director, Loss Prevention, for Best Products. "The greater exposure is with employee theft." For this reason, many companies spend the majority of their loss prevention resources on this area.

Of course, retailers cannot overlook the problem of shoplifting. According to our survey, customers accounted for 93 percent of the apprehensions in 1990. The actual dollars in losses cannot be accurately calculated; however, the total shrinkage of our participants was $1.4 billion at retail, and if customers accounted for at least 60 percent of it, we can estimate that shoplifting accounted for approximately $840 million in losses. Compounding the customer problem is the fact that, according to Lew Shealy, it is more expensive to control shoplifting.

Civil recovery is one popular way to address both employee and customer theft. According to the executives we spoke with, the restitution procedure is an effective deterrent, plus it generates revenue. In many cases, civil restitution revenues are funding the loss prevention program. With the retail economy in a continuing slump, a self-supporting functional area is no small thing.

Overall Findings

Note: The overall findings exclude the supermarket retailers who participated in the survey.

Shrinkage At retail, overall shrinkage as a percent of sales decreased on a same respondent basis by six percent in 1990, from 2.22 percent to 2.08 percent. Shrinkage declined for each revenue group as well, with the greatest decline occurring among companies with revenues of $100–$399 million; these companies' shrinkage dipped by 12 percent.

At cost, shrinkage decreased, from 1.73 percent to 1.58 percent. On a same-respondent basis, shrinkage decreased from 1.73 to 1.68, a three percent decline. Shrinkage at cost increased, however, for all companies with revenues of $100 million or more.

In 1990, total dollars lost to shrinkage at retail was $1.4 billion (based on 70 companies). The average loss was $20.1 million, up from $19 million in 1989. The total lost at cost averaged $10.8 million, up from $9.1 million in 1989.

On a same-respondent basis, real dollar shrinkage at cost increased by 23 percent; at retail, it increased by eight percent.

The highest shrinkage departments for general merchandise were fashion accessories and costume jewelry, at 6.45 percent. The low-shrink department was shoes, at 1.65 percent.

Some 74 percent of retailers reported that they had a targeted shrinkage goal, and the larger the company the more likely they were to have a goal. What was the goal? At retail, it was 1.84 percent. At cost, it was 1.15 percent. The shrinkage goal at retail was 12 percent below the actual shrinkage reported. The at-cost goal was 27 percent below the actual shrink percentage.

Companies that did not meet their shrinkage goals were most likely to have the loss prevention department investigate the cause of the shrinkage. The next most popular step was to implement additional loss prevention controls, followed by an investigation by the internal audit/shrinkage control department.

Expenses and Capital Expenditures On a same-respondent basis, loss prevention expenses as a percent of sales increased to 0.34 percent in 1990 from 0.33 percent in 1989, a three percent rise. Companies with revenues of $100 million–$399 million had the highest expenses at 0.41 percent. Department store respondents had the highest expenses as a percent of sales—0.47 percent—and drug chains had the lowest expenses at 0.21 percent.

People costs accounted for the lion's share of loss prevention expenses—63 percent. The segment with the highest people-related expenses was department stores, at 80 percent. The specialty apparel and specialty hardlines respondents had a survey low of 52 percent. For companies with revenues of $1 billion or more, people costs accounted for 74 percent of loss prevention expenses. For companies with revenues below $100 million, however, "other" security costs accounted for 56 percent of loss prevention expenses, with the largest portion, 29 percent, going for alarms and physical facilities.

Breakdown of Security and Loss Prevention Expenses

(Based on 120 responses)

People Cost:		Other Security Cost:	
Employee guards/detectives	20%	Alarms & physical facilities	19%
External guards/detectives	8	CCTV lease/rent/depreciation	4
Prevention employees other than guards/detectives	26	EAS lease/rent/depreciation	8
Outside services	4	Other electronic equipment lease/rent/depreciation	1
Incentive and reward programs	3	Other	5
Employee awareness programs	2		
Total people cost	63%	Total other security cost	37%

Pie chart: 63% / 37%

Apprehensions and Dollars Recovered

	Customers		Employees	
	1990	1989	1990	1989
Total number of survey participants	136	136	136	136
Total aggregate apprehensions	405,988 (93)	394,410 (89)	29,920 (100)	30,199 (94)
Total value of merchandise recovered at retail (in $ thousands)	$21,662 (85)	$19,327 (81)	$14,611 (89)	$13,178 (85)
Total value of unrecovered merchandise employees admitted to stealing at retail (in $ thousands)	NA	NA	$16,632 (69)	$11,730 (63)
Average value of merchandise recovered per apprehension at retail	$184 (79)	$223 (76)	$730 (85)	$625 (80)

( ) = Number of responses to this question
NA = Information is not applicable

Security Devices

	Devices Presently Utilized	Company Plans on Implementing in the Future	Four Most Effective Security Devices				Four Least Effective Security Devices			
			#1	#2	#3	#4	#1	#2	#3	#4
Total responses to the question	126	64	112	108	107	102	95	86	81	78
Employee awareness programs	83%	14%	35%	14%	9%	8%	1%	3%	7%	4%
POS systems	72	19	9	13	16	10	4	5	6	5
CCTV	71	9	13	10	15	8	5	5	9	5
Guards/detectives	63	—	11	12	8	10	4	3	2	9
Incentive programs	63	14	4	9	11	13	2	5	6	8
Mirrors	58	2	—	1	3	2	38	7	4	4
Lock boxes, cables & chains	55	2	3	6	8	4	2	12	15	9
Limited access areas	54	—	—	6	5	1	8	10	10	5
EAS non-ink type tags	49	8	13	6	7	12	2	5	2	8
Security fixtures	47	8	2	1	1	3	5	9	10	5
Employee package control programs	46	5	1	3	2	6	5	10	6	8
Pre-employment honesty testing	44	19	4	5	3	7	3	9	2	5
Exception monitoring software	40	38	3	8	5	8	2	—	4	6
Observation booths	31	2	—	—	—	2	4	5	7	4
Drug testing	29	25	1	4	4	6	4	3	5	5
Fitting room attendants	19	2	—	—	2	—	2	3	1	5
EAS ink type tags	10	14	2	—	2	1	1	2	1	1
Subliminal behavior packages	1	8	—	—	—	—	5	2	1	4
Other	8	—	—	4	—	1	—	—	—	—

Reprinted with permission from Ernst & Young. *Source:* The Ernst & Young/IMRA Survey of Retail Loss Prevention Trends (January 1992).

Capital expenditures averaged $522,000 per company (based on 90 companies) in 1990. On a same-respondent basis, capital expenditures increased by 23 percent. Mass merchant/general merchandise retailers had the highest average capital expenditures, $1.1 million, and specialty hardliners had the lowest average, $134,000. EAS equipment accounted for the greatest percentage of overall capital expenditures, 39 percent. CCTV accounted for 29 percent, POS systems accounted for 11 percent, security fixtures accounted for 10 percent, and other electronic equipment accounted for eight percent.

Apprehensions The respondents apprehended a total of 436,000 people in 1990—406,000 customers and 30,000 employees. Respondents apprehended an average of 4,365 customers and 299 employees per company. The average value of merchandise recovered at retail, however, was $255,000 per company from customer apprehensions, and $164,000 per company from employee apprehensions. Employees, then, accounted for only about seven percent of the apprehensions but approximately 38 percent of the dollars recovered.

Also, employees admitted to stealing another $241,000 at retail per company that was not recovered.

Security Devices The most frequently used security device was employee awareness programs (83 percent). This was followed by POS systems (72 percent), closed circuit television (71 percent), guards/detectives (63 percent), and incentive programs (63 percent).

The National Retail Security Survey (1991), *Security* Magazine

Three tables are presented here that illustrate the use of loss prevention personnel and loss prevention systems. Note that personnel and systems are applicable to combat both internal losses and the shoplifting problem.

Table A Use of Loss Prevention Personnel, National Retail Security Survey '91

	Department Store	Discount Store	Specialty Apparel	Specialty Hard Goods	Specialty Other	Home Centers	Drug Store	Grocery, Etc.	Overall Percent
Honesty Shoppers	53.4%	48.6%	41.7%	53.8%	58.9%	47.3%	75.0%	62.1%	53.8%
Fitting Room Attendants	42.4%	62.1%	32.8%	0.0%	0.0%	0.0%	0.0%	0.0%	19.4%
Observation Booths	60.2%	89.1%	40.3%	43.5%	51.7%	68.4%	83.3%	66.7%	25.2%
Plain Clothes Detectives	87.6%	86.4%	14.9%	12.8%	19.6%	36.8%	50.0%	65.1%	46.8%
Uniform Guards	17.8%	32.4%	35.8%	25.6%	42.8%	31.5%	52.7%	54.5%	36.8%

Percentages take into account the 37 stores that are classified as "other" (8.0% of total) but that are not mentioned in the table.

© 1992, *Security Magazine*. Reprinted with permission.

Table B Number of LP (Loss Prevention) Employees per $100 Million in Annual Sales, National Retail Security Survey '91

	Department Store	Discount Store	Specialty Apparel	Specialty Hard Goods	Specialty Other	Home Centers	Drug Store	Grocery, Etc.
Less than 5	16.7%	43.2%	56.9%	61.3%	56.3%	37.9%	55.8%	40.0%
5 to 15	16.7%	16.2%	19.6%	22.6%	25.0%	13.8%	20.5%	28.0%
16 to 25	28.6%	16.2%	3.9%	9.7%	8.3%	27.6%	2.3%	12.0%
More than 25	38.0%	35.2%	19.6%	12.9%	10.4%	20.7%	20.5%	20.0%
	42	38	63	38	49	29	44	25

Number of LP Employees per Store

	Department Store	Discount Store	Specialty Apparel	Specialty Hard Goods	Specialty Other	Home Centers	Drug Store	Grocery, Etc.
0	14.1%	7.0%	71.6%	77.3%	82.1%	64.7%	68.3%	70.0%
1 to 2	18.3%	32.0%	19.0%	15.8%	12.5%	32.4%	20.6%	26.0%
3	19.7%	6.0%	3.2%	2.6%	3.6%	0.0%	4.8%	0.0%
4 to 5	21.2%	8.6%	3.2%	5.2%	1.8%	2.9%	4.8%	4.0%
More than 5	26.7%	8.6%	0.0%	0.6%	0.0%	0.0%	1.6%	0.0%

© 1992, *Security Magazine*. Reprinted with permission.

Table C Use of Loss Prevention Systems, National Retail Security Survey '91

	Department Store	Discount Store	Specialty Apparel	Specialty Hard Goods	Specialty Other	Home Centers	Drug Store	Grocery, Etc.	Overall Percent
Ink/Dye Tags	19.1%	2.7%	16.4%	0.0%	5.3%	0.0%	5.5%	1.5%	8.3%
Electronic Security Tags	36.9%	45.9%	65.6%	38.4%	41.0%	34.2%	47.2%	21.1%	40.0%
Visible Live CCTV	65.7%	64.8%	29.8%	61.5%	60.7%	65.7%	61.1%	71.2%	60.0%
Visible Simulated CCTV	17.8%	32.4%	25.4%	20.5%	17.8%	31.5%	27.7%	25.7%	24.8%
Covert CCTV	68.4%	62.1%	28.3%	33.3%	42.8%	42.1%	52.7%	51.5%	43.8%
Observation Mirrors	60.2%	89.1%	40.3%	43.5%	51.7%	68.4%	83.3%	66.6%	53.6%
Cables, Locks and Chains	87.6%	72.9%	56.7%	58.9%	44.6%	75.3%	38.8%	54.5%	62.8%
Subliminal Messaging Systems	0.0%	2.7%	2.9%	5.1%	3.5%	0.0%	5.5%	0.0%	1.9%
Security Display Fixtures	52.0%	35.1%	19.4%	30.7%	33.9%	47.3%	30.5%	15.1%	33.3%
Merchandise Alarms	56.1%	48.6%	25.3%	20.5%	23.2%	44.7%	36.1%	19.7%	35.3%
Average Number of Systems	4.6	4.4	3.1	3.1	3.1	4.1	3.9	3.3	

Percentages take into account the 37 stores that are classified as "other" (8.0% of total) but that are not mentioned in the table.

© 1992, *Security* Magazine. Reprinted with permission.

APPENDIX B

The Americans With Disabilities Act

Introduction

The Americans with Disabilities Act of 1990 (ADA) makes it unlawful to discriminate in employment against a qualified individual with a disability. The ADA also outlaws discrimination against individuals with disabilities in State and local government services, public accommodations, transportation and telecommunications. This information explains the part of the ADA that prohibits job discrimination. This part of the law is enforced by the U.S. Equal Employment Opportunity Commission (EEOC) and State and local civil rights enforcement agencies that work with the Commission.

Are You Covered?

Job discrimination against people with disabilities is illegal if practiced by:

- private employers,
- state and local governments,
- employment agencies,
- labor organizations, and
- labor-management committees.

The part of the ADA enforced by the EEOC outlaws job discrimination by:

Source: U.S. Equal Employment Opportunity Commission, *The Americans With Disabilities Act* (Washington, DC: U.S. Government Printing Office, 1991).

- all employers, including state and local government employers, with 25 or more employees after July 26, 1992, and
- all employers, including state and local government employers, with 15 or more employees after July 26, 1994.

Another part of the ADA, enforced by the U.S. Department of Justice (DOJ), prohibits discrimination in state and local government programs and activities, including job discrimination by all state and local governments, regardless of the number of employees, after January 26, 1992.

Because the ADA gives responsibilities to both EEOC and DOJ for employment by state and local governments, these agencies will coordinate the federal enforcement effort. In addition, since some private and governmental employers are already covered by nondiscrimination and affirmative action requirements under the Rehabilitation Act of 1973, EEOC, DOJ, and the Department of Labor also will coordinate the enforcement effort under the ADA and the Rehabilitation Act.

What Employment Practices Are Covered?

The ADA makes it unlawful to discriminate in all employment practices such as:

- recruitment
- hiring
- promotion
- training
- lay-off
- pay
- firing
- job assignments
- leave
- benefit
- all other employment related activities.

The ADA prohibits an employer from retaliating against an applicant or employee for asserting his rights under the ADA. The Act also makes it unlawful to discriminate against an applicant or employee, whether disabled or not, because of the individual's family, business, social or other relationship or association with an individual with a disability.

Who Is Protected?

Title I of the ADA protects qualified individuals with disabilities from employment discrimination. Under the ADA, a person has a disability if he has a *physical or mental impairment* that *substantially limits* a *major life activity.* The ADA also protects individuals who have a *record of* a substantially limiting impairment, and people who are *regarded as* having a substantially limiting impairment.

To be protected under the ADA, an individual must have, have a record of, or be regarded as having a *substantial,* as opposed to a minor, impairment. A substantial impairment is one that significantly limits or restricts a *major life activity* such as hearing, seeing, speaking, breathing, performing manual tasks, walking, caring for oneself, learning or working.

An individual with a disability must also be qualified to perform the *essential functions* of the job with or without *reasonable accommodation,* in order to be protected by the ADA. This means that the applicant or employee must:

- satisfy your job requirements for educational background, employment experience, skills, licenses, and any other qualification standards that are job related; and
- be able to perform those tasks that are essential to the job, with or without reasonable accommodation.

The ADA does not interfere with your right to hire the best qualified applicant. Nor does the ADA impose any affirmative action obligations. The ADA simply prohibits you from discriminating against a qualified applicant or employee because of her disability.

How Are Essential Functions Determined?

Essential functions are the basic job duties that an employee must be able to perform, with or without reasonable accommodation. You should carefully examine each job to determine which functions or tasks are essential to performance. (This is particularly important before taking an employment action such as recruiting, advertising, hiring, promoting or firing).

Factors to consider in determining if a function is essential include:

- whether the reason the position exists is to perform that function,
- the number of other employees available to perform the function or among whom the performance of the function can be distributed, and
- the degree of expertise or skill required to perform the function.

Your judgment as to which functions are essential, and a written job description prepared before advertising or interviewing for a job will be considered by EEOC as evidence of essential functions. Other kinds of evidence that EEOC will consider include:

- actual work experience of present or past employees in the job,
- time spent performing a function,

- consequences of not requiring that an employee perform a function, and
- terms of a collective bargaining agreement.

What Are My Obligations to Provide Reasonable Accommodations?

Reasonable accommodation is any change or adjustment to a job or work environment that permits a qualified applicant or employee with a disability to participate in the job application process, to perform the essential functions of a job, or to enjoy benefits and privileges of employment equal to those enjoyed by employees without disabilities. For example, reasonable accommodation may include:

- acquiring or modifying equipment or devices,
- job restructuring,
- part-time or modified work schedules,
- reassignment to a vacant position,
- adjusting or modifying examinations, training materials or policies,
- providing readers and interpreters, and
- making the workplace readily accessible to and usable by people with disabilities.

Reasonable accommodation also must be made to enable an individual with a disability to participate in the application process, and to enjoy benefits and privileges of employment equal to those available to other employees.

It is a violation of the ADA to fail to provide reasonable accommodation to the *known* physical or mental limitations of a qualified individual with a disability, unless to do so would impose an undue hardship on the operation of your business. Undue hardship means that the accommodation would require significant difficulty or expense.

What Is the Best Way to Identify a Reasonable Accommodation?

Frequently, when a qualified individual with a disability requests a reasonable accommodation, the appropriate accommodation is obvious. The individual may suggest a reasonable accommodation based upon her own life or work experience. However, when the appropriate accommodation is not readily apparent, you must make a reasonable effort to identify one. The best way to do this is to consult informally with the applicant or employee about potential accommodations that would enable the individual to participate in the application process or perform the essential functions of the job. If this consultation does not identify an appropriate accommodation, you may contact the EEOC, state or local vocational rehabilitation agencies, or state or local organizations representing or providing services to individuals with disabilities. Another resource is the Job Accommodation Network (JAN). JAN is a free consultant service that helps employers make individualized accommodations. The telephone number is 1–800–526–7234.

When Does a Reasonable Accommodation Become an Undue Hardship?

It is not necessary to provide a reasonable accommodation if doing so would cause an *undue hardship*. Undue hardship means that an accommodation would be unduly costly, extensive, substantial or disruptive, or would fundamentally alter the nature or operation of the business. Among the factors to be considered in determining whether an accommodation is an undue hardship are the cost of the accommodation, the employer's size, financial resources and the nature and structure of its operation.

If a particular accommodation would be an undue hardship, you must try to identify another accommodation that will not pose such a hardship. If cost causes the undue hardship, you must also consider whether funding for an accommodation is available from an outside source, such as a vocational rehabilitation agency, and if the cost of providing the accommodation can be offset by state or federal tax credits or deductions. You must also give the applicant or employee with a disability the opportunity to provide the accommodation or pay for the portion of the accommodation that constitutes an undue hardship.

Can I Require Medical Examinations or Ask Questions About an Individual's Disability?

It is unlawful:

- to ask an applicant whether she is disabled or about the nature or severity of a disability, or
- to require the applicant to take a medical examination before making a job offer.

You can ask an applicant questions about ability to perform job-related functions, as long as the questions are not phrased in terms of a disability. You can also ask an applicant to describe or to demonstrate how, with or without reasonable accommodation, the applicant will perform job-related functions.

After a job offer is made and prior to the commencement of employment duties, you may require that an applicant take a medical examination if everyone who will be working in the job category must also take the examination. You may condition the job offer on the results of the medical examination. However, if an individual is not hired because a medical examination reveals the existence of a disability, you must be able to show that the reasons for exclusion are job related and necessary for conduct of your business. You also must be able to show that there was no reasonable accommodation that would have made it possible for the individual to perform the essential job functions.

Once you have hired an applicant, you cannot require a medical examination or ask an employee questions about disability unless you can show that these requirements are job related and necessary for the conduct of your business. You may conduct voluntary medical examinations that are part of an employee health program.

The results of all medical examinations or information from inquiries about a disability must be kept confidential, and maintained in separate medical files. You may provide medical information required by state workers' compensation laws to the agencies that administer such laws.

Do Individuals Who Use Drugs Illegally Have Rights Under the ADA?

Anyone who is currently using drugs illegally is not protected by the ADA and may be denied employment or fired on the basis of such use. The ADA does not prevent employers from testing applicants or employees for current illegal drug use, or from making employment decisions based on verifiable results. A test for the illegal use of drugs is not considered a medical examination under the ADA; therefore, it is not a prohibited pre-employment medical examination, and you will not have to show that the administration of the test to employees is job related and consistent with business necessity. The ADA does not encourage, authorize or prohibit drug tests.

How Will the ADA Be Enforced and What Are the Available Remedies?

The provisions of the ADA which prohibit job discrimination will be enforced by the U.S. Equal Employment Opportunity Commission. After July 26, 1992, individuals who believe they have been discriminated against on the basis of their disability can file a charge with the Commission at any of its offices located throughout the United States. A charge of discrimination must be filed within 180 days of the discrimination, unless there is a state or local law that also provides relief for the discrimination on the basis of disability. In most cases where there is such a law, the complainant has 300 days to file a charge.

The Commission will investigate and initially attempt to resolve the charge through conciliation, following the same procedures used to handle charges of discrimination filed under Title VII of the Civil Rights Act of 1964. The ADA also incorporates the remedies contained in Title VII. These remedies include hiring, promotion, reinstatement, back pay, and attorney's fees. Reasonable accommodation is also available as a remedy under the ADA.

How Will EEOC Help Employers Who Want to Comply with the ADA?

The Commission believes that employers want to comply with the ADA, and that if they are given sufficient information on how to comply, they will do so voluntarily.

Accordingly, the Commission will conduct an active technical assistance program to promote voluntary compliance with the ADA. This program will be designed to help employers understand their responsibilities and assist people with disabilities to understand their rights and the law.

In January 1992, EEOC will publish a Technical Assistance Manual, providing practical application of legal requirements to specific employment activities, with a directory of resources to aid compliance. EEOC will publish other educational materials, provide training on the law for employers and for people with disabilities, and participate in meetings and training programs of other organizations. EEOC staff also will respond to individual requests for information and assistance. The Commission's technical assistance program will be separate and distinct from its enforcement responsibilities. Employers who seek information or assistance from the Commission will not be subject to any enforcement action because of such inquiries.

The Commission also recognizes that differences and disputes about the ADA requirements may arise between employers and people with disabilities as a result of misunderstandings. Such disputes frequently can be resolved more effectively through informal negotiation or mediation procedures, rather than through the formal enforcement process of the ADA. Accordingly, EEOC will encourage efforts to settle such differences through alternative dispute resolution, providing that such efforts do not deprive any individual of legal rights provided by the statute.

Additional Questions and Answers on the Americans with Disabilities Act

Q. What is the relationship between the ADA and the Rehabilitation Act of 1973?

A. The Rehabilitation Act of 1973 prohibits discrimination on the basis of handicap by the federal government, federal contractors and by recipients of federal financial assistance. If you were covered by the Rehabilitation Act prior to the passage of the ADA, the ADA will not affect that coverage. Many of the provisions contained in the ADA are based on Section 504 of the Rehabilitation Act and its implementing regulations. If you are receiving federal financial assistance and are in compliance with Section 504, you are probably in compliance with the ADA requirements affecting employment except in those areas where the ADA contains additional requirements. Your nondiscrimination requirements as a federal contractor under Section 503 of the Rehabilitation Act will be essentially the same as those under the ADA; however, you will continue to have additional affirmative action requirements under Section 503 that do not exist under the ADA.

Q. **If I have several qualified applicants for a job, does the ADA require that I hire the applicant with a disability?**

A. No. You may hire the most qualified applicant. The ADA only makes it unlawful for you to discriminate against a qualified individual with a disability on the basis of disability.

Q. **One of my employees is a diabetic, but takes insulin daily to control his diabetes. As a result, the diabetes has no significant impact on his employment. Is he protected by the ADA?**

A. Yes. The determination as to whether a person has a disability under the ADA is made without regard to mitigating measures, such as medications, auxiliary aids and reasonable accommodations. If an individual has an impairment that substantially limits a major life activity, she is protected under the ADA, regardless of the fact that the disease or condition or its effects may be corrected or controlled.

Q. **One of my employees has a broken arm that will heal but is temporarily unable to perform the essential functions of his job as a mechanic. Is this employee protected by the ADA?**

A. No. Although this employee does have an impairment, it does not substantially limit a major life activity if it is of limited duration and will have no long term effect.

Q. **Am I obligated to provide a reasonable accommodation for an individual if I am unaware of her physical or mental impairment?**

A. No. An employer's obligation to provide reasonable accommodation applies only to *known* physical or mental limitations. However, this does not mean that an applicant or employee must always inform you of a disability. If a disability is obvious, e.g., the applicant uses a wheelchair, the employer "knows" of the disability even if the applicant never mentions it.

Q. **How do I determine whether a reasonable accommodation is appropriate and the type of accommodation that should be made available?**

A. The requirement generally will be triggered by a request from an individual with a disability, who frequently can suggest an appropriate accommodation. Accommodations must be made on a case-by-case basis, because the nature and extent of a disabling condition and the requirements of the job will vary. The principal test in selecting a particular type of accommodation is that of *effectiveness*, i.e., whether the accommodation will enable the person with a disability to perform the essential functions of the job. It need not be the best accommodation, or the accommodation the individual with a disability would prefer, although primary consideration should be given to the preference of the individual involved. However, as the employer, you have the discretion to choose between effective accommodations, and you may select one that is least expensive or easier to provide.

Q. When must I consider reassigning an employee with a disability to another job as a reasonable accommodation?

A. When an employee with a disability is unable to perform her present job even with the provision of a reasonable accommodation, you must consider reassigning the employee to an existing position that she can perform with or without a reasonable accommodation. The requirement to consider reassignment applies only to employees and not to applicants. You are not required to create a position or to bump another employee in order to create a vacancy. Nor are you required to promote an employee with a disability to a higher level position.

Q. What if an applicant or employee refuses to accept an accommodation that I offer?

A. The ADA provides that an employer cannot require a qualified individual with a disability to accept an accommodation that is neither requested nor needed by the individual. However, if a necessary reasonable accommodation is refused, the individual may be considered not qualified.

Q. If our business has a fitness room for its employees, must it be accessible to employees with disabilities?

A. Yes. Under the ADA, workers with disabilities must have equal access to all benefits and privileges of employment that are available to similarly situated employees without disabilities. The duty to provide reasonable accommodation applies to all nonwork facilities provided or maintained by you for your employees. This includes cafeterias, lounges, auditoriums, company-provided transportation and counseling services. If making an existing facility accessible would be an undue hardship, you must provide a comparable facility that will enable a person with a disability to enjoy benefits and privileges of employment similar to those enjoyed by other employees, unless this would be an undue hardship.

Q. If I contract for a consulting firm to develop a training course for my employees, and the firm arranges for the course to be held at a hotel that is inaccessible to one of my employees, am I liable under the ADA?

A. Yes. An employer may not do through a contractual or other relationship what it is prohibited from doing directly. You would be required to provide a location that is readily accessible to, and usable by your employee with a disability unless to do so would create an undue hardship.

Q. **What are my responsibilities as an employer for making my facilities accessible?**

A. As an employer, you are responsible under Title I of the ADA for making facilities accessible to qualified applicants and employees with disabilities as a reasonable accommodation, unless this would cause undue hardship. Accessibility must be provided to enable a qualified applicant to participate in the application process, to enable a qualified individual to perform essential job functions and to enable an employee with a disability to enjoy benefits and privileges available to other employees. However, if your business is a place of public accommodation (such as a restaurant, retail store or bank) you have different obligations to provide accessibility to the general public, under Title III of the ADA. Title III also will require places of public accommodation and commercial facilities (such as office buildings, factories and warehouses) to provide accessibility in new construction or when making alterations to existing structures. Further information on these requirements may be obtained from the U.S. Department of Justice, which enforces Title III.

Q. **Under the ADA, can I refuse to hire an individual or fire a current employee who uses drugs illegally?**

A. Yes. Individuals who currently use drugs illegally are specifically excluded from the ADA's protections. However, the ADA does not exclude persons who have successfully completed or are currently in a rehabilitation program and are no longer illegally using drugs, and persons erroneously regarded as engaging in the illegal use of drugs.

Q. **Does the ADA cover people with AIDS?**

A. Yes. The legislative history indicates that Congress intended the ADA to protect persons with AIDs and HIV disease from discrimination.

Q. **Can I consider health and safety in deciding whether to hire an applicant or retain an employee with a disability?**

A. The ADA permits an employer to require that an individual not pose a direct threat to the health and safety of the individual or others in the workplace. A direct threat means a significant risk of substantial harm. You cannot refuse to hire or fire an individual because of a slightly increased risk of harm to himself or others. Nor can you do so based on a speculative or remote risk. The determination that an individual poses a direct threat must be based on objective, factual evidence regarding the individual's present ability to perform essential job functions. If an applicant or employee with a disability poses a direct threat to the health or safety of himself or others, you must consider whether the risk can be eliminated or reduced to an acceptable level with a reasonable accommodation.

Q. Am I required to provide additional insurance for employees with disabilities?

A. No. The ADA only requires that you provide an employee with a disability equal access to whatever health insurance coverage you provide to other employees. For example, if your health insurance coverage for certain treatments is limited to a specified number per year, and an employee, because of a disability, needs more than the specified number, the ADA does not require that you provide additional coverage to meet that employee's health insurance needs. The ADA also does not require changes in insurance plans that exclude or limit coverage for pre-existing conditions.

Q. Does the ADA require that I post a notice explaining its requirements?

A. The ADA requires that you post a notice in an accessible format to applicants, employees and members of labor organizations, describing the provisions of the Act. EEOC will provide employers with a poster summarizing these and other federal legal requirements for nondiscrimination. EEOC will also provide guidance on making this information available in accessible formats for people with disabilities.

For more specific information about ADA requirements affecting *employment* contact:

Equal Employment Opportunity Commission
1801 L Street, NW
Washington, DC 20507
(202) 663-4900 (Voice)
(800) 800-3302 (TDD)
(202) 663-4494 (TDD for 202 Area Code)

For more specific information about ADA requirements affecting *public accommodations and state and local government services* contact:

Department of Justice
Office on the Americans with Disabilities Act
Civil Rights Division
P.O. Box 66118
Washington, DC 20035-6118
(202) 514-0301 (Voice)
(202) 514-0381 (TDD)
(202) 514-6193 (Electronic Bulletin Board)

For more specific information about requirements for *accessible design in new construction and alterations* contact:

Architectural and Transportation Barriers Compliance Board
1111 18th Street, NW
Suite 501
Washington, DC 20036
800-USA-ABLE
800-USA-ABLE (TDD)

For more specific information about ADA requirements affecting *transportation* contact:

Department of Transportation
400 Seventh Street, SW
Washington, DC 20590
(202) 366-9305
(202) 755-7687 (TDD)

For more specific information about ADA requirements for *telecommunications* contact:

Federal Communications Commission
1919 M Street, NW
Washington, DC 20554
(202) 632-7260
(202) 632-6999 (TDD)

For more specific information about federal disability-related *tax credits and deductions for business* contact:

Internal Revenue Service
Department of the Treasury
1111 Constitution Avenue, NW
Washington, DC 20044
(202) 566-2000

This booklet is available in Braille, large print, audiotape and electronic file on computer disk. To obtain accessible formats call the Office of Equal Employment Opportunity on (202) 663-4395 (voice) or (202) 663-4399 (TDD), or write to this office at 1801 L Street, N.W., Washington, D.C. 20507.

Index

Ability tests, 68
Accountability, 121–22
Accounting, 122
Age Discrimination in Employment Act (1967), 55
Alarms
 application of, 231–32
 components of, 226
 effectiveness of, 226
 false, 234, 252–53, 268
 sensors, 226–31
 shoplifting and, 158, 160
 signaling systems, 232–34
Albermarle Paper Co. v. J. Moody, 56
Alcohol abuse, 319–20
American Psychological Association, 71
American Society for Industrial Security, 29
Americans with Disabilities Act (ADA) (1990)
 description of, 342–53
 job applicant screening and, 72
 physical security and, 224–25
 purpose of, 47, 55–56
Andrews v. City of Philadelphia, 46
Application forms, job, 61–62
Aptitude tests, 68
Armed Power Strips and Boxes, 152
Arthur Young & Co., 140–41
Assault, 34–35
Associated Locksmiths of America (ALOA), 214–15
Athena Research Corp., 257
Atmospherics, 202
Audits/auditing
 employee theft and, 122
 security planning, 27

Background checks, 64–67
Bad checks, 86
 case examples, 88, 92
 preventive measures, 89–91
 recovery from, 89
 traveler's checks, 90
 used by professional criminals, 88
Bakke v. University of California, 56
Battery, 35
Berlin, Peter, 107
A. M. Best Co., 290
Bill of Rights, 164
Bona fide occupational qualification (BFOQ), 63
Breach of contract, 34
Bull, James L., 257
Burger King, 305–7
Burglars, characteristics and techniques of, 240–44
Burglary
 case problems, 270
 defenses against, 244–47
 definition of, 240
 police and false alarms, 252–53
 procedures following a, 251–52
 safes and, 247–51
 statistics on, 240
Burns, Dan, 14–16
Buros Institute of Mental Measurement, 71
Business Watch, 269–70

Cameras, pinhole lens, 174
Capacitance sensors, 230
Card-operated lock, 222
Carroll, John, 141
Cash registers
 computerized, 80–82, 84
 electronic, 80
 mechanical, 79–80
 stealing from, 83–84
CCTV. *See* Closed-circuit television
Centers for Disease Control, 291
Cepco, 152
Chain organizations, definition of, 4

Chain Store Age Executive, 71
Chapman v. Atlantic Zayre Inc., 172
Charged coupled device (CCD) cameras, 158
Checkpoint Systems' Impulse Program, 151
Chiera, Louis, 152
Child Protection and Toy Safety Act (1969), 33
Cipher lock, 222
Civil recovery, shoplifting and, 195–96
Civil Rights Act (1964), Title VII
  creation of, 33, 55
  credit checks and, 67–68
  drug testing and, 70
Civil rights claim, case example, 45–46
Clark, John P., 115, 116, 121
Clayton Act (1914), 32
Closed-circuit television (CCTV)
  effectiveness of, 211
  employee theft and, 126
  monitoring of sales via, 82, 113
  scanning and wanding of data and, 81
  shoplifting and, 157–58
Combination lock, 219
Community crime prevention programs, 268–70
Computerized cash registers, 80–82, 84
Computers, used by investigators, 165
Consumer Credit Protection Act (1969), 32–33
Contract investigations, 163, 177
Convenience Store Security Act (1990), 258
Conversion, 36
Counterfeiting, 96, 98
Court testimony, preparing for, 169–70
Credit card fraud
  case examples, 93–94, 95–96, 101–2
  preventive measures, 94–95
  types of losses, 92–93
Credit checks, 67–68
Cressey, Donald R., 117
Crime analysis, security planning and use of, 18–19
Crime insurance, 279–89
Crimes associated with retailing, 4–7
Crime Stoppers, 269
Crow, Wayman J., 257
Currency switch, 96

D'Addario, Francis J., 18–19
Damages, 40–41
Databases
  job applicant screening and, 66–67
  used by investigators, 165
Deadbolt lock, 215–19

DeAngelis v. Jamesway Department Store, 171–72
Deep pocket theory, 39–40
Defamation, 36–37
Demand letter, 196, 197
Depositions, 43–44
DiLonardo, Robert, 153
Disasters, 303–5
Disk tumbler, 221
Display windows, 203
Doors, 223–24, 299
Drug abuse
  company program guidelines, 317–19
  employee assistance programs, 319–20
  employee education programs, 320
  internal investigations, 324–25
  legal issues, 323–24
  role of supervisors, 320–22
Drug Enforcement Administration, 317
Drug tests/testing
  job applicant screening and, 70–71
  questions to consider, 322–23
Dual technology devices, 230
Duston, Robert, 109–10, 119, 183

Eckerd Drug, 11–13
Eldridge, Benjamin, 6
Electrical switches, 226
Electromechanical locks, 222–23
Electronic article surveillance (EAS), 126
  effectiveness of, 150
  at hypermarkets, 156–57
  magnetic, 148
  microwave, 147–48
  radio frequency, 148
  selecting, 152
  source tagging, 151
  tagging strategies, 149–50, 151, 153
  types of tags, 152–53
Electronic cash registers (ECRs), 80
Electronic data interchange (EDI), 326
Electronic funds transfer system (EFTS), 326
Electronic mail (E-mail), job applicant screening and, 67
Elevated surfaces, checklist, 298
Embezzlement, 109, 115
Emergency exit locks, 222
Emotional distress, infliction of, 35
Employee assistance programs (EAPs), 319–20
Employee education programs, 320
Employee Polygraph Protection Act (EPPA) (1988), 57, 164, 179

INDEX

Employee theft
- case examples, 108–9, 110–13
- costs of, 109–10
- investigation of, 170–83
- methods used, 113–14, 115
- preventing, 113–15
- prosecution decision for, 182–83
- reasons for stealing, 116–17
- signs of, 115
- who are employee thieves, 116

Employee theft countermeasures
- accountability, accounting, and auditing, 121–22
- additional strategies, 126–27
- case problems, 127, 130
- human resources programs, 120
- job applicant screening, 65–67
- management support, 119–20
- physical security, 126
- planning and budgeting, 120
- policies and procedures, 120–21
- reporting and reward programs, 122–25
- satisfying employee needs, 117–19
- signs, 125

Equal Employment Opportunity Act (1972), 55
Equal Pay Act (1963), 55
Ernst & Young, 331–36
Exiting or egress, checklist, 298–99
Experimental control group, 25–26

Factory Mutual, 289
Fair Credit Reporting Act, 68
Fair Labor Standards Act (1938), 33, 57
Fairmount Fair Mall, 235–36
False imprisonment or arrest, 35
Family Educational Rights and Privacy Act (1974), 65
Fastop, 25–26
FBI
- National Crime Information Center of, 253
- National Fraudulent Check File of, 88

Federal Crime Insurance Program, 279–89
Federal Insurance Administration, 279
Federal Insurance Contribution Act (1937), 57
Federal Trade Commission (FTC), 32
Federal Trade Commission Act (1914), 32
Federal Wage and Hour Law, 33
Fences, 210
Fiber optics, 231
Fielding, Henry, 5
Fire Fighters Local Union 1784 v. Stotts, 57
Fire protection/prevention, checklist, 295–96, 302–3

Fitting room attendants, shoplifting and role of, 146
Florida, robberies in, 258–59
Fluid tags, 153, 154
Fluorescent lamps, 236
Fort Worth Town Center Mall, 313

Gable, Myron, 71
Gangs, 314–17
Garcia, Enrique, 258
Glass breakage detectors, 227
Griffin, Kenneth, 259
Griggs v. Duke Power, 56

Hall, Freddie Lee, 259
Hallcrest Report II, 109
Harris v. Temple, 92
Hazardous substances communication, 300–301
Hollinger, Richard C., 115, 116, 121
Hollon, Charles J., 71
Honesty tests, 69–70
Human needs, hierarchy of, 118
Human resources
- *See also* Job applicant screening; Training
- job analysis and, 59, 61
- legislation and court decisions regarding, 54–57
- problems in retailing, 53–54
- recruiting and, 61
- scope of, 53

Hunter, Ronald D., 257–58
Hypermarkets, 4, 156–57

Illinois Retail Merchants Association, 141
Incandescent lamps, 236
Infrared photoelectric sensors, 228
Ink tags, 153
Insurance
- *See also* Risk management
- boiler and machinery, 279
- business interruption, 278
- classification of insurers, 290
- crime, 279
- example of commercial crime insurance policy, 279–89
- fidelity bonds, 279
- glass, 279
- group, 279
- key person, 279
- liability, 277
- loss prevention, 289–90
- property, 277

reviewing coverage, 290
statistics on, 276–77
workers' compensation, 277–78
Intelligence tests, 69
Intentional torts, 34–37
Internal theft. *See* Employee theft
International Council of Shopping Centers (ICSC), 309–10, 312, 314
Interviewing guidelines for investigators, 165–67
Interviews, job applicant screening and, 62–64
Intrusion detectors, 210
Invasion of privacy, 36
Inventories, 104–6
Investigation(s)
  cameras for, 174
  case examples, 171–72, 175–77, 188–89, 194–95, 199
  case problems, 198–99
  contract, 163, 177
  definition of, 162
  of employee theft, 170–83
  proper testing procedures, 179–82
  proprietary, 163, 177
  questions to ask regarding, 162–63
  recorders for, 174
  of shoplifting, 183–97
  statistics on methods used in, 196
  undercover, 177–78
  video alarm systems for, 174
Investigative skills
  court testimony, 169–70
  interviewing, 165–67
  knowledge of legal system and citizens' rights, 164
  knowledge of sources of information, 164–65
  report writing, 167–69
Investigative tools, 174

Jackie Ross v. Wal-Mart Stores, Inc., 188–89
Jamb peeling, 242
Job analysis, 59, 61
Job applicant screening
  Americans with Disabilities Act and, 72
  application forms, 61–62
  background checks, 64–67
  case examples of, 65–66
  case problems, 77
  choosing methods of, 71–72
  credit checks, 67–68
  databases, 66–67
  electronic mail, 67
  internal theft prevented by, 65–67

  interviews, 62–64
  legislation and court decisions regarding, 54–57
  private investigators, 67
  purpose of, 57
  recruiting and, 61
  selection procedures, 61–65
  testing, 68–71
Job rotation, 77
Just-in-time (JIT) systems, 326

Kay-Bee Toy Stores, 14–16
Keller, Leonard, 178
Key-in-knob lock, 215
Klein, Jerry, 151
Kleptomaniac, 133
Knogo, 152

Ladders, checklist for portable, 299–300
Larson, John A., 178
Laws
  federal, 32–33
  investigators and knowledge of, 164
  local and state, 31–32
  regarding human resources, 54–57
Lawsuits, preparing for, 43–44
Layout patterns, store, 204–5
Lever tumbler, 221–22
Levy, Michael, 103
Liabilities, civil
  case examples, 38, 42–43, 44–46, 49
  case problems, 48–49
  damages, 40–41
  forms for release from, 186–87
  intentional torts, 34–37
  malpractice, 39
  negligence, 37–39, 41–42
  strict liability, 40
  types of, 33, 34
  vicarious liability, 39–40
Liabilities, criminal, 47–48
Liability insurance, 277
Lighting
  benefits of, 234–36
  store design and interior, 203
  types of, 236–37
Lipsett v. University of Puerto Rico, 46
Lives of Remarkable Criminals, The, 5
Lock(s)
  case example, 219–20
  early types of, 212–13
  effectiveness of, 210
  electromechanical, 222–23
  key controls, 222–23

mechanical, 215-20
mechanisms, 220-22
selecting, 213-15
Lombroso, Cesare, 178
Loss prevention
definition of, 8
purpose of, 289-90
Loss Prevention through Crime Analysis (D'Addario), 18

McNees, M. Patrick, 142
Magnetic contact switches, 226
Maietta v. United Parcel Service, Inc., 199
Malicious prosecution, 35-36
Malpractice, 39
Management Information Systems (MISs), 79
Management support
employee theft and, 119-20
shoplifting and, 144
Marketing
security planning and, 27-29, 207-8
shoplifting and, 139-40
Maslow, Abraham, 118
Mastercard International, 92
Material handling, checklist, 301
Mechanical locks, 215-20
Mental Measurements Yearbook, 71
Merchant Police of England, 5
Mercury vapor lamps, 237
Metal halide lamps, 237
Metallic foil, 226
Metropolitan Police Act, 6
Microwave motion detectors, 229-30
Moak, Gary, 141
Modus operandi (MO) (method of operation), 165
Moore v. May Department Stores Co., 76
Mortise lock, 219
Motion detectors, 227-31
Murphy, D. J. I., 141-42

Nasim v. Tandy Corp., 102
National Coalition to Prevent Shoplifting, 132
National Council on Compensation Insurance, 278
National Crime Prevention Institute, 29
National Fire Protection Association (NFPA), 24, 289, 302
National Institute for Drug Abuse (NIDA), 70, 323
National Institute for Occupational Safety and Health (NIOSH), 291
National Institute of Justice, 116
National Labor Relations Act (1935), 57
National Lighting Bureau, 235
National Retail Federation, 29
National Retail Security Survey, 107, 114, 120, 196, 336-41
Needs, hierarchy of human, 118
Negligence, 37-39, 41-42
Neighborhood watch, 269
Networking, 165
NLRB v. Weingarten inc., 172
North Dakota Retail Theft Act, 192-93
Northwest Plaza, 313

Occupational Safety and Health Act (1970), 57, 291
Occupational Safety and Health Administration (OSHA), 24
description of safety standards, 291-301
On-the-job training, 76-77
Openings, checklist for floor and wall, 297
Operation identification, 268-69
Orientation programs, 75
Our Rival the Rascal (Eldridge and Watts), 6

Padlock, 219, 220
Park Fair Mall, 313
Passive infrared (PIR) motion detectors, 227-28
Peel, Robert, 5
Personality tests, 69
Physical security
Americans with Disabilities Act and, 224-25
case problems, 237
employee theft and, 126
importance of testing, 209-11
planning, 212
shoplifting and, 146-47
Pilferage, 109
Pin tumbler, 221
Point-of-sale (POS)
bad checks, 86, 88-92
case problems, 100-101
cash registers, 79-82, 83
computerized cash registers, 80-82, 84
counterfeiting, 96, 98
credit card fraud, 92-96
preventing losses at, 84-86
protection features from use of, 82
refund fraud, 98-99
scanning and wanding of data, 80-81
stealing from cash registers, 83-84
summary of vulnerabilities, 99-100

types of losses occurring at, 82–83
Universal Product Code, 81–82
Policies and procedures, employee theft and, 120–21
Polygraphs, 178
 proper testing procedures, 179–82
Pressure mats, 227
Private investigators, use of, 67
Probable cause hearing, 194
Property insurance, 277
Proprietary investigations, 163, 177
Prosecution decision
 for employee theft, 182–83
 for shoplifting, 193–94
Psychological stress evaluator (PSE), 178–79

Quick response (QR) delivery system, 326

Rabidue v. Osceola Refining Co., 46
Radtke v. Everett, 46
Range DRF Overhead System, 152
Ray, JoAnn, 141
REACT International, 269
Recorders, time-lapse, 174
Refund fraud, 98–99
Rehabilitation Act (1973), 55
Reporting and reward programs, employee theft and, 122–25
Report writing, 167–69
Research/feedback, security planning and, 24–26
Respondeat superior, 39–40
Retailing
 concept, 7
 history of, 3–4
 mix, 7
 objectives and problems, 9–10
 strategy, 7
Retail Management (Levy and Weitz), 103
Return on investment (ROI), security planning and, 21–23
Revco Drug Stores, 89
Reward programs
 employee theft and, 122–25
 shoplifting and, 145
Rim lock, 219
Risk analysis, security planning and, 20–21
Risk assumption, 273–74
Risk abatement, 274
Risk management
 See also Insurance
 case example, 305–7
 case problems, 307
 definition of, 273
 strategies, 273–74
Risk managers, duties of, 274–76
Risk retention, 274
Risk spreading, 274
Risk transfer, 274
Robbers, characteristics and techniques of, 253, 256
Robbery
 case examples, 258–59
 case problems, 270
 defenses against, 259–65
 definition of, 240, 253
 planning and research on, 256–59
 police and false alarms, 268
 procedures after a, 266–67
 procedures during a, 265–66
 statistics on, 253
"Robbery as Robbers See It," 257
"Robbery Deterence: An Applied Behavioral Science Demonstration," 257
Robinson-Patman Act (1936), 32
Rosabel Brown v. J. C. Penney Co., Inc., 43
Ross Stores, 124
Ruffin, Mack, 259

Safes
 burglary-resistant/money, 248
 effectiveness of, 210–11
 fire-resistant/record, 247–48
 methods for opening, 249, 251
 UL classification of, 248–49, 250
Safety, description of OSHA standards, 291–301
Salespeople, shoplifting and role of, 144–45
Scanning data, 80–81
Scientific method, use of, 26
Scott v. Sears, Roebuck & Co., 46
Screen sensors, 230–31
Sears, Richard W., 3
Security
 charge of negligent, 41–42
 definition of, 8
 surveys, 331–42
 training, 77
Security, 64, 70, 196, 336–41
Security and Crime Prevention, 245
Security Letter, 257
Security Management, 132, 193
Security officers, shoplifting and role of, 146
Security planning
 audits, 27
 case examples of, 11–16

case problems, 29–30
from a systems perspective, 18–19
guidelines, 16–17
importance of, 11
information sources, 29
marketing, 27–29
questions during, 17–18
research/feedback and, 24–26
return on investment and, 21–23
risk analysis and, 20–21
standards, 23–24
Security posts, 211
Security Tag Systems, 151
Sekurlabel, 151
Self-insurance, 274
Sensormatic's SpeedStation, 152
Sensors, 226–31
Sexual harassment, case examples, 46
Shealy, Lew, 11–13
Shepard, Ira M., 109–10, 119, 183
Sherman Antitrust Act (1890), 32
Shoplifters
  behavior of, 136–37
  types of, 133, 136
Shoplifters Anonymous, 160
Shoplifting
  case examples, 138, 188–89, 194–95
  case problems, 160–61
  civil recovery and, 195–96
  countermeasures, 126
  database information on, 66
  definition of, 132
  earliest accounts of, 4–5
  evaluating antishoplifting strategies, 142
  forms for release from civil liability, 186–87
  how to reduce, 138–39
  investigation of, 183–97
  investigative report, 186
  losses from, 132
  marketing techniques and problems with, 139–40
  prosecution decision for, 193–94
  reasons for, 133
  research on, 140–42
Shoplifting countermeasures
  additional strategies, 160
  alarms, 158, 160
  charged coupled device cameras, 158
  closed-circuit television, 157–58
  electronic article surveillance, 126, 147–57
  fitting room attendants, role of, 146
  management support, 144

physical security, 146–47
reward programs, 145
salespeople, role of, 144–45
security officers, role of, 146
socialization of employees, 143–44
store detectives, 145–46
Shopping malls, 309–14, 327–29
Shrinkage/shrink
  See also under type of
  defining, 103
  inventories and, 104–6
  perceptions of, 107–8
Shrinkage Control (Berlin), 107
Signs, employee theft and, 125
Site selection/design, factors to consider, 201
Socialization of employees, 143–44, 245, 247
Sodium lamps, 236
Source tagging, 151
Southland Corp., 257
Squealer, 152
Stairs and stairways, checklist, 297–98
Stajer Corp., 152
Standards, security planning, 23–24
State v. Daye, 132
Store design
  atmospherics, 202
  case problems, 237
  display windows, 203
  layout patterns, 204–5
  lighting, 203
  merchandise fixtures, 204
  open front, 202, 207
  security problems with, 205–8
  security recommendations for, 208–9
  sound, 203
Store detectives, use of, 145–46
Stores Mutual Association (SMA), 66
Strict liability, 40
"Study of Safety and Security Requirements for 'At-Risk Businesses'," 258
Substance abuse. *See* Alcohol abuse; Drug abuse
Superstores, 4
Supervisors, drug abuse and role of, 320–22
Surveillance, 165
Swanson, Richard N., 258

Tampering, product, 33
Target hardening, 223, 257, 268
Target marketing, 28
Technology, role of, 325–27
Terrorism, 33–34
Tests/testing job applicants
  ability, 68

aptitude, 68
drug, 70–71
honesty, 69–70
intelligence, 69
personality, 69
proper procedures for polygraph, 179–82
reliability and validity of, 71
Theft/thieves
   See also Employee theft
   database information on, 66
   prevented by applicant screening, 65–67
Theft by Employees in Work Organizations (Clark and Hollinger), 116
Thieves at Work (Shepard and Duston), 109–10, 119
3M, 152
Time-recording lock, 220
Torts, intentional, 34–37
Training
   benefits of, 75
   case example, 76
   case problems, 77
   designing, 75–76
   methods, 76–77
   objectives of, 74
   on-the-job, 76–77
   orientation programs, 75
   security, 77
   videos, 77
Traveler's checks, 90
Trespass to personal property, 36
Trespass to real property, 36

Ultrasonic motion detectors, 228
Undercover investigations, 177–78

Underwriters Laboratory (UL), 24, 225, 248, 289
Uniform Crime Report, 132, 202, 240, 241, 253
U.S. Department of Commerce, 139–40, 215
U.S. Department of Justice, 151, 315, 316, 317
U.S. Department of Labor, 291
Universal Product Code (UPC), 81–82, 326
University of Chicago, 317

Vassallo v. Clover, 46
Vendors, losses from, 114–15
Vibration sensors, 230
Vicarious liability, 39–40
Video(s)
   alarm systems, 174
   training, 77
Visa International, 92

Wafer tumbler, 221
Walkways, checklist, 296–97
Wal-mart, 188–89
Wanding data, 80–81
Ward, Aaron Montgomery, 3–4
Warded lock, 220–21
Washington v. Davis, 56
Watts, William, 6
Weaver, Frances, 141
Weber v. Kaiser, 56–57
Webster v. Dieringer's Variety, Inc., 199
Weitz, Barton A., 103
Wight, Stu, 151
Windows, 225
Woodfield Shopping Center, 312–13
Work environment, checklist, 296
Workers' compensation insurance, 277–78

Printed in the United States
124325LV00003B/22/A